The World in Your Head

A Gestalt View of the Mechanism of Conscious Experience

The World in Your Head

A Gestalt View of the Mechanism
of Conscious Experience

Steven Lehar
Schepens Eye Research Institute, Boston

 LAWRENCE ERLBAUM ASSOCIATES, PUBLISHERS
2003   Mahwah, New Jersey   London

Editor: Bill Webber
Editorial Assistant: Kristin Duch
Cover Design: Kathryn Houghtaling Lacey
Textbook Production Manager: Paul Smolenski
Text and Cover Printer: Sheridan Books, Inc.

Camera ready copy for this book was provided by the author.

Lawrence Erlbaum Associates, Inc., Publishers
10 Industrial Avenue
Mahwah, New Jersey 07430

Library of Congress Cataloging-in-Publication Data

Lehar, Steve.
The world in your head : a Gestalt view of the mechanism of conscious
    experience / Steve Lehar.

      p. cm.

    Includes bibliographical references and index.
    ISBN 0-8058-4176-8 (alk. paper)
    1. Perception. 2. Consciousness. 3. Gestalt psychology.   I. Title.
    BF311 .L44   2002
    153.7—dc21   2002016472
                                                      CIP

Books published by Lawrence Erlbaum Associates are printed on acid-
free paper, and their bindings are chosen for strength and durability.

Printed in the United States of America
10 9 8 7 6 5 4 3 2 1

I would like to thank the many people who helped to make this book possible. In the first place I must thank my great uncle Franz Lehár and the Lehár Succession LLC for providing funding for my research. I also thank Eli Peli and the Schepens Eye Research Institute for having the vision to see the merit in my work, and for providing office space and facilities. I would also like to thank Richard Held for his continued encouragement and support through the many years of this project, and Bill Webber and Lawrence Erlbaum Associates for having the courage to take on such an unusual project. I am also deeply endebted to a number of friends and colleagues for the intellectual stimulation of our many debates and discussions and/or shared psychonautical adventures that played such a critical role in the inspiration behind this book. That list includes, but is by no means limited to, Frank Guenther, Andy Worth, Krishna Govindarajan, Dan Cruthirds, Joe Enis, Josh Seims, Tim Howells, Niall McLoughlin, John Reynolds, Gary Bradski, Matthew Sordillo, Peter Eggleston, and Benoit Deshailes. Finally I extend the warmest thanks to my loving wife Ginny, for her enduring faith and endless encouragement through the many years that it took to produce this book.

Contents

Preface

The workings of the human mind and brain represents one of the last great frontiers in human knowledge. For our understanding of the brain today is in a state where physics was before Newton, or astronomy before Galileo. For many years I have felt a strong attraction to this field of knowledge because unlike other branches of science, this one remains wide open to armchair philosophy and novel theoretical approaches. I have always suspected that introspection can offer useful insights into the workings of the brain. How could it possibly be otherwise? Curiously, I was to discover that this is very much a minority view, most experts in the field today seem to think that perception gives us knowledge of the world, rather than of the brain, and that observations made introspectively are somehow suspect, being hopelessly subjective and impossible to verify. My first entry into this field was by way of image processing and artificial intelligence. There is no better introduction to the problems of natural vision than attempting to solve the problem with computers. For the computer has, in the digital image, all of the information in that image in the form of explicit numerical data. And yet the problem of extracting useful information from that data turns out to be extraordinarily difficult. For although the computer can detect simple features easily enough, such as image edges, an edge detection algorithm tends to find thousands of edges in a typical natural scene, most of which are spurious, either texture lines, or shadows, or irregular fragmented surfaces that are hopelessly confused. Furthermore, many of the most significant edges are often missing, being occluded by foreground objects, or having insufficient contrast with the background, and many significant edges contain gaps, kinks, multiple contours, contrast reversals, etc. The next step of making sense of configurations of edges remains largely an unsolved problem except in the most controlled visual environments. In my experience with image processing I began to get the impression that the farther we progress with complex algorithms designed to analyze the image data with ever more sophisticated strategies, the more brittle and rigid and cantankerous our algorithms seem to become. I began to see that there is a fundamental difference between the properties of natural vision, as exhibited even by the lowly house fly, and the rigid deterministic approach to vision represented by the digital computer. The little fly, with its tiny pinpoint of a brain, dodging effortlessly between the tangled branches of a shrub in dappled sunlight and in gusty cross-winds, seems to thumb its nose at our lofty algorithms and expensive hardware that can, at best, guide a van loaded with the latest in computer equipment at a snail's pace down a clearly demarcated road, even then occasionally running astray. It became clear to me that nature was hiding some very simple elegant secret in biological vision, whose operational principles are entirely different from digital computation.

While I was employed doing image processing and artificial intelligence, I happened into a talk by Stephen Grossberg in which he presented an interesting approach to investigating biological vision. Grossberg's approach was to study the properties of visual illusions, and attempt to replicate those illusions with computer algorithms. For if we can replicate the properties of the visual illusions, this surely will offer insights into the nature of early visual processing in biological vision. This approach is particularly appealing because some illusions seem simple in principle, and therefore offer a good starting point for modeling visual perception, and yet other illusions exhibit an exquisite subtlety and complexity, and therefore those illusions promise a glimpse into those most mysterious and enigmatic aspects of visual processing whose operational principles remain to be discovered. I was so enamored of this approach that I quit my job in image processing and joined the Ph.D. program at Boston University in Grossberg's department.

The study of visual processing by way of visual illusions was an approach championed by the Gestalt movement. Gestalt theory, I discovered, seemed to capture the essence of that elusive principle of computation that is so difficult to express in computational terms. In fact the early Gestaltists had made a concerted effort to characterize exactly those kinds of phenomena that are impossible to express in terms of local or atomistic computational strategies as in the digital computer. There has been considerable cross-fertilization of ideas in recent decades between theories of artificial and biological computation, and many of the concepts in computer image processing, such as spatial convolutions with spatial kernels, have found parallels in neural network theory, in the form of patterned receptive fields. The limitations of computer image processing algorithms therefore reflect corresponding problems in neural network theory. For the spatial receptive field is no different in principle from a template matching scheme, a concept whose limitations are well known. It seemed to me therefore that many of the limitations of artificial vision system were also problems for neural network theory. The principal difficulty involves the most central element in neural network theory, i.e. the concept that neurons behave as quasi-independent processors with strictly segregated input and output channels. This atomistic concept of local processors, sometimes known as the Neuron Doctrine, is the antithesis of the holistic global computational paradigm suggested by Gestalt theory. I discovered however that my concerns with the neuron doctrine were not generally shared by others in the field, most researchers seeming to believe that the properties of the neuron are so well established experimentally that all that remains to be discovered is the proper arrangement of these elemental processors to account for the observed properties of perception. I felt that I was virtually alone in my conviction that the fundamental principles of neural function remain to be discovered.

In my own Ph.D. thesis work I proposed a Harmonic Resonance theory to explain a number of visual illusions which were difficult to account for in conventional neural terms. I thought I had made a very significant discovery of a completely new principle of neurocomputation that promised an answer to those troublesome Gestalt aspects of perception. While I was permitted to graduate from Boston University with my Harmonic Resonance thesis, Grossberg and others remained unconvinced, seeing no need to abandon the well established concepts of neuroscience. Furthermore, to my surprise, I found that all my attempts to get my thesis work published were rebuffed. It seems that the conventional notion of neurocomputation by way of spatial receptive fields has been accepted for so long that it would take extraordinary evidence to convince neuroscientists of the extraordinary hypothesis that the neuron doctrine is not sufficient to account for the phenomena of visual experience. That extraordinary evidence was available however, and was plain for all to see. The problem was that people, including myself at the time, were looking right at it without ever seeing it. It was a classic case of not seeing the forest for the trees, for the extraordinary evidence of visual processing is plainly evident in the world of conscious experience.

I remember very vividly the first time I came to realize the truth of *indirect realism*. I was sitting in my armchair at home, practicing the exercise I now call *introspective retrogression*, trying to see where in the world that I see around me could I find evidence of the properties of my visual cortex. I knew that without my cortex I could see nothing at all, and that therefore in some sense this image of the world around me was itself somehow produced by my cortex, but while in my cortex, it was also at the same time out in the world around me. It seemed that the world around me had a dual character, it was both the real world, and a perceptual world, and that the two appeared to be somehow superimposed. There was a curious paradox wrapped up in this idea of perception that I just could not seem to get straight, for how could the world of perception escape the confines of my head to appear in the world around me? Then one day it hit me all of a sudden like a lightning bolt, in the form of a vivid mental image. Suddenly I could see in my mind's eye that the world I saw around me, including the picture of myself sitting in my chair, was merely an image generated inside my head, and therefore it could not be out in the world. In other words, out beyond the walls and floor and ceiling of the room I saw around me, was the inner surface of my true physical skull, and beyond that skull was an inconceivably immense remote external world, of which this world that was in my experience was merely a miniature virtual-reality replica. It was no new fact that I had suddenly learned, for my answers to most questions about perception would have been about the same as before that insight. And yet there was a fundamental shift in my perspective that has colored all of my subsequent thinking on perception. For what I could now see was that the brain is capable of generating vivid three-dimensional images of a fully spatial world, like the one I see around me right now. There is no way that a hierarchy of independent neural processors, however they might be arranged, could possibly account for this world of internal reality as I experience it.

I came running into school the day after my great introspective discovery, only to find that nobody knew what the hell I was talking about. The idea of an enormous world out there above the dome of the sky, they said, was just plain absurd. I had endless debates with colleagues on this issue, to the point where I was forbidden to bring up the topic any more in social settings, because I was getting to be a bore. I found it incredible that I should be the only person to have seen into the illusion of conscious experience, and incredible that others could not see it as clearly as I did, now that I was there to point it out to them. For as incredible as my hypothesis might seem, the alternative was even more incredible, for it suggests that we can somehow be aware of the world directly, as if bypassing the representational machinery in the brain, in violation of everything we know about the laws of physics.

In the year after my Ph.D. I went back to the library and began to read the original Gestalt texts in the words of the Gestalt masters themselves. I discovered to my surprise and relief that I was not alone, but that the Gestaltists themselves had made that same discovery decades ago, and had embodied it in the Gestalt principle of isomorphism. But in the intervening decades, this great secret of vision had somehow been forgotten! How could something of such significance have vanished from contemporary psychology and neuroscience almost without a trace? For despite the strong emphasis on Gestalt theory in Grossberg's department at Boston University, I had never once heard mention of the principle of isomorphism, or that the world of experience is all contained inside your head. These aspects of Gestalt theory have been largely forgotten even by those who consider themselves proponents of Gestalt theory. The issue of indirect realism is not only rejected by contemporary neuroscience, it is no longer even considered a valid topic of discussion. In the rare texts where the issue is mentioned at all, it is usually passed off as a pseudoproblem that had been resolved long ago.

Further searching through the library turned up some writings by Bertrand Russell, who made exactly the same argument for isomorphism, but without any mention of Gestalt theory, since Russell argued the point from first principles. Finally I discovered the writings of Immanuel Kant, and found that it was he who had first articulated this idea over two centuries ago. So it was an old idea that I was dealing with after all, although curiously it seems to be an idea that has had to be rediscovered again and again by different generations of thinkers, because the idea has never taken hold to become a part of the established body of scientific knowledge. It was a great relief for me to see that this idea had such a noble and ancient heritage, for I was so convinced of its irrefutable truth, that should I be mistaken, I would also necessarily be completely mad, as some of my colleagues were beginning to believe. It is an idea which is both very obvious at some level, and yet at the same time almost impossible to conceive, and both Wolfgang Köhler and Bertrand Russell had expressed exasperation in their attempts to convince others of its irrefutable truth. And yet, there are other ideas that are equally difficult to conceive which have made their way into accepted science. For example the idea that the world is round, and that people on the underside do not fall off it, or that solid matter is composed mostly of empty space, and the dimensions of our universe, both at the micro and the macro level are truly beyond the ability of anyone to fully comprehend. It is difficult for us to realize retrospectively how absurd these ideas must have seemed to others when they were first proposed. Nevertheless these ideas have entered into the mainstream of science, and are even taught to high school students as properties of the physical world. I believe therefore that the idea that there are two worlds of reality is an idea that will one day be taught to children in school, as one of the essential facts that make sense of our experience of this world. The objective of this book is to make that day come sooner rather than later. For as long as we maintain the direct realist view that the world we see around us is the world itself, we can never make any significant progress in understanding the mechanism of conscious experience.

Chapter 1

The Two Worlds of Reality

The brain is wider than the sky,
For, put them side by side,
The one the other will contain
With ease, and you besides.
                    —Emily Dickenson

THE PHILOSOPHICAL DIVIDE IN THEORIES OF VISION

The scientific investigation into the nature of biological vision has been plagued over the centuries by a persistent confusion over a central philosophical issue. Simply stated, this is the question of whether the world we see around us is the real world itself, or whether it is merely a copy of the world presented to consciousness by our brain in response to input from our senses. In philosophical terms, this is the distinction between *direct realism* and *indirect realism*. Although not much discussed in contemporary neuroscience, this issue is of the utmost significance to our understanding of the nature of visual processing. Although the issue is most often either avoided altogether, or passed off as a pseudoproblem, it is very real and very significant. The frequent evasive handling of it can be traced to the fact that current theories of neurocomputation are often based implicitly on the direct realist view that the world we see around us is the world itself. This view, however, is demonstrably wrong on logical grounds, and therefore most theories of visual processing and representation can be shown to be founded on false assumptions.

The direct realist view, also known as *naive realism*, is the natural intuitive understanding of vision that we accept without question from the earliest days of childhood. When we see an object, such as this book that you hold in your hands, the vivid spatial experience of the book is assumed to be the book itself. This assumption is supported by the fact that the book is not merely an image, but appears as a solid three-dimensional object that emits sounds when we flip its pages, emits an odor of pulp and ink, and produces a vivid spatial sensation of shape, volume, texture, and weight as we manipulate it in our hands. Our belief in the reality of our perceived world is continually reaffirmed by the stability and permanence of objects we perceive in the world. Nevertheless, there are deep logical problems with the direct realist view that cannot be ignored if we are ever to understand the true nature of perceptual processing.

The problem arises if we accept the modern materialistic view of the brain as the organ of consciousness. According to this view, every aspect of visual experience is a consequence of electrochemical interactions within our physical brain in response to stimulation from the eyes. In other words, there is a direct correspondence between the physical state of the brain, and the corresponding subjective experience, such that a change of a particular sort in the physical brain state results in a change in the subjective experience. Conversely, any change in the subjective experience reflects some kind of change in the underlying brain state. It follows therefore that a percept can be viewed in two different contexts, either from the objective external context, as a pattern of electrochemical activity in the physical brain expressed in terms of neurophysiological variables such as electrical voltages or neural spiking frequencies, or from the internal subjective context, where that same percept is viewed as a subjective experience expressed in terms of subjective variables such as perceived color, shape, motion, and so on. Like the two faces of a coin, these very different entities can be identified as merely different manifestations of the same underlying structure. The dual nature of a percept is analogous to the representation of data in a digital computer, where a pattern of voltages present in a particular memory register can represent some meaningful information, either a numerical value, or a brightness value in an image, or a character of text, or what have you, when viewed from inside the appropriate software environment. When viewed in external physical terms, those same data take the form of voltages or currents in particular parts of the machine.

This materialistic view of perception, which is generally accepted in modern neuroscience, is at odds with a most fundamental property of visual experience: the fact that objects of the visual world are experienced as outside of ourselves, in the world itself, rather than within our brain where we assume the neurophysiological state to be located within our head. (See Russell, 1927, Harrison, 1989, and Smythies, 1994, for insightful discussion of the problem and its implications.) The flow of visual information is exclusively unidirectional, from the world through the eye to the brain. The causal chain of vision clearly shows that the brain cannot experience the world out beyond the sensory surface, but can register only the data transmitted to it from the sensory organs. In other words, if your subjective experience of the vivid spatial percept of this book corresponds to physical processes occurring within your brain, then in a very real sense this book too, as you perceive it, is also necessarily located within your physical brain. A percept cannot escape the confines of our physical brain into the world around us any more than the pattern of voltages in a digital computer can escape the confines of particular wires and registers within the physical mechanism.

Neither can we explain the external nature of perception by the fact that internal patterns of energy in our physical brain are connected to external objects and surfaces by reference, any more than the voltages encoded in a computer register can be considered external to a computer just because they refer to the external values that they represent. Although a sensor may record an external quantity in an internal register or variable in a computer, from the internal perspective of the software running on that computer, only the internal value of that variable can be "seen," or can possibly influence the operation of that software. In exactly analogous manner, the pattern of electrochemical activity that corresponds to our conscious experience can take a form that reflects the properties of external objects, but our consciousness is necessarily confined to the experience of those internal effigies of external objects, rather than of external objects themselves. Yet we observe in subjective experience the perceptual structures and surfaces of our world of experience as present external to our bodies, as if superimposed on the external world in a manner that appears to have no correspondence to the manner of representation in a digital computer.

It is the external nature of perception that has led many philosophers through the ages to conclude that there is something deeply mysterious about consciousness, which is forever beyond our capacity to fully comprehend. As Searle (1992) explained, when we attempt to observe consciousness, we see nothing but whatever it is we are conscious of; there is no distinction between the observation and the thing observed. It seems impossible in principle to endow a robotic intelligence with the powers of external perception the way we experience our own visual world, for a robot cannot in principle experience the world directly, but only through the image projected by the world on the sensory surface of the robot's electronic eye. Unless we invoke mystical processes beyond the bounds of science, this same limitation must also hold for human and animal perception: that is, we can only know what occurs within our brain, which is the organ of conscious experience. How then can we explain the external nature of the visual world as observed in subjective experience?

KANT'S INSIGHT: DUAL NATURE OF REALITY

The solution to this paradox was discovered centuries ago by Immanuel Kant (1781) with the concept of indirect realism. Kant argued that there are in fact two worlds of reality, which he called the *nouminal* and the *phenomenal* worlds. The nouminal world is the objective external world, which is the source of the light that stimulates the retina. This is the world studied by science, and is populated by invisible entities such as atoms, electrons, and various forms of radiation. The phenomenal world is the internal perceptual world of conscious experience, which is a copy of the external world of objective reality constructed in our brain on the basis of the image received from the retina. The only way we can perceive the nouminal world is by its effects on the phenomenal world. Therefore the "world" we experience as external to our bodies is not actually the world itself, but only an internal virtual reality replica of that world generated by perceptual processes within our head.

The distinction between these two views of perception is illustrated schematically in Fig. 1.1. In the direct realist view, your perceptual experience of the world around you as you sit reading this book is identified as the world itself, that is, you perceive yourself where you sit, surrounded by your physical environment, as suggested in Fig. 1.1A. In the indirect realist view of perception, the world you see around you is identified as a miniature perceptual copy of the world contained within your real physical head, as suggested schematically in Fig. 1.1B. The nouminal world and your nouminal head are depicted in dashed lines, to indicate that these entities are invisible to your direct experience.

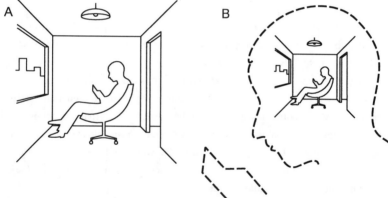

Fig. 1.1 (A) Your perceptual experience of the world as you sit reading this book, as conceptualized in the direct realist view of perception. (B) The true situation as conceived in the philosophy of indirect realism, where your percept of the world around you is identified as an internal pattern in your head, with the real external world (shown in dashed lines) being beyond your direct experience.

According to this view, consciousness is indeed directly observable, contrary to Searle's contention, for the objects we experience as being in the world around us are the products or "output" of consciousness rather than the "input" to it, and the experience of a three-dimensional object occupying some portion of perceived space is also a direct observation of consciousness; only in a secondary fashion is that percept also representative of an objective external entity. This remarkable insight into the true nature of reality ranks with those other great revolutions in our view of our place in the cosmos, such as the fact that the earth is round rather than flat as it appears locally, or that the earth rotates under the sun rather than the reverse as it appears from the earth's surface, or that solid objects contain more empty space than solid matter, as they appear perceptually. However, although Kant's great insight is now more than two centuries old, this basic fact of human experience is not generally taught in school. Even more remarkably, neither is it generally known or even discussed in those sciences where it would be of the utmost relevance. Instead, theories of perception and neural representation continue to be advanced that are based either explicitly or implicitly on direct realist assumptions.

The reason for the persistent confusion over this issue is that Kant's insight is particularly difficult to visualize or to explain in unambiguous terms. For example, even the description of the causal chain of vision is itself somewhat ambiguous, because it can be interpreted in two alternative ways. Consider the statement that light from this page stimulates an image in your eye, which in turn promotes the formation of a percept of the page up in your brain. The ambiguity inherent in this statement can be revealed by the question, "Where is the percept?" There are two alternative correct answers to this question, although each is correct in a different spatial context. One answer is that the percept is up in your head (the one you point to when asked to point to your head), which is correct in the external or direct realist context of your perceived head being identified with your objective physical head, and because your visual cortex is contained within your head, that must also be the location of the patterns of energy corresponding to your percept of the page. The problem with this answer, however, is that no percept is experienced within your head where you imagine your visual cortex to be located. The other correct answer is that the percept of the page is right here in front of you where you experience the image of a page. This answer is correct in the internal spatial context of the entire perceived world around you being within your head. However, the problem with this answer is that there is now no evidence of the objective external page that serves as the source of the light. The problem is that the vivid spatial structure you see before you is serving two mutually inconsistent roles, both as a mental icon representing the objective external page that is the original source of the light, and as an icon of the final percept of the page inside your head, thus, the page you see before you represents both ends of the causal chain, and our mental image of the problem switches effortlessly between the internal and external contexts to focus on each end of the causal chain in turn. It is this automatic switching of mental context that makes this issue so elusive, because it hinders a consideration of the problem as a whole.

INTROSPECTIVE RETROGRESSION

The distinction between the nouminal and phenomenal worlds can be clarified with an exercise in phenomenology I call *introspective retrogression*. In fact, it was while performing this exercise that I first encountered the truth of indirect realism. Suppose that you are watching a ball game on television. It is possible, while watching the game, to redirect your attention from the game itself to the glowing phosphor dots on your television screen. This attentional shift can be made without moving the eyes, or even changing their focus, because you are looking at exactly the same thing, the television screen, but you have stepped backward conceptually from the game being recorded, to the screen that presents the recorded data. By careful analysis of the picture it is possible to separate out features that belong to the game itself, such as the images of the ball and the players, from features that belong to the screen, such as the glowing phosphor dots that twinkle and scintillate as the moving images pass over them. It may even be possible to identify features introduced by components in the long chain of transmission between the ball game and your screen. For example, raindrops on the protective glass plate in front of the television camera can be identified as being between the ball game and the photosensor array of the television camera. If a dark pixel-sized spot were observed on the screen that remained fixed despite panning and zooming of the scene, this blemish might reflect either a bad pixel in the photosensor array of the recording camera or perhaps faulty phosphor dots on your own screen. If, however, the bad pixel disappeared when you changed channels, or when the view of the ball game switched to a different camera, then the blemish could be identified with a camera at the transmitting end rather than the screen at the receiving end. Speckles of "snow" on the television screen can be identified with the electrical noise from household appliances if that noise correlates with the operation of those appliances. All of the factors along the long chain of transmission between the camera and the screen are collapsed onto the picture on the screen. By careful analysis, these factors can often be separated and assigned to specific points along the transmission chain.

Now step further back from the screen to the retina of your own eye that is viewing the scene. Where in your view of the scene around you is the evidence of the retina on which the scene is recorded? Everyone knows the experience of temporarily bleaching the retina by looking at a camera flash, or staring at a bright light bulb, which leaves a darkened after-image in your visual field. The fact that this after-image moves with your eyes as you glance around the room indicates that it is anchored in the retina. And yet that moving fleck appears not at the spot where you believe your retina to be located, but rather beyond the retina, out in the world itself. The entire scene that you see around you is therefore downstream of the retina. If the camera flash were in the form of an erect arrow, the image of this light on the retina would be inverted by the lens to form an inverted arrow on your physical retina, where it could in principle be viewed from the outside using an ophthalmoscope, at the same time that it is perceived subjectively from the inside. But your subjective experience of that inverted after-image appears right-side-up. This clearly indicates that the subjective world is oriented parallel to the inverted retinal image rather than to the erect external world. The image you experience on your own retina therefore appears subjectively *not* at the point at the back of your eyeball where you suppose your retina to be, but rather it is seen in the entire scene that appears to be out beyond your eye, out in the world around you.

Now to retrogress one more step, consider: Where in the visual world do we see evidence of the visual cortex? Again, it is no good looking at the back of your head, where you believe the cortex to be located, because all you see there is an imageless void. The image itself is again to be found out in the world you see around you. There is a very interesting perceptual phenomenon known as Emmert's Law (Coren, et al., 1994). When you experience a bleaching of the retina due to a bright light, the after-image of that light is seen in depth at the same distance as the surface against which it is viewed. When you look at your hand three inches from your face, the after-image appears as a tiny fleck on the surface of your hand. When you look at distant mountains, on the other hand, the after-image becomes a huge blob, blotting out many acres of the mountain side. The size of the after-image on the retina of course remains constant in terms of visual angle. Nevertheless, it appears to change with its perceived distance, appearing small when perceived close, and large when perceived far.

This phenomenon can help us factor out the retinal from the cortical contribution to the perceived world, for it shows us that the retinal image, which is two-dimensional and without depth, is perceived nevertheless as a depth percept, and that therefore this depth component must be added to the scene by cortical processing. If you can picture the world you see around you as a flat two-dimensional projection (which is not easy to do) then you are viewing the retinal component of the scene. When viewing the more natural three-dimensional percept, you are viewing the cortical component of the scene. In a very real sense, therefore, the world you see around you is not the world itself, but rather a pattern of activity in your own visual cortex. By observing the nature of the world you see around you therefore, you are observing the nature of the representation of a visual scene in the visual cortex, together with any visual artifacts introduced along the chain of transmission from the object you view to its representation in the cortex. It is only in secondary fashion that that percept is also representative of the more remote external world of objective reality.

A DOUBLE MENTAL IMAGE REFLECTS TWO WORLDS OF REALITY

There is a curious paradox in this view of the world you perceive around you as a double entity, which is identified simultaneously with both ends of the causal chain of vision. I propose an alternative mental image to disambiguate the two spatial contexts that are so easily confused: Out beyond the farthest things you can perceive in all directions, that is, above the dome of the sky, and below the solid earth under your feet, or beyond the walls, floor, and ceiling of the room you see around you, is located the inner surface of your true physical skull. And beyond that skull is an unimaginably immense external world of which the world you see around you is merely a miniature internal replica. This can only mean that the head you have come to know as your own is not your true physical head, but merely a miniature perceptual copy of your head in a perceptual copy of the world, all of which is contained within your real head in the external objective world. In other words, the vivid spatial experience of the world you see around you is the miniature world depicted in Fig. 1.1B, and is therefore completely contained within your nouminal head in the nouminal world. This mental image is more than just a metaphorical device, for the perceived and objective worlds are not spatially superimposed, as is assumed in the direct realist model, but the perceived world is completely contained within your head in the objective world. Although this statement can only be true in a topological, rather than a strictly topographical sense, the advantage of this mental image is that it provides two separate and distinct icons for the separate and distinct internal and external worlds, which can now coexist within the same mental image. This no longer allows the automatic switching between spatial contexts that tends to confuse the issue. Furthermore, this insight emphasizes the indisputable fact that every aspect of the solid spatial world that we perceive to surround us is in fact primarily a manifestation of activity within an internal representation, and only in secondary fashion is it also representative of more distant objects and events in the external world.

I have found a curious dichotomy in the response of colleagues in discussions on this issue. When I say that everything you perceive is inside your head, they are apt to reply, "Why of course, but that is so obvious it need hardly be stated." When, on the other hand, I turn that statement around and say that their physical skull is located out beyond the farthest things they can perceive around them, to this they object, "Impossible! You must be mad!" And yet the two statements are logically identical! How can it be that the one is blindingly obvious while the other seems patently absurd? This provocative formulation of the issue in the double mental image is my contribution to the debate, for it brings into sharper focus a concept that is difficult to address in more abstracted terms. This issue demonstrates the value of the mental image, or of a vivid spatial analogy, as a vehicle for expressing certain spatial concepts in a way that is difficult to formulate in more abstracted terms. This concept is used extensively throughout this book.

THE RADAR CONTROLLER ANALOGY

Another mental image that can be helpful in clarifying this issue is the analogy of a radar controller, who directs air traffic by radio based on a pattern of "blips" on the radar screen representing the aircraft under his control. The controller talks to the blips on his screen through a microphone, hears their reply in his earphones, and observes their responses to his commands in the miniature world of the radar scope. Our world of perceptual experience is analogous to the world of the radar screen, except that unlike the radar controller, we have no way to peek behind the curtain of the illusion and see the world directly as it is. As in the case of perception, the spatial coordinates of the radar scope are decoupled from those of the external world, in that the orientation of the scope itself relative to the external world is entirely irrelevant to its function. For example the controller can be seated with the north of his scope oriented facing south in external coordinates, without the slightest adverse effect on the controller's performance of his duties. The discrepancy between the internal and external coordinates would only become apparent to the controller if an aircraft were to manifest itself to him directly, instead of through the radar screen. For example if an aircraft were to "buzz the tower" so close that the sound of its engines could be heard directly through the walls of the control tower, the controller might be surprised to hear the noise due to a blip approaching from the left on the scope, being heard approaching from the right in the control room.

There is an interesting phenomenon called the *pressure phosphene* that reveals a similar discrepancy between internal and external coordinates in perception. Press your fingertip gently against your eyeball through the eyelid, touching the eyeball at a point opposite the retina, which covers mostly the posterior half of the eyeball. This is most easily accomplished by rotating the eye all the way to the upper left, for example, and touching the lower-rightmost portion of the eyeball, tucking your finger into the edge of the eye socket. Wiggle your finger while doing this, and you will see a visual sensation that looks like a moving dark patch. This feature is caused by the direct physical stimulation of the cells in the retina due to flexing of the elastic wall of the eyeball, which generates a retinal signal as if in response to a visual stimulus. In essence, you are seeing the pressure of your fingertip "from the inside," expressed as a visual sensation. What is interesting is that the visual sensation appears on the *opposite* side to the one stimulated by the finger. For example if you stimulate the lower right corner of the eyeball, the pressure phosphene will appear in the upper left corner of the visual field. The conventional explanation for this phenomenon is that when pressing on the lower right of the eyeball, you stimulate the portion of the retina that would normally be illuminated by light from the upper-left quadrant in the external world. Although this explanation is true enough as far as it goes, it does not address the fact that the pressure image is in register with the external world, whereas the light image is inverted by the optics of the eye. Therefore it is the entire visual scene you see around you that is inverted relative to the external world, whereas the pressure phosphene more accurately represents the true location of your finger in external coordinates. But the image of your finger tip seen visually appears in perfect register with the somatosensory experience of the location of your finger. This means that our somatosensory experience must also be inverted to remain in register with the inverted visual image. The pressure phosphene therefore is in fact a remote signal directly from the external world without inversion, exactly analogous to the sound of the airplane heard through the control room wall.

AN ANALOGICAL PARADIGM OF REPRESENTATION

Once we recognize the world of experience for what it really is, it becomes clearly evident that the representational strategy used by the brain is an *analogical* one. In other words, objects and surfaces are represented in the brain *not* by an abstract symbolic code, as suggested in the propositional paradigm, nor are they encoded by the activation of individual cells or groups of cells representing particular features detected in the scene, as suggested in the neural network or feature detection paradigm. Instead, objects are represented in the brain by constructing full spatial effigies of them that appear to us for all the world like the objects themselves—or at least so it seems to us only because we have never seen those objects in their raw form, but only through our perceptual representations of them. Indeed, the only reason why this very obvious fact of perception has been so often overlooked is because the illusion is so compelling that we tend to mistake the world of perception for the real world of which it is merely a copy. This is a classic case of not seeing the forest for the trees, for the evidence for the nature of perceptual representation in the brain has been right before us all along, cleverly disguised as objects and surfaces in a virtual world that we take to be reality. So, for example, when I stand before a table, the light reflected from that table into my eye produces an image on my retina, but my conscious experience of that table is not of a flat two-dimensional image; rather, my brain fabricates a three-dimensional replica of that table carefully tailored to exactly match the retinal image, and presents that replica in an internal perceptual space that includes a model of my environment around me, with a miniature copy of my own body at the center of that environment. The model table is located in the same relation to the model of my body as the real table is to my real body in external space. The perception or consciousness of the table therefore is identically equal to the appearance of the effigy of the table in my perceptual representation, and the experience of that internal effigy is the closest I can ever come to having the experience of the physical table itself.

This raises the question of why the brain goes to the trouble of constructing an internal replica of the external world, and why that replica has to be presented as a vivid spatial structure instead of some kind of abstract symbolic code. It also raises the philosophical question of who is viewing that internal replica of the external world. If the presence of an internal model of the world required a little man, or "homunculus," in your brain to observe it, that little man would itself have to have an even smaller man in its little head, resulting in an infinite regress of observers within observers. But the internal model of the external world is not constructed so as to be viewed by an internal observer; rather, the internal model is a data structure in the brain, just like any data in a computer, with the sole exception that these data are expressed in explicit spatial form. If a picture in the head required a homunculus to view it, then the same argument would hold for any other form of information in the brain, which would also require a homunculus to read or interpret that information. In fact, any internal representation need only be available to other internal processes rather than to a miniature copy of the whole brain. The reason the brain expresses perceptual experience in explicit spatial form must be because the brain possesses spatial computational algorithms capable of processing that spatial information. In fact, the nature of those spatial algorithms is itself open to phenomenological examination, as I show shortly. But first, in order to illustrate the meaning of a spatial computation that operates on spatial data, I present another spatial analogy, as an extension to the analogy of the radar controller.

THE PLOTTING-ROOM ANALOGY

During the Battle of Britain in the Second World War, Britain's Fighter Command used a plotting room as a central clearinghouse for assembling information on both incoming German bombers and defending British fighters, gathered from a variety of diverse sources. A chain of radar stations set up along the coast would detect the range, bearing, and altitude of invading bomber formations, and this information was continually communicated to the Fighter Command plotting room. British fighter squadrons sent up to attack the bombers reported their own position and altitude by radio, and squadrons on the ground telephoned in their strength and state of readiness. Additional information was provided by the Observer Corps, from positions throughout the British Isles. The Observer Corps would report friendly or hostile aircraft in their area that were either observed visually or detected by sound with the aid of large acoustical dishes. Additional information was gathered by triangulating the radio transmissions from friendly and hostile aircraft, using radio direction-finding equipment. All of this information was transmitted to the central plotting room, where it was collated, verified, and cross-checked, before being presented to controllers to help them organize the defense. The information was presented in the plotting room in graphical form, on a large table map viewed by controllers from a balcony above. Symbolic tokens representing the position, strength, and altitudes of friendly and hostile formations were moved about on the map by WAAFs (Women's Auxiliary Air Force personnel) equipped with croupier's rakes, in order to maintain an up-to-date graphical depiction of the battle as it unfolded.

The symbols representing aircraft on the plotting-room map did not distinguish between aircraft detected by radar as opposed to those sighted visually, or detected acoustically, because the information of the sensory source of the data was irrelevant to the function of the plotting room. The same token was used therefore to represent a formation of bombers as it was detected initially by radar, then tracked by visual and acoustical observation, and finally confirmed by radio reports from the fighter squadrons sent out to intercept it. The functional principle behind this concept of plotting information is directly analogous to the strategy used for perceptual representation in the brain.

AN ANALOGICAL ALGORITHM

the plotting-room analogy diverges from perception in that the plotting room does indeed have a "homunculus" or homunculi, in the form of the plotting-room controllers, who issue orders to their fighter squadrons based on their observations of the plotting room map. However, the idea of a central clearinghouse for assembling sensory information from a diverse array of sensory sources in a unified representation is just as useful for an automated system as it is for one designed for human operators. The automated system need only be equipped with the appropriate spatial algorithms to make use of that spatial data. The fact that a spatial or analogical form was chosen for the plotting room suggests that this form of information is more easily processed by the human mind than a more symbolic or abstracted representation, which in turn suggests that the mind employs a spatial computational strategy that works well with spatial or analogical data.

In order to clarify the meaning of a spatial algorithm that operates on spatial data, I next describe a hypothetical mechanism designed to replace the human controllers in the Fighter Command plotting room. The general principle of operation of that mechanism, I propose, reflects the principle behind human perception and how it relates to behavior. A squadron of fighters sent to intercept a fleet of invading bombers should be directed to close with the enemy. This objective could be expressed in the plotting room model as a force of attraction, like a magnetic or electrostatic force, that pulls the fighter squadron token in the direction of the approaching bomber formation token on the plotting room map. However, the token cannot move directly in response to that force. Instead, that attractive force is automatically translated into instructions for the squadron to fly in the direction indicated by that attractive force, and the force is only relieved or satisfied as the radio, radar, and Observer Corps reports confirm the actual movement of the squadron in the desired direction. Only then is that movement reflected in the movement of its token on the plotting-room map. The force of attraction between the squadron token and that of the bomber formation in the plotting room model represents an analogical computational strategy or algorithm, designed to convert a perceptual representation, the spatial model, into a behavioral response, represented by the command for the squadron to fly in the direction indicated by the force of attraction. The feedback loop between the perceived environment and the behavioral response that it provokes is mediated through actual behavior in the external world, as reflected in sensory or "somatosensory" confirmation of that behavior back in the perceptual model.

The spatial model of the battle on the plotting room map represents the best guess, based on sensory evidence, of the actual configuration of the forces in the real world outside. Therefore, when a formation of aircraft is believed to be in motion, its token is advanced automatically based on its estimated speed and direction, even in the absence of direct reports, to produce a running estimate of its location at all times. To demonstrate the power of this kind of computational strategy, let us delve a little deeper into the plotting-room analogy and refine the mechanism to show how it can be designed to be somewhat more intelligent.

When intercepting a moving target such as a bomber formation in flight, it is best to approach it not directly, but with a certain amount of "lead," just as a marksman leads a moving target by aiming for a point slightly ahead of it. Therefore the bomber formation is best intercepted by approaching the point toward which it appears to be headed. This too can be calculated with a spatial algorithm by using the recent history of the motion of the bomber formation to produce a "leading token" placed in front of the moving bomber token in the direction that it appears to be moving, advanced by a distance proportional to the estimated speed of the bomber formation. The leading token therefore represents the presumed future position of the moving formation a certain interval of time into the future. The fighter squadron token should be designed to be attracted to this leading token, rather than to the token representing the present or last known position of the bomber formation. But in the real situation the invading bombers would often change course in an attempt to throw off the defense. It was important therefore to try to anticipate likely target areas, and to position the defending fighters between the bombers and their likely objectives. This behavior could be achieved by marking likely target areas, such as industrial cities, airports, or factories, with a weaker attractive force to draw friendly fighter squadron tokens toward them. This force, in conjunction with the stronger attraction to the hostile bombers, induces the fighters to tend to position themselves between the approaching bombers and their possible targets, or to deviate their course towards those potential targets on their way to the attacking bombers, and then to approach the bombers from that direction. Fighter squadrons could also be designed to exert an influence on one another. For example, if it is desired that different squadrons accumulate into larger formations before engaging the bomber streams (the "big wing" strategy favored by Wing Commander Douglas Bader), the individual fighter squadron tokens could be equipped with a mutually attractive force, which tends to pull different squadrons toward each other on their way to the bomber formations whenever convenient, making them coalesce into larger clumps. If, on the other hand, it is desired to distribute the fighters more uniformly across the enemy formations, the fighter squadron tokens could be given a mutually repulsive force, which would tend to keep them spread out to cover more territory defensively. Additional forces or influences could be added to produce even more complex behavior. For example, as a fighter squadron begins to exhaust its fuel and/or ammunition, its behavior pattern should be inverted, to produce a force of repulsion from enemy formations, and attraction back toward its home base, to induce it to refuel and rearm at the nearest opportunity. With this kind of mechanism in place, fighter squadrons would be automatically commanded to take off, approach the enemy, attack, and return to base, all without human intervention.

The mechanism just described is of course rather primitive, and would need a good deal of refinement to be at all practical, to say nothing of the difficulties involved in building and maintaining a dynamic analog model equipped with spatial fieldlike forces. But the computational principle demonstrated by this fanciful analogy is very powerful. It represents a parallel analogical spatial computation that takes place in a spatial medium, a concept that is quite unlike the paradigm of digital computation, whose operational principles are discrete, symbolic, and sequential.

There are several significant advantages to this style of computation. Unlike the digital decision sequence with its complex chains of Boolean logic, the analogical computation can be easily modified by inserting additional constraints into the model. For example if the fighters were required to avoid areas of intense friendly antiaircraft activity, this additional constraint can be added to the system by simply marking those regions with a repulsive force that will tend to push the fighter squadron tokens away from those regions without interfering with their other spatial constraints. Because the proposed mechanism is parallel and analog in nature, any number of additional spatial constraints can be imposed on the system in similar manner, and each fighter squadron token automatically responds to the sum total of all of the analog forces acting on it in parallel. In an equivalent Boolean system, every additional constraint added after the fact would require reexamination of every Boolean decision in the system, each of which would have to be modified to accommodate every combination of possible contingencies. In other words adding or removing constraints after the fact in a Boolean logic system is an error-prone and time-consuming business requiring the attention of an intelligent programmer, whereas in the analogical representation spatial constraints are relatively easy to manipulate independently, and the final behavior automatically takes account of all of those spatial influences simultaneously. The analogical paradigm also permits behavior that is governed by extended fieldlike influences in a manner that is awkward to emulate in the Boolean paradigm.

ANALOGICAL VERSUS SEQUENTIAL LOGIC

The analogical and discrete paradigms of computation have very different characters. The Boolean sequential logic system is characterized by a jerky robotic kind of behavior, due to the sharp decision thresholds and discrete on/off nature of the computation. The analogical system on the other hand exhibits a kind of smooth interpolated motion characteristic of biological behavior. Of course, a digital system can be contrived to emulate an analogical one (as is true for the converse also), and indeed computer simulations of weather systems, aircraft in flight, and other analog physical systems offer examples of how this can be done. But perhaps the greatest advantage of the analogical paradigm is that it suffers no degradation in performance as the system is scaled up to include hundreds or thousands of spatial constraints simultaneously, whereas the digital simulation gets bogged down easily, because those constraints must be handled in sequence in long chains of Boolean logic. The analogical paradigm is therefore particularly advantageous for the most complex computational problems that require simultaneous consideration of innumerable factors, where the digital sequential algorithm becomes intractable. It is also advantageous in problems involving extended fields of influence, such as seeking an optimal path through irregular terrain.

There are, however, cases in which a Boolean or sequential component is required in a control system—for example if it is required to direct a squadron to proceed to a point B by way of an intermediate point A. This kind of sequential logic can be incorporated in the analogical representation by installing an attractive force to point A that remains active only until the squadron token arrives there, at which point that force is turned off, and an attractive force is applied to point B instead. Or perhaps the attractive force can fade out gradually at point A in analog fashion as the squadron token approaches, while a new force fades in at point B, allowing the squadron to cut the corner with a smooth curving trajectory instead of a sharp turn, or to adapt the curve of their turn to account for other spatial influences. A similar logical decision process would be required for a squadron to select its target. If a squadron token were to experience an equal attraction to two or more bomber formations simultaneously, that would cause it to intercept some point between them. Therefore the squadron token should be designed to select one bomber formation token from the rest, and then feel an attractive force to that one exclusively.

THE DIFFERENTIAL ANALYZER

In the 1950s Vannevar Bush at MIT developed a mechanical analog computer that, although rapidly made obsolete by the emergence of the new digital electronic computer, nevertheless demonstrated some intriguing computational principles that are unique to that paradigm and suggestive of the nature of biological computation. The *differential analyzer*, as the machine was called (see Fifer, 1961, for a thorough review of analog computation), consisted of an array of parallel shafts that rotated on finely machined bearings, mounted on a table. Each shaft represented a variable whose value was encoded by the total angle that the shaft had rotated from some reference angle or origin. The shafts were interconnected by orthogonal cross-shafts through a variety of ingenious mechanical devices that performed various mathematical operations, such as addition, multiplication, integration, and so on. For example, if one shaft represented a variable x, and another represented t, a third shaft y could be defined to represent $y = \int x\, dt$ by connecting it by cross-shafts to the other two shafts through a mechanical integrator mechanism. The integrator expressed the integral function in literal analog fashion, so that the rotation of shaft y was always literally equal to $\int x\, dt$, however shafts x and t happened to be turned. Thus the variable y took on its meaning not just by definition, but by its functional connection to the rest of the machine. More complex differential equations were built up in this manner from simpler elements to arbitrary levels of complexity, to solve dynamic equations that were prohibitively computational-intensive by other means known at that time. Virtually any physical system that can be expressed as a differential equation can thus be simulated in physical analogy by the differential analyzer.

The differential analyzer was not easy to program, for it required a different mechanical configuration of shafts and gears for every equation that it was set to solve, so the device was rapidly superseded first by the more flexible analog electronic computer, and then by the even more programmable digital computer. But the differential analyzer exhibits some unique characteristics that demonstrate the power of the analogical paradigm. Although the mechanism was generally used as an input/output device, with certain variables being fixed as input in order to compute an output value on other free variables, this kind of mechanism can in principle be operated just as well in reverse, by turning the output shafts and observing the resultant rotation of the input shafts, thereby performing the inverse function of the original one. More generally, once a particular functional relationship between variables has been established in the mechanism, any combination of these variables can be fixed, to observe the effects on the values, or degrees of freedom, of the remaining free variables. Because there is no need to specify variables in advance as either "input" or "output," the input to the system can be provided by whatever variables are currently available, seamlessly switching from one source to another, just as human perception switches between visual, somatosensory, auditory, or tactile input modalities, using whatever sensory input happens to be currently available. In fact, even in the absence of *any* input, the differential analyzer can continue to model the system it is configured to model, this time decoupled from the external world, like a freewheeling hallucination, or dream, whose dynamic unfolding follows the kinds of laws of motion and causality normally observed in the external world which it is designed to model.

Variables can also be given an intermediate status between fixed and free, by means of mechanical spring forces that tend to push or drive them in a particular direction. For example, if a variable is connected to a particular system so as to represent a measure of economy, or profit, or any other measure of desirable attribute of the modeled system, a spring force can then be applied to that shaft to express the desire to maximize that economy or profit or whatever, and that desire force will be propagated to all of the other free variables in the system as communicated through the intermediate functional transformation mechanisms. In fact, any number of spring forces can be applied to any number of the variables in the system to express even more complex combinations of constraints, and the dynamic state of the system will evolve under the collective action of all of those physical constraints communicated in parallel back and forth through the system. This kind of system can therefore even address problems which are mathematically underconstrained, by installing gentle spring forces that pull the system state toward any desired quadrant of the solution space.

This concept of computation does not have the input/output structure characteristic of so many of our mathematical and computational formalisms, for the influences between the variables propagate through the system in all directions simultaneously. Similarly, it is somewhat misleading to describe human behavior as an output based on a sensory input, for human behavior is a continuously changing response to a continuously changing sensory environment, mediated by a continuously changing perceptual representation of that environment.

INTERNAL VERSUS EXTERNAL REPRESENTATION

The analogical spatial strategy just presented is reminiscent of the kind of computation suggested by Braitenberg (1984) in his book *Vehicles*. Braitenberg described very simple vehicles that exhibit a kind of animal-like behavior by way of very simple analog control systems. For example, Braitenberg described a light-seeking vehicle equipped with two photocells connected to two electric motors that power two driving wheels. In the presence of light, the current from the photocells drives the vehicle forward, but if the light distribution is nonuniform and one photocell receives more light than the other, the vehicle will turn either toward or away from the light, depending on how the photocells are wired to the wheels. One configuration produces a vehicle that exhibits light-seeking behavior, like a moth around a candle flame, whereas with the wires reversed the same vehicle will exhibit light-avoiding behavior, like a cockroach scurrying for cover when the lights come on. The behavior of these simple vehicles is governed by the spatial field defined by the intensity profile of the ambient light, and therefore, like the analogical paradigm, this type of vehicle also performs a spatial computation in a spatial medium. However in the case of Braitenberg's vehicles, the spatial medium is the external world itself, rather than an internal replica of it. Rodney Brooks (1991) elevated this concept to a general principle of robotics, whose objective is "intelligence without representation." Brooks argued that there is no need for a robotic vehicle to possess an internal replica of the external world, because the world can serve as a representation of itself. O'Regan (1992) extended this argument to human perception, and insisted that the brain does not maintain an internal model of the external world, because the world itself can be accessed as if it were an internal memory, except that it happens to be external to the organism. Nevertheless, information from the world can be extracted directly from the world whenever needed, just like a data access of an internal memory store.

There is a fundamental flaw with this concept of perceptual processing, at least as a description of human perception. For unless we invoke mystical processes beyond the bounds of science, then surely our conscious experience of the world must be limited to that which is explicitly represented in the physical brain. In the case of Braitenberg's vehicles, that consciousness would correspond to the experience of only two values: the brightness detected by the two photocells. The conscious decision-making processes of the vehicle (if it can be called such) would be restricted to responding to those two values with two corresponding motor signals. These four values therefore represent the maximum possible content of the vehicle's "conscious experience." The vehicle has no idea of its location or orientation in space, and its complex spatial behavior is more a property of the world around it than of anything going on in its "brain."

Similarly, if the world is indeed accessed as an external memory, as suggested by O'Regan, our conscious experience cannot extend to portions of that external memory that are not currently being "accessed," or copied into an internal representation in the brain. We should never see in visual consciousness the world around us as a structural whole, but only as a sequence of local fragments that change with each visual saccade. But this description is inconsistent with our subjective experience, for when we stand in a space, like a room, we experience the volume of the room around us as a simultaneously present whole, every volumetric point of which exists as a separate parallel entity in our conscious experience, even in monocular viewing. Braitenberg's vehicles can be programmed to go to the center of a room by placing a light at that location, but the vehicle cannot conceive of the void of the room around it or conceptualize its center, for those are spatial concepts that require a spatial understanding. On the other hand, we can see the walls, floor, and ceiling of a room around us simultaneously, embedded in a perceived space, and we can conceptualize any point in the space of that room in three dimensions without having to actually move there ourselves. We can program ourselves to follow a wall at a certain distance, or to walk along the center of a path or corridor, or to pick a path of least resistance through irregular terrain, taking account simultaneously of every region of rough and smooth ground. The world of visual experience therefore clearly demonstrates that we possess an internal map of external space like the Fighter Command plotting room, and the world we see around us is exactly that internal representation.

SYMBOL GROUNDING BY SPATIAL ANALOGY

The analogical spatial paradigm offers a solution to some of the most enduring and troublesome problems of perception. Although the construction and maintenance of a spatial model of external reality is a formidable computational challenge (see chap. 4 through 6 and chap. 10), the rewards that it offers make the effort very much worth the trouble. The greatest difficulty with a more abstracted or symbolic approach to perception has always been the question of how to make use of that abstracted knowledge. This issue was known as the *symbol grounding problem* (Harnad, 1990) in the propositional paradigm of representation promoted by the artificial intelligence (AI) movement. The problem of vision, as conceptualized in AI, involves a transformation of the two-dimensional visual input into a propositional or symbolic representation. For example, an image of a street scene would be decomposed into a list of items recognized in that scene, such as "street," "car," "person," and so on, as well as the relations between those items. Each of these symbolic tags or labels is linked to the region of the input image to which it pertains. The two-dimensional image is thereby carved up into a mosaic of distinct regions, by a process of segmentation (Ballard & Brown, 1982, pp. 6–12), with each region being linked to the symbolic label by which it is identified.

Setting aside the practical issues of how such a system can be made to work as intended (which itself turns out to be a formidable problem), this manner of representing world information is difficult to translate into practical interaction with the world. The algorithm does not "see" the street in the input image as we do, but rather it sees only a two-dimensional mosaic of irregular patches connected to symbolic labels. Consider the problem faced by a robotic vehicle designed to find a mailbox on the street and post a letter in it. Even if an image region is identified as a mailbox, it is hard to imagine how that information could be used by the robot to navigate down the street to the mailbox, avoiding obstacles along the way. What is prominently absent from this system is a three-dimensional consciousness of the street as a spatial structure, the very information that is so essential for practical navigation through the world. A similar representational problem is seen in neural network theories that explain visual perception as the "lighting up" of a constellation of "feature detector" nodes in response to a visual stimulus.

An analogical representation of the street, on the other hand, would involve a three-dimensional spatial model, like a painted cardboard replica of the street complete with a model of the robot's own body at the center of the scene. It is the existence of such a three-dimensional replica of the world in an internal model that, I propose, constitutes the act of "seeing" the street. Setting aside the issue of how such a model can be constructed from the two-dimensional image (which is also a formidable problem), making practical use of such a representation is much easier than for a symbolic or abstracted representation. Once the mailbox effigy in the model is recognized as such, it can be marked with an attractive force, and that force in turn draws the effigy of the robot's body toward the effigy of the mailbox in the spatial model. Obstacles along the way are marked with negative fields of influence, and the spatial algorithm to get to the mailbox is to follow the fields of force, like a charged particle responding to a pattern of electric fields.

The analogical paradigm can also be employed to compute the more detailed control signals to the robot's wheels. The forward force on the model of the robot's body applies a torque force to the model wheels, but the model wheels cannot respond to that force directly. Instead, that torque in the model is interpreted as a motor command to the wheels of the larger robot to turn, and as larger wheels begin to turn in response to that command, that turning is duplicated in the turning of the model wheels, as if responding directly to the original force in the model world. Side forces to steer the robot around obstacles can be computed in a similar fashion. A side force on the model robot should be interpreted as a steering torque, like the torque on the pivot of a caster wheel. That pivoting torque in the model is interpreted as a steering command to pivot the larger wheels, and the steering of the larger wheels is then reflected in the steering of the model wheels also. The forces impelling the model robot through the model world are thereby transformed into motor commands to navigate the real robot through the real world. However, obstacles in the real world that might block the larger wheels from turning or pivoting as commanded would prevent their smaller replicas from turning also, thereby communicating the constraints of the external world back in to the internal model. Unlike Braitenberg's vehicles, this robot has a spatial "consciousness" or awareness of the structure of the world around it, for it can feel the simultaneous influence of all the visible surfaces in the scene, which jointly influence its motor behavior. For example the robot navigating between obstacles in its path feels the repulsive influence of all of them simultaneously, and is thereby induced to take the path of least resistance weaving between them like a skier on a slalom course, on the way to the attractive target point. Our own conscious experience clearly has this spatial property, for we are constantly aware of the distance to every visible object or surface in our visual world, and we can voluntarily control our position in relation to those surfaces, although what we are actually "seeing" is an internal replica of the world rather than the world itself.

The idea of motor planning as a spatial computation has been proposed in *field theories* of motor control, as discussed in chapter 10, in which the intention to walk toward a particular objective in space is expressed as a fieldlike force of attraction, or *valence*, between a model of the body, and a model of the target, expressed in a spatial model of the local environment. The target is marked with a positive valence, whereas obstacles along the way are marked with negative valence. When we see an attractive stimulus—for example, a tempting delicacy in a shop window at a time when we happen to be hungry—our subjective impression of being physically drawn toward that stimulus is not only metaphorically true, but I propose that this subjective impression is a veridical manifestation of the mental mechanism that drives our motor response. For the complex combination of joint motions responsible for deviating our path towards the shop window is computed in spatial fashion in a spatial model of the world, exactly as we experience it to occur in subjective consciousness.

Indeed, the spatial configuration of the positive and negative valence fields evoked by a particular spatial environment can be inferred from observation of their effects on behavior, in the same way that the pattern of an electric field can be mapped out by its effects on moving charged particles. For example, the negative valence field due to an obstacle such as a sawhorse placed on a busy sidewalk can be mapped by observing its effect on the paths of people walking by. The moving stream of humanity divides to pass around the obstacle like water flowing around a rock in a stream in response to the negative valence field projected by that obstacle. Although the influence of this obstacle is observed in external space, the spatial field that produces that behavioral response actually occurs in the spatial models in the brains of each of the passers-by individually.

Another example of a spatial computational strategy can be formulated for the problem of targeting a multijointed limb, that is, specifying the multiple angles required of the individual joints of the limb in order to direct its end-effector to a target point in three-dimensional space. This is a complex trigonometrical problem that is underconstrained. However, a simple solution to this complex problem can be found by building a scale model of the multijointed limb in a scale model of the environment in which the limb is to operate. The joint angles required to direct the limb toward a target point can be computed by simply pulling the end-effector of the model arm in the direction of the target point in the modeled environment, and recording how the model arm reacts to this pull. Sensors installed at each individual joint in the model arm can be used to measure the individual joint angles, and those angles in turn can be used as command signals to the corresponding joints of the actual arm to be moved. The complex trigonometrical problem of the multijointed limb is therefore solved by analogy, as a spatial computation in a spatial medium.

There is evidence to suggest that this kind of strategy is employed in biological motion. For when a person reaches for an object in space, a person's body tends to bend in a graceful arc, whose total deflection is evenly distributed among the various joints to define a smooth curving posture. Thus, the motor strategy serves to minimize a configural constraint expressed in three-dimensional space, implicating a spatial computational strategy. The dynamic properties of motor control are also most simply expressed in an external spatial context: The motion of a person's hand while moving toward the target describes a smooth arc in space and time, accelerating uniformly through the first half of the path, and decelerating to a graceful stop through the second half. In other words, the observed behavior is exactly as if the person's body were indeed responding lawfully to a spatial force of attraction between the hand and the target object in three-dimensional space, which in turn suggests that a spatial computational strategy is being used to achieve that result. Further evidence comes from the subjective experience of motor planning, for we are unaware of the individual joint motions when planning such a move, but rather our experience is more like a force of attraction that seems to pull our hand toward the target object, and the joints in our arm seem to simply follow our hand as it responds to that pull. This computational strategy generalizes to any configuration of limbs with any number of joints, as well as to continuous limbs like a snake's body or an elephant's trunk. This same strategy also applies globally to the motion of the body as a whole through the environment.

The analogical concept of perceptual computation couples the functions of sensory and motor processing by way of an interface expressed neither in sensory nor in motor terms, but in a modality-independent structural code representing objects and surfaces of the external world. Perceptual processes construct the volumetric spatial model based on information provided by the sensory input. Attentional and motivational processes mark objects or regions of that model with positive and negative valence, and those regions in turn project spatial valence fields that pervade the volumetric void of the perceived world like the electric fields projected by charged objects. Motor processes then compute the response of a structural model of the body to the valence fields expressed in the structural model of the surrounding environment.

STRUCTURAL PROPERTIES OF THE SPATIAL MODEL

If the world of conscious experience, in both its structural and functional aspects, is a veridical manifestation of processes taking place in the physical brain, as it must of necessity be, this in turn validates a phenomenological approach to the investigation of biological computation. The phenomenological approach offers a unique perspective into the workings of the mind, which in turn sets constraints for the corresponding workings of the brain. Phenomenological examination reveals that the perceptual model of the external world is more than a mere replica of the visible surfaces in the world, but rather it is a meaningful decomposition of those surfaces into coherent objects, and those objects are perceived to extend beyond their visible surfaces. we experience objects perceptually not as the hollow facade defined by their visible front surfaces, but as complete volumetric wholes which we perceive to extend in depth, and whose outer surfaces are perceived to enclose the perceived object even around its hidden rear face. For example your view of the front face of this book in your hands generates a percept of the book as a solid spatial object, whose hidden rear faces are filled in or reified from the information of the visible front face, as well as from the sensation of the rear face sampled at discrete points by your fingers, with the help of your general knowledge of the shape of books. Thought and knowledge are often discussed as if they were nonspatial abstractions. The phenomenological approach reveals that thought can also take the form of volumetric structures that appear in a volumetric model of space. This is plainly evident for "perceptual thoughts," as seen in the volumes and surfaces of the phenomenal world. However, phenomenology also reveals the existence of more abstract mental constructs that are nevertheless experienced as volumetric spatial forms. Although the hidden portions of an object are experienced in an invisible or ghostly *amodal* manner (Michotte, Thinés, & Crabbé, 1991), the percept of those hidden portions is nevertheless a volumetric spatial structure, for it is possible to reach back behind an object like a sphere or cylinder, or the back of this book, and indicate with your palm the approximate location and surface orientation at any sample point on the hidden surface, based only on the view of the visible front face of that object. This exercise, which I call *morphomimesis*, provides evidence for the rich spatial structure in perceptual experience. Although your hand can mime only one such invisible surface at a time, the entire hidden structure of a perceived object is experienced simultaneously as a structural volume embedded in perceived space, as indicated by the shape your hand takes as you prepare to grasp the book by its hidden rear face. Similarly, when an object is partially occluded by a foreground object, like the portion of the world hidden behind this book, we perceive it to exist nevertheless as a perceptual whole, with the missing portions filled in perceptually where we know them to exist. Again, the information encoded in that perceptual experience is expressed in an invisible amodal form, but the spatial structure of that experience can again be revealed by morphomimesis.

A similar form of perceptual reification is seen in the percept of the world hidden behind your head. That world is also experienced as a vivid spatial void occupied by the spatial structures of the floor on which you stand, or the chair on which you sit, as well as the walls that enclose the room behind your back, extrapolated from the visible portions of those surfaces that fall within the visual field. That is why we can reach back to scratch our ear, or pick up a coffee cup or pencil from a surface behind us without necessarily having to look back to guide our hand to its target. Much of this information is usually acquired from earlier views of those now-hidden surfaces. But whether it is learned or immediately perceived, that information is nevertheless encoded in explicit spatial form, like a structural model of the room around you that extends into space behind you, if only in a fuzzy probabilistic, but essentially spatial, manner.

FUNCTIONAL PROPERTIES OF THE SPATIAL MODEL

In order for the perceptual model of the world to be a meaningful representation of it, the model must be more than just a structural replica of the configuration of objects and surfaces, but the model must also replicate the essential laws and forces of the world to lend meaning to observed motions in the world. we not only perceive objects to possess color, shape, and size, but we also experience them to posses mass and weight and impenetrability, as well as permanence, in the sense that we do not expect them to spontaneously appear or disappear without cause. Again, these aspects of knowledge are usually considered to be nonspatial abstractions. However, the properties such as mass and impenetrability are perceived to pervade a specific volume of perceived space corresponding exactly to the volume of the perceived object to which they apply. These higher order properties that we perceive objects to posses in various combinations have a direct influence on our understanding of their behavior when observed in perception, as well as on our predictions of the possible behavior of those objects under hypothetical circumstances. For example, if a moving object that is perceived to have a certain shape and color disappears momentarily behind an occluder, it is expected to reappear at the other side with the same shape and color, and at the precise moment determined by its perceived velocity and the length of the occluded path. In other words, the object is tracked perceptually even while concealed behind the occluder, as a volumetric image of a particular shape, color, location, and velocity, although the percept is experienced in amodal form through the occlusion. If a moving object is observed racing toward a solid wall, its perceived momentum and impenetrability result in an expectation that it will impact the wall with an audible report, after which it will be expected to either be flattened or shattered by the impact, or to bounce back elastically after contact with the wall, depending on the properties of the material of which it is perceived to be composed. If no such change is observed after the collision, this will result in a fundamental change in the perceived properties of that object. For example, if the object passes effortlessly through the wall, the object will suddenly be perceived to be insubstantial, like a ghost, or the beam of a searchlight; that is, it will lose its perceived impenetrability. If, on the other hand, the object stops dead on contact with the wall, it will immediately lose its perceived mass, like a block of Styrofoam striking a sticky surface. If it smashes powerfully through the wall, it will be perceived to be massive. Similarly, objects perceived to have weight are expected perceptually to accelerate toward the ground whenever they are perceived to be unsupported, whereas objects that are observed to hover with no visible means of support are perceived to be weightless like a balloon. The perceived higher order properties of objects can therefore be considered as a perceptual shorthand that predicts the motions of those objects under a wide variety different circumstances, whereas those properties themselves are inferred from the observed behavior of their object.

The perceptual model of the external world therefore is a direct physical analog of the world, akin to a physical model constructed of components that posses actual mass and weight and impenetrability, although in the brain those objects must be composed of nothing more than patterns of electrochemical activation that somehow mimic those external forces and properties. Because the objects of which the perceived world is constructed exert simulated forces on each other, some configurations of perceived objects will be more stable than others. For example, the percept of a solid block of granite floating over the ground with no visible means of support exerts a powerful downward force of simulated gravity in the perceptual representation. But if the sensory stimulus that produces the percept is static, then either the synthetic gravity in the perceptual model must be balanced by an imagined upward force of invisible support, or the granite must lose its perceived weight. Either of these perceptual interpretations is unlikely in the real world, and therefore that percept will be unstable, as if seeking out a more reasonable explanation. The percept of a granite block resting on the ground, on the other hand, is a more stable configuration, because the simulated forces of gravity and support are symmetrically balanced, and therefore no unseen or improbable forces are needed to stabilize the percept. According to this analogical view of perception, a meaningful understanding of the world corresponds to the construction of a functional copy of the world in an internal representation, complete with functional forces and laws of motion that replicate the laws and forces of the physical world. The physical laws embodied in the perceptual mechanism do not correspond exactly to the laws of physics as discovered by science, encoding instead what is known as *naive physics*, that is, physical principles as they are understood intuitively by the nonscientist.

ABSTRACT THOUGHT AND COGNITION

The higher order functions of cognition and mental imagery can also be studied by introspective observation. Mental images often take the form of solid three-dimensional objects that can move about in space, and those images can be manipulated under voluntary control in order to test various spatial hypotheses—for example, when picturing a new arrangement of furniture, or planning a construction project. The nature of the mental image is itself amodal, like the ghostly percept of the hidden rear faces of objects. But the spatial reality and volumetric nature of the mental image can also be demonstrated by morphomimesis, such as by polishing the imaginary faces of an imagined sphere or cube with your hands, using sweeping motions that conform to the invisible surfaces of the imagined form wherever you choose to locate it in perceived space. The ability to manipulate such imaginary spatial constructs offers clear evidence for the spatial nature of at least some cognitive abstractions.

In chapter 9 I propose that amodal perception, as of occluded objects in the world, is a primitive or lower form of mental imagery, and that mental imagery and cognition evolved from that lower level function of amodal perception. The idea of mental imagery as the essential principle behind cognition enjoyed more popularity in the early days of psychology, before modern notions of neurocomputation rendered it neurophysiologically implausible. Besides the troublesome issue of how thoughts can take the form of three-dimensional spatial structures, there was always the deeper problem of how abstract ideas could possibly be encoded as a mental image. In chapter 9 I propose a solution to this issue, again based on phenomenological observation: Although the mental image of an abstract concept such as "furniture" is experienced as a fuzzy nonspatial form, that abstraction can also be reified under voluntary control, to appear as a particular piece of furniture, such as a chair, and that chair can be further reified to appear in the mental image at any desired orientation, location, and scale, as well as in any color or furniture style. It is the very flexibility and indeterminate nature of the abstract mental image that give it its power of abstraction, for the abstraction, even in its most indeterminate form, can be processed in mental manipulations—for example when imagining an unspecified piece of furniture standing in a corner of a real room, or imagining a "thing" resting in your hand. The fuzzy, indeterminate nature of the mental abstraction therefore should not be taken as evidence for its nonspatial nature, but only as evidence for its fuzzy, indeterminate nature. The mental abstraction appears as a kind of probabilistic superposition of multiple possible shapes, but spatial shapes nonetheless, that can under voluntary control be reified in any or all of their dimensions of variability, or manipulated in indeterminate form as fuzzy, probabilistic entities.

NEUROPHYSIOLOGICAL CONSIDERATIONS

At some level the properties of subjective experience as outlined here, such as the vivid spatial nature of the world of perception and the analogical influences they exert on our behavior, are so plainly manifest in everyday experience as to hardly require psychophysical confirmation. However, theories of perceptual processing very rarely take account of these most obvious properties of experience. The reason for this is that these properties are inconsistent with contemporary understanding of neurophysiology. Ever since Santiago y Cajal confirmed the cellular basis of the nervous system, a concept known as the *neuron doctrine* has come to dominate psychology. The input/output function of the neural dendrites and axon, together with the relatively slow transmission across the chemical synapse, suggests that neurons operate as quasi-independent processors in a sequential or hierarchical architecture that processes information in well defined processing streams. This idea was captured by Sherrington's evocative image of the brain as "an *enchanted loom* where millions of flashing shuttles weave a dissolving pattern, always a meaningful pattern though never an abiding one" (Sherrington, 1941, p. 173).

However, the neuron doctrine is inconsistent with the properties of the subjective experience of vision. Our experience of a visual scene is not at all like an assembly of abstract features, or millions of flashing shuttles, but rather our percept of the world is characterized by a stable and abiding experience of solid volumes, bounded by colored surfaces, embedded in a spatial void. There is a dimensional mismatch between this world of volumes and surfaces and the constellation of discrete activations suggested by the neuron doctrine. Far from being a reduced or abstracted featural decomposition of the world, the world of perceptual experience encodes more explicit spatial information than the sensory stimulus on which it is based. There is no accounting in the neuron doctrine for this constructive or generative aspect of perceptual processing. Sherrington himself acknowledged this disparity between physiology and phenomenology (Sherrington, 1941, p. 228-229).

Contemporary neuroscience therefore finds itself in a state of serious crisis, for the more we learn about the details of neurophysiology, the farther we seem to get from an explanation of the most fundamental properties of the world of visual experience. This has led neuroscientists in recent decades to tend to ignore the subjective conscious experience of vision, and to adopt by default a naive realist view that excludes the phenomenal world from the set of data to be explained by neuroscience. In fact, the "bottom-up" approach that works upward from the properties of neurons measured neurophysiologically and the "top-down" approach that works downward from the subjective experience of perception are equally valid and complementary approaches to the investigation of the visual mechanism. Both approaches are essential because each approach offers a view of the problem from its own unique perspective. Eventually these opposite approaches to the problem must meet somewhere in the middle. However, to date, the gap between them remains as large as it ever was. I propose that the problem is a paradigmatic one: one that cannot be resolved by simply specifying the right neural network architecture. The atomistic concept of computation embodied in the neuron doctrine must itself be replaced by a more holistic paradigm.

If the neuron doctrine concept of neurocomputation is indeed in doubt, what is there to replace it? How are we to model the computational operations of perception in the absence of a plausible neurophysiological theory to define the elements of which our model is to be composed? In this book I present a *perceptual modeling* approach, as discussed in chapter 2. I propose to model the percept as it is experienced subjectively, rather than the neurophysiological mechanism by which that experience is supposedly subserved. This is only an interim solution, for ultimately the neurophysiological basis of neurocomputation must also be identified. However, the perceptual modeling approach can help to quantify the information processing apparent in perception, as a necessary prerequisite for a search for a neurophysiological mechanism that can perform the equivalent computational transformation. This approach leads to a very different view of perceptual processing than that suggested by the neural network approach inspired by neurophysiology. In chapters 4 through 6 I present a model of the computational transformations manifest in perceptual processing expressed in terms that are independent of any particular theory of neural representation. The model reveals the unique computational principles that are operative in perception.

HARMONIC RESONANCE THEORY

The properties of perceptual processing revealed by the perceptual modeling approach are deeply perplexing, not only in terms of the underlying neurophysiological mechanism, but even in more general terms of theories of computation and representation. The holistic global aspect of perception identified by Gestalt theory represents the polar opposite to the atomistic sequential processing strategy embodied both in the neuron doctrine and in the paradigm of digital computation. The preattentive nature of Gestalt phenomena and their universality across individuals independent of past visual experience suggest that these enigmatic Gestalt phenomena reflect a fundamental aspect of perceptual computation. No significant progress can possibly be made in our understanding of perceptual processing until the computational principles behind Gestalt theory have been identified.

In fact, there is one physical phenomenon that exhibits exactly those same enigmatic Gestalt properties. That is the phenomenon of *harmonic resonance*, or patterns of standing waves in a resonating system. In chapter 8 I present a harmonic resonance theory of neurocomputation as an alternative to the neuron doctrine paradigm. Like the spatial receptive field of the neuron doctrine, the standing wave defines a spatial pattern in the neural substrate. Unlike the receptive field model, the spatial pattern defined by harmonic resonance is not a rigid templatelike entity hard-wired in a cell's receptive field, but a more elastic, adaptive mechanism, like a rubber template, that automatically deforms to match any deformation of the input pattern.

Harmonic resonance also exhibits invariances in a unique form. In a circular-symmetric resonating system like a circular flute, or in a spherical resonating cavity, the pattern of standing waves within that cavity can rotate freely within that cavity while maintaining its structural integrity and characteristic form. This offers an explanation for the rotation invariance observed in perception that has been so difficult to account for in conventional neurocomputational terms.

Another unique property of harmonic resonance is that resonances in different modules or subsystems tend to couple with each other to produce a single global resonance that synchronizes the individual resonances in the subsystems in such a way that a modulation of the resonance in one subsystem will be communicated immediately and in parallel to all the other subsystems of the coupled system. This unique property of harmonic resonance offers a new perspective on the question of the "binding problem" and the unity of the conscious experience, as discussed in chapters 6 and 8. This concept also offers an explanation for the global resonances observed across the entire cortex in electroencephalogram (EEG) recordings. Furthermore, harmonic resonance offers a functional explanation for the phenomenon of coherent oscillations observed across widely separated cortical areas, a phenomenon that is somewhat problematic for the neuron doctrine, because the phase of spiking activity should not be preserved across the chemical synapse. According to the harmonic resonance model, this synchronous activity is not a signal in its own right between individual neurons, but is an epiphenomenon of a global standing-wave pattern that spans those remote cortical areas.

The harmonic resonance model therefore offers a computational principle with unique holistic properties suggestive of many aspects of perception. I propose therefore that harmonic resonance is the computational principle behind the enigmatic holistic properties of perception identified by Gestalt theory.

A PSYCHO-AESTHETIC HYPOTHESIS

The harmonic resonance theory of neurocomputation also accounts for a number of other curious aspects of human experience that have been difficult to account for in conventional neural terms. The most prominent characteristics of harmonic resonance are symmetry and periodicity of the standing-wave patterns, both in space and in time. It turns out that symmetry and periodicity have very special significance in human experience, for these properties are ubiquitous in human aesthetics, as seen in the symmetrical and periodic patterns of design used in all cultures throughout human history to decorate clothing, pots, tools, and other artifacts, especially items of special symbolic or religious significance. Symmetry and periodicity are also prominent features of architecture, music, poetry, rhythm, and dance. In chapter 11 I propose a *psycho-aesthetic hypothesis*, whereby any principles of aesthetics that are found to be universal across all human cultures are thereby indicative of properties that are fundamental to the human mind itself, rather than being a cultural heritage. I propose therefore that the symmetry and periodicity in art and music are aesthetically pleasing exactly because they are easily encoded in the periodic basis function offered by the harmonic resonance representation.

The harmonic resonance theory also suggests an explanation for one of the most enduring mysteries of human experience: the question of why resonances in musical instruments and the rhythmic beating of drums can often evoke the deepest emotional response in the human soul. I propose that the musical instrument represents man's first modest success at replicating the physical principle behind biological computation, and that the strong emotional response evoked by these inanimate resonances reflects an unconscious recognition of the essential affinity between mind and music.

Chapter 2

The Dimensions of Conscious Experience

PERCEPTUAL MODELING VERSUS NEURAL MODELING

The task of perceptual psychology is a formidable one, for the nature of visual experience is so rich and complex that it defies reduction to computational terms. The models of visual processing proposed to date address only the very simplest or lowest levels of perception, and shed no light at all on the more complex and mysterious aspects of perception. It has become fashionable in recent decades to express models of visual perception in the form of neural network models, even models formulated to explain psychophysical rather than neurophysiological data. However, there is a problem inherent in modeling perceptual phenomena with neural models, because psychophysical experiments specifically measure the subjective conscious experience of perception, as opposed to a neurophysiological state. Until a mapping is established between subjective experience and the corresponding neurophysiological state, there is no way to verify whether the neural model has correctly replicated the perceptual phenomenon.

I propose therefore a *perceptual modeling* as opposed to neural modeling approach: that is, to model the information apparent in the subjective percept rather than the objective state of the physical mechanism of perception. Whatever the neurophysiological mechanism that corresponds to any subjective experience, the information encoded in that physiological state must be equivalent to the information apparent in the subjective percept. Unlike a neural network model, the output of a perceptual model can be matched directly to psychophysical data, as well as to the subjective experience of perception. This perceptual modeling approach must eventually converge with neurophysiological knowledge, at which point it will be possible to map the perceptual variables of brightness, color, and so on to neurophysiological variables such as spiking frequency or ionic concentration.

THE PSYCHOPHYSICAL POSTULATE

The true nature of external reality is in principle forever beyond our capacity to fully comprehend. On the other hand, the internal representation of perceptual data encoded in the brain, the nature of that information is plain, as long as we recognize the world before us for what it really is: an internal perceptual representation, rather than the objective world of which it is merely a copy. Although we cannot observe directly the physical medium by which perceptual information is encoded in the brain, we can observe the information encoded in that medium, expressed in terms of the variables of subjective experience. By analogy with the digital computer, there is no way for a program running on a computer to determine from the content of a particular data array whether those data are encoded in the form of electrical voltages in transistors, or magnetic fields on a ferromagnetic medium, or microscopic pits on an optical storage medium like a compact disk device, and so on. However by performing the appropriate tests, the program can determine the dimensions of those data, for example, the precision of each data item and the total number of items stored. In other words, the program can determine the informational content of the data, but not the physical storage medium by which those data are expressed in the physical machine. The same principle must also hold in perceptual experience, as originally proposed by Müller (1896) in a hypothesis that has come to be known as the *psychophysical postulate*. Müller argued that because the subjective experience of perception is encoded in some neurophysiological state, the dimensions of conscious experience cannot possibly be any greater than the dimensions of the corresponding neurophysiological state by which that experience is encoded in the brain. Therefore it is possible by direct phenomenological observation to determine the dimensions of conscious experience, and thereby to infer the dimensions of the information encoded neurophysiologically in the brain.

THE GESTALT PRINCIPLE OF ISOMORPHISM

The Gestalt principle of isomorphism states explicitly what is merely implied by Müller's psychophysical postulate. In the case of structured experience, equal dimensionality between the subjective experience and its neurophysiological correlate implies similarity of structure or form. For example, the percept of a filled-in colored surface, whether real or illusory, encodes a separate and distinct experience of color at every distinct spatial location within that surface to a particular resolution. Each point of that surface is not experienced in isolation, but in its proper spatial relation to every other point in the perceived surface. In other words the experience is extended in (at least) two dimensions, and therefore the neurophysiological correlate of that experience must also encode (at least) two dimensions of perceptual information.

The mapping of phenomenal color space was established by the method of *multidimensional scaling* (Coren et al., 1994, p. 57), in which color values are ordered in psychophysical studies based on their perceived similarity, to determine which colors are judged to be nearest to each other, or which colors are judged to be between which other colors in phenomenal color space. A similar procedure could just as well be applied to spatial perception to determine the mapping of phenomenal space. If two points in a perceived surface are judged psychophysically to be nearer to each other when they are actually nearer, and farther when they are actually farther, and if other spatial relations such as between-ness are also preserved phenomenally, this provides direct evidence that phenomenal space is mapped in a spatial representation that preserves those spatial relations in the stimulus. The outcome of this proposed experiment is so obvious it need hardly be performed. And yet its implication, that our phenomenal representation of space is spatially mapped, is not often considered in contemporary theories of spatial representation.

The isomorphism required by Gestalt theory is not a strict *structural* isomorphism—that is, a literal isomorphism in the physical structure of the representation—but merely a *functional* isomorphism, a behavior of the system *as if* it were physically isomorphic (Köhler, 1947, pp. 57-64). The exact geometrical configuration of perceptual storage in the brain cannot be observed phenomenologically any more than the configuration of silicon chips on a memory card can be determined by software examination of the data stored within those chips. Nevertheless, the mapping between the stored perceptual image and the corresponding spatial percept must be preserved, as in the case of the digital image, so that every stored color value is meaningfully related to its rightful place in the spatial percept.

A functional isomorphism must also preserve the functional transformations observed in perception, and the exact requirements for a functional isomorphism depend on the functionality in question. For example, when a colored surface is perceived to translate coherently across perceived space, the corresponding color values in the perceptual representation of that surface must also translate coherently through the perceptual map. If that memory is discontinuous, like a digital image distributed across separate memory chips on a printed circuit board, then the perceptual representation of that moving surface must jump seamlessly across those discontinuities in order to account for the subjective experience of a continuous translation across the visual field. In other words, a functional isomorphism requires a functional connectivity in the representation as if a structurally isomorphic memory were warped, distorted, or fragmented while preserving the functional connectivity between its component parts. Although this kind of functionality is often more efficiently implemented in a topographically organized map that requires shorter connections between adjacent elements, that is not a strict requirement. A similar efficiency can be had in a *topologically* organized map, where neighborhood relations are preserved but with absolute distances distorted. In any case, an argument for *structural* or *topological* isomorphism is an argument of representational efficiency and simplicity, rather than of logical necessity. A *functional* isomorphism, on the other hand, is strictly required in order to account for the properties of the perceptual world as observed subjectively.

Furthermore, even for a representation that is functionally but not structurally isomorphic, descriptions of the functional transformations performed in that representation are most simply expressed in their structurally isomorphic form, just as a panning or scrolling function in image data is most simply expressed as a spatial shifting of image data, even when that shifting is actually performed in hardware in a nonisomorphic memory array. In the present discussion, therefore, our concern is chiefly with the functional architecture of perception—that is, a description of the spatial transformations observed in perception, whatever form those transformations might take in the physical brain—and those transformations are most simply described as if taking place in a physically isomorphic space.

INTROSPECTION AND THE STRUCTURALIST TRADITION

The scientific investigation of the subjective experience of perception, or introspection, marked the birth of psychology as a science distinct from philosophy and biology, for psychology is defined as the science of the psyche, or mind, and neurophysiology only enters into the picture to provide a physical substrate for mind. However, from the outset, certain problems emerged with respect to the procedure of introspective analysis. Introspection as a branch of psychology was pioneered by the Introspectionist, or Structuralist, movement (Wundt, 1873-1874, Titchener, 1898), so named because their stated objective was to study the structure of conscious experience. A principal concern of the Structuralists was to distinguish the elements of consciousness, derived most immediately from the sensory stimulus, from higher level perceptual or cognitive inferences drawn from that experience. For example, a rectangular table top viewed in perspective projects a trapezoidal image on the retina, due to perspective foreshortening. However, the naive observer is naturally inclined to discount the perspective distortion and to report the table top as rectangular rather than trapezoidal in shape. The Structuralists therefore placed great emphasis on the proper training of the introspective observer, in order to avoid what they dubbed the *stimulus error*—reporting the way we know an object to be objectively, as opposed to the way it appears to consciousness in its most raw or elemental form. In the process, however, the Structuralists imposed on their observations their own preconceived notion that the lowest or most fundamental level of conscious experience must be similar dimensionally to the raw sensory stimulus, and therefore the trained introspective observer endeavored to observe exclusively the two-dimensional component of the visual experience and to ignore the three-dimensional inferential structure apparently built on it by perceptual and cognitive processes. The difficulty with this procedure is that the lower level aspects of perception appear indistinguishable perceptually from the higher level cognitive components, and therefore the observations of introspection must depend on one's preconceived notions of what is permissible to observe. This resulted in inconsistencies between introspective observations, even between observers trained in the same procedure. As a result of this historical legacy, introspection earned a reputation for being hopelessly subjective, and to this day introspection is still considered somewhat disreputable as a serious scientific procedure.

The Gestalt movement challenged the assumptions behind introspectionism and introduced a different form of introspection. If we observe the world around us without bias, as it presents itself to consciousness, it becomes immediately apparent that the world we perceive is by no means a two-dimensional projection, but appears as a solid three-dimensional world. The depth component of the perceived world is not due to some kind of inference based on the two-dimensional stimulus, but rather, even in monocular viewing, the world appears primarily as a volumetric depth percept. In fact, it takes considerable training for an artist to learn to extract the two-dimensional projection from the three-dimensional world of visual experience, as required to produce a perspective sketch. It is thus the two-dimensional projection that must be inferred from the three-dimensional percept, rather than the other way around. The introspective procedure of the Structuralists therefore was not really a true introspection, but a biased introspection based on a knowledge of the geometry of the retina. If an artist were commissioned to create an accurate depiction of the subjective experience of a visual scene, the closest approximation to the information present in that experience would be some kind of three-dimensional painted construct, like a museum diorama, or a theatre set, or like the painted cardboard models made by architects to give an impression of the buildings they plan to construct. When viewed through a window that hides their connection to the rest of the world, such constructs can be indistinguishable from the percept of a real scene, which suggests that the informational content of those painted models is similar to that of the corresponding spatial percept. The Gestalt approach suggests exactly this kind of data structure being encoded in the brain, and that in turn suggests that there is a great deal of perceptual processing that occurs below the level of consciousness, where the two-dimensional retinal image is transformed into the three-dimensional percept. The lowest level of conscious experience therefore is already far removed from the retinal representation, containing a great deal more explicit spatial information than that present at the sensory surface.

A QUANTITATIVE PHENOMENOLOGY

We know the information that is present on the retinal surface. That information appears as a spatial pattern of light intensity projected on a two-dimensional surface, just as on the photosensor array of a video camera. Exactly which aspects of this image are extracted by retinal processing cannot be said with certainty, but the information available for extraction can be determined objectively, and therefore we can describe with some precision the input available to visual processing. The dimensions of conscious experience, or the "output" of perceptual processing, can also be determined by careful examination of the phenomenal world. The transformation of perception can therefore be described as a transformation from the two-dimensional retinal stimulus to the three-dimensional percept generated from that image.

Immanuel Kant described the experience of vision as a spatial void, within which colored regions are experienced as representing surfaces and objects of the world. Every point on every visible surface is perceived at an explicit spatial location in three dimensions, and all of the visible points on a perceived object like a cube or a sphere, or this book, are perceived simultaneously in the form of continuous surfaces in depth. The perception of multiple transparent surfaces, as well as the experience of empty space between the observer and a visible surface, reveals that multiple depth values can be perceived at any spatial location. I propose to model the information in perception as a computational transformation from a two-dimensional colored image (or two images in the binocular case) to a three-dimensional volumetric data structure in which every point can encode either the experience of transparency, or the experience of a perceived color at that location. The appearance of a color value at some point in this representational manifold corresponds *by definition* to the subjective experience of that color at the corresponding point in phenomenal space. If we can describe the formation of this volumetric data structure from the two-dimensional retinal image as a computational transformation, we will have quantified the information processing apparent in perception, as a necessary prerequisite to the search for a neurophysiological mechanism that can perform that same transformation.

It is not necessary for the perceptual model to actually become colored to represent the experience of color at some point in space, any more than the electrical voltages that encode the pixel values of a colored digital image are in any sense colored in themselves. All that is required is that the information content in the representation of color be equal to the informational content of the perceptual experience. Although this solution leaves unresolved the fundamental philosophical issue of the ultimate nature of consciousness, it does allow us to quantify the information encoded in conscious experience, an approach that has served psychology well in the past.

THE FUNCTION OF CONSCIOUS EXPERIENCE

There is much discussion in philosophy about the possible function of conscious experience, and whether it is an epiphenomenon that has no direct functional value. The issue is highlighted with the notion of the hypothetical "zombie" whose behavior as observed externally is identical to that of normal people, except that this zombie supposedly lacks all conscious experience. This notion sounds very peculiar from the indirect realist perspective. Once we accept that the world which appears to be external to our bodies is in fact an internal data structure in our physical brain, the notion of the zombie as proposed becomes a contradiction in terms. A zombie that does not possess an internal picture of the world around it could not possibly walk about in the world avoiding obstacles as we do. Without a conscious memory of where it had just been, and a conscious intent of where it would like to go next, the zombie would behave much as we do when we are in an unconscious state: It would lie inert and immobile, with neither the incentive nor the capacity for action.

The notion of this kind of zombie presupposes a distinction between the structural aspects of the perceived world, which are supposedly a reflection of the objective spatial properties of the world, and the subjective qualia with which those perceptual structures are somehow painted or clothed. This harkens back to an old distinction drawn by Locke, between the primary and secondary qualities of perception. However, Immanuel Kant (1781/1991) argued that the perception of space and the perception of time are themselves a priori intuitions; they are a kind of quale used by the mind to express the structure of external reality. Therefore the fact that the world of experience appears as a volumetric spatial structure is itself an aspect of conscious experience, rather than (or in addition to) a veridical manifestation of the true nature of the external world.

The notion of the hypothetical zombie therefore is impossible in principle, because it is impossible to have any perceptual experience in the absence of some subjective   qualia by which   that experience is expressed. Qualia are the carriers of the information experienced in perception (Rosenberg, 1999), just as electromagnetic waves are the carriers of radio and television signals. Again, information theory can help clarify the central role of qualia in perceptual representation. Information is defined independent of the physical medium by which it is carried, whether it be electromagnetic radiation, electrical voltages on a wire, or characters on a printed page, or some other way. However, in every case there must be some physical medium to carry that information, for it is impossible for information to exist without a physical carrier of some kind. A similar principle holds on the subjective side of the mind/brain barrier, where the information encoded in perceptual experience is carried by modulations of some subjective quale, whether it be variations of hue, brightness, saturation, pitch, heat or cold, pleasure or pain, and so on. The notion of experience without qualia to support it is as impossible as the notion of information without any physical medium or mechanism to carry that information. The zombie argument therefore is circular, for it presupposes the possibility of behavior in the absence of experience to demonstrate that behavior and experience are theoretically separable. The functional purpose of conscious experience therefore is to provide an internal replica of the external world in order to guide our behavior through the world, for otherwise we would have no knowledge of the structure of the world, or of our location within it.

This view of qualia as the carriers of the information in conscious experience casts a new light on the concept of primary and secondary qualities of perception. Although all of conscious experience is necessarily "secondary" in Locke's sense, there are nevertheless certain aspects of conscious experience that are a secondary manifestation of the actual configuration of external reality, such as the spatial structures in conscious experience, at least when perception is veridical, that is, nonillusory. Other aspects of phenomenal experience are entirely "secondary," such as the qualia for color, pleasure, or pain, in the sense that they represent an arbitrary mapping that has no direct correspondence to external reality. For example, the position of a glowing phosphor "blip" on a radar scope is a "primary" manifestation of the location of an aircraft in external space, although expressed in a distorted miniature representation, whereas the green color and fuzzy shape of that blip are entirely secondary qualities of this representation, corresponding to the actual mechanism of the representation, rather than to any property of the external world. The "secondary qualities" of perception are a direct manifestation of the actual mechanism of your own brain, as viewed "from the inside". The phenomenal quale of the color red, for example, is not a quality of some ethereal "mind stuff," but rather it is an observed property of the actual mechanism of the physical brain, used to represent light of longer wavelengths detected in the external world.

THE CARTESIAN THEATRE AND THE HOMUNCULUS PROBLEM

This "picture-in-the-head" or "Cartesian theatre" concept of visual representation has been criticized on the grounds that there would have to be a miniature observer to view this miniature internal scene, resulting in an infinite regress of observers within observers. Pinker (1984, p. 38) pointed out, however, that there is no need for an internal observer of the scene, because the internal representation is simply a data structure like any other data in a computer, except that these data are expressed in spatial form. In fact, any information encoded in the brain needs only to be available to other internal processes, rather than to a miniature copy of the whole brain. To deny the spatial nature of the perceptual representation in the brain is to deny the spatial nature so clearly evident in the world we perceive around us.

To paraphrase Descartes, it is not only the existence of myself that is verified by the fact that I think, but when I experience the vivid spatial presence of objects in the phenomenal world, those objects are certain to exist, at least in the form of a subjective experience, with properties as I experience them to have—that is, location, spatial extension, color, and shape. I think them, therefore they exist. All that remains uncertain is whether those percepts exist also as objective external objects as well as internal perceptual ones, and whether their perceived properties correspond to objective properties. But their existence in my internal perceptual world is beyond question if I experience them, even if only as a hallucination.

BOUNDED NATURE OF THE PERCEPTUAL WORLD

The idea of perception as a literal volumetric replica of the world inside your head immediately raises the question of boundedness—that is, how an explicit spatial representation can encode the infinity of external space in a finite volumetric system. The solution to this problem can be found by inspection. Phenomenological examination reveals that perceived space is not infinite but is bounded. This can be seen most clearly in the night sky, where the distant stars produce a domelike percept that presents the stars at equal distance from the observer, and that distance is perceived to be less than infinite. The lower half of perceptual space is usually filled with a percept of the ground underfoot, but it too becomes hemispherical when viewed from far enough above the surface, for example, from an airplane or a hot-air balloon. The dome of the sky above and the bowl of the earth below therefore define a finite, approximately spherical space (Heelan, 1983) that encodes distances out to infinity within a representational structure that is both finite and bounded. Although the properties of perceived space are approximately Euclidean near the body, there are peculiar global distortions evident in perceived space that provide clear evidence of the phenomenal world being an internal rather than external entity.

THE PHENOMENON OF PERSPECTIVE

Consider the phenomenon of perspective, as seen for example when standing on a long straight road that stretches to the horizon in a straight line in opposite directions. The sides of the road appear to converge to a point both up ahead and back behind, but while converging, they are also perceived to pass to either side of the percipient, and at the same time, the road is perceived to be straight and parallel throughout its entire length. This property of perceived space is so familiar in everyday experience as to seem totally unremarkable. And yet this most prominent violation of Euclidean geometry offers clear evidence for the non-Euclidean nature of perceived space. For the two sides of the road must therefore in some sense be perceived as being bowed, and yet while bowed, they are also perceived as being straight. This can only mean that the space within which we perceive the road to be embedded, must itself be curved.

What does it mean for a space to be curved? If it is the space itself that is curved, rather than just the objects within that space, then it is the definition of straightness itself that is curved in that space. In other words, if the space were filled with a set of grid lines marking straight lines with uniform spacing, those lines themselves would be curved rather than straight, as they are in Euclidean space. However, the curvature would not be apparent to creatures who live in that curved space, because the curves that are followed by those grid lines are the very definition of straightess in that space. In other words, a curved object in that curved space would be defined as perfectly straight, as long as the curvature of the object exactly matched the curvature of the space it was in. If you are having difficulty picturing this paradoxical concept, and suspect that it embodies a contradiction in terms, just look at phenomenal perspective, which has exactly that paradoxical property. Phenomenal perspective embodies that same contradiction in terms, with parallel lines meeting at two points while passing to either side of the percipient, and while being at the same time straight and parallel and equidistant throughout their length. This absurd contradiction is clearly not a property of the physical world, which is measurably Euclidean, at least at the familiar scale of our everyday environment. Therefore that curvature must be a property of perceived space, thereby confirming that perceived space is not the same as the external space of which it is an imperfect replica.

In fact, the observed warping of perceived space is exactly the property that allows the finite representational space to encode an infinite external space. This property is achieved by using a variable representational scale: the ratio of the physical distance in the perceptual representation relative to the distance in external space that it represents. This scale is observed to vary as a function of distance from the center of our perceived world, such that objects close to the body are encoded at a larger representational scale than objects in the distance, and beyond a certain limiting distance the representational scale, at least in the depth dimension, falls to zero, that is, objects beyond a certain distance lose all perceptual depth. This is seen, for example, where the sun and moon and distant mountains appear as if cut out of paper and pasted against the dome of the sky.

The distortion of perceived space is suggested in Fig. 2.1A, which depicts the perceptual representation for a man walking down a road. The phenomenon of perspective is by definition a transformation from a three-dimensional world through a focal point to a two-dimensional surface. The appearance of perspective on the retinal surface therefore is no

Fig. 2.1   (A) The perceptual representation of a man walking down a long straight road. The sides of the road are perceived to be parallel and equidistant throughout their length, yet at the same time they are perceived to converge to a point both up ahead and behind, and that point is perceived at a distance that is less than infinite. This peculiar violation of Euclidean geometry is perhaps the strongest evidence for the internal nature of the perceived world, for it shows evidence of the perspective projection due to the optics of the eye, out in the world around us, although in a unique form. (B) A peculiar property of this warped representation is that its two-dimensional projection is identical to the two-dimensional perspective projection of the corresponding Euclidean space that it represents.

mystery, and is similar in principle to the image formed by the lens in a camera. What is remarkable in perception is the perspective that is observed not on a two-dimensional surface, but somehow embedded in the three-dimensional space of our perceptual world. Nowhere in the objective world of external reality is there anything that is remotely similar to the phenomenon of perspective as we experience it phenomenologically, where a perspective foreshortening is observed not on a two-dimensional image, but in three dimensions on a solid volumetric object. The appearance of perspective in the three-dimensional world we perceive around us is perhaps the strongest evidence for the internal nature of the world of experience, for it shows that the world that appears to be the source of the light that enters our eye must actually be downstream of the retina, because it exhibits the traces of perspective distortion imposed by the lens of the eye, although in a completely different form.

This view of perspective offers an explanation for another otherwise paradoxical but familiar property of perceived space whereby more distant objects are perceived to be smaller, and yet at the same time are perceived as undiminished in size. This corresponds to the difference in subject's reports depending on whether they are given *objective* versus *projective* instruction (Coren et al., 1994, p. 500) in how to report their observations, showing that both types of information are available perceptually. This duality in size perception is often described as a cognitive compensation for the foreshortening of perspective, as if the perceptual representation of more distant objects is indeed smaller, but is somehow labeled with the correct size as some kind of symbolic tag representing objective size attached to each object in perception. However, this kind of explanation is misleading, for the objective measure of size is not a discrete quantity attached to individual objects, but is more of a continuum, or gradient of difference between objective and projective size, that varies monotonically as a function of distance from the egocentric point. In other words, this phenomenon is best described as a warping of the space itself within which the objects are represented, so that objects that are warped coherently along with the space in which they are embedded appear undistorted perceptually. The mathematical form of this warping is discussed in more detail in chapter 4.

The bizarrely warped space of subjective experience has another interesting property, which is that the two-dimensional projection of this warped representational space, projected radially from the center, is identical to the two-dimensional perspective projection of the corresponding Euclidean world that it represents, as suggested in Fig. 2.1B. In other words, a photograph taken from the center of this distorted model world would be identical to a photograph taken from the corresponding point in the external world. This makes this particular representation a convenient format for what is, after all, the primary function of visual perception, which is to reconstruct a full three-dimensional model of the external world based on its two-dimensional retinal projection.

THE EMBODIED PERCIPIENT

This model of spatial representation emphasizes another aspect of perception that is often ignored in models of vision: that our percept of the world includes a percept of our own body within that world, and our body is located at a very special location at the center of that world, and it remains at the center of perceived space even as we move about in the external world. Perception is embodied by its very nature, for the percept of our body is the only thing that gives an objective measure of scale in the world.

This fact became evident in dramatic form when the Apollo astronauts were required to hover to a landing on the lunar surface by visual reference. The texture of the lunar surface appears similar through a wide range of spatial scales, and therefore it is impossible to judge the height of the craft as is done on earth, by the scale of familiar objects such as trees, houses, and cars. A man standing on the moon, on the other hand, has a vivid sense of his height of eye, due to the somatosensory feel of the ground against his feet, and this senation provides an objective measure of scale for the entire visual scene. In the words of Protagoras, man is the measure of all things. The little man at the center of the spherical world of perception therefore is not a miniature observer of the internal scene, but is itself a spatial percept, constructed of the same perceptual material as the rest of the spatial scene, for that scene would be incomplete without a replica of the percipient's own body in his perceived world.

Chapter 3

The Enigma of Gestalt Phenomena

A GESTALT REVIVAL

In the contemporary literature, Gestalt theory is associated chiefly with a number of visual illusions, as well as with Wertheimer's laws of perceptual grouping. However, there is little discussion today of the fundamental principles of visual processing revealed by those Gestalt illusions and grouping laws. In fact, the properties of perception identified by Gestalt theory remain as mysterious today in computational terms as they were when they were originally introduced almost a century ago.

There were several reasons for the general decline in popularity of Gestalt theory in psychology, beginning around the 1950s. The first and most serious was the failure of Gestalt theory to propose a viable computational mechanism to account for the global nature of perception and the properties of emergence and reification. The second was the refinement of the single-cell recording technique, which shifted the theoretical emphasis from fieldlike theories of whole aspects of perception to pointlike theories of neural response. There is a security and comfort to be found in the objectivity of direct electrical measurements of the nervous system, for that approach avoids the thorny philosophical issues inherent in the study of conscious experience. Finally, Gestalt theory was dealt another blow with the remarkable success of the digital computer, a device whose operational principles represent the polar opposite to the Gestalt way of thinking, by breaking every computational problem into a sequence of simple steps that are each computed in isolation from the problem as a whole. In the heady days of the early artificial intelligence movement, the problem of vision was considered all but solved, so much so that researchers working on visual recognition felt it unnecessary to emulate biological vision systems, but set out to reinvent visual processing from first principles using digital computation. It has taken decades of experience with the digital computer to reveal the fundamental limitations of the atomistic strategy embodied in that paradigm of computation, and thereby to bring about a new appreciation for the remarkable capacity embodied in biological vision systems, even those of the simpler animals. The time has come to revisit Gestalt theory and to reevaluate its findings in the light of this new perspective.

WERTHEIMER'S LAWS OF PERCEPTUAL GROUPING

Wertheimer's laws of perceptual grouping (Wertheimer, 1923), some of which are illustrated in Fig. 3.1, demonstrate the holistic aspect of perception which are difficult to

45

explain in terms of the atomistic model of neural processing. In Fig. 3.1A, the dots segregate spontaneously into two groups based on their similarity of shape and size, thus demonstrating the principle of perceptual grouping by similarity. A similar grouping is also observed between elements that are similar in color or motion or texture. Although it is simple enough to define the rules for such a perceptual segmentation in any particular case, those rules do not generalize easily to other cases. Figure 3.1B demonstrates grouping by proximity, although the proximity required for perceptual grouping is not defined in absolute terms but in terms of some kind of relative proximity of a form that is also difficult to express in explicit laws. Figure 3.1C demonstrates grouping by"good continuation": that is, those dots that are perceived to lie along a continuous path are perceived as a separate entity, distinct from the other dots in the figure. Figure 3.1D depicts grouping by closure, such that the dots are segregated perceptually based on their tendency to outline enclosed forms. Figure 3.1E demonstrates grouping by symmetry. This figure was constructed by replicating an irregular arrangement of dots in a fourfold symmetry about a center. Figure 3.1F depicts the same basic pattern, this time replicated in a periodic array, thereby demonstrating the Gestalt law of periodicity.

The properties of the stimulus reflected in these grouping laws exhibit global configural qualities that are difficult to define algorithmically. The facts that these perceptual organizations are experienced immediately, are beyond the reach of cognitive analysis or intervention, and are independent of an individual's past visual experience suggest that these represent low-level spatial interactions between the elements of perception that provide concrete evidence for the nature of the computational algorithm of natural vision. However, despite the apparently lawful nature of these phenomena, the exact laws behind them remain elusive, mostly because those laws appear in a form that is difficult to express in the reductionist form familiar to scientific analysis. There are many more Gestalt laws of perceptual grouping that have been identified, all of them exhibiting this same elusive holistic nature. There is a need to devise a new formalism to express these holistic aspects of perceptual computation in order to quantify the properties of the perceptual transformation.

EMERGENCE

The most significant general property of perception identified by Gestalt theory was a holistic, or global-first, aspect of perception in which the global configuration of a stimulus is often perceived in the absence of its local component features. Figure 3.2 shows a picture that is familiar in vision circles, one that reveals the principle of emergence in a most compelling form. For those who have never seen this picture before, it appears initially as a random pattern of irregular shapes. A remarkable transformation is

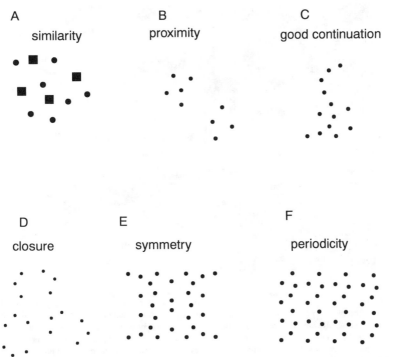

Figure 3.1   Examples of some of Wertheimer's laws of perceptual grouping: (A) similarity, (B) proximity, (C) good continuation, (D) closure, (E) symmetry, and (F) periodicity. Although these groupings are experienced preattentively, it is difficult to devise explicit rules that predict the grouping percept for arbitrary figures.

observed in this percept as soon as one recognizes the subject of the picture as a dalmation dog in patchy sunlight in the shade of overhanging trees. The outlines of the dog are defined by a large number of apparently chance alignments of irregular edges. What is remarkable about this percept is that the dog is perceived so vividly despite the fact that much of its perimeter is missing. Furthermore, visual edges that form a part of the perimeter of the dog are locally indistinguishable from other less significant edges. Therefore any local portion of this image does not contain the information necessary to distinguish significant from insignificant edges. This figure therefore reveals a kind of processing different from the atomistic approach suggested by feature detection theory, for in this image global features are detected as a whole, rather than as an assembly of local parts. No computational algorithm has ever been devised that can handle the level of visual ambiguity present in the dog picture.

Fig. 3.2 The dog picture is familiar in vision circles, for it demonstrates the principle of emergence in perception. The local regions of this image do not contain sufficient information to distinguish significant form contours from insignificant noisy edges. As soon as the picture is recognized as that of a dog in the dappled sunshine under overhanging trees, the contours of the dog pop out perceptually, filling in visual edges even in regions where no edges are present in the input.

In his discussion of the dog picture, Marr (1982, pp. 100–101) suggested that this image represents a special case of top-down influence, which is only of secondary importance in early visual processing. However, the dog picture simply reveals in exaggerated form a principle of visual processing that is found in all visual recognition. The only reason this ambiguity is not readily apparent is that recognition usually occurs so rapidly that all we experience consciously is the final percept, neatly segmented into clearly defined figure and ground. The ambiguity in more common imagery can be revealed, however, by viewing randomly selected points in randomly selected photographs of natural scenes through a *reduction screen*—that is, a small aperture in an opaque sheet laid over the photograph so as to reveal only one local portion of the image at a time. Viewing through the reduction screen, it is impossible to distinguish significant form edges in the image from insignificant or spurious edges such as texture lines in grass, tree, or fabric patterns, or the edges due to cast shadows or attached shadows, specular reflections, and so on. If it is impossible to identify the significant form edges that define the perimeter of objects, then it is impossible to recognize those objects with the kind of deterministic algorithm suggested by Marr. This problem is well known in the field of artificial image recognition algorithms that begin with local edge detection. The fact that even a human observer cannot identify the significant form edges through a reduction screen indicates that it is not the choice of featural representation that is lacking in the digital algorithms, but the information of global significance is simply not available in the local context, even under the scrutiny of the full human visual system. This in turn demonstrates that there must be some kind of global process at work in visual recognition, which operates on the image as a whole, rather than in a piecewise manner building up from local features. The principle of emergence is commonly seen in a natural environment of trees and shrubs, whose irregular tangle of branches and leaves offer no solid perimeter on which a feature detection algorithm can reliably operate, and yet the global configurations of these objects are readily perceived both by humans and even simple animals.

The principle of emergence, sometimes expressed as the Platonic motto "The whole is more than the mere sum of its parts," suggests some kind of magical mystical process whereby perceptual structure appears out of nowhere. However, Wolfgang Köhler (1924) argued that there is no magic in emergence; the principle of emergence is seen in many physical systems, including the way that electric charge distributes itself throughout a conductor, or water seeks its own level in a vessel. Perhaps the most familiar Gestalt example of emergence in a physical system is the soap bubble (Koffka, 1935). The spherical shape of a soap bubble is not encoded in the form of a spherical template or abstract mathematical code, but rather the form emerges from the parallel action of innumerable local forces of surface tension acting in unison. This concept is demonstrated most clearly in the soap-bubble computer in which a closed loop of wire is bent into some arbitrary three-dimensional shape, and then dipped into soapy water to form a bubble surface. The forces of surface tension cause the bubble surface to draw in on itself, resulting at equilibrium in a surface that automatically computes the minimum spanning surface for the given perimeter. In simple cases this minimal surface can also be derived analytically, but for more complex or irregularly shaped perimeters the problem may have no closed-form solution. Nevertheless, the bubble computer solves this problem for virtually any shaped perimeter instantaneously, and the time required for the computation is essentially independent of the exact shape of the perimeter.

A similar emergent principle is observed in spline curve interpolation. In the days of wooden shipbuilding the smooth curves of the hull were computed by bending flexible wooden splines around spikes driven into the floor of the lofting room at discrete reference points which were located by scaling up measurements from the drafting plans. The spline computes its globally smooth curvature by a parallel relaxation of the multiple forces of stiffness active at all points along the length of the spline simultaneously.

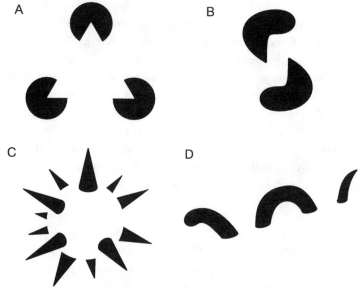

Fig. 3.3 (A) The Kanizsa triangle. (B) Tse's volumetric worm. (C) Idesawa's spiky sphere. (D) Tse's "sea monster." These illusions reveal the constructive or generative function of perception, for the percept encodes more explicit spatial information than the retinal stimulus on which the percept is based.

There are two features that characterize emergent phenomena: parallelism and dynamics. The parallel aspect of emergence is the fact that multiple tiny forces act on the system in unison, and the most emergent systems are also continuous, or fieldlike in nature, as in the case of the soap bubble whose surface and the forces acting within it essentially define a continuum. Many wave phenomena also exhibit the continuous aspect of emergence, for example, diffraction patterns and holography, whose final patterns depend on the total contribution of all of its elements. The dynamic aspect of emergence is reflected in the fact that the final global state is not computed in a single pass, but continuously, like a relaxation to equilibrium in a dynamic system model. In other words the forces acting on the system induce a change in the system configuration, and that change in turn modifies the forces acting on the system. The system configuration and the forces that drive it therefore are changing continuously in time until equilibrium is attained, at which point the system remains in a state of dynamic equilibrium; that is, its static state belies a dynamic balance of forces ready to spring back into motion as soon as the balance is upset. In computer simulations the emergent system has to be quantized into discrete elements, whose dynamic evolution is simulated in discrete time steps, where the forces acting on the system are assumed to be constant over a very short time interval. At the end of that interval the new system configuration is used to calculate the new forces for the next time interval, and the calculation is repeated through as many iterations as required to reach equilibrium. Computer simulations of emergent phenomena even as simple as a bubble surface can be computationally very expensive, and inevitably suffer from artifacts due to quantization in space and time. Thus, many problems that are considered mathematically or computationally intractable are actually perfectly computable, given the proper analog dynamic mechanism to perform the computation by emergence. Gestalt theory suggests that the computations of visual perception have this emergent character.

REIFICATION

The Kanizsa figure (Kanizsa, 1979) shown in Fig. 3.3A, is one of the most familiar illusions introduced by Gestalt theory. In this figure the triangular configuration is not only recognized as being present in the image, but that triangle is filled in perceptually, producing visual edges in places where no edges are present in the input. Furthermore, the illusory triangle is filled in with a white that is brighter than the white background of the figure. Finally, the figure produces a perceptual segmentation in depth, with the three Pac-Man features appearing as complete circles, completing amodally behind an occluding white triangle. In more recent work, Tse (1998, 1999) extended this concept with a set of even more sophisticated illusions such as those shown in Fig. 3.3B through 3.3D, in which the illusory percept takes the form of a three-dimensional volume. These figures demonstrate that the visual system performs a perceptual *reification*,[1] a filling-in of a more complete and explicit perceptual entity based on a less complete visual input. The spatial reification of a two-dimensional stimulus into a solid three-dimensional percept is also observed in the dog picture of Fig. 3.2, where the shape of the dog pops out of the picture with a specific three-dimensional slope defined perceptually at every point on the dog's back. The identification of this generative or constructive aspect of perception was one of the most significant achievements of Gestalt theory.

MULTISTABILITY

Multistability in perception is direct evidence for multistability in the brain. A familiar example of multistability in perception is seen in the Necker cube, shown in Fig. 3.4A. Prolonged viewing of this stimulus results in spontaneous reversals, in which the entire percept is observed to invert in depth. The reversals can be controlled somewhat by fixating on one or the other internal vertex, which has a tendency to pop into a convex vertex percept. In this reversal, every point on the percept is observed to shift to a different location in depth. Figure 3.4B shows the famous faces/vase illusion introduced by Rubin (1958), where the contour is perceived to belong always to the foreground object or

---

1. Webster: re-ify [L *res* thing]: to regard something abstract as a material thing.

A   B

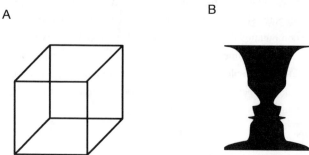

Fig. 3.4   (A) The Necker cube. (B) Rubin's faces/vase illusion. These illusions reveal the multistability of perception, which in turn shows that vision is not a sequential process from input to percept, but is more of a dynamic system whose equilibrium states represent the final percept.

objects. Even more compelling examples of multistability are seen in surrealistic paintings by Salvator Dali, and etchings by Escher, in which large and complex regions of the image are seen to invert perceptually, losing all resemblance to their former appearance (Attneave, 1971). The significance for theories of visual processing is that perception cannot be considered as simply a feed-forward processing performed on the visual input to produce a perceptual output, as it is sometimes characterized in computational models of vision, but rather perception must involve some kind of dynamic process whose stable states represent the final percept. The spontaneous reversals in these illusions demonstrate that the perceptual process is active continuously, and exists in a state of dynamic balance whose apparent stability or static character when viewing an unambiguous stimulus is somewhat illusory.

INVARIANCE

A central focus of Gestalt theory was the issue of invariance: how the essential structural character of an object is recognized immediately and effortlessly when presented in a great variety of different aspects and viewing conditions. For example, the structures depicted in Fig. 3.5A are immediately recognized as the same essential shape independent of translation, rotation, and scale. These shapes are immediately distinguishable from the shapes in Fig. 3.5B, which are constructed of the same basic elements. Recognition also appears invariant to distortions due to perspective and elastic deformation, as seen in Fig. 3.5C, and the structural form is even recognized when constructed of different low-level featural elements as shown in Fig. 3.5D. Not only are all of these shapes recognized despite these various distortions, but we perceive the distortion itself just as clearly as the shape it distorts. For example, for each of the elastic or perspective distortions shown in Fig. 3.5C, we can predict how that same distortion would affect the shape of a cube or pyramid to which it was applied. Invariance in perception is a general principal that is

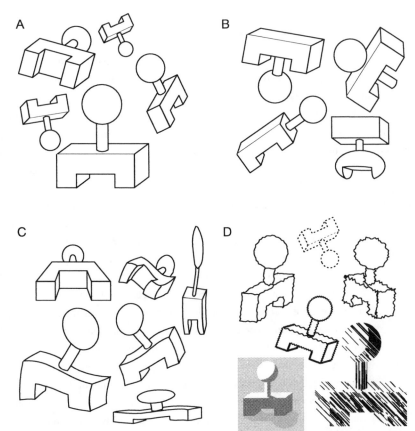

Fig. 3.5   (A) The basic structural form of a simple object is recognized immediately independent of rotation, translation, and scale, as seen in this example which is easily distinguished from (B) similar shapes composed of different configurations of the same basic elements. (C) Recognition also occurs independent of perspective or elastic deformations, and (D) independent of the characteristics of the low-level edges or texture elements of which the stimulus is composed.

observed also in different modalities—for example, in the perception of color and brightness, where the color of an object is generally judged independent of the color of the light falling on it. Snow is perceived as white even when viewed at sunset, where the side facing the sun is measurably yellow or orange, whereas the side away from the sun is actually blue from the diffuse illumination of the sky. It takes considerable training for artists to learn to depict these colors photographically as they appear in the visual stimulus, as opposed to the way they appear perceptually, which is how they are most often painted by children and amateurs, who tend to paint the snow white. Invariance is also observed in other sensory modalities. In the auditory mode, melodies are recognized independent of the absolute pitch of the music that carries them, and words are recognized independent of the voices that form them.

The preattentive ease with which these invariances are handled in visual recognition suggests that invariance is fundamental to the visual representation. However, it is difficult to imagine how such invariance can be achieved computationally in a recognition system except by providing detectors sensitive to every possible variation in the stimulus and connecting them all to a single recognition response node. That approach leads to a combinatorial explosion in the required number of detectors. For example, a visual detector tuned to respond to a particular character, like the letter "E," can be defined as a template shaped like the letter "E" that is scanned electronically over the entire visual scene searching for its "E" feature at every spatial location. The detector would also have to be scanned at every possible orientation and at a range of spatial scales for the response to be invariant to rotation and scale. But the scanning would have to account not only for each of these individual variations, but also for every combination of those variations—for example, to recognize a letter that is rotated and translated and scaled to some degree. The problem becomes rapidly intractable even for a relatively small number of featural variations. Furthermore, the perceptual reification observed in Fig. 3.3 suggests that the recognized form is reified in the context of the partial input that gives rise to it, in a manner that is difficult to account for in terms of conventional neurophysiology. Feature-based theories of recognition have been proposed in which the local elements are detected first, and then the configuration of those elements results in recognition of the global form. The problem with this approach can be seen in Fig. 3.5D, where the same structure is recognized even when composed of different elemental features. Invariance in perception and recognition is one of the deepest enigmas of natural vision, and no real progress can possibly be made in understanding visual processing without accounting for invariance as a fundamental property of the system.

BRAIN ANCHORING

Phenomenological examination of the visual world shows it to rotate relative to our perceived head as our head turns relative to the world. Furthermore, objects within the perceived world move coherently relative to the background while maintaining their perceptual integrity as discrete objects, even when they disappear momentarily behind occluding foreground objects. If we assume that the structural percept of the world is represented by a spatial pattern of activation of some sort in the tissue of the brain, this suggests that the internal representation of external objects and surfaces is not anchored to the tissue of the brain, as suggested by current concepts of neural representation, but is free to rotate coherently relative to the neural substrate, as suggested in Köhler's field theory (Köhler & Held, 1947). In other words, the perceptual picture of the world can move relative to the representational substrate, and discrete patterns of perceptual structure can move relative to that background while maintaining their perceptual integrity and recognized identity, like the words scrolling across the array of light bulbs on an old fashioned cinema marquee.

This issue of brain anchoring is so troublesome that it is often cited as a counterargument for an isomorphic representation, because it is difficult to conceive of the solid spatial percept of the surrounding world having to be reconstructed anew in all its rich spatial detail with every turn of the head or blink of the eyes. However, the fact that this reconstruction occurs can be verified phenomenologically, as long as we recognize the truth of indirect realism. Therefore, this property too must be expressed in models of visual representation.

AMODAL PERCEPTION

There is another aspect of perception whose significance was recognized by Gestalt theory but receives little mention in the contemporary literature. This is the phenomenon of amodal perception (Michotte, Thinés, & Crabbé, 1991), or the perception of spatial structure that is not associated with any particular sensory modality. For example, a book lying on a table is perceived to lie on a complete table top whose surface is continuous under the book and whose color and surface texture are experienced perceptually as continuous under the book, even though there is no sensory stimulus corresponding to the occluded portion of that surface. The hidden rear faces of objects are also perceived amodally, as observed by Gibson (Reed, 1988) and the Gestaltists (Kanizsa 1979; Arnheim, 1969a, p. 86). For example, a sphere is not perceived as the hemisphere presented by its visible surface, but is experienced as a complete sphere, even though the percipient is aware that the rear surface is hidden from view. Similarly, an object partially occluded by a foreground object is perceived to be complete behind the occluder. These phenomena indicate that it is possible to perceive spatial structure in the absence of physical stimulation.

One reason why amodal perception has been so readily overlooked is that the nature of the amodal percept is so insensible and insubstantial that it is likely to be mistaken for a purely cognitive abstraction. In fact, I argue in chapter 9 that the amodal percept is intermediate between perception and cognition, having the sharply defined spatial definition of the former, and the insensible character of the latter. The spatial definition of the amodal percept can be revealed by a process I call *morphomimesis*. If you stand in front of a pillar, it is possible to indicate with the palm of your hand the approximate location and orientation of the hidden rear surface of the pillar at different sample points with a sweep of your palms, even for an artificial pillar built like a hollow facade, with a curved front face but no rear face. The ability to perform this kind of manual miming confirms the existence of a high-resolution, fully reified spatial representation of the form of the pillar in your brain, which encodes the same information as a full spatial replica, or internal model of the pillar, including its hidden rear surfaces.

PERCEPTION OUTSIDE THE VISUAL FIELD

The experience of perception suggests that visual space includes a percept of the world outside of the visual field, including the world behind the head. In other words, the head is treated as an occluder of the world behind the head, and the final percept is of a spherical space surrounding the body, only part of which corresponds to the visual field. Parts of the visual world that are currently outside of the visual field are experienced amodally, that is, in the absence of a vivid impression of color and visual detail. However, the world behind the head is experienced as a spatial structure, as can be demonstrated with a backward step. A step (whether forward or backward) requires an accurate knowledge of the height and orientation of the ground at the point of contact. This becomes evident whenever a step encounters an unexpected change in surface height or orientation, even of as little as an inch or two, which inevitably results in a stumble. A backward step without a stumble therefore is like a *pedal* morphomimesis, in that it indicates that the stepper has knowledge of these parameters within about an inch or two. Both Gibson (Reed 1988) and the Gestaltists (Kanizsa, 1979; Tampieri, 1956; Attneave & Farrar, 1977; Arnheim, 1969a, p. 86) fully appreciated the significance of this aspect of amodal perception.

MAKING SENSE OF GESTALT PHENOMENA

It is small wonder that in the face of this formidable array of most enigmatic properties, theories of vision have generally been restricted to simplistic models of isolated aspects of the problem in a piecemeal manner. However, this does not in any way justify the fact that the Gestalt properties of perception, discovered and identified almost a century ago, are so little discussed in the contemporary literature. Our failure to find a neurophysiological explanation for Gestalt phenomena does not suggest that no such explanation exists, only that we must be looking for it in the wrong places. The enigmatic nature of Gestalt phenomena highlights the importance of the search for a computational mechanism that exhibits these same properties. In fact, any model that fails to address the Gestalt phenomena of perception is worse than no model at all, for it is a diversion from the real issues of perception.

The usual analytical approach of breaking a complex problem into simpler pieces is only valid when those pieces are functionally independent. A model of an emergent system must take into account the global nature of the process and must model all the relevant components that contribute to the emergent state. In the case of visual perception, this is a formidable undertaking, for the various Gestalt aspects of perception, emergence, reification, multistability, invariance, brain anchoring, amodal perception, and so on are not separable modules to be modeled individually, but are different aspects of a single unified dynamic mechanism. There is no evidence in the behavior of an isolated neural cell that gives any clue as to how these global properties are achieved. How then are we to begin to model these properties in the absence of a viable computational paradigm to provide the building blocks for the construction of a model of visual processing?

This is where the perceptual modeling approach can be of value. Even in the absence of a computational mechanism, it is possible to provide a quantitative perceptual model that describes the dynamic properties of the percept as observed phenomenally. This is an interim solution, for ultimately the neurophysiological mechanism will also have to be identified. However, the perceptual model serves to constrain the search for a neural mechanism that exhibits those same properties. The beauty of the perceptual modeling approach is that even in the absence of a specific neurophysiological mechanism with the required properties, a perceptual model can be designed with whatever properties are required to account for the observed phenomena, without regard to neurophysiological plausibility or computational efficiency, only to perceptual accuracy.

For example, emergence and spatial reification can be incorporated in the perceptual model by specifying that the three-dimensional surface and volume percept emerges in the perceptual manifold by the collective action of innumerable local forces in a manner analogous to the formation of a bubble surface, and those local forces can be described with respect to their effects on the perceptual representation as observed phenomenally, as opposed to their physical instantiation in the brain. This concept is elaborated in the next chapter. Multistability is thereby related to emergence, because it too suggests a dynamic process proceeding to equilibrium, but with the proviso that there need not be only a single equilibrium state—there can be many, and the spontaneous reversals as observed in the Necker cube suggest some kind of habituation or dynamic depletion and recovery process, which destabilizes any perceptual state that has been active for too long.

In order to account for amodal perception, another state must be defined in the perceptual manifold to represent volumes of solid matter in the absence of a visual sensation. A percept of a sphere would therefore be represented as a visible hemispherical front face, and this percept in turn would stimulate the emergence of an invisible spherical volume in the perceptual manifold corresponding to the amodal percept of the whole sphere. Similarly, a cylinder like a pillar is perceived as complete despite the fact that only its front surface is visible. The amodal structure therefore represents the object as a whole in a format that is independent of any particular sensory modality. This allows a variety of sensory stimuli to contribute to a single spatial percept, as was demonstrated by Galli (1932), who showed that a stroboscopic motion stimulus composed of different sense modalities, such as light and sound, or light and contact, is perceived as a single moving object.

The issue of brain anchoring, so troublesome in a neural network model, is addressed in the perceptual model by stating that the spatial pattern of the volumetric percept is not anchored to the perceptual matrix, but can rotate and translate freely within it. For example, when we turn our head, the subjective experience suggests that the image of the world in the perceptual representation rotates freely with respect to the representational substrate, so that the picture of the world in the perceptual space remains locked onto the coordinates of the external world even as the substance of the brain rotates around it, just as the image on the photosensor array of a video camera remains oriented to the world outside the camera as the camera pans across a scene. Whatever the neurophysiological reality behind this performance, these are the properties of the experience of perception, and therefore they must be the reflected in the perceptual model.

The property of invariance can also be expressed in the perceptual model. For example, rotation invariance can be quantified by proposing that the spatial structure of a perceived object and its orientation are encoded as separable variables. This would allow the structural representation to be updated progressively from successive views of an object that is rotating through a range of orientations. However, the rotation invariance property does not mean that the encoded form has no defined orientation, but rather that the perceived form is presented to consciousness at the orientation and rate of rotation that the external object is currently perceived to possess. In other words, when viewing a rotating object, like a person doing a cartwheel, or a skater spinning about her vertical axis, every part of that visual stimulus is used to update the corresponding part of the internal percept even as that percept rotates within the perceptual manifold to remain in synchrony with the rotation of the external object. So, for example, the characteristics of the skater's body are built up from the full-face, half-face, and profile views observed as the skater rotates, and those characteristics continue to be perceived amodally when the skater rotates away from the viewer, and would be expected to reappear with the same characteristics as the skater completes her turn. The property of translation invariance can be similarly quantified in the representation by proposing that the structural representation can be updated from a stimulus that is translating across the sensory surface, to update a perceptual effigy that translates with respect to the representational manifold. This property is required to account for the structural constancy of the perceived world as it scrolls past a percipient walking through a scene, with each element of that scene following the curved perspective lines suggested in Fig. 2.1, expanding outwards from a point up ahead, and collapsing back to a point behind, as would be seen in a cartoon movie rendition of that figure. However, recognition of an object's characteristic form remains constant through these gyrations of its perceptual image. This invariance property can also be expressed in a perceptual model, as described in chapter 6.

The fundamental invariance of such a representation offers an explanation for another property of visual perception, namely; the way that the individual impressions left by each visual saccade are observed to appear phenomenally at the appropriate location within the global framework of visual space depending on the direction of gaze. For example, when we look up, the retinal image is used to update our percept of the sky overhead, whereas when we look down, that same image updates our percept of the ground underfoot. This property can be quantified in the perceptual model by proposing that the sensory image from the retina is projected into the perceptual manifold in a direction that takes account of the current direction of gaze. The percept of the surrounding environment therefore serves as a kind of three-dimensional frame buffer expressed in global coordinates, which accumulates the information gathered in successive visual saccades and maintains an image of that external environment in the proper orientation relative to a spatial model of the body, compensating for body rotations or translations through the world. Portions of the environment that have not been updated recently gradually fade from perceptual memory, which is why it is easy to bump one's head after bending for some time under an overhanging shelf, or why it is possible to advance safely only a few steps after closing one's eyes while walking.

PLAUSIBILITY CONSIDERATIONS

The neurophysiological studies of the cortex using single-cell recordings might appear to be inconsistent with the nonanchored representation suggested by phenomenology. However, an argument can be made for the adaptive value of a neural representation of the external world that could break free of the tissue of the sensory or cortical substrate in order to lock on to the more meaningful coordinates of the external world, if only a plausible mechanism could be conceived to achieve this useful property. The issue therefore is whether we have enough knowledge about the theory of information-processing systems to make a judgement about the plausibility of such a rotation-invariant representation of spatial structure. The history of psychology is replete with examples of plausibility arguments based on the limited technology of the time that were later invalidated by the emergence of new technologies. The outstanding achievements of modern technology, especially in the field of information-processing systems, might seem to justify our confidence to judge the plausibility of proposed processing algorithms.

Yet despite the remarkable capabilities of modern computers, there remain certain classes of problems that appear to be fundamentally beyond the capacity of the digital computer. In fact, the very problems that are most difficult for computers to address, such as extraction of spatial structure from a visual scene, especially in the presence of attached shadows, cast shadows, specular reflections, occlusions, and perspective distortions, as well as the problems of navigation in a natural environment, defined by irregular and fragmented forms, and so on, are problems that are routinely handled by biological vision systems, even those of simpler animals. On the other hand, the kinds of problems that are easily solved by computers, such as perfect recall of vast quantities of meaningless data, perfect memory over indefinite periods, detection of the tiniest variation in otherwise identical data, and exact repeatability of even the most complex computations, are the kinds of problems that are inordinately difficult for biological intelligence, even that of the most complex of animals.

It is therefore safe to conclude that the computational principles of biological vision are fundamentally different from those of digital computation. Thus, plausibility arguments predicated on contemporary concepts of what is computable are not applicable to biological vision. Indeed, this is the strongest argument for a perceptual modeling approach in order to quantify the computational properties of the perceptual transformation unbiased by our preconceived notions of computational plausibility based on a computer technology that is fundamentally dissimilar to biological computation.

Chapter 4

The Computational Mechanism of Perception

GENERAL PRINCIPLES OF THE PERCEPTUAL TRANSFORMATION

The basic function of visual perception can be described as the transformation from a two-dimensional retinal image, or a pair of images in the binocular case, to a solid three-dimensional percept. Figure 4.1A depicts a two-dimensional stimulus that produces a three-dimensional percept of a solid cube complete in three dimensions. For simplicity, a simple line drawing is depicted in the figure, but the argument applies more appropriately to a view of a real cube observed in the world. Every point on every visible surface of the percept is experienced at a specific location in depth, and each of those surfaces is experienced as a planar continuum, with a specific three-dimensional slope in depth. The information in this perceptual experience can therefore be expressed as a three-dimensional model, as suggested in Fig. 4.1B, constructed on the basis of the input image in Fig. 4.1A. The percept also includes an amodal representation of the hidden rear face of the cube, which appears to be similar to the visible front face, that is, with equal sides and orthogonal angles. The transformation from a two-dimensional image space to a three-dimensional perceptual space is known as the *inverse optics* problem, because the intent is to reverse the optical projection in the eye, in which three-dimensional information from the world is collapsed by the optics of the eye into a two-dimensional image. However, the inverse optics problem is underconstrained, for there are an infinite number of possible three-dimensional configurations that can give rise to the same two-dimensional projection. How does the visual system select from this infinite range of possible percepts to produce the single perceptual interpretation observed phenomenally?

The answer to this question is of central significance to understanding the principles behind perception, for it reveals a computational strategy quite unlike anything devised by mankind, and certainly unlike the algorithmic decision sequences embodied in the paradigm of digital computation. The transformation observed in visual perception gives us the clearest insight into the nature of this unique computational strategy. I propose that the principles of emergence, reification, and multistability are intimately involved in this reconstruction, and that in fact these Gestalt properties are exactly the properties needed for the visual system to address the fundamental ambiguities inherent in reflected light imagery.

The principle behind the perceptual transformation can be expressed in general terms as follows. For any given visual input there is an infinite range of possible configurations of

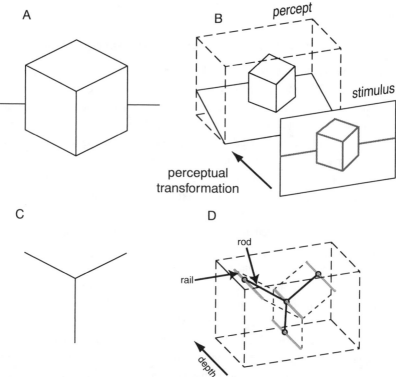

Fig. 4.1   (A) A line drawing stimulates a volumetric spatial percept with an explicit depth value at every point on every visible surface, and an amodal percept of hidden rear surfaces. (B) Perception viewed as a transformation from a two-dimensional stimulus to a three-dimensional percept. (C) The central "Y" vertex from (A), which tends to be perceived as a corner in depth. (D) A dynamic rod-and-rail model of the emergence of the depth percept in (C) by relaxation of local constraints.

objects in the external world that could have given rise to that same stimulus. The configuration of the stimulus constrains the range of those possible perceptual interpretations to those that line up with the stimulus in the two dimensions of the retinal image. Now although each individual interpretation within that range is equally likely with respect to the stimulus, some of those perceptual alternatives are intrinsically more likely than others, in the sense that they are more typical of objects commonly found in the world. I propose that the perceptual representation has the property that the more likely structural configurations are also more stable in the perceptual representation, and therefore the procedure used by the visual system is to essentially construct or reify all possible interpretations of a visual stimulus in parallel, as constrained by the configuration of the input, and then to select from that range of possible percepts the most stable perceptual configuration by a process of emergence. In other words, perception can be viewed as the computation of the intersection of two sets of constraints, which might be called *extrinsic* versus *intrinsic* constraints. The extrinsic constraints are those defined by the visual stimulus, whereas the intrinsic constraints are those defined by the structure of the percept. The configuration of the input encodes the extrinsic constraints, whereas the stability of the perceptual representation encodes the intrinsic constraints.

Arnheim (1969a) presented an insightful analysis of this concept, which can be reformulated as follows. Consider (for simplicity) just the central "Y" vertex of Fig. 4.1A depicted in Fig. 4.1C. Arnheim proposed that the extrinsic constraints of inverse optics can be expressed for this stimulus using a rod-and-rail analogy as shown in Fig. 4.1D. The three rods, representing the three edges in the visual input, are constrained in two dimensions to the configuration seen in the input, but are free to slide in depth along four rails. The rods must be elastic between their endpoints, so that they can expand and contract in length. By sliding along the rails, the rods can take on any of the infinite three-dimensional configurations corresponding to the two-dimensional input of Fig. 4.1C. For example, the final percept could theoretically range from a percept of a convex vertex protruding from the depth of the page, to a concave vertex intruding into the depth of the page, with a continuum of intermediate perceptual states between these limits.

There are other possibilities beyond these—for example, percepts where each of the three rods is at a different depth and therefore they do not meet in the middle of the stimulus. However, these alternative perceptual states are not all equally likely to be experienced. Hochberg and Brooks (1960) showed that the final percept is the one that exhibits the greatest simplicity, or prägnanz. In the case of the vertex of Fig. 4.1C, the percept tends to appear as three rods whose ends coincide in depth at the center and meet at a mutual right angle, defining either a concave or convex corner. This reduces the infinite range of possible configurations to two discrete perceptual states. This constraint can be expressed emergently in the rod and rail model by joining the three rods flexibly at the central vertex, and installing spring forces that tend to hold the three rods at mutual right angles at the vertex. With this mechanism in place to define the intrinsic or structural constraints, the rod-and-rail model becomes a dynamic system that slides in depth along the rails, and this system is bistable between a concave and convex right angled percept, as observed phenomenally in Fig. 4.1C. Although this model reveals the dynamic interaction between intrinsic and extrinsic constraints, this particular analogy is hard-wired to modeling the percept of the triangular vertex of Fig. 4.1C. I next develop a more general model that operates on this same dynamic principle but is designed to handle arbitrary input patterns.

A GESTALT BUBBLE MODEL

For the perceptual representation I propose a volumetric block or matrix of dynamic computational elements, as suggested in Fig. 4.2A, each of which can exist in one of two states, transparent or opaque, with opaque-state units being active at all points in the volume of perceptual space where a colored surface is experienced. In other words, upon viewing a stimulus like Fig. 4.1A, the perceptual representation of this stimulus is modeled as a three-dimensional pattern of opaque state units embedded in the volume of the perceptual matrix in exactly the configuration observed in the subjective percept when viewing Fig, 4.1A, that is, with opaque-state elements at all points in the volumetric space that are within a perceived surface in three dimensions, as suggested in Fig. 4.1B. All other elements in the block are in the transparent state to represent the experience of the spatial void within which perceived objects are perceived to be embedded.

More generally, opaque state elements should also encode the subjective dimensions of color, that is, hue, intensity, and saturation, and intermediate states between transparent and opaque would be required to account for the perception of semitransparent surfaces, although for now, the discussion is limited to two states and the monochromatic case. The transformation of perception can now be defined as the turning on of the appropriate pattern of elements in this volumetric representation in response to the visual input, in order to replicate the three-dimensional configuration of surfaces experienced in the subjective percept.

SURFACE PERCEPT INTERPOLATION

The perceived surfaces due to a stimulus like Fig. 4.1A appear to span the structure of the percept defined by the edges in the stimulus, somewhat like a milky bubble surface clinging to a cubical wire frame. Although the featureless portions of the stimulus between the visual edges offer no explicit visual information, a continuous surface is perceived within those regions, as well as across the white background behind the block figure, with a specific depth and surface orientation value encoded explicitly at each point in the percept. This three-dimensional surface interpolation function can be expressed in the perceptual model by assigning to every element in the opaque state a surface orientation value in three dimensions, and by defining a dynamic interaction between opaque state units to fill in the region between them with a continuous surface percept.

In order to express this process as an emergent one, the dynamics of this surface interpolation function must be defined in terms of local fieldlike forces analogous to the local forces of surface tension active at any point in a soap bubble. Figure 4.2C depicts an opaque state unit representing a local portion of a perceived surface at a specific three-

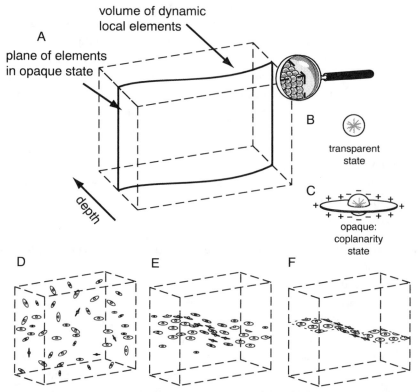

Fig. 4.2   (A) The Gestalt bubble model consisting of a block of dynamic local elements which can be in one of two states. (B) The transparent state, with no neighborhood interactions, and (C) the opaque state representing the perception of an opaque surface at that point at a particular orientation. The local surface percept tends to propagate outward in coplanar fashion, to produce complete perceived surfaces. (D) Given a random initial distribution of states throughout the matrix, any initial inhomogeneity will tend to feed back on itself, amplifying the activity of elements within the plane and rotating their planes of influence closer to the plane of the emerging surface, while suppressing elements outside of the plane to the transparent state. (E and F) Eventually a single dynamic surface will emerge, which remains free to shift, stretch, and flex, like a bubble surface.

dimensional location and with a specific surface orientation. The planar field of this element, depicted somewhat like a planetary ring in Fig. 4.2C, represents both the perceived surface represented by this element, and a fieldlike influence propagated by that element to adjacent units. This planar field fades smoothly with distance from the center, in this case with a Gaussian function. The effect of this field is to recruit adjacent elements within that field of influence to take on a similar state—that is, to induce transparent state units to switch to the opaque state, and opaque-state units to rotate toward a similar surface orientation value. The final state and orientation taken on by any element are computed as a spatial average or weighted sum of the states of neighboring units as communicated through their planar fields of influence, with the greatest influence from nearby opaque elements in the matrix. The influence is reciprocal between neighboring elements, thereby defining a circular relation as suggested by the principle of emergence. In order to prevent runaway positive feedback and uncontrolled propagation of surface signal, an inhibitory dynamic is also incorporated in order to suppress surface formation out of the plane of the emergent surface, by endowing the local field of each unit with an inhibitory field in order to suppress the opaque state in neighboring elements in all directions outside of the plane of its local field. The mathematical specification of the local field of influence between opaque-state units is outlined in greater detail in the appendix. However, the intent of the model is expressed more naturally in the global properties as described here, so the details of the local field influences are presented as only one possible implementation of the concept, provided in order to ground this somewhat nebulous idea in more concrete terms.

The global properties of the system due to the local interactions should unfold as follows. Imagine that initially all of the elements in the matrix are assigned randomly to either the transparent or the opaque state, with random surface orientations for opaque-state elements, as suggested in Fig. 4.2D. The mutual fieldlike influences between these elements would tend to amplify any initial inhomogeneity, in which a group of opaque-state units happen to be aligned in an approximate plane. As this plane of active units feeds back on its own activation, the orientations of its elements would conform ever closer to that of the emergent plane, whereas elements outside of the plane would be suppressed to the transparent state, as suggested in Fig. 4.2E. This would result in the emergence of a single plane of opaque-state units as a dynamic global pattern of activation embedded in the volume of the matrix, as suggested in Fig. 4.2F. That surface would be free to flex and stretch much like a bubble surface, although unlike a real bubble, this surface is defined not as a physical membrane, but as a dynamic sheet of active elements embedded in the matrix. This volumetric surface interpolation function will now serve as the backdrop to an emergent reconstruction of the spatial percept around a three-dimensional skeleton or framework constructed on the basis of the visual edges in the scene.

LOCAL EFFECTS OF A VISUAL EDGE

A visual edge can be perceived as an object in its own right, like a thin rod or wire surrounded by empty space. More often, however, an edge is seen as a discontinuity in a surface, either as a corner or fold, or perhaps as an occlusion edge like the outer perimeter of a flat figure viewed against a more distant background. The interaction between a visual edge and a perceived surface can therefore be modeled as follows. The two-dimensional

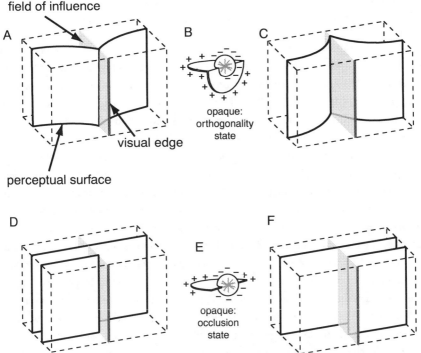

Fig. 4.3   (A) A visual edge projects a field of influence into the depth dimension of the perceptual matrix, which changes the dynamic behavior of opaque-state elements within that field of influence from the coplanarity state to (B), the orthogonality state, which completes the perceived surface through a right angled corner coincident with the visual edge. (C) The corner percept can occur either in convex or concave form. (D) Alternatively, the visual edge can promote an occlusion percept by inducing opaque-state elements to change to (E), the occlusion state, with a coplanar field extending in one direction only. (F) This percept too can occur either in left-over-right or right-over-left forms. The final effect of a visual edge therefore is to produce a multistable percept that can alternate spontaneously among the four states shown in (A), (C), (D), and (F).

edge from the retinal stimulus projects a different kind of field of influence into the depth dimension of the volumetric matrix, as suggested by the gray shading in Fig. 4.3A, to represent the three-dimensional locus of all possible edges that project to the two-dimensional edge in the image. In other words, this field expresses the inverse optics probability field or extrinsic constraint due to a single visual edge. Wherever this field intersects opaque-state elements in the volume of the matrix, it changes the shape of their local fields of influence from a coplanar interaction to an orthogonal, or corner, interaction as suggested by the local force field in Fig. 4.3B. The corner of this field should align parallel to the visual edge, but should otherwise remain unconstrained in orientation except by interactions with adjacent opaque units. This means that the corner percept could just as well emerge in a concave configuration as shown in Fig. 4.3C, and in fact the entire perceived corner would be free to tilt backward or forward in depth.

Visual edges can also denote occlusion, so opaque-state elements can also exist in an occlusion state, with a coplanarity interaction in one direction only, as suggested by the occlusion field in Fig. 4.3E. This would promote the emergence of an occlusion percept along the visual edge as suggested in Fig. 4.3D, with a foreground surface occluding a more distant background surface, and again, there is another possible occlusion percept depicted in Fig. 4.3F, with a right-over-left occlusion instead of left-over right. Therefore, in the presence of a single visual edge, a local element in the opaque state should have an equal probability of changing into the orthogonality or occlusion state, with the orthogonal or occlusion edge aligned parallel to the inducing visual edge. Once a visual edge has been "accounted for" perceptually, as a corner or occlusion percept at some depth, it should not influence the perceptual interpretation of other surfaces at different depths. Therefore the influence of the field projected by the visual edge shown in Fig. 4.3D and 4.3F expires at the depth of the nearer surface for which it accounts, having no influence on the farther surface in depth. In order to account for the fact that edges tend to be perceived in the same configuration throughout their entire length, elements in the orthogonal state should tend to promote orthogonality in adjacent elements along the perceived corner, whereas elements in the occlusion state promote occlusion along that edge, although the whole edge may change state back and forth as a unit in a multistable manner. Therefore the local effects of a visual edge result in a multistable percept that alternates randomly between the states depicted in Fig. 4.3, A, C, D, and F, each of which is free to drift in and out in depth and rotate back and forth through any orientation in depth. However, the final configuration selected by the system would depend not only on the local image region depicted in Fig. 4.3, but also on forces from adjacent regions of the image, in order to fuse the orthogonal or occlusion state percept seamlessly into nearby coplanar surface percepts. The appendix presents a more detailed mathematical description of how these orthogonality and occlusion fields might be defined.

GLOBAL EFFECTS OF CONFIGURATIONS OF EDGES

Visual illusions like the Kanizsa figure shown in Fig. 3.3A suggest that edges in a stimulus that are in a collinear configuration tend to link up in perceptual space to define a larger global edge connecting the local edges. This kind of collinear boundary completion is expressed in this model as a physical process analogous to the propagation of a crack or fold in a physical medium. A visual edge that fades gradually produces a crease in the perceptual medium that tends to propagate outward beyond the edge as suggested in Fig. 4.4A. If two such edges are found in a collinear configuration, the perceptual surface will tend to crease or fold between them, as suggested in Fig. 4.4B. This tendency is accentuated if additional evidence from adjacent regions support this configuration, as in the case of Fig. 4.4C where fading horizontal lines are seen to link up across the figure to create a percept of a folded surface in depth, which would otherwise appear as a regular hexagon in the plane of the page. Alternatively, the fading visual edge might promote an occlusion percept as suggested in Fig. 4.4D, and a collinear arrangement of such edges would promote a perceptual scission as suggested in Fig. 4.4E, with a foreground surface breaking away in front of an occluded background surface. This perceptual phenomenon is observed in Fig. 4.4F.

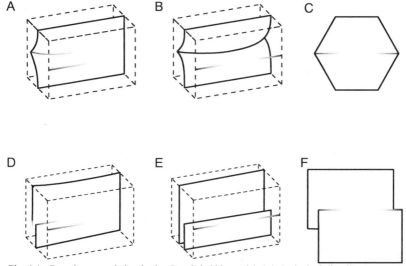

Fig. 4.4   Boundary completion in the Gestalt bubble model. (A) A single fading line creates a crease in the perceptual surface. (B) Two fading lines generate a crease joining them, especially when (C) the spatial context is consistent with this interpretation as seen in this figure. (D) Alternatively, a fading line can promote an occlusion percept, which (E) tends to join up with other edges in a collinear configuration, especially when (F) the spatial context is consistent with this interpretation.

Gestalt theory emphasized the significance of closure as a prominent factor in perceptual segmentation, because an enclosed contour is seen to promote a figure/ground segregation (Koffka, 1935, p. 178). For example, an outline square tends to be seen as a square surface in front of a background surface that is complete and continuous behind the square, as suggested in the perceptual model depicted in Fig. 4.5A. The problem is that closure is a Gestalt-like quality defined by a global configuration that is difficult to specify in terms of any local featural requirements, especially in the case of irregular or fragmented contours as seen in Fig. 4.5B. In this model an enclosed contour breaks away a piece of the perceptual surface, completing the background amodally behind the occluding foreground figure. In the presence of irregular or fragmented edges the influence of the individual edge fragments act collectively to break the perceptual surface along that contour as suggested in Fig. 4.5C, like the breaking of a physical surface that is weakened along an irregular line of cracks or holes. The final scission of figure from ground is therefore driven not so much by the exact path of the individual irregular edges, as it is by the global configuration of the emergent gestalt. This computational mechanism therefore embodies the central insight of Gestalt theory, that the holistic global aspects of perception suggest a holistic global process in the perceptual mechanism in which segmentation occurs by the simultaneous action of innumerable local forces that all contribute to the final perceptual state.

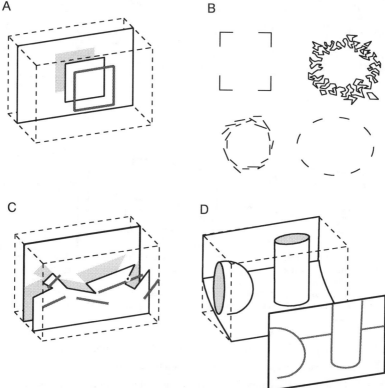

Fig. 4.5   (A) The perception of closure and figure/ground segregation are explained in the Gestalt bubble model exactly as perceived, in this case as a foreground square in front of a background surface that completes behind the square. (B) Even irregular and fragmented surfaces produce a figure/ground segregation. (C) The perceived boundary of the fragmented figure follows the global emergent gestalt rather than the exact path of individual edges. (D) Closure is also defined in three dimensions, as the tendency for objects to be perceived as enclosed in depth.

The phenomenon of closure in perception applies just as well to three dimensions, as the tendency for objects to be perceived as enclosed in depth, forming complete "bubbles" of enclosed perceptual volumes with modal front faces and amodal rear surfaces, as suggested in Fig. 4.5D. This suggests a three-dimensional "clumping" force by which perceived surfaces tend to close up to form perceived wholes, a concept that lies at the very heart of Gestalt theory, for a gestalt (a German word for which there is no direct English translation) represents a complete whole or form, like an object distinct from its environment.

VERTICES AND INTERSECTIONS

In the case of vertices or intersections between visual edges, the different edges interact with one another favoring the percept of a single vertex at that point. For example, the three edges defining the three-way "Y" vertex shown in Fig. 4.1C promote the percept of a single three-dimensional corner, whose depth profile depends on whether the corner is perceived as convex or concave. In the case of Fig. 4.1A, the cubical percept constrains the central "Y" vertex as a convex rather than as a concave trihedral percept. I propose that this dynamic behavior can be implemented using the same kinds of local field forces described in the appendix to promote mutually orthogonal completion in three dimensions, wherever visual edges meet at an angle in two dimensions.

Figure 4.6A depicts the three-dimensional influence of the two-dimensional Y vertex when projected on the front face of the volumetric matrix. Each plane of this three-planed structure promotes the emergence of a corner or occlusion percept at some depth within that plane. But the effects due to these individual edges are not independent. Consider, for example, first the vertical edge projecting from the bottom of the vertex. By itself, this edge might produce a folded percept as suggested in Fig. 4.6B, which could occur through a range of depths, and at various orientations in depth. But the two angled planes of this percept each intersect the other two fields of influence due to the other two edges of the stimulus, as suggested in Fig. 4.6B, thus favoring the emergence of those edges' perceptual folds at that same depth, resulting in a single trihedral percept at some depth in the volumetric matrix, as suggested in Fig. 4.6C. Any dimension of this percept that is not explicitly specified or constrained by the visual input remains unconstrained. In other words, the trihedral percept is embedded in the volumetric matrix in such a way that its three-component corner percepts are free to slide inward or outward in depth, to rotate through a small range of angles, and to flip in bistable manner between a convex and concave trihedral configuration. The model now expresses the multistability of the rod-and-rail analogy shown in Fig. 4.1D, but in a more generalized form that is no longer hard-wired to the Y-vertex input shown in Fig. 4.1C, but can accommodate any arbitrary

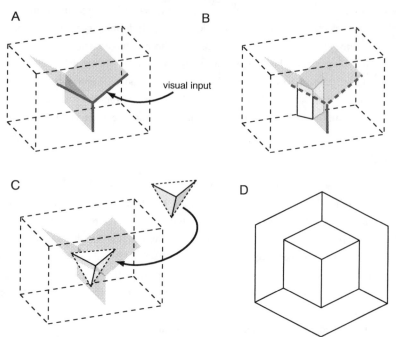

Fig. 4.6 (A) The three-dimensional field of influence due to a two-dimensional Y vertex projected into the depth dimension of the volumetric matrix. (B) Each field of influence—for example, the one due to the vertical edge—stimulates a folded surface percept. The folded surface intersects the other fields of influence due to the other two edges, thereby tending to produce a percept of a single corner. (C) One of many possible emergent surface percepts in response to that stimulus, in the form of a convex trihedral surface percept. (D) The percept can also be of a concave trihedral corner, as seen sometimes at the center of this bistable figure.

configuration of lines in the input image. A local visual feature like an isolated Y vertex generally exhibits a larger number of stable states, whereas in the context of adjacent features the number of stable solutions is often diminished. This explains why the cubical percept of Fig. 4.1A is stable, whereas its central Y vertex alone as shown in Fig. 4.1C is bistable. The fundamental multistability of Fig. 4.1A can be revealed by the addition of a different spatial context, as depicted in Fig. 4.6D.

PERSPECTIVE CUES

Perspective cues offer another example of a computation that is inordinately complicated in most models. However, in a fully reified spatial model, perspective can be computed relatively easily with only a small change in the geometry of the model. Figure 4.7A shows a trapezoid stimulus, which has a tendency to be perceived in depth; that is, the shorter top side tends to be perceived as being the same length as the longer base, but apparently diminished by perspective. Arnheim (1969a) suggested a simple distortion to the volumetric model to account for this phenomenon, which can be reformulated as follows. The height and width of the volumetric matrix are diminished as a function of depth, as suggested in Fig. 4.7B, transforming the block shape into a truncated pyramid that tapers in depth. However, the vertical and horizontal dimensions represented by that space are not diminished; in other words, the larger front face and the smaller rear face of the volumetric structure represent equal areas in perceived space, by unequal areas in representational space, as suggested by the converging grid lines in the figure. All of the spatial interactions just described, such as the collinear propagation of corner and occlusion percepts, would be similarly distorted in this space.

Even the angular measure of orthogonality is distorted somewhat by this transformation. For example, the perceived cube depicted in the solid volume of Fig. 4.7B is metrically shrunken in height and width as a function of depth, but because this shrinking is in the same proportion as the shrinking of the space itself, the depicted irregular cube represents a percept of a regular cube with equal sides and orthogonal faces. On the other hand, the propagation of the field of influence in depth due to a two-dimensional visual input does not shrink with depth. A projection of the trapezoid of Fig. 4.7A would occur in this model as depicted in Fig. 4.7C, projecting the trapezoidal form backward in parallel, independent of the convergence of the space around it. The shaded surfaces in Fig. 4.7C therefore represent the locus of all possible spatial interpretations of the two-dimensional edges of the trapezoid stimulus of Fig. 4.7A. For example, one possible perceptual interpretation is of a trapezoid in the plane of the page, which can be perceived to be either nearer or farther in depth, but because the size scale shrinks as a function of depth, the percept will be experienced as larger in absolute size (as measured against the shrunken spatial scale) when perceived as farther away, and as smaller in absolute size (as measured against the expanded scale) when perceived to be closer in depth. This corresponds to the phenomenon known as *Emmert's law* (Coren et al. 1994), whereby a retinal after-image appears larger when viewed against a distant background than when viewed against a nearer background.

There are also an infinite number of alternative perceptual interpretations of the trapezoidal stimulus, some of which are depicted by the shaded lines of Fig. 4.7D. Most of these alternative percepts are geometrically irregular, representing figures with unequal sides and odd angles. But of all these possibilities, there is one special case, depicted in black lines in Fig. 4.7D, in which the convergence of the sides of the perceived form happens to coincide exactly with the convergence of the space itself. In other words, the nearer and farther horizontal edges of this perceptual interpretation span exactly the same number of units in the converging reference grid of the distorted spatial representation.

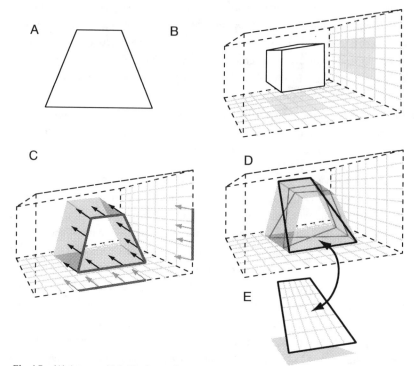

Fig. 4.7   (A) A trapezoidal stimulus tends to be perceived as a rectangle viewed in perspective. (B) The perspective modified spatial representation whose dimensions are shrunken in height and breadth as a function of depth. (C) The projection of a field of influence into depth of the two-dimensional trapezoidal stimulus does not shrink with depth but is projected in parallel. (D) Several possible perceptual interpretations of the trapezoidal stimulus (darker gray), one of which (depicted in black outline) represents a regular rectangle viewed in perspective, because the convergence of its sides exactly matches the convergence of the space itself. (E) The distorted reference grid is projected onto the distorted surface to show how it is perceived to be both distorted, and at the same time perceived to be rectangular, exactly as observed in perception.

Therefore this particular percept represents a regular rectangle viewed in perspective, with parallel sides and right angled corners. This is shown in Fig. 4.7E, where the distorted reference grid has been projected onto the sloping trapezoidal surface to show how it is both perceived to be distorted by perspective, and at the same time perceived to be an undistorted rectangle. This paradoxical property, clearly evident in the subjective experience of perspective, can be expressed in quantitative terms as a distortion of the perceptual reference grid to match the distortion of perspective.

BOUNDING THE REPRESENTATION

An explicit volumetric representation of perceived space as proposed here must necessarily be bounded in some way in order to allow a finite representational space to map to the infinity of external space, as suggested in Fig. 2.1. The nonlinear compression of the depth dimension observed in phenomenal space can be modeled mathematically with a vergence measure, which maps the infinity of Euclidean distance into a finite bounded range, as suggested in Fig. 4.8A.This produces a representation reminiscent of museum dioramas, like the one depicted in Fig. 4.8B, where objects in the foreground are represented in full depth, but the depth dimension gets increasingly compressed with distance from the viewer, eventually collapsing into a flat plane corresponding to the background. This vergence measure is presented here merely as a nonlinear compression of depth in a monocular spatial representation, as opposed to a real vergence value measured in a binocular system, although this system could of course serve both purposes in biological vision. Assuming unit separation between the eyes in a binocular system, this compression is defined by the equation

$$v = 2 \; \text{atan}(1/2r)$$

where v is the vergence measure of depth, and r is the Euclidean range, or distance in depth. Actually, because vergence is large at short range and smaller at long range, it is actually the "π-compliment" vergence measure ρ that is used in the representation, where $\rho = (\pi - v)$, and ρ ranges from 0 at $r = 0$, to π at $r = \infty$.

What does this kind of compression mean in an isomorphic representation? If the perceptual frame of reference is compressed along with the objects in that space, then the compression need not be perceptually apparent. Figure 4.8C depicts this kind of compressed reference grid. The unequal intervals between adjacent grid lines in depth define intervals that are perceived to be of equal length, so the flattened cubes defined by the distorted grid would appear perceptually as regular cubes, of equal height, breadth, and depth. This compression of the reference grid to match the compression of space would, in a mathematical system with infinite resolution, completely conceal the compression from the percipient. In a real physical implementation there are two effects of this compression that would remain apparent perceptually, due to the fact that the spatial matrix itself would have to have a finite perceptual resolution. The resolution of depth within this space is reduced as a function of depth, and beyond a certain limiting depth, all objects are perceived to be flattened into two dimensions, with zero extent in depth. This phenomenon is observed perceptually, where the sun, moon, and distant mountains appear as if they are pasted against the flat dome of the sky.

The other two dimensions of space can also be bounded by converting the x and y of Euclidean space into azimuth and elevation angles, α and β, producing an angle/angle/vergence representation, as shown in Fig. 4.9A. Mathematically this transformation

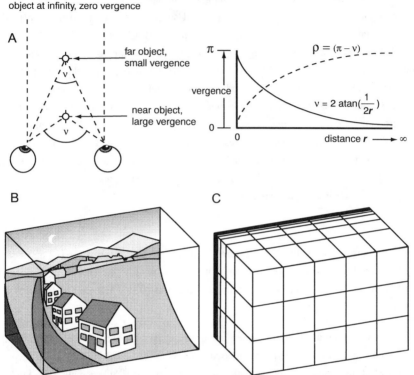

Fig. 4.8   (A) A vergence representation maps infinite distance into a finite range. (B) This produces a mapping reminiscent of a museum diorama. (C) The compressed reference grid in this compressed space defines intervals that are perceived to be of uniform size.

converts the point $P(\alpha,\beta,r)$ in polar coordinates to point $Q(\alpha,\beta,\rho)$ in this bounded spherical representation. In other words, azimuth and elevation angles are preserved by this transformation, and the radial distance in depth r is compressed to the vergence representation ρ as already described. This spherical coordinate system has the ecological advantage that the space near the body is represented at the highest spatial resolution, whereas the less important, more distant parts of space are represented at lower resolution. All depths beyond a certain radial distance are mapped to the surface of the representation which corresponds to perceptual infinity.

The mathematical form of this distortion is depicted in Fig. 4.9B, where the distorted grid depicts the perceptual representation of an infinite Cartesian grid with horizontal and vertical grid lines spaced at equal intervals. This geometrical transformation from the infinite Cartesian grid actually represents a unique kind of perspective transformation on the Cartesian grid. In other words, the transformed space looks like a perspective view of a Cartesian grid when viewed from inside, with all parallel lines converging to a point in

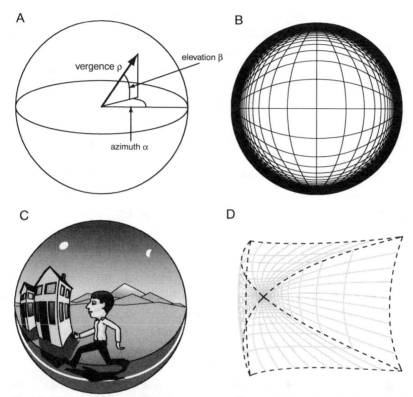

Fig. 4.9   (A) An azimuth/elevation/vergence representation maps the infinity of three-dimensional Euclidean space into a finite perceptual space. (B) The deformation of the infinite Cartesian grid caused by the perspective transformation of the azimuth/elevation/vergence representation. (C) A view of a man walking down a road represented in the perspective distorted space. (D) A section of the spherical space depicted in the same format as the perspective distorted space shown in Fig. 4.7.

opposite directions. The significance of this observation is that by mapping space into a perspective-distorted grid, the distortion of perspective is removed, in the same way that plotting log data on a log plot removes the logarithmic component of the data. Figure 4.9C shows how this space would represent the perceptual experience of a man walking down a road. If the distorted reference grid of Fig. 4.9B is used to measure lines and distances in Fig. 4.9C, the bowed line of the road on which the man is walking is aligned with the bowed reference grid and is therefore perceived to be straight. Therefore, the distortion of straight lines into curves in the perceptual representation is not immediately apparent to the percipient, because the lines are perceived to be straight. Similarly, the walls of the two houses shown in Fig. 4.9C which bow outward from the observer, conform to the distortion of the reference grid and are therefore perceived to be straight and vertical. Likewise, the nearer and farther houses are perceived to be of approximately equal height and depth in objective size, because they span the same number of grid lines in the perspective distorted grid, and yet at the same time the farther house is also perceived to be smaller in projective size, as observed also in perception. However, in a global sense there are peculiar distortions that are apparent to the percipient, caused by this deformation of Euclidean space: Although the sides of the road are perceived to be parallel, they are also perceived to meet at a point on the horizon. The fact that two lines can be perceived to be both straight and parallel and yet to converge to a point both in front of and behind the percipient indicates that our internal representation itself must be curved. The proposed representation of space has exactly this property. Parallel lines do not extend to infinity but meet at a point beyond which they are no longer represented. Likewise, the vertical walls of the houses in Fig. 4.9C bow outward away from the observer, but in doing so they follow the curvature of the reference lines in the grid of Fig. 4.9B and are therefore perceived as being both straight and vertical.

Evidence for the spherical nature of perceived space dates back to observations by Helmholtz (1925). A subject in a dark room is presented with a horizontal line of point lights at eye level in the frontoparallel plane and is instructed to adjust their displacement in depth, one by one, until they are perceived to lie in a straight line in depth. The result is a line of lights that curves inward towards the observer, with the amount of curvature being a function of the distance of the line of lights from the observer. Helmholtz recognized this phenomenon as evidence of the non-Euclidean nature of perceived space. The Hillebrand–Blumenfeld *alley experiments* (Hillebrand, 1902; Blumenfeld, 1913) extended this work with different configurations of lights, and mathematical analysis of the results (Luneburg, 1950; Blank, 1958) characterized the nature of perceived space as Riemannian with constant Gaussian curvature (for a review see Graham, 1965; Foley, 1978; and Indow, 1991). In other words, perceived space bows outward from the observer, with the greatest distortion observed proximal to the body, as suggested by the Gestalt bubble model.

Because curved lines in this spherical representation represent straight lines in external space, all of the spatial interactions discussed in the previous section, including the coplanar interactions, and collinear creasing of perceived surfaces, must follow the grain or curvature of collinearity defined within this distorted coordinate system. The distance scale encoded in the grid of Fig. 4.9B replaces the regularly spaced Cartesian grid by a nonlinear collapsing grid whose intervals are spaced ever closer as they approach perceptual infinity but nevertheless represent equal intervals in external space. This nonlinear collapsing scale thereby provides an objective measure of distance in the perspective-distorted perceptual world. For example, the houses in Fig. 4.9C would be perceived to be of approximately the same size and depth, although the farther house is experienced at a lower perceptual resolution. An interesting property of this representation is that different points on the bounding surface of the spherical representation represent different directions in space. All parallel lines that point in a particular direction converge to the same surface point representing that direction.

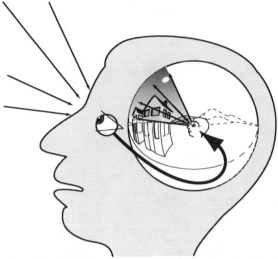

Fig. 4.10   The image from the retina is projected into the perceptual sphere from the center outward, as an inverse analog of the cone of light that enters the eye in the external world, taking into account eye, head, and body orientation in order to update the appropriate portion of perceptual space depending on the direction of gaze. Whatever the neurophysiological mechanism behind this incredible projective function, these are the observed properties of phenomenal perception.

Figure 4.9D depicts how a slice of Euclidean space of fixed height and width would appear in the perceptual sphere, extending to perceptual infinity in one direction, like a slice cut from the spherical representation of Fig. 4.9C. This slice is similar to the truncated pyramid shape shown in Fig. 4.7B, with the difference that the horizontal and vertical scale of representational space diminishes in a nonlinear fashion as a function of distance in depth. In other words, the sides of the pyramid in Fig. 4.9D converge in curves rather than in straight lines, and the pyramid is no longer truncated, but extends in depth all the way to the vanishing point at representational infinity. An input image is projected into this spherical space using the same principles as before. The two-dimensional image from the spherical surface of the retina is copied onto a spherical surface in front of the eyeball of the perceptual effigy, from whence the image is projected radially outward in an expanding cone into the depth dimension as suggested in the internal perceptual world depicted in Fig. 4.10, as an inverse analog of the cone of light received from the world by the eye. Eye, head, and body orientation relative to the external world are taken into account in order to direct the visual projection of the retinal image into the appropriate sector of perceived space, as determined from proprioceptive and kinesthetic sensations in order to update the image of the body configuration relative to external space.

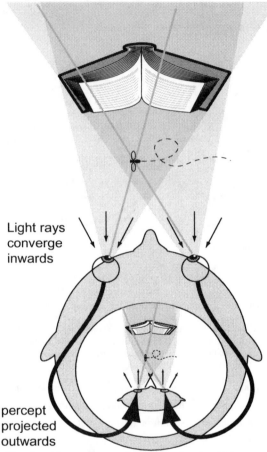

Fig. 4.11 For binocular vision, each eye projects its own image out into perceptual space, where the intersection of those projections fixes the three-dimensional location of the emergent percept by triangulation.

BINOCULAR AND MULTIOCULAR VISION

The model of visual perception just developed was presented as a monocular model. The generality of this approach to vision is that the concept can be readily extended to account for binocular, or even multiocular, vision, with the eyes arranged in arbitrary configurations, simply by inserting the additional eyes in the proper location and orientation in the perceptual homunculus. Each eye projects its visual image outward into perceived space as described earlier. Whenever two cones from different eyes intersect in perceptual space, both cones contribute to the formation of the structural percept in the binocular region of intersection, as suggested in Fig. 4.11. This concept of binocular vision by projection from two directions has been proposed and elaborated by a number of authors, including Boring (1933), Charnwood (1951), Kaufman (1974), Julesz (1971), and Marr and Poggio (1976), where it is known generally as the *projection field theory* of binocular vision.

The principal difficulty with any model of binocular vision involves an issue known as the *correspondence problem*. In order to triangulate between two images of the same feature viewed from the two eyes, it is necessary first to identify features in each eye sufficient to match the corresponding features across the left and right images. This problem was highlighted in dramatic form by Julesz (1971) with the introduction of the *random dot stereogram*, in which a binocular percept of surfaces in depth is achieved from random dot patterns presented to each eye. Different regions of the random dots are coherently shifted left or right in one image relative to the other, in order to produce distinct regions with different disparity. The fact that this stimulus produces a vivid experience of binocular depth presents somewhat of a chicken-and-egg problem for models of binocular vision, for in order to calculate the disparity between regions of the stimulus, individual dots must somehow be matched up between the two images, a task that is very difficult with the random dot stimulus, given the uniformly random distribution of the dots. The only feature readily identifiable for matching between the two eyes is the disparity feature, but that feature can only be detected after the match has occured. Julesz correctly identified this as a problem requiring an emergent solution, and he proposed a dynamic relaxation model similar in principle to the approach proposed here.

The present approach addresses both monocular and binocular perception, and employs the same essential principle in each case: that the depth ambiguity inherent in the two-dimensional stimulus is reified as a probability field extending into the depth dimension, and the final percept is computed by emergence from this probability field or, in the binocular case, from the intersection in depth of two such probability fields. In other words, the intersection of the extrinsic constraints specified by each eye in the three-dimensional matrix eliminates much of the depth ambiguity inherent in a monocular view.

A NEW MATHEMATICS

The perceptual modeling just developed reveals general principles that are more significant than the details of the particular perceptual interactions described. In fact, those details, which are necessarily somewhat speculative, are presented principally in order to exemplify these more general principles in concrete terms. One principle suggested by this modeling is that the visual system exhibits a unique way of expressing uncertainty by an expansion of the percept throughout the range of uncertainty, resulting in a spatial probability field, or fuzzy superposition of every possible perceptual state within the range of uncertainty, as expressed in the extrinsic constraints. Intrinsic constraints work to collapse that probability field into a smaller number of, or at best a single discrete state. For example, the depth ambiguity inherent in a monocularly viewed edge is expressed in the model as a spatial probability field that presents that edge at every possible depth, and orientation in depth simultaneously throughout the volume of perceived space that projects to that edge, as suggested by the gray shaded region in Fig. 4.3A. This same principle is extended through further reification, for the perceptual implications of a visual edge are that it suggests a transition between surfaces, and therefore the perceptual mechanism attempts to reify not only a percept of every edge at every possible depth, but also every possible configuration of surfaces consistent with each of those possible edges in depth, all pursued in parallel as a continuous probability field. The final percept is then selected from that infinite set by finding that configuration of surfaces whose reification encounters the greatest global support from more distant regions of the perceptual field. A typical two-dimensional visual scene thus generates a fantastically complex array of hypothesized edges and surfaces in three dimensions, which project outward by extrapolation, and inward by interpolation, seeking out confirmation of higher order structures hidden in the scene, although the salience or strength of those probability fields is progressively attenuated as they spread outward from the stimulus from which they were spawned.

The ability of the visual system to express multiple possible alternatives as a continuous probability field represents a unique form of generalization, similar in some sense to the generalization seen in algebra, where an abstract variable x can take on any possible value in the range of real numbers. However, unlike the practice of algebra, which performs manipulations on variables like x in an abstracted symbolic form, perception treats the variable x as a reified expansion of all of its possible values simultaneously. In other words, x is not processed as a single abstracted symbol, but as a spatial probability field in the form of a diffuse line expanding outward along the x axis. Perception operates by calculating the intersections, or joint probability distribution of all such variables in parallel, to allow the final percept to emerge within the regions of highest perceptual probability, under the guidance of intrinsic constraints.

Like a probability density function, the salience or intensity of a variable in perception is inversely proportional to its spatial extent. Therefore the infinite patterns of reification triggered by a visual stimulus are initially so thin and tenuous as to be subliminal and

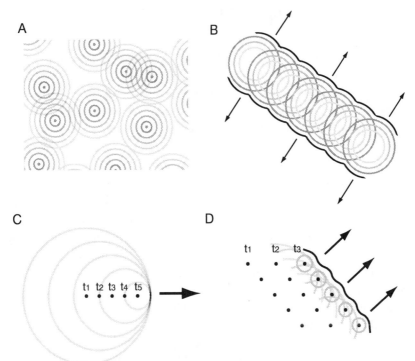

Fig. 4.12   The properties of wave propagation demonstrate an emergent diffuse style of spatial interaction suggestive of emergence in perception. (A) Raindrops striking a pond create an incoherent pattern of radiating rings, that generally cancel by destructive interference. (B) If a line of raindrops strike the pond simultaneously, their expanding rings would collectively define an advancing wavefront propagating at right angles to the line of drops. (C) If the raindrops arrive along a line at equal intervals in space and time, their collective action defines a wavefront propagating along the line of drops. (D) Lines of raindrops arrriving coherently along an oblique front generate an emergent wavefront along that oblique front. These properties suggest a unique holistic principle of computation in perception.

fleeting in consciousness. The percept becomes progressively more salient as its range of variation is reduced. The logical operations of perception are therefore spatial rather than symbolic manipulations, which reveal a novel form of spatial reasoning in which every possible implication of a feature or set of features is pursued in parallel. A key aspect of this Gestalt style of spatial logic is that decisions as to the validity of local spatial hypotheses are postponed as late as possible in the process, rather than being decided early based on local evidence, as is the practice in the feature detection paradigm. This allows a confluence of multiple pieces of very weak evidence, which would otherwise have been eliminated early in the process, to work together to support a global hypothesis that is consistent with all of the available evidence. This, it would seem, is the very essence of emergence, as observed in the percept of the dog picture.

APPARENT MOTION PHENOMENON

This unique principle of computation is also evident in the phenomenon of apparent motion, the phenomenon that inspired much of Wertheimer's thinking on the computational mechanism of perception. Apparent motion is obtained in its most simple form by the alternate flashing of two adjacent lights, which creates the percept of a single light that jumps back and forth between the two points. There are two significant aspects of this perceptual phenomenon. In the first place, the percept is clearly illusory, for a motion is perceived where there is no motion in the stimulus, which demonstrates the generative or constructive aspect of perception. The other significant aspect of this illusion is that the percept appears to be reconstructed "backward in time." The percept of a single light flashing once is experienced veridically as a single flash. On the other hand, when this is accompanied by a subsequent flash nearby, the percept is of a moving light that is experienced to be in motion from the moment that the first light turns on. However, until the second light appears, there is no way for the visual system to know whether another light is going to appear, or at what time or in what direction it might appear. Therefore the appearance of the moving percept synchronized with the appearance of the first light seems to have been reconstructed after the second light made its appearance, in apparent violation of the law of causality.

This paradoxical property can be explained in terms of a computation of spatial logic by reification. The sudden appearance of a light, or any other visual feature, can mean that a new object has suddenly come into being. However, it is also possible that a formerly occluded object has suddenly been exposed to view, which suggests a relative motion between the new object and its former occluder. Instead of making an a priori decision based on this local stimulus evidence, the visual system pursues all alternative interpretations simultaneously, as follows. The appearance of the first light creates a percept of a sudden appearance, and simultaneously a percept of rapid expansion outward from that point, because an expansion expresses motion in all directions simultaneously. Furthermore, that expansion is expressed through a range of speeds simultaneously, expanding outward both slowly and quickly and at every intermediate speed from the point of sudden appearance. This perceptual hypothesis is expressed as a transient spatial probability field, whose perceptual salience remains weak as long as it remains distributed among many alternative possibilities. If no further stimulus is encountered, the expansion percept eventually fades from consciousness due to lack of confirmation of any of its "predictions," leaving only the sudden appearance component of the original percept, which is not disconfirmed by the nonappearance of later features. This reduction of perceptual alternatives results in a corresponding increase in salience of the single remaining alternative. However, the decision of the system to accept the sudden appearance interpretation does not need to be propagated "backward in time," for the perceptual hypothesis of a sudden appearance had been active all along since the first appearance of the light. All that is required after the failure of other lights to appear is the elimination of the alternative unsupported interpretations.

If, on the other hand, the first light is followed closely by a second one, the conjunction of the expansion percept due to the second stimulus, together with the expansion percept of the first light, results in the reinforcement of the single expansion percept whose direction and rate of expansion take it exactly to the location of the second light at the moment that it appears. In other words, the single perceptual interpretation of a motion from the first light to the second, at a speed and direction that exactly match the time interval between the two stimuli, is the only component of the original compound percept to survive after the appearance of the second stimulus, resulting in an experience "after the fact" of a directed motion from the first light to the second at a constant velocity. Again, the event does not have to be reconstructed "backward in time," because the event was already represented in this form from the moment of appearance of the first light. All that is required is the elimination of all competing hypotheses that are inconsistent with the pair of observations separated in space and time, like the collapse of a wave function in quantum mechanics to a single classical state.

Although the stimulus for the apparent motion phenomenon is reduced to its minimal form for a clear demonstration of the principle, in more typical natural scenes the motion of an extended object behind a fragmented occluder like a shrub, or a perforated screen, produces a cacophony of appearances and disappearances of features at irregular intervals in space and time. This visual chaos is ordered by the visual system by generating a separate expanding percept from every local edge fragment as it appears in the stimulus, like the expanding rings seen on the surface of a pond during a rain shower, emanating from every point of impact of a raindrop. The individual drops in a rain shower are distributed randomly in space and time, and therefore the expanding rings that they generate generally cancel each other by interference, as suggested in Fig. 4.12A. However, if these raindrops, or appearance events, were to occur in a synchronized global pattern, the global wave patterns produced by interference between the local expanding waves would reflect that global structure. For example if a number of drops arrayed in a straight line were to strike the pond simultaneously, the expanding rings caused by every individual drop would merge into a larger coherent wavefront, which is straight and parallel to the line defined by the drops, and propagates outward from the line at right angles to it, as shown in Fig. 4.12B. This follows from the behavior of light, and other waves, in which a wavefront can be considered as a line of point sources, each radiating wavefronts in expanding rings. Alternatively, if the raindrops were to strike the pond successively along a line at equal intervals in space and time, the resulting wave pattern due to constructive interference would produce a wavefront traveling along the line of drops, as suggested in Fig. 4.12C, because each new drop arrives just as the wave from the previous drops reach that point. Likewise, if several lines of drops arrive in sequence, advancing along an oblique front as suggested in Fig. 4.12D, their collective action produces an emerging wavefront propagating at right angles to the oblique front, as suggested by the arrows in Fig. 4.12D. The coherent wavefront would even emerge if the drops arrive in a more random pattern, like the pattern of appearance events occasioned by a visual edge moving behind a fragmented occluder like a shrub, with the coherence of the underlying edge being reconstructed by the collective action of the expanding rings stimulated by each appearance event.

Although the details of this spatial computation remain to be specified more precisely, the general concept suggested by apparent motion is that the global organizational principle in perception seems to have a diffuse spatial nature that allows the simultaneous reification of innumerable spatiotemporal hypotheses in parallel as expanding probability fields, each of which makes specific spatiotemporal "predictions" about later events at particular places and times. Those hypotheses that receive confirmation by subsequent features consistent with their predictions survive, and the rest fade quietly from memory. All that is required is a neurophysiologically plausible mechanism that is consistent with this unconventional form of spatial reasoning.

The properties of wave propagation demonstrate how coherent global patterns of motion distributed across isolated local stimuli can in principle all contribute to a single perceptual interpretation. The computational principle behind this concept of perceptual processing cannot be meaningfully reduced to an equivalent Turing machine description without losing its most significant properties. Therefore, this general concept of spatial logic represents a unique computational principle unlike any other principle of computation devised by mankind. This is what Wertheimer meant when he said that a *new mathematics* would have to be developed to express the computational principles behind perception. In chapter 8 I present a harmonic resonance theory to provide a possible mechanism to account for this unique holistic style of spatial computation.

DEPTH FROM TEXTURE AND MOTION

This same general principle of perceptual computation offers an interesting new perspective on a number of other deeply perplexing perceptual phenomena. Consider the perception of depth from texture, as shown for example in Fig. 4.13A. Again, the two-dimensional stimulus is expanded or reified in depth to express the extrinsic constraints of the stimulus, as suggested by the gray shading in Fig. 4.13B. The volumetric matrix of perceptual space then tries every possible spatial interpretation of the stimulus in parallel. For example, one interpretation is of a surface at some depth within the frontoparallel plane, as shown in Fig. 4.13B; in this perceptual interpretation, the dots of the stimulus are assumed to lie within the plane of that surface in depth. However, this percept exhibits a nonuniform distribution of texture elements throughout its surface. The surface percept shown in Fig. 4.13C, on the other hand, exhibits a uniform distribution of texture elements throughout its surface, as measured against the perspective-distorted reference grid. This is seen in Fig. 4.13D, which shows the perceptual reference scale projected onto the sloping perceived surface. This perceptual interpretation is therefore simpler, in an information-theoretical sense, and is therefore favored by the intrinsic constraints. For this regularity to be detected in this special case requires that it be reified volumetrically, because the regularity in its texture pattern cannot be found until the reification is performed.

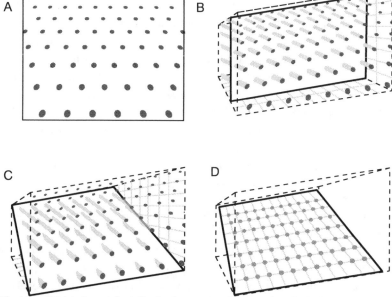

Fig. 4.13   (A) A texture gradient stimulus that promotes the perception of a sloping plane in depth. (B) If interpreted in the plane of the page, this suggests a nonuniform spacing of texture elements. (C) When interpreted at the proper slope in depth, the same texture maps to a uniform spacing in the perceptual representation, because the closer spaced dots at the top of the pattern map to a greater distance in depth, where (D) the spatial scale of the representation is correspondingly reduced, so that the closer spacing of the texture elements is perceived as a uniform spacing, rendered at reduced spatial resolution.

The same general principle can also be invoked to explain the phenomenon of structure from motion, where a solid three-dimensional percept is experienced while viewing a two-dimensional stimulus. For example, when viewing a two-dimensional projection of a random cluster of dots in three-dimensional space, the perceptual experience of that projection remains flat as long as the dots remain stationary. However if the cluster is rotated rigidly about some arbitrary axis in three dimensions, every component dot describes an elliptical path in the two dimensional projection, as suggested in Fig. 4.14A. Because every stimulus dot projects a spatial probability field into the depth dimension of perceptual space, the effect of the rigid rotation in depth of each dot about the center causes the linear probability field projected by each stimulus dot to sweep out an elliptical cylinder in depth, as shown by the gray shading in Fig. 4.14A. This elliptical cylindrical field represents the full range of possible perceptual interpretations suggested by one selected dot of the stimulus, from which intrinsic constraints then select the simplest interpretation.

For example, one possible set of interpretations is of an elliptical rotation parallel to the frontoparallel plane, as suggested by the elliptical arrows in Fig. 4.14A. This represents the most literal interpretation of the two-dimensional stimulus as a two-dimensional rotation at some depth. However, there is also an infinite range of alternative possibilities, as suggested by the light shaded ellipses in Fig. 4.14B, involving trajectories that circulate in depth, most of which follow elliptical paths of every possible eccentricity and orientation in depth, rotating at nonuniform rates about their centers. But of all of these different interpretations, there is a subset of special cases in which the rotation is circular in depth, as suggested by the black circle depicted in Fig. 4.14B, and this rotation would be at a uniform rate about the center. Because uniform circular motion is simpler than nonuniform elliptical motion, this percept will be favored by the intrinsic constraints.

In fact, there is a full range of such circular motion interpretations of the elliptical stimulus trace occurring through the full range of depth, so the selection of the subset exhibiting uniform circular motion results in this range of circular motions appearing simultaneously in the perceptual matrix, as suggested in Fig. 4.14C. There is a further perspective ambiguity, because the circular rotation can be perceived as viewed from either above or below, which allows another set of equally likely perceptual interpretations of the circular motion at the other angle of tilt, as suggested in Fig. 4.14D. The final percept therefore is bistable between the two alternative perspectives, either one of which remains unconstrained in depth.

The perceptual computation just described occurs simultaneously and in parallel for all of the dots in the rotating cluster. Due to the parallel nature of the computation, there is no

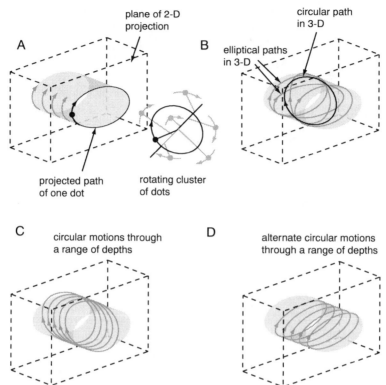

Fig. 4.14   Structure from motion of a random cluster of dots in rotation, computed by spatial reification. (A) Each dot of a random cluster of dots rotating in three dimensions projects an elliptical path in perspective. This ellipse is reified into the perceptual matrix as an elliptical cylinder in depth that represents every possible spatial interpretation of the two-dimensional projection. (B) Several possible paths (depicted in darker gray) represent ellipses in three dimensions with irregular rates of rotation. Of these, one special case (depicted in black) represents a circular rotation at uniform rate about the center. (C) This special case can actually emerge through a range of different depths, while (D) another set of circular paths corresponds to an alternative interpretation of the same stimulus as a circular rotation viewed from below instead of above. The final percept will therefore be bistable between the two states shown in (C and D).

additional computational load for larger numbers of dots. In fact, having more dots actually helps the computation, as each dot further constrains the range of perceptual alternatives, thereby helping to collapse the percept to a single spatial interpretation. There is a general principle behind this Gestalt approach to perception, seen in all of the diverse phenomena of spatial perception; apparent motion, depth from texture, and depth from motion. The dimensions of the perceptual representation match the dimensions of the external world, the distal stimulus, rather than those of the sensory surface, or the proximal stimulus. Perceptual computations are performed as spatial field-like operations in this volumetric representational space. The recovery of three-dimensional structural information from the two-dimensional retinal stimulus is achieved by first reifying all of the spatial and spatiotemporal implications suggested by the stimulus in the perceptual representation, and then selecting from that infinite set of possible reconstructions, the one that exhibits the most perceptual simplicity, or prägnanz.

Chapter 5

The Perception of Illumination

FUNDAMENTAL AMBIGUITIES IN REFLECTED LIGHT IMAGERY

The perception of light is unlike the perception of other aspects of the visual world, because light is the medium or carrier of visual information. This poses a fundamental problem in visual perception, for it is impossible in principle to distinguish in the pattern of light on the retinal surface those features that are due to the three-dimensional structure of the world from artifacts of the process of illumination, such as the direction and strength and pattern of illumination striking the visual scene, as well as those secondary artifacts due to the interaction between light and the world it illuminates—for example, the sharp edges due to attached shadows and cast shadows, visual features caused by reflection and refraction, and edges due to abrupt changes in surface reflectance unrelated to geometrical form. These various optical influences are hopelessly confounded in the two-dimensional projection on the retina. The existence of these fundamental problems with visual imagery explains why decades of the most intensive research in artificial vision systems have failed to produce a practical system that can operate reliably in any but the most controlled visual environments.

The approach most often proposed to address this formidable challenge has been to break the problem into separate domains, and to propose analytical solutions based on physical principles that apply within each domain. We find in the vision literature, therefore, computational algorithms for extracting shape from shading, shape from motion, shape from binocular disparity, shape from line drawings, and so on, with the environmental conditions tightly restricted within each of those specialized domains in order to keep the solutions mathematically tractable. However, the more general problem of shape from reflected-light imagery remains largely unsolved, especially when it includes arbitrary configurations of illumination and illuminated objects, transparent and mirrored surfaces, and irregular or fragmented surfaces, as found commonly in natural scenes.

The solution suggested by Gestalt theory is found using an entirely different strategy: by solving all of these problems in parallel rather than individually. These problems are not separable, but are inextricably intertwined, and therefore the solution to any to one of them depends on the solution to all the others. The secret of the Gestalt approach is that it represents a probabilistic or statistical, rather than analytic, approach to the problem, and therefore combining information from a variety of disparate sources does not make the problem more difficult, as in the analytical approach, but actually makes it easier, because each additional source of information further constrains the range of possible solutions.

In this chapter I show how this principle applies to the problem of determining the structure of the world and that of the structure of the light illuminating that world simultaneously. Combining these two problems offers a more robust solution than either one can offer by itself. This same principle applies also to other perceptual modalities, such as the integration of auditory, somatosensory, kinesthetic, and proprioceptive information, which when combined with visual information results in such a stable and reliable model of the world that it has taken centuries to see through the illusion and to recognize the world around us for the internal representation that it is.

BRIGHTNESS, LIGHTNESS, AND ILLUMINANCE

When light is reflected from a surface to form an image on the retina, there is a fundamental ambiguity with respect to the brightness at any point in the image, because it is impossible to determine with any certainty what proportion of that light is due to the reflectance of the surface, as opposed to the intensity of the light illuminating that surface. A solution can be found in the fact that the patterns of reflectance and illumination on an object typically exhibit different characteristic patterns. The reflectance of an object is typically uniform across the different surfaces and facets of the object, at least for simple objects composed of uniform material, whereas the pattern of illumination is generally nonuniform, exhibiting highlights and shadows that reflect the inhomogeneity of the pattern of illumination. This is shown schematically in Fig. 5.1A. The objective of the perceptual processes therefore is to perform a perceptual scission, as suggested in Fig. 5.1A, in order to factor illuminance from reflectance in the brightness image. To do this, every point in the volumetric matrix must be able to represent three local variables: one each for brightness, lightness (i.e., perceived reflectance or surface color), and illuminance. The brightness value is known from the brightness in the input image. All that remains is to apportion that brightness in some ratio between lightness and illuminance at each point on an opaque surface. The more of the brightness that is attributed to surface lightness, the less that brightness can be due to illuminance, and vice versa. This relationship between the three variables can be expressed as a dynamic circuit present at each point in a perceptual model, as suggested in Fig. 5.1B, where the dark circles represent nodes, or dynamic variables that can each range in value from 0 to 1, to represent the values of the three variables of brightness, lightness, and illuminance at each point in the volumetric matrix. The brightness node feeds activation equally to the lightness and illuminance nodes, but the mutually inhibitory relation between those nodes ensures that the more activation is experienced by one, the more it suppresses the other.

Therefore the lightness and illuminance nodes are in a state of dynamic balance energized by the brightness node, which expresses the dynamic constraints among the three variables. However, the equation remains underconstrained locally; that is, for any given brightness value, the lightness and illuminance values can seesaw alternately to distribute that brightness value in some ratio between them.

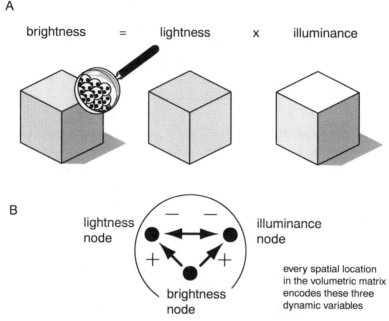

Fig. 5.1   (A) The pattern of brightness of an object is a combination of its lightness, (i.e., perceived reflectance) and its illuminance. The objective of brightness perception is to factor these two components from the brightness image. (B) The situation can be modeled dynamically by providing three nodes (black circles) at every point in the percept (white circles) representing the three variables, with a mutually inhibitory relation between the brightness and lightness nodes, such that the more brightness that is attributed to lightness, the less is attributed to illuminance at each point.

The additional constraints required to resolve the ambiguity can be found in the spatial configurations of lightness and illuminance throughout the perceived figure. Because the lightness of the object tends to be uniform over the figure, an estimate of the overall lightness value can be calculated as an average of the brightness over the whole figure, whereas the illuminance value can be estimated by the difference in brightness from one side of the figure to the other, and how that pattern of illuminance relates to the global illumination profile. These two factors are next addressed in turn.

The average lightness of the figure can be calculated in analog emergent fashion by connecting all of the individual lightness nodes to each other throughout the surface or volume of the visual gestalt and allowing lightness values to diffuse freely from node to node, like a gas distributing itself uniformly within a closed container. In other words, every lightness node tends to take on the average value of its locally connected neighbors, which at equilibrium will result in a uniform lightness distribution throughout the connected region. Each lightness node receives some greater or lesser activation from its corresponding brightness node, depending on whether it is on a sunny or shady surface of the block. The average lightness, as calculated by the spatial diffusion, tends to take on the average brightness signal received across all of the lightness nodes. This spatial diffusion of lightness value expresses the constraint that lightness tends to be uniform within a single Gestalt. In the simple example shown in Fig. 5.1, this constraint is sufficient to perform the perceptual scission illustrated, for the overall brightness that is common across the whole block elevates the value of the lightness nodes uniformly across the whole figure. Wherever the brightness is greater than this uniform average lightness, the illuminance nodes are forced to higher values, as on the sunny side of the block, whereas in places where the brightness is lower than the average lightness value, the illuminance nodes are forced to lower values, as on the shady side of the block.

THE PERCEPTION OF ILLUMINATION

The calculation of surface brightness just described depends on an assumption of uniform object reflectance, which does not hold in all cases. Therefore, any additional constraints available from other sources can help resolve residual ambiguities in those cases. The other source of information can be found in the pattern of illumination. The information in a visual scene concerning the pattern of illumination available perceptually can be determined phenomenologically. Consider the stimulus depicted in Fig. 5.2A. This image produces a bistable percept in which each pair of dark and light panels can be seen as either a convex or concave corner. (The spontaneous reversal of this kind of figure can be controlled somewhat by fixating on one vertex, which will then tend to be seen as convex.) When a single pair of panels is isolated, as in Fig. 5.2B, the percept becomes tristable— that is, it can be seen as either a convex corner, depicted in Fig. 5.2C, or a concave corner, as in Fig. 5.2D, or as a pair of diamond-shaped tiles in the plane of the page, as suggested in Fig. 5.2E. In an isomorphic model this change between the three stable states would be accompanied by a corresponding change in the state of the internal spatial representation. What is interesting in this percept is how the perception of the spatial structure is seen to influence the perception of the illuminant of the scene. When the scene is viewed as a convex corner the illuminant is perceived to the left, whereas when the scene is viewed as a concave corner the illuminant is perceived to the right. When seen as two diamond-shaped tiles the illuminant becomes irrelevant, because the difference in brightness between the two tiles is now seen as a difference in reflectance rather than a difference in illumination. This example reveals the intimate connection between the perception of structure, surface lightness, and illuminant.

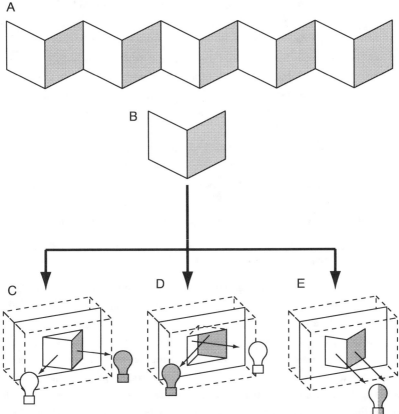

Fig. 5.2 (A) This figure produces a bistable percept whose spontaneous reversal is seen to simultaneously reverse the perceived direction of illumination. (B) Isolation of one pair of panels from the figure results in a tri-stable percept, whose three states correspond to (C) a convex corner illuminated from the left, (D) a concave corner illuminated from the right, or (E) two diamond-shaped tiles in the plane of the page with no percept of illumination. This phenomenon reveals the close coupling between the perception of structure and illumination, as well as perceived surface reflectance.

REVERSE RAY TRACING

The principle of isomorphism suggests that we model the percept as it appears subjectively. The subjective experience of Fig. 5.2B includes an awareness of a source of illumination from one side or the other, although that illuminant is perceived amodally, like the region outside the visual field. The percept is a spatial one, however, as it is easy to point in the approximate direction of the perceived illumination source. I propose therefore a *reverse ray-tracing* algorithm that calculates a percept of the likely illumination profile from the appearance of a scene. Consider the case when the figure is seen as a convex corner, as shown in Fig. 5.2C. The "sunny side" surface would propagate a percept of bright illuminant to the left, whereas the "shady side" surface would propagate a perception of "dark illuminant" to the right, or the percept of reduced illumination from that direction. When the spatial configuration of the figure reverses as in Fig. 5.2D, the percept of the illumination profile is automatically reversed. In the case of the flat percept of two diamond-shaped tiles, as shown in Fig. 5.2E, both surfaces project back to the same direction of illumination and therefore their influences cancel. Because the difference in surface brightness can no longer be attributed to a difference in illumination, it must be due to surface lightness, or perceived reflectance. This phenomenon thus suggests a bidirectional coupling between the illuminance nodes in a spatial percept, and the value of a perceived illumination source, that takes into account the direction of that illumination relative to the particular surface. A bright illuminant would be expected to increase the brightness of surfaces directed toward it, and conversely a bright surface angled in a certain direction suggests a bright illumination source in that direction.

THE PERCEPTION OF GLOBAL ILLUMINATION

Points on the surface of the perceptual sphere represent directions in visual space, and the connectivity of the distorted representation is such that all parallel lines meet at a point on the bounding surface of the sphere. This architecture offers a means of calculating the perceived illumination from every direction in space based on the configuration of the perceived scene. Suppose that the pattern of collinearity represented in the reference grid is designed to model the physical propagation of light through space. In other words, any local element that is in the transparent state, when receiving a signal representing light from any direction, responds by passing that signal straight through the element following the lines of collinearity defined in the perspective distorted space. This way, light signals generated by a modeled light source will propagate along the curves in the representation so as to simulate the propagation of light along straight lines in Euclidean space. If a point on the surface of the perceptual sphere is designated as a light source, that light signal will propagate throughout the volume of the perceptual sphere as shown in Fig. 5.3A. This model therefore is capable of modeling or simulating the illumination of a scene by a light source at infinity, or any nearer location within the perceptual sphere. Whenever the light signal encounters a perceived surface (i.e., elements in the opaque state), the elements representing that surface take on a surface illuminance value that is proportional to the total illumination striking that surface from all directions to which that surface is exposed.

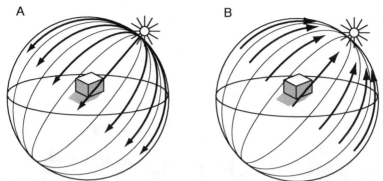

Fig. 5.3   (A) A model of a perceived illumination source on the surface of the perceptual sphere propagates light signal throughout the volume of the perceptual sphere, illuminating all exposed opaque surfaces in that representation. (B) A reverse ray tracing from every opaque surface in the space projects back to a percept of the illuminant apparently responsible for the observed illumination of the scene.

The ray tracing performed by the model should also operate in the reverse direction, taking the perceived surface brightness signals from every point in the scene, and propagating them backward along the reverse light paths to produce a percept of the illumination profile. This calculation represents a spatial inference about the likely illumination profile responsible for the pattern of illuminance observed in the scene. In the scene depicted in Fig. 5.3B, for example, the illuminated surfaces that are pointing upward to the right produce by reverse ray tracing a percept of a bright illuminant in that direction, while the shady surfaces in the same scene project a percept of dark illuminant in the opposite direction. This description is only approximate, however, because a brightly lit surface does not imply illumination exclusively from the normal direction. The illumination could actually be coming from a range of angles near the normal, so the probability distribution of the possible illuminants suggested by a bright surface defines a spherical cosine function centered on the surface normal. The global illumination profile is calculated as the sum of all such probability distributions from every surface in the scene. For example, Fig. 5.4A represents the spherical cosine illuminant distribution suggested by the bright horizontal surfaces in the scene, with a brightness peak at the zenith, normal to those surfaces; Fig. 5.4B represents the illuminant distribution due to the bright and dark vertical surfaces, which suggests two brightness and two darkness peaks in the general direction of the four surface normals. Figure 5.4C represents the total illuminant percept calculated by summing all of the individual component illuminant profiles, which produces an illuminant distribution with a single brightness peak in the upper-right quadrant.

The final perceived illumination profile therefore is only approximate, although it would clearly distinguish between a uniform versus a strongly polarized illumination profile. The block depicted in Fig. 5.3 and 5.4 is shown (for clarity) at the center of the sphere, although that point would normally be occupied by the body percept of the percipient. However, the same block displaced from the center in any direction would generate the same illuminant percept, as all parallel lines in this representation project to the same point on the surface of the representation.

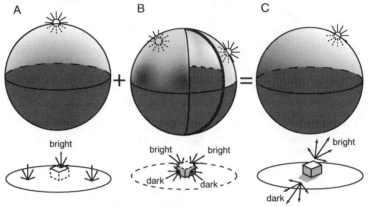

Fig. 5.4   The illumination profile suggested by (A) the bright horizontal surfaces of the scene, plus (B) the bright and dark vertical surfaces of the scene, are summed to produce (C) the combined illumination profile suggested by the whole scene. The lower hemisphere is occluded by the percept of the ground plane, and therefore gets no illumination information.

A PARALLEL RELAXATION

The forward and reverse ray-tracing calculations operate simultaneously and in parallel to produce by relaxation a single, globally coherent percept of both the perceived scene and the illumination profile of that scene. For example, if the panels in Fig. 5.2A or Fig. 5.2B are perceived to be part of the same surface, there will be a tendency to see them as the same lightness, or surface reflectance, even though they appear of different brightness. This tendency corresponds to the spatial diffusion of lightness signal in the lightness image that tends to unify the lightness percept within the bounds of a single gestalt. This unity, however, can only be achieved by assuming different illumination levels for each panel, to account for the observed difference in brightness. The different surface illuminances in the two panels in turn project, by reverse ray tracing, two different hypotheses of the illumination strength in two different directions, producing a percept of a strongly polarized illumination profile. The illumination profile in turn projects by forward ray tracing to illuminate the brighter panel more than the darker panel. In other words, the entire percept is self-consistent, and therefore reinforces itself by positive feedback between the spatial and the illuminant percepts.

The same process in the case of the flat percept of Fig. 5.2E produces a different result. Initially, it too might begin with an assumption of uniform lightness across both panels, which in turn projects two different illuminance signals of different strengths, but in this spatial percept the perceived panels are parallel, so the two illuminant hypotheses are back-projected in the same direction, where the light and dark illuminant signals cancel, producing a percept of a uniform, nonpolarized illumination profile. This uniform illumination in turn illuminates the two panels equally, by forward ray tracing. This results in a conflict between the reverse ray-traced unequal illuminant and the forward-traced equal illuminant, so this time the feedback is in conflict with the initial hypothesis. As the surface illuminance signal in the two panels becomes equal, a scission occurs in the surface lightness signal to account for the difference in surface brightness. In other words, the brightness assimilation between the two panels gives way to a brightness contrast between them, resulting in a percept of two uniform surfaces of different surface reflectance.

What was described as a step-by-step process here would actually unfold in one smooth step, during which all possible interpretations of form and illuminant are pursued simultaneously, and the one that survives after feedback is the one that receives the greatest global support. The winning percept in turn suppresses the alternative interpretations by reification of its own interpretation in every surface and illuminant in the representation.

GENERAL PROPERTIES

In its most general form, the model presented here suggests that perception involves the construction of an internal spatial analog of external objects and processes. Because the spatial structures encoded in the representation emerge in response to different visual modalities, the representation itself is therefore essentially modality independent, expressing the elements of perception in terms of objects and surfaces in the external world, rather than in terms of any particular visual modality, as in the case of the plotting-room analogy presented in chapter 1. The lowest level of perceptual representation therefore—the structural representation of objects and surfaces in a scene—serves as the common interface, or lingua franca between different visual modalities, such as color, binocular disparity, and motion.

Figure 5.5 shows how even a relatively simple three-dimensional scene can produce an alarmingly complex two-dimensional pattern of light. Factors such as the presence of multiple light sources, transparency, specular reflections, mirrored surfaces, attached shadows, cast shadows, and mutual illumination interact with one another to produce complex patterns of light that are virtually impossible to disentangle in a two-dimensional or $2^1/_2$-dimensional context. Yet if such a three-dimensional scene is encoded within an internal three-dimensional model, those same complex patterns of shadow and shine can be readily calculated by replicating the physical propagation of light through the model. In fact, Fig. 5.5 was generated in exactly this manner, by a computer ray-tracing algorithm[1] that models the complex intersecting light paths through a three-dimensional model of the scene.

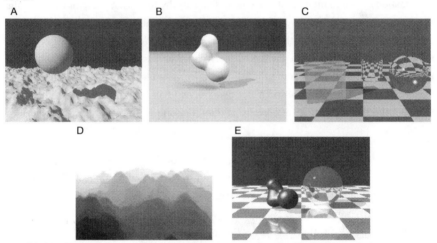

Fig. 5.5   These images, generated by a computer ray tracing algorithm (POV-Ray), demonstrate the power of the human visual system to make sense of (A) attached shadows and cast shadows, (B) concentrated and diffuse illumination, (C) transparency and refraction, (D) atmospheric depth cue, and (E) specular reflection and mirrored surfaces.

The most difficult computational task faced by a computer ray-tracing algorithm is the sheer number of light rays from every point on every source that must all be traced out in all directions in sequence, as they are reflected, refracted, absorbed, and reemitted through the various substances and surfaces in the modeled scene. This problem is addressed in the general model by proposing a parallel ray-tracing algorithm that follows all light paths simultaneously, so that the mere presence of a modeled scene in the representation automatically generates a predicted two-dimensional image of the scene as it would appear on the retinal surface. That predicted image is automatically updated even as the spatial percept pops back and forth between alternative stable states. The real power of this approach is that the local behavior of individual rays of light is relatively easy to model through absorption, reflection, refraction, and reemission, so the complex two-dimensional projection of a scene emerges by the parallel action of a multitude of

---

1. POV-Ray. This excellent program is available free of charge from http://www.POVray.org/

relatively simple local computations. Like a computer ray-tracing algorithm, therefore, the model inherits from the properties of physical light the more complex secondary properties observed in the global pattern of light due to a visual scene. The model can thus account for the perception of self-luminance and mutual illumination, simply by accurately modeling the propagation of light through space.

If the model accurately replicates the propagation of light, it will also automatically calculate shadows cast by opaque objects as seen in Fig. 5.5A, because the model inherits the properties of shadows from the properties of physical light. Furthermore, the model would automatically handle attached shadows, shadows cast by one object on another, and detached shadows, even when the cast shadow falls on a broken or irregular surface. These phenomena, often problematic for more conventional image-interpretation algorithms, are inherited automatically by the Gestalt bubble model from the physical properties of light.

If the model accurately replicates a well-defined, localized light source, then it would also automatically replicate the behavior of a diffuse light source, which would cast fuzzy shadows instead of sharp-edged shadows. Conversely, if the perception of sharp-edged shadows in a scene results, by reverse ray tracing, in a perceptual inference of a well-defined light source, a similar scene with fuzzy shadows throughout would automatically result in a perceptual inference of a fuzzy or diffuse light source, as seen in Fig. 5.5B.

If the perceptual representation is endowed with color—that is, opaque-state units and the propagating light signal are allowed to represent the additional variables of hue and saturation at every point—then a colored illumination profile will automatically result in the perceptual inference of a colored illuminant. For example, if all convex objects in a scene exhibit a red highlight on one side and a blue highlight on the other, whereas objects perceived to be concave exhibit the reverse pattern of highlights, this would be reified by reverse ray tracing to the percept of red and blue illuminants from opposite directions. Once the pattern of illumination is determined from certain surfaces in the scene, the inferred illumination will in turn help distinguish convex from concave objects in the rest of the scene based on the pattern of highlights they exhibit.

The perception of transparency, often problematic for models of perception, is again handled naturally by the Gestalt bubble model with the minor modification of allowing matrix elements to take on intermediate values between transparent and opaque, thus allowing them to model some ratio of transmittance and reflectance, as seen in Fig. 5.5C. Also evident in that figure is the perception of multiple depth planes, where the front and rear surfaces of the transparent objects are seen as complete surfaces in front of more distant background surfaces. With another minor change, transparent objects might be modeled to deflect the modeled light passing through them, replicating another aspect of the behavior of physical light, and thus accounting for the perception of refraction, as seen also in Fig. 5.5C. The patterns of luminance on the transparent glass objects are not perceived as properties of those surfaces, but as properties of more distant surfaces through the glass, which is where they are registered in the perceptual model of the experience.

If the clear atmosphere in the perceptual sphere is given a slight bluish opacity, then the modeled light transmitted by elements in the semitransparent state would take on a bluish tint in proportion to the distance traveled by the modeled light through the modeled atmospheric haze. More distant objects will thereby automatically tend to appear more blue than nearer objects. Conversely, a landscape of rolling green hills that become more blue with perceived distance from the observer tends to be interpreted perceptually as being of a uniform green, with the blue tint being attributed to the filtering effect of the semitransparent atmosphere, as suggested in monochrome form in Fig. 5.5D. Hence the blue component of an object otherwise expected to be green would serve as a cue to the distance to that object. By the simple measure of endowing the modeled atmosphere with a slight opacity, this model thus automatically inherits the capacity to interpret the atmospheric depth cue or *aerial perspective* (Coren, Ward, & Enns, 1994), and that interpretation is expressed in the form of an explicit spatial model.

Specular reflections from polished surfaces have long been recognized as an important cue both to the shape of the illuminated object and to the nature and direction of the illuminating light source. This property can be added to the Gestalt bubble model by allowing opaque-state units to take on a gloss value, and by modeling glossy surfaces to reflect some proportion of incident light coherently, rather than reemitting it in a diffuse manner, as shown in Fig. 5.5E. A surface with 100% gloss would be modeled as a perfect mirror, coherently reflecting a whole section of the perceived scene. Again, the patterns of light and dark observed on a mirrored surface are attributed not to the surface itself, but to other surfaces displaced in the direction of the perceived reflection.

Many of the perceptual phenomena addressed by this model have been deeply problematic for other computational models of perception, even when addressed individually and in isolation. Although a full set of equations characterizing the present model remains to be specified, the real promise of this approach is that it is capable of addressing these most problematic issues, even where they interact with one another. The reliability of the Gestalt approach to perception stems from the fact that matching between visual features encoded in perception and visual features present on the retina is presumed to occur not at the level of the sensory image, where these various influences are hopelessly confounded,

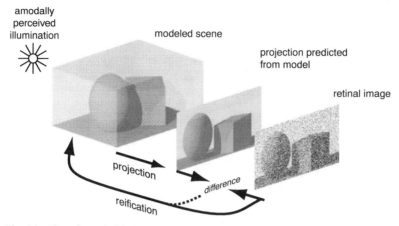

amodally
perceived
illumination

modeled scene

projection predicted
from model

retinal image

projection

difference

reification

Fig. 5.6   The noisy retinal image is used to construct a three-dimensional model of perceived surfaces and illuminants by reification. That perceptual model in turn is used to create a two-dimensional projection of the modeled scene. The projection is then compared with the retinal image, and the differences between them are used to update the modeled scene, in order to minimize the differences between its predicted projection and the retinal input.

but at the level of the model of physical space. The sequence of perceptual processing, depicted in Fig. 5.6, can be summarized as follows. Initially the retinal image, which is probably very noisy, and is known to contain gaps such as the blind spot, and portions occluded by retinal veins, is projected into the volume of the perceptual representation where it defines a set of extrinsic constraints. These, in combination with intrinsic constraints, generate one or more possibly mutually contradictory perceptual interpretations of that input in the form of three-dimensional spatial structures constructed by reification from the two-dimensional retinal stimulus. The spatial structures in turn project back toward the retinal image by top-down feedback, as suggested in Fig. 5.6, where they are expressed in the form of a two-dimensional image representing the predicted view of the modeled scene as it should appear from the perspective of the percipient. This predicted back-projection is then matched against the retinal input, which reinforces reified features that are consistent with the retinal image, while suppressing those that are not. This bottom-up/top-down resonance continues in analog fashion, continually updating the three-dimensional model so as to minimize the differences between its two-dimensional projection and the retinal input. The retinal image therefore never enters consciousness directly, but only by way of its influence on the three-dimensional percept of the world derived from it.

Chapter 6

Recognition versus Completion

PATTERN COMPLETION BY INFORMATON THEORY

The model of perceptual processing developed thus far has focused on the principle of reification, or the perceptual generation of filled-in surfaces and objects in an internal representation of external reality. However this is not to deny the significance of the inverse of reification, which is the abstractive function of perception, in which extended features in the sensory stimulus are reduced to some kind of symbolic code, as required for the storage of perceived objects and events in memory, or for their communication through language. Historically, abstraction has been generally considered as the principle, if not the only, function of perception. This process is often described as occurring in stages from lower to higher levels of cortical representation, much like a sequence of image-processing steps in a machine vision algorithm. Typically, such algorithms begin with the detection of edges, and then proceed to the detection of corners or vertices defined by the intersection of edges, then on to the identification of surfaces and volumes, as delimited by their bounding vertices, and so forth. The ultimate objective is to attach some kind of symbolic label to different objects in the scene as a model of visual recognition, as described for example by Ballard and Brown (1982) for computer vision, and by Marr (1982) and Biederman (1987) for natural vision. However, this concept of visual processing ignores the reification function of perception, as identified by Gestalt theory and as elaborated in previous chapters. In fact, I propose that abstraction and reification are complementary functions in perception, for the abstract code defines the pattern or skeleton of the percept to be filled in by reification processes.

Attneave (1954) proposed that the representational code for visual form used in human perception can be deduced from principles of information theory. This theory explains how information can be compressed, for example, in digital communications in order to minimize the amount of data that must be sent along a transmission line. Information theory describes how redundancy, or repeating patterns, can be eliminated from a signal using information compression. For example, an image containing large regions of uniform pixel values can be compressed without loss of information by sending each string of identical pixels as just two values, one to encode the value of the repeating pixel, and the other to record how many identical pixels are in the string. Similarly, two-dimensional geometrical forms of uniform surface color can be transmitted by a coded descriptor of their shape, together with a single value to encode their color. The amount of compression that can be achieved depends on the nature of the image. The more regularity is contained in the image, the greater is the opportunity for information compression. The optimal type of compression to be used on an image depends on the type of regularity present in the image in question. For example, an image containing symmetrical or periodic patterns can be compressed by encoding one unit of the repeating pattern, together with coded instructions for how to replicate that unit in order to restore the complete pattern.

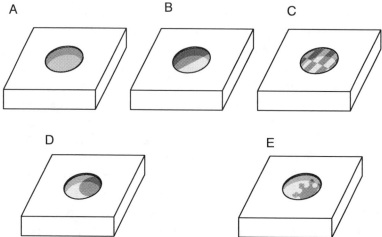

Fig. 6.1   (A) A local portion of a surface viewed through an aperture creates an amodal percept of a continuous surface extending outward from the visible portion. (B) If the visible portion contains a visual edge, that edge is perceived amodally to extend outward in both directions, dividing the two regions of different color, by the principle of good continuation. (C) If the edge has no defined contrast polarity, then the amodally completed edge also has no defined contrast polarity, unless, as in this case, the contrast reversals are periodic, in which case the pattern is perceived to complete with the same periodicity. (D) Amodal completion also respects the Gestalt principle of closure and (E) the Gestalt principle of symmetry in the completion of the amodal percept.

Attneave proposed that the Gestalt laws of perceptual grouping provide evidence of information compression in perception. The laws of similarity, proximity, good continuation, symmetry, common fate, and so on represent regularities in the visual world that offer an opportunity for information compression, and the fact that these properties are found significant in perception suggests that these regularities are indeed exploited by natural vision systems. Figure 6.1A shows a local portion of a surface viewed through a circular aperture. The surface seen through the aperture is not perceived as an isolated patch, but rather as a visible portion of a larger surface, the rest of which is perceived amodally behind the occluding screen. Furthermore, phenomenological examination of this amodal percept suggests that the hidden portions of that surface are perceived to be similar to the visible portion, with the same color and texture, although the confidence of this percept seems to diminish somewhat with distance from the visible portion of the surface. This kind of deduction is commonly assumed to be a cognitive process. However, whether it is labeled as cognitive or amodal-perceptual, the deduction can be described as a spatial image or fieldlike data structure extrapolated outward from the visible portion of the surface by a process that can be modeled by a spatial diffusion, as suggested in the diffusion of perceived lightness discussed in the previous chapter. The lightness diffusion in that model can be seen as a computational implementation of the Gestalt principles of similarity and proximity, extending a similar surface percept outward to proximal locations from the modally perceived region. The structural or spatial nature of this inference becomes more evident in the example shown in Fig. 6.1B, where the contrast edge is perceived amodally to continue beyond the aperture in both directions by the Gestalt principle of good continuation—that is, by extrapolation of the visual edge out into the occluded portions of the scene, in conjunction with the similarity and proximity principles applied to fill in the dark and bright surfaces on either side of the extrapolated edge. This type of collinear extrapolation can therefore be modeled by a *directed diffusion* process, as proposed by Lehar (1994), that projects the visual edge outward as a linear extension in both directions, and the confidence of this extension fades with distance like a spatial probability field. When contrast reversals are encountered across a visual edge, as seen in Fig. 6.1C, the edge is still inferred to continue into the occluded region, but this time like an edge in an outline drawing, with a linear form but without a specific contrast polarity. However, if the contrast reversals are periodic, as shown in this example, then this periodicity itself reflects a regularity in the visual stimulus that can be used in the construction of the spatial inference by the Gestalt principle of periodicity. Similarly, the Gestalt principle of closure would tend to complete the form in Fig. 6.1D, whereas symmetry would suggest the completion of Fig. 6.2E. These intuitive insights into the structure of the amodal percept can be easily tested psychophysically by asking subjects viewing images like those in Fig. 6.1 to guess the brightness values at various sample points on the hidden surfaces, in a manner similar to the procedure used by Attneave (1954).

Even longer range completion is observed with perceptual interpolation between regions of spatial information, as shown in Fig. 6.2. This interpolation appears to be of the same nature as the interpolation observed in modal illusory phenomena such as the Kanizsa figure, with the sole difference that the interpolated structures are amodal rather than modal in nature. The extrapolation and interpolation observed in Figs. 6.1 and 6.2 are therefore examples of perceptual reification, revealing a generative or constructive aspect of perception. However, this reification must presuppose a certain abstraction also, because the reification must conform to the patterns of regularity detected in the visible portions of the scene. There is a general principle evident in this manifestation of perceptual processing: that the visual system attempts to complete spatial structure into unseen portions of the scene based on the implicit assumption that the visible portion is a *representative sample* of the hidden parts of the scene.

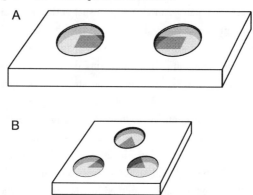

Fig. 6.2   Amodal completion produces an even more stable perceptual completion across longer distances by interpolation inward between visible portions of the scene than by extrapolation outward.

PATTERN COMPLETION IN THREE DIMENSIONS

The *representative sample principle* holds also in the perception of the hidden portions of three-dimensional objects, such as the shapes shown in Fig. 6.3, which are experienced phenomenally as enclosed volumes in three dimensions, complete with an amodal percept of their hidden rear faces, constructed by completion of the regular pattern observed on their visible front faces. In the case of more regular shapes, such as Fig. 6.3A through 6.3C, the amodal percept could in theory be quite precise mathematically, although there is still a probabilistic component to the amodal percept because there is no guarantee that the regularity must necessarily hold through the hidden portions of the figure. The perceptual experience of the rear face of these objects is no more than a likely assumption in the absence of contradictory evidence, but a spatial assumption, nonetheless, that can be described as a three-dimensional spatial probability field. The resolution of the amodal percept also appears to be less than the resolution of the modal front face; for example, it is difficult to precisely locate individual spikes on the amodal side of the percept of Fig. 6.3D, even though that surface is perceived nevertheless as studded with spikes of a specific size and average spacing. The amodal completion of the shapes in Fig. 6.3E and Fig. 6.3F are even more probabilistic in nature, due to the irregularity of the visible front surface. However, these amodal percepts are also spatial structures, because it would be possible to measure a three-dimensional probability field defined by the likelihood that a subject would guess any point in three-dimensional space as being inside or outside of the three-dimensional figure from the view of its visible front face. A psychophysical study of amodal completion could even be performed using line drawing stimuli like Fig. 6.3E, where the subject would be required to judge whether the tip of the pointer is inside or outside the volume of the perceived house, which again would likely reveal a fieldlike amodal structure stimulated by the visible portions of the line drawing. The structure of the amodal percept is therefore lawfully related to the shape of the visible front surface, as constructed by perceptual processes.

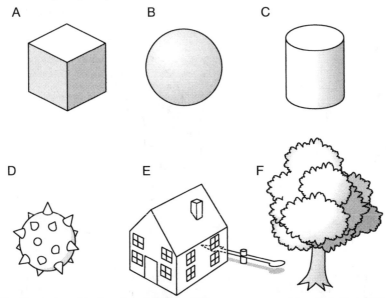

Fig. 6.3   A view of the front face of different objects generates an amodal percept of their hidden rear faces. This percept is like a spatial field, in that if a subject were given full three-dimensional models of these objects built as hollow facades with the rear faces missing, the subjects could easily indicate with their hand the perceived spatial extent of those hidden rear surfaces, like a three-dimensional probability field whose shape is determined by the perceived shape of the visible front faces. Alternatively, a subject viewing a stimulus like the house drawing in (E) could be asked to estimate whether the tip of the pointer is inside or outside the volume of the house.

A common criticism of Gestalt theory is that it attempts to explain everything in terms of perceptual interactions and does not give sufficient consideration to cognitive factors and to learning from experience. This is a misunderstanding of the Gestalt message, however, which is not to discount the influence of cognitive factors; rather, Gestalt theory suggests that there is no clear dividing line between perceptual and cognitive functions, because cognitive functions are similar in principle to perceptual functions, and differ from them only in degree of complexity rather than by their nature. Figure 6.3E is a case in point, for although our experience with houses is a strong factor in our expectations about the shape of their rear faces, I propose that that cognitive expectation is not expressed in the form of purely abstract concepts in a symbolic mental code, but the cognitive inference also has a spatial character much like the objects of amodal perception. The cognitive component is also more readily manipulated by conscious intent. For example, the amodal percept of the back of the house can be made to pop outward if we are given the additional cognitive information that there is a deck or sun room attached to the back of the house. However, this thought too is expressed as a spatial structure, albeit a somewhat nebulous and uncertain one. The relation between cognition and amodal perception is elaborated in chapter 9.

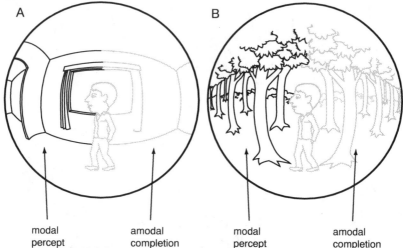

| modal | amodal | modal | amodal |
| percept | completion | percept | completion |

Fig. 6.4   The amodal completion of the hidden half of objects applies also to the hidden half of the world behind the head, which is also completed perceptually by an assumption of similarity with the visible front half, exactly as in the case of the hidden rear faces of objects.

COMPLETION BEHIND THE HEAD

The same kind of pattern completion can also be applied to the spatial percept of the world behind the head, based on the same general principle that the world within the visual field is a representative sample of the world all around. Therefore in the absence of contradictory evidence, this assumption is a useful working hypothesis until proven otherwise. For example, a view of the internal corner of a room seen in the visual field suggests a possible configuration for the rest of the room, as suggested in Fig. 6.4A, by the very same principle as that used with a view of a cube from the outside, as in Fig. 6.3A. Of course, there is no guarantee that a room should be necessarily square, or that the percipient is necessarily located at its center, and therefore the amodal percept of the room behind the head would often be more vaguely specified than suggested in Fig. 6.4A. However, in a real situation the extent and aspect ratio of the room would have been observed when first entering it, and those proportions would be generally preserved to some level of accuracy in the amodal percept as the person walks about in the room and turns in different directions. This can be demonstrated by morphomimesis, by entering an unfamiliar room, and after a brief initial glance, it is possible to turn around and walk backward, and indicate with your palms the approximate location and surface orientation of various walls behind you at various sample points while viewing only the world in front of you, although you are likely to stumble over smaller obstacles like furniture, indicating that these are not mapped with great precision, but are experienced as a vague probability field. Attneave and Farrar (1977) demonstrated how psychophysical experiments can be designed to measure the amodal perception of surfaces in the hidden portion of the perceptual field. Perceptual completion is not confined to the visual modality, but is seen also in the somatosensory domain. When a blind man, or a man in pitch darkness stands in an unfamiliar space, the sensation of contact between his feet and the floor stimulates a percept of a surrounding space over a floor, or ground plane, whose structural characteristics—hardness, irregularity, and so on—as felt through his feet are extrapolated outward from the point of contact by the representative sample principle, although the certainty of this percept fades with distance from the point of contact. If the man advances slowly with arms outstretched, the perceived space expands around him with his advance. The first contact of his hand with a wall produces an immediate amodal spatial experience of a wall extending outward in coplanar fashion from the point of contact, and the salience or certainty of that percept fades with distance from the point of contact. The man can turn and walk parallel to the wall, verifying its continuity with occasional contact with his hand, and his amodal percept of the wall expands progressively as he advances along the wall, merging with a matching percept of the floor extrapolated from the sensory contact through the feet. If he encounters a second wall at right angles to the first, the amodal percept becomes one of a trihedral corner between two walls and the floor, and perhaps a vague sense of closure, that is, of being inside an enclosed room, although the size of the room remains vague and ill-defined. Young infants first beginning to walk experience difficulty with this kind of perceptual reification, frequently bumping their heads on overhanging shelves or table tops. In the case of an outdoor space the same principle can also be applied. For example, a view of a forest as suggested in Fig. 6.4B would suggest, in the absence of contradictory evidence, that the forest is expected to continue in similar fashion with a similar periodicity of trees, although the irregular spacing of the trees within the visual field and the variation among individual trees would not allow a precise prediction of the exact location of the trees outside the visual field. Nevertheless, the information about the approximate tree size, shape, and spacing seen up ahead would be very helpful in making sense of the visual stimulus if the man were to turn around suddenly and look at the world behind him, for the only information he would then need to encode from that view is the difference between what he sees and what he expected to see.

As the man progresses forward through the woods, the modal percept translates coherently into the amodal field behind the head, thereby constantly updating the amodal portion of the perceptual field that only fades gradually if the man stopped his forward progress without looking around. This is why people generally gaze ahead while walking, but when they stop, after an interval, they usually begin to look around them at regular intervals, to refresh their mental image of the world around and behind them. The more geometrical world of our man-made environment—for example a city street, or a corridor in a building—can be completed amodally more easily than a natural scene, which may explain in part why we prefer order and regularity in our artificial environments.

Fig. 6.5   A cube can be abstracted to its plane faces that bound the volume of the cube. Those faces can be further abstracted to the straight lines that bound them. The lines can also be abstracted to the pair of points that bound their endpoints at the vertices of the cube, and finally the pattern of vertices can be abstracted to an eightfold pattern of vertices about a center of symmetry. That eightfold symmetry encodes the cubical form, independent of rotation, translation, or scale.

ABSTRACTION AS DERIVATIVE, REIFICATION AS INTEGRAL

The principles of information theory would suggest that the spatial information of the world can be encoded in most compressed form by encoding the points of transition, or places where the regularity of the pattern of the visual world is broken, in order to avoid redundancy in the representational code. In the case of a solid cube embedded in empty space, the transition from the solid substance of the cube to the empty space around it occurs at the surface of the cube, and therefore the volumetric percept of the cube can be encoded by that three-dimensional surface alone. This obviates the need to explicitly encode the solid volumes of either the object or the space around it. The surface of the cube in turn is defined by plane faces, within which the pattern of the surface is regular, and therefore those faces need not be explicitly encoded point for point, but can be abbreviated to the three-dimensional corner-edges where the different facets of the cube meet, defining a three-dimensional wire frame like a Necker cube. The corner-edges themselves contain further redundancy, and therefore they too can be expressed more compactly terms of their two endpoints. The entire cube can therefore be encoded by the three-dimensional location of the eight corners of the cube. But those eight corners themselves define a regular pattern when viewed from the special location of the center of the cube, from which point the corners can be defined by eight identical vectors pointing outward from the center, as suggested in Fig. 6.5.

The reduction of the cube to this minimal representation is the process of abstraction in perception corresponding to compression in information theory. A complementary process of reification represents the inverse of abstraction, which, like a decompression algorithm in information theory, serves to reconstruct the perceptual image of the cube from the abstracted information. Given the compact information of the cube as an angular solid with an eightfold symmetry at a particular location and orientation in space, eight identical vectors can be constructed equally spaced in solid angle around the central point located somewhere in perceptual space. Each of these vectors defines the endpoints of the 12 linear corners of the cube, and these corner-edges in turn define the bounds of the flat surfaces of the cube, and those surfaces in turn separate the volumes of space that are inside versus outside of the cube.

I propose that the principle behind the perceptual transformation is a simultaneous and continuous process of abstraction and reification. The visible front faces of objects in the world are first reified from the visual stimulus, as described in chapter 4. As these hollow shells, or visual facades, emerge in the volume of perceptual space, a symmetry detection mechanism marks any centers of symmetry in the volumetric matrix, and that compressed encoding in turn serves to regenerate the hidden portions of those facades to match their visible front faces, resulting in a solid three-dimensional amodal core with a hollow modal face on the visible side.

For example, the presence of a section of a spherical shell in the modal representation would produce a symmetry response at the spherical center of that surface, as suggested in Fig. 6.6A, and that response in turn would stimulate an amodal percept of the rest of the spherical shape, as suggested in dashed lines in that figure. Similarly, a portion of a cylindrical surface would promote the amodal completion of the rest of the cylindrical form, as suggested in Fig. 6.6B, and that cylinder would also tend to propagate outward along its cylindrical axis in both directions, as suggested in Fig. 6.6C, extrapolating the detected pattern of symmetry. A section of a planar surface would tend to propagate in planar fashion, as suggested in Fig. 6.6D, and as discussed in the coplanar propagation of surface percept also in chapter 4. Angular shapes such as cubes, pyramids, tetrahedrons, dodecahedrons, and so on would also find simple expression in a symmetry-based descriptor, which would explain the perceptual significance of the platonic solids, as recognized already in ancient Greek science. Figure 6.6E shows schematically how a simple scene would be reified in perception, with the modal front faces of the foreground objects stimulating an amodal completion of their hidden rear surfaces. Notice how these

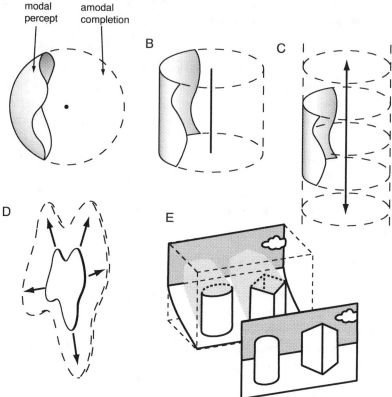

Fig. 6.6   The basic function of perception can be described as a simultaneous abstraction of perceived forms to their axis of central symmetry, together with a reification of that pattern of symmetry to construct an amodal completion of the percept based on the perceived regularity. A spherical surface (A) is completed as a whole sphere; a cylindrical surface (B) is completed to a full cylinder; and that cylinder is extrapolated (C) along its axis in both directions. (D) A planar surface is extrapolated outward in the plane. (E) Perceptual reification of a simple scene, showing amodal completion of hidden rear surfaces. Notice the amodal "shadows" cast by foreground objects, which require background surfaces to be completed through the occlusion from their visible portions.

foreground objects cast amodal "shadows" across the space that they occlude, which requires amodal completion to complete those background surfaces based on their visible portions.

INVARIANCE IN PERCEPTION

When we observe a geometrical figure, like a cube, translating and rotating, and scaling by perspective as it moves about in the visual field, our recognition of that form remains constant throughout the gyrations of that form, and our recognition of that form is located within the percept of the cube—that is, the recognition is spatially localized to the recognized object. This kind of invariance can be quantified in the perceptual model by defining the recognition mechanism in a distributed form. In other words, the mechanism that recognizes the cubical form is replicated at every spatial location in the volumetric matrix, so that the cubical response to the percept remains continually active while that cube is present in the visual field. Therefore that cubical response is not encoded by a single detector mechanism, but jumps continuously from one detector to the next, as the percept translates across the perceptual manifold, remaining always at the center of the moving cubical percept. This is analogous to the way that color is represented on a color television monitor, where each discrete point on the screen is equipped with three colored phosphor dots for red, green, and blue (RGB), which in combination are able to express the full gamut of colors in RGB space at any point on the screen. A spot of a particular color moving across the screen is represented by a synchronized flashing of the phosphor dots on the screen, with the dots turning on and off again as the colored spot passes through.

A symmetry measure suggests how this kind of distributed encoding of spatial form might be expressed in general terms. The eightfold symmetry descriptor of the cubical form is by its nature invariant to rotation and scale, and replicating this detector throughout the volume of the perceptual sphere adds also a translation invariance. For example, a descriptor of geometrical form based on the pattern of symmetry of the objects' vertices might define a basis set of geometrical forms as suggested in Fig. 6.7A, where the forms are depicted in a sequence based on their number of vertices. In essence this is akin to a three-dimensional Fourier descriptor of solid geometrical form, and as such, it can encode any configuration of vertices, not just those of regular solids whose vertices are equally spaced in solid angle from the center. The encoding of more asymmetrical forms is achieved by combinations of the primitives for the regular geometric forms. For example, Fig 6.7B shows the effects of adding a first harmonic or unilateral symmetry component to the second, third, and fourth harmonic patterns of directional periodicity, which tends to stretch out those shapes asymmetrically in one direction, whereas Fig. 67C shows the effect of adding a second harmonic, or bilateral symmetry, to the third and fourth harmonic forms, which stretches them out in two oppositely oriented directions. The amount of distortion caused by these combinations depends on the relative magnitudes or coefficients of the component harmonics of the composite form.

The appearance of a triangular form anywhere in the visual field, for example, would promote the emergence of a third harmonic, or "3" as the central symmetry value of this shape, and that response would remain continually active at the center of that triangle wherever it translates or rotates or scales through the perceived scene, whereas a square

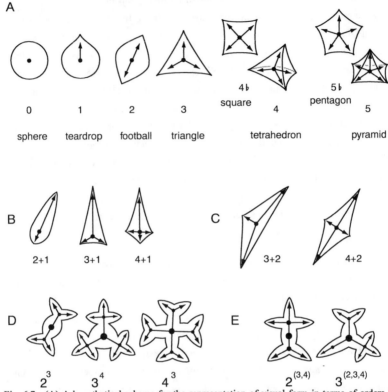

Fig. 6.7   (A) A hypothetical scheme for the representation of visual form in terms of orders of symmetry of its vertices about a center, indicated by the number below each figure. The forms themselves are reified from the abstracted configuration of vertices by a process analogous to inflating a bubble surface around a wire frame skeleton. (B) A first harmonic modifier stretches these shapes in one direction, whereas (C) a second harmonic modifier stretches them in two opposite directions. (D) More complex compound forms can be defined by a hierarchical code that expresses a central and peripheral symmetry. (E) An even more general code expresses different peripheral symmetries on each branch of the central symmetry.

would evoke a symmetry value of "4," located at the center of the perceived square. Additional parameters could express variations on this basic scheme. For example, a magnitude term could define the size of the represented shape, and a *bloat* parameter (to borrow a term from Adobe Illustrator) might define the magnitude of expansion from the central axis skeleton, analogous to the pressure inside a bubble. For example progressive reduction of the bloat value would convert a second-order symmetry from a football shape, to a needle, to a single line or bidirectional vector, as suggested by the central axis vector in Fig. 6.7A, whereas the teardrop shape with zero bloat defines a unidirectional vector, and the triangle becomes three equally spaced vectors from the center, and so on.

The vectors, or central skeletons of these forms, therefore correspond to the shape with bloat value zero.

There is psychophysical evidence that supports some kind of central axis skeleton representation of visual form. Palmer (1985) discussed the perceptual tendency towards local and global symmetry, which defines a central skeleton of a geometrical form in the manner of a medial axis transform (Blum, 1973; Marr, 1977; Kovács, Fehér, & Julesz, 1997). The central axis percept has been related to psychophysical phenomena such as the accuracy of locating a point on a figure (Attneave, 1955b), the perceptually "random," as well as the aesthetic placement of points on a figure (Hollingsworth-Lisanby & Lockhead, 1991; Psotka, 1978), and lowered detection thresholds for features located on such a medial axis (Kovács & Julesz, 1995).

ENCODING HIGHER ORDER PATTERNS OF SPATIAL STRUCTURE

The code defined in terms of symmetry just outlined applies only to shapes that are organized around a single center. However, the same concept can be extended to more complex forms in a hierarchical manner, expressed as symmetries of symmetries, or peripheral symmetries organized around a central symmetry. For example, the first shape shown in Fig. 6.7D exhibits a bilateral symmetry, superimposed on which is a more peripheral threefold symmetry represented by the "Y"-vertex features that appear at opposite ends of the shape. The shape of this figure can therefore be expressed in a hierarchical code of the form 2^3. Figure 6.7D also shows the shapes for the hierarchical codes 3^4 and 4^3. An even more general code would allow for different peripheral symmetries at each branch of the central symmetry, as suggested in Fig. 6.7E, in which the number of peripheral symmetries for each form matches the value of the central symmetry.

The details of the shape code presented here are both vague and highly speculative. However, this particular code is only one possible coding scheme, presented only to demonstrate by example the more significant aspects of what is being proposed here, namely, that whatever the code used in human shape recognition, it must be fundamentally invariant to rotation, translation, and scale, to account for invariance in recognition, and yet it must also incorporate reification with abstraction—that is, when a part of a pattern is seen, perception fills in the missing portions following the basic pattern suggested by the visible portions. Therefore this abstract code can be conceived to appear spontaneously in the volumetric center of perceived objects in the perceptual manifold in the same manner as already described for simple platonic solids.

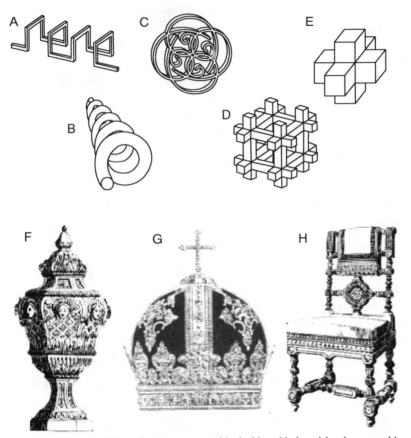

Fig. 6.8 (A through E) Several patterns expressed in the hierarchical spatial code proposed by Leeuwenberg based on principles of information theory. (F through H) Typical ornamental designs incorporate hierarchical patterns of symmetry and periodicity in a manner that is suggestive of a similar code in perception.

Lieeuwenberg (1971) proposed a more intricate scheme to encode patterns of spatial structure, based on the same Gestalt interpretation of information theory and its relation to the representative sample principle. The basic concept behind Leeuwenberg's code is similar to the "turtle graphics" concept of drawing expressed as a sequence of moves and turns. For example, a square is defined by four moves and four turns of 90 degrees each. By defining special "outer product" turns, Leeuwenberg's code escapes from the two-dimensional page to define full three-dimensional patterns. For example the blocky spiral form shown in Fig. 6.8A is defined by a square (as defined earlier) that is swept through space at right angles to the plane of the square, to produce a tube with square cross section. Segments of this tube are then interspersed at regular intervals with a series of outer product turns, whose periodic pattern defines the global form of the blocky spiral. The entire pattern can therefore be expressed in a compact hierarchical code. The Gestalt idea expressed in Leeuwenberg's code is that each level of the code defines an infinite pattern, which allows higher levels of the code to encode only the discontinuities, or breaks in the pattern, defined at the lower levels. This relates to the representative sample principle because a finite sample of a pattern automatically suggests a more extensive pattern extrapolated outward from the given sample. For example, the expanding helix shown in Fig. 6.8B is defined by a circle swept at right angles to its plane to define a circular cross-section pipe, and that pipe in turn follows a higher order helical spiral pattern by expanding the radius of its turn at a uniform rate. Any local portion of this expanding helix therefore contains the information of the whole shape, which can thereby be reconstructed from a local sample by the representational sample principle.

Leeuwenberg also employs notions of symmetry and periodicity, as seen for example in Fig. 6.8C, which is defined by a rectangular cross-section tube swept in an expanding spiral path, and a finite section of this spiral is then replicated through a fourfold symmetry about a center. Other examples of symmetrical and hierarchical patterns expressed in Leeuwenberg's code are shown in Fig. 6.8D and Fig. 6.8E. Each of these patterns has a specific information content as expressed in Leeuwenberg's code. Psychophysical studies (Handel & Garner, 1966) showed that this kind of regularity correlates with the perceptual effort required to encode these patterns; that is, the number of patterns confused with each other increases as a function of the information content. The information-theoretic basis of this coding scheme favors the kind of symmetry and periodicity of the patterns that can be efficiently expressed in this code, and the symmetries and periodicities render the patterns aesthetically pleasing.

It has long been recognized that the perception of musical form is also related to the representative sample principle, for a finite sample of a melodic pattern suggests an infinite pattern by extrapolation, and subsequent violations of that expectation as the melody develops merely suggest more complex, higher order compound patterns in a hierarchical code. Lieeuwenberg proposed a variation of his code of visual form for the perception of structure in musical form, that reveals similar hierarchical patterns of symmetry and periodicity. In chapter 11 I present the psycho-aesthetic hypothesis, which suggests that aspects of visual form that are universally judged to be aesthetically pleasing are evidence of the geometrical primitives of the human visual code. Symmetry and periodicity are prominent in all decorative art across cultures and throughout history, especially in ornamental design, such as the patterns shown in Fig. 6.8, F–H, which exhibit the kind of hierarchical symmetry suggested in Fig. 6.7E, expressed as reified volumetric solids. Note how the regularity inherent in these ornamental structures specifies to a large extent the exact patterns perceived amodally through the hidden portions of these figures. In chapter 8 I present a harmonic resonance theory of visual representation, in which I propose that visual pattern is encoded in terms of patterns of standing waves in the neural substrate. This is consistent with the symmetry code already described, and which has a natural tendency to complete patterns of symmetry and periodicity as observed in amodal perception.

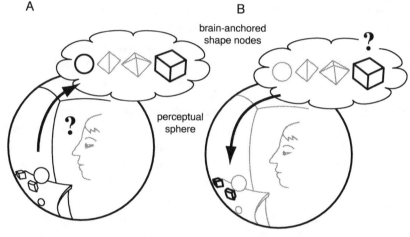

Fig. 6.9   (A) The platonic solids depicted in the "thought clouds" here represent a separate brain-anchored representation of geometrical form, which is coupled to the perceptual sphere in such a way that the presence of one or more exemplars of any particular shape in the perceptual field lights up the corresponding shape node, as if in answer to the question "What do you see?" (B): The system works in reverse also, where a top-down priming of the invariant concept "cube" in turn "lights up" or draws attention to all cubes currently present in the perceptual field, whatever their rotation, translation, or scale, as if in answer to the question "Where are the cubes?" The answer to the question is presented in the perceptual world where the cubes themselves are observed to lie.

BRAIN-ANCHORED ACCESS TO INVARIANT CODE

There is a problem with the nonanchored concept of recognition developed earlier, for there is no single location in the representation where the information about objects detected in the scene can be found. This problem becomes evident when considering a motor response—for example, when a subject is instructed to press a key whenever a particular shape is seen anywhere in the visual field. The motor response must ultimately be expressed in the brain-anchored form of a signal to the specific muscle that will result in the keypress. This suggests that despite the invariant code necessary at one level of the representation, there must also be a brain-anchored copy of this code available for the motor response. However problematic this might be for a neurophysiological model, this functionality can be expressed in the perceptual model by proposing a separate brain-anchored code to represent the presence of particular geometrical forms wherever they might appear in the perceptual manifold.

This concept is depicted schematically in Fig. 6.9, where the array of platonic solids shown in the "thought cloud" above the perceptual sphere represents an array of brain-anchored invariant shape nodes at some fixed location in the brain. Each of these nodes is connected to every point in the volume of the perceptual sphere, so that the brain-anchored shape node will light up whenever one or more exemplars of its characteristic form appears anywhere within the perceptual manifold. Because there are spheres and cubes currently present in the perceptual manifold in Fig. 6.9A, recognition of this fact is expressed in the brain-anchored code by the lighting up of the sphere and cube nodes, suggested schematically in Fig. 6.9A by the bold outlines. In answer to the question "What shapes do you perceive?" suggested by the question mark in Fig. 6.9A, the system need only check the response of these invariant nodes, which in this case would produce the response "spheres and cubes." The response of these brain-anchored nodes is thereby invariant to rotation, translation, and scale.

In order to account for perceptual reification, the system should also be able to operate in top-down mode, as for example in response to the question, "Where are the cubes?" The answer is found by priming the invariant cube node top-down, as suggested by the bold outlines in the brain-anchored code in Fig. 6.9B, and this in turn highlights all of the cubes in the perceptual sphere, whatever their orientation, location, or scale, as suggested by the bold outlines in the perceptual sphere in Fig. 6.9B. Similarly, a top-down priming of the invariant sphere node would highlight all of the spheres in the perceptual manifold. Whatever the neurophysiological mechanism by which the invariant node is connected to the objects in perception, this model at least offers a functional description of invariance as observed in recognition, in order to constrain the search for a neurophysiological mechanism with the required properties. In chapter 8 I propose a computational principle to account for this improbable transformation in the form of a harmonic resonance, or standing wave representation.

ENCODING IRREGULAR FORMS

The forms of nature are generally far more complex than the regular geometric forms that appear in man-made artifacts. For example, the complexity of the irregular tangle of branches and twigs of a tree seems to overwhelm the visual system, because all that detail cannot possibly be absorbed in a single glance. Phenomenological examination reveals two distinct levels of encoding observed in such complex percepts, sometimes called sensory versus epistemic perception. At the lower level of immediate experience, the branches and twigs are perceived with near-photographic fidelity and are rendered perceptually in full three-dimensional depth, especially in binocular viewing, or with the benefit of motion parallax, although the detail is only rendered at the highest resolution near the center of the visual field, as is also evident phenomenologically. However, that level of complexity is not preserved in all its detail from one glance to the next, for if a tree is replaced by a similar tree in the moment that we blink, we do not notice the difference, as demonstrated by the phenomenon of *change blindness* (Grimes, 1996; Rensink, O'Regan, & Clark, 1997; Simons & Levin, 1997). This suggests that the lower level of most immediate experience encodes much greater depth of detail than can be stored in short-term memory. If two similar trees are compared side by side, as shown in Fig. 6.10, A and B, a first glance suggests that they are identical, and the differences in detail are revealed only by a sequential part-by-part comparison. This is the way in which an artist would copy a tree (when the intention is photographic accuracy), connecting one branch or twig to the next in sequence to build up the complete picture on the page. The artist demonstrates the capacity of short-term memory for visual forms by the amount of detail she carries to the paper with each glance at the tree.

A   B

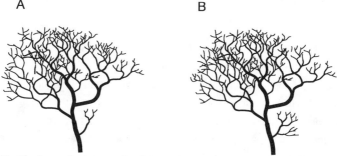

Fig. 6.10   The forms of nature are often far more complex than can be assimilated with a single glance, as demonstrated here by the fact that it takes intensive scrutiny and a serial search to discover the differences between trees (A) and (B). However, the limitation is one of short-term memory when glancing from one tree to the other. Phenomenological observation suggests that the full extent of detail in a figure like this is indeed present in immediate consciousness. This can be verified by treating the two trees as left and right eye images of a stereo pair. Fusing these two images makes the tiny differences between them pop out in parallel, showing that the full detail must be present in immediate consciousness, even if it does not penetrate to short-term memory.

However, although the initial glance does not capture all of the detail of the tree, a complex and convoluted spatial percept is experienced nonetheless at a lower level of immediate experience. This raises the question of whether that convoluted percept is a veridical facsimile of the actual image of the tree, or whether a region of the visual field is somehow labeled as "complex and convoluted," without an actual replica of every branch and twig that we seem to experience consciously. The question therefore is whether consciousness is an illusion that is actually much simpler than it seems. If we are to believe the evidence of our conscious experience itself, then the complex tangle of twigs and branches experienced when viewing Fig. 6.10 must be present in the brain in a form that is isomorphic with the way that we perceive it. However, this is difficult to confirm psychophysically, because the level of complexity overwhelms the code of short-term memory, and therefore we can only report on the aspects of that experience that are encoded in short-term memory. But the issue can be approached from another direction. If Fig. 6.10A and Fig. 6.10B are taken as a stereo pair and fused binocularly as left and right eye images, all of the minute differences between them pop out immediately and in parallel (as soon as the fusion is complete), indicating that those features must have been present in consciousness in all their spatial detail, although encoded at a lower, more immediate level of consciousness that does not pass through the bottleneck of short-term memory to receive a full abstract encoding for every component of that complex scene.

Further support for this view comes from the phenomenon of *eidetic memory*, seen in people with the rare ability to remember whole pages of text or complex scenes in a single glance or very brief presentation. If these people can commit the rich conscious experience to short-term or long-term memory, it is more likely that their gift is a special form of memory that can record a normal conscious experience, rather than a special form of consciousness that encodes more visual detail than our own, as well as a larger capacity memory to store that extra detail.

There has been a great deal of interest recently in the phenomenon of *change blindness* (Grimes, 1996; Rensink et al., 1997; Simons & Levin, 1997), where the appearance or disappearance of prominent objects in a visual scene goes unnoticed by subjects viewing that scene in a video recording, if the moment of change is masked by a few frames of video noise. This kind of finding is always received with great enthusiasm by the vision community, for it seems to confirm the reductionist notion that the complexity of conscious experience is an illusion, and that in fact the visual information encoded in the brain is considerably simpler than it appears subjectively, thus confirming the naive realist view of perception that so greatly simplifies the job of proposing computational models of perception. However, change blindness experiments do not measure the content of conscious experience, for they involve a comparison of a presently experienced scene with a short-term memory of a scene from the immediate past. Therefore any feature that was not encoded in short-term memory would not be noticed as missing from the currently experienced scene. The common confusion in psychology of the content of short-term memory with the content of consciousness can be traced to the naive realist view that the vivid spatial scene experienced in immediate consciousness is not actually present in the brain, but is identified as the external world itself which is the source of the light that forms the retinal image, because it is observed to exist outside of the body rather than inside the brain. However, the indirect realist hypothesis reveals than anything that enters consciousness must therefore have entered the internal representation of the brain, including the rich spatial percept of the world that we experience to surround us.

It is curious how an ornamental structure, like those depicted in Fig. 6.8F through 6.8H, appears in some sense more complex than the irregular branching pattern seen in Fig. 6.10, although the latter clearly contains more information in the information-theoretical sense. I propose that this phenomenon can be explained by the fact that the complexity of the tree apparent at the level of immediate consciousness overwhelms the higher level code, and is therefore abbreviated in short or long-term memory to a code for the shape of the global gestalt. This can be expressed, even after the briefest glance, as a trunk topped by a cloud of "irregular branching structure," a form that is typical of naive art and children's depictions of trees in which the irregular top is reduced to a simpler spherical or triangular form, filled in with a uniform leafy or twiggy texture. In this sense, the internal representation of the ornamental form is indeed more complex: The regularities in its structure penetrate to higher levels of consciousness even in a single glance than does the irregular pattern of the tree, which, although more complex in immediate consciousness, is expressed in a simpler code at the higher level abstract representation.

A similar phenomenon is revealed by stimuli composed of patterns of dots, like those seen on dice. When the number of dots is small enough, their number is perceived immediately and in parallel, especially when they are organized into regular geometrical arrangements, as are the dots on dice. When the number of dots gets much above 6, 7, or 8, and especially if they are arranged in a random cluster, it becomes much more difficult to count them in parallel in a single glance, although of course any number of dots can be counted sequentially. The immediate spatial percept of such a larger group of dots is therefore a percept of "a cluster of" dots, which would not be distinguishable preattentively from a similar cluster that was only slightly greater or lesser in number, although global configural aspects of such clusters, such as the spatial extent or aspect ratio of the whole, or symmetry and periodicity of the dots, are perceived in immediate conscious experience.

THE RELATION BETWEEN RECOGNITION AND PERCEPTION

Given the insights just developed, let us now return to the more general issue of the functional nature of recognition and how it relates to the function of perception. The functional role of recognition is elucidated by the condition of visual agnosia. Farah (1990) drew a distinction between two forms of agnosia that she called *apperceptive* agnosia and *associative* agnosia. Apperceptive agnosia is the more serious and debilitating condition, for the apperceptive agnosic cannot make spatial sense of the visual world. Such a patient can list the individual features that she observes in an object but cannot integrate those features into a spatially coherent whole. For example, when presented with a line drawing of a bicycle, the agnosic might identify individual parts, like a pedal, or a spoked wheel, but cannot tell whether she is viewing a picture of a complete bicycle or an assortment of disassembled parts. Agnosics cannot, for example, count the number of wheels, or see how those wheels are configured in relation to each other. Apperceptive agnosics will attempt to identify an object by a process of adding up visual impressions, performing the integration of features cognitively rather than spatially. For example, such patients often use color to identify objects, mistaking vanilla ice cream for scrambled eggs, and a piece of white soap for a piece of paper. These patients therefore seem to have normal sensory function, but a perceptual dysfunction. What is missing in the apperceptive agnosic is the functionality described in chapter 4, where visual features are integrated into three-dimensional spatial structures that can be used for practical interaction with the world. Visual agnosia is perplexing for the naive realist, because it would seem to be impossible to see the wheels of a bicycle without seeing also where they are. According to naive realism, vision involves the detection of objects out in the world itself—that is, they appear at the location that they actually occupy in external space. The indirect realist perspective, on the other hand, reveals that the very space in which objects appear in perception is itself a data structure or representation in the brain, without which there can be no coherent framework in which the objects of perception can appear. The experience of the apperceptive agnosic is what would be expected if vision operated as proposed by O'Regan (1992), without an internal spatial representation in which individual visual impressions can be stored in their proper relation to each other in a global context. When the agnosic patient glances from one bicycle wheel to another, each is perceived in isolation, with no spatial relation to the rest of the scene, so the agnosic cannot tell whether the wheel she is seeing at one moment is the same as the one seen a moment earlier. The experience of the apperceptive agnosic must be somewhat like a cubist painting that shows disconnected fragments of the visual world.

The condition of associative agnosia is a very different phenomenon. In this condition, the patient is able to integrate the visual world into a coherent whole, but in this case their deficit lies in the fact that they are unable to recognize the objects in the world. This condition therefore represents successful perception, but a failure of recognition. For example, "The Man Who Mistook his Wife for a Hat," in Oliver Sacks's book of that title (Sacks, 1985), could walk down the street on his way to work, avoiding obstacles along the way, without being able to identify the obstacles he was avoiding. The subjective experience of this condition must be somewhat like living in a world made exclusively of papier maché, composed of objects and surfaces with irregular contours but unrecognizable forms. The objects and surfaces can be seen perfectly clearly as spatial structures, but they cannot be identified as anything beyond irregular blobs. When the man from Sacks's story was preparing to leave the neurologist's office at the end of a visit, he saw an irregular form about the size and shape of a coat stand, and attempted to retrieve his hat from the top of it, unaware that the form he was seeing was actually that of his wife. Although this condition is highly inconvenient, it is by no means as debilitating as that of the apperceptive agnosic, who is denied the experience of the visual world as a structured spatial whole. Because the associative agnosic seems to have an intact perceptual function, but lacks the function of recognition, this condition is very helpful in clarifying the functional role of recognition.

What would it take for Oliver Sacks's patient to recognize an object as a human form? According to the propositional paradigm, and the feature detection paradigm, recognition amounts to the lighting up of a symbolic label in the brain, as if the irregular papier maché blob present in visual consciousness were labeled as are the parts in an anatomical illustration, with little arrows that point to "head" and "eye" and "ear" at particular points on the otherwise amorphous or unrecognizable form. Marr (1982) and Biederman (1987) suggested that the visual form is also broken down into geometrical primitives, so for example the head might be indicated with a pointer labeled "sphere" and the torso might be labeled "cylinder". But although this concept has a certain intuitive appeal, there is something fundamentally missing from this notion of perception. When we see a head as being generally spherical, this is more than merely a symbolic label attached to the head; rather, we see the head itself as an approximate sphere, as if the sphere itself, in reified form, is somehow incorporated into the percept of the head. In other words what is missing in the abstractionist view of recognition is the reification component.

I propose that visual recognition does involve a decomposition of a spatial structure into geometrical primitives as suggested by Marr and Biederman, but that decomposition occurs by reification, approximately as follows. When viewing a human body, the initial impression might be of an irregular pillar, somewhat like the papier maché form seen by the associative agnosic. Because the top end of that pillar is somewhat rounded on a narrow neck, this quasi-spherical shape triggers a recognition of its spherical form by the activation of an invariant "sphere node," and the activation of that node in turn emphasizes and completes the spherical form of that part of the body. In other words, as the head is recognized as being somewhat spherical, that recognition in turn makes the head portion of the spatial percept actually become more spherical, rounding out both its visible front and its hidden rear faces by modal and amodal completion. This completion in turn brings into stark contrast portions of the retinal image that differ significantly from that spherical form. For example, because the head is not really spherical, being narrower from ear to ear, the spherical descriptor of it bulges out anomalously at both sides of the head where the head is actually narrower than the sphere. This anomaly can be corrected by modifying the spherical descriptor as an oblate spheroid with a particular aspect ratio that best matches the evidence of the retinal image. With this anomaly taken care of, the next most salient anomaly is seen at the front of the head, where the jaw protrudes from the oblate spheroid, extending out of it like a separate form. If the perceived person has a "square jaw," that protruding shape might be characterized as a rounded cube partially embedded and blended into the bottom half of the oblate sphere. This cubical percept in turn lights up an invariant cube node with a "rounded" modifier, and that node in turn feeds back down to make the square jaw even more square or cubical in the spatial percept, again to match the sensory stimulus.

With the spherical top and cubical bottom of the head accounted for, the next salient anomaly might be the nose, which protrudes prominently from both the spherical and cubical percepts. The nose in turn might be characterized as a triangular slab poking out of the front of the face. This lights up a triangular slab node in the invariant representation, also with a "rounded" modifier, and that node in turn amplifies or enhances the triangular slabularity of that part of the face in the three-dimensional percept under construction. So as each geometrical component of the face is recognized, that component appears also in the spatial percept, and perceptual recognition proceeds to the next most salient feature that violates the current geometrical characterization of the form, progressively refining the percept to ever higher accuracy from coarse outline to fine detail until the three-dimensional percept exactly matches the two-dimensional retinal stimulus. The relations between the geometrical primitives must also be encoded in the representation. So the head should be encoded not just as "sphere and cube" but "sphere over cube," and the nose as "triangular slab protruding from sphere over cube," and so on, so that the reification of that compound concept reconstructs those forms in their proper relation to each other. The simplified geometrical forms seen in the sculptures of modern art often illustrate the nature of this kind of decomposition of the human form into simplified geometrical primitives.

I propose therefore that the function of recognition serves a dual purpose. First, it offers a symbolic representation of the forms present in perception expressed in terms of geometric primitives, which can be used for verbal processing or for encoding a perceptual experience in memory in compact form. The other equally important function of recognition is to refine the spatial percept constructed out of reified renditions of those same geometrical primitives. In other words, the higher level code for visual form is not merely a symbolic abstraction, but a precise parametric specification that is used to instruct the perceptual mechanism how to construct that particular spatial percept. That same abstract code is thereby also capable of regenerating the percept top-down in mental imagery or imagination. The symbolic nodes that encode the geometric primitives in perception are meaningless by themselves in isolation from the perceptual mechanism, for those nodes only take on the meaning of the concepts that they represent by their ability to reify those spatial concepts in the perceptual representation, just as the meaning of the various variables in Vannevar Bush's differential analyzer take on their meaning by their functional connection to the rest of the machine. I propose therefore that the mechanism that morphs the initially irregular pillarlike percept into a high resolution detailed rendition of a human form is part and parcel of the mechanism that recognizes that pillarlike structure as a human form. This constructive or generative capacity represents the most significant and meaningful aspect of the function of recognition, without which true recognition cannot really occur. Only by means of this generative function of higher level recognition does the amorphous papier maché world of the associative agnosic becomes sculpted into the intricately articulated and detailed world of our own visual experience.

Gestalt theory suggests that there is no sharp distinction between perception and cognition, but that they differ in degree rather than in kind. Visual agnosia supports this view; in fact, agnosias do not segregate neatly into apperceptive and associative forms, but form a continuum that includes intermediate forms in which simple object recognition is preserved while complex objects cannot be distinguished. Indeed, Sacks's patient could recognize simple geometrical primitives like the Euclidean solids, and could describe more complex forms in terms of their component primitives. The perceptual function can therefore be seen as a more primitive form of recognition, which breaks down or organizes the world in terms of more primitive features such as cubes, spheres, planes, and other euclidean solids. These lower level primitives are in turn used in combination to express the higher order patterns of visual form that we normally associate with the function of visual recognition.

THE PERCEPTION OF PHYSICAL LAWS

The discussion up to this point has presented the function of perception as of recovering and reconstructing the geometrical structure of objects in the field of view. But perception does much more than that. The objects of perception are also observed to possess perceived mass, weight, hardness or softness, and physical qualities such as perceived malleability or brittleness. In fact, the world of perception appears as a complete spatial replica of the physical world that mimics the laws and forces of external reality, as well as its structure and appearance. For example, a view of a block suspended in midair with no visible means of support promotes the emergence in perception of a spatial replica of that block, which by default takes on a perceived weight whose magnitude depends on the substance of which the block is perceived to be composed. This perceived weight pulls the perceived block downward toward the perceived ground by the force of perceived gravity, as an internal force that duplicates the action of the physical force that it represents. However, if the sensory view of that block fails to fall toward the ground, the perceived block must also be prevented from falling toward the perceived ground in the internal representation. This can be done either by providing some invisible means of support—for example a perceived jet of air, or magnetic levitation—or the perceived block must lose its perceived weight in order to allow it to continue to hover in the perceptual representation. Similarly, an object in motion is perceived by default to have a certain momentum, so that if it disappears momentarily behind an occluder, it will be expected to reappear at the proper time from the other side. If it fails to reappear, it will be perceived to have collided invisibly with something behind the occluder. The moving percept therefore behaves very much like the physical object that it represents. The perceived higher order properties of objects therefore appear to be a kind of perceptual shorthand that encodes the possible behavior of perceived objects in hypothetical or imaginary circumstances; conversely, those higher order properties are induced from the observed behavior of the perceived object. As long as the objects in the world around us behave as expected, based on the properties we perceive them to possess, they attract little attention. However, as soon as an object is observed to violate our perceptual expectations, that immediately draws our attention to that object, in the hope that careful scrutiny of its extraordinary behavior will help us update our mental model of its true nature. Objects that continue to violate physical laws as we perceive them are then automatically perceived to be animated and autonomous, which puts them into a completely different category with regard to our expectations of their possible future behavior.

The idea that our understanding of the laws of naive physics have a perceptual basis is supported by Michotte's investigations (1963) of the perception of causality. Michotte showed that the perception that one object caused another to move depends not on cognitive factors, but on the precise timing of events in the stimulus, much as in the phenomenon of apparent motion. Experiments by Heider and Simmel (1944) showed that moving displays of simple shapes such as squares and triangles moving about and interacting in specific ways were consistently judged by subjects in personal terms, with one figure being judged as aggressive, bad tempered, and so on, and another figure judged as frightened, meek, or helpless. These personalized characteristics also provide a kind of short hand descriptor to make sense of these higher order properties of the motion of those objects, this time for animated or autonomous objects, in order to help us understand or predict their behavior in different circumstances or occasions. Like Michotte, Heider and Simmel suggested that causal impressions were given by the spatial, temporal, and figural aspects of the display, suggesting a low-level perceptual function.

This concept of perceptual representation suggests that Newton's laws of motion are properties of the perceived world as much as they are of the physical world, and that therefore Newton's discovery of these laws was as much an act of introspection as it was of external observation. In chapter 11 I propose that the laws of mathematics too are properties of the mind rather than of the world of physical matter, and that therefore mathematical invention also has a large component of introspective discovery. Leeuwenberg (1971) discussed the similarity between Newton's dynamic laws of motion and the static laws of visual structure. For example, the tendency to see a local edge as part of a larger global edge by the representative sample principle, or the Gestalt principle of good continuation, is a static analog to Newton's first law of motion, that an object tends to continue in uniform motion unless acted on by a force. A more literal dynamic version of Newton's first law is also seen in motion perception, where an object that disappears behind an occluder is expected to reappear at the other side. Newton's second law of motion, which describes the motion of a body under uniform acceleration, is comparable to the perceptual tendency to extrapolate the uniform or lawful change of a pattern in perception, as seen in the spiral forms in Fig. 6.8B, whose static rate of expansion is expected perceptually to continue at the same rate in the absence of contradictory evidence. Leeuwenberg also related Newton's law of action and reaction to the perceptual tendency toward symmetry. For example, in the percept of a block resting on the ground, the forces of weight and support are balanced in a symmetrical opposition, which lends stability to the percept by virtue of its greater prägnanz. The asymmetrical percept of the hovering block, on the other hand, cries out for another force to restore the balance. Newton's laws of motion therefore can be viewed as dynamic variations of the Gestalt principles such as good continuation, symmetry, and so on. These laws are intrinsic properties of the perceptual representation that have developed to help us encode a complex spatiotemporal pattern of experience in the simpler, or more succinct terms of perceived objects and the dynamic relations between them.

This concept of perceptual function also makes a statement about epistemology, or the theory of knowledge. According to this view, to know a rock, for example, is to know its weight and mass and hardness, and to be able to predict its behavior when dropped or thrown, or when struck against another rock, or to notice that something is awry when a rock is observed to behave in an extraordinary or unlawful manner. I propose that this knowledge is expressed in very literal form in the brain, as the capacity to construct a virtual replica of a rock in perception, and to match the dynamic behavior of that rock against the dynamic image of a rock present in the visual field. Knowledge of the world corresponds to the possession of an internal dynamic model of the world, complete with a replica of the physical forces, laws of motion, and material properties of that world.

Chapter 7

Relation to Neurophysiology

RELATING THE PERCEPTUAL MODEL TO NEUROPHYSIOLOGY

Up until this point the discussion of the mechanism of perception has been presented exclusively in perceptual modeling terms. However, eventually the perceptual model has to relate back to neurophysiology. How can the volumetric spatial world of phenomenal experience, whose boundaries appear so regular and spherical, possibly map to the irregular wrinkled two-dimensional surface of the cerebral cortex? Unless we can at least form some kind of mental image of the spatial relation between the nouminal brain and the phenomenal world, the perceptual model remains detached from our knowledge of the world, like a disconnected image hanging in space. I propose to make the connection between the two worlds of reality by elaborating the perceptual model developed so far, to show how the unity of perceptual experience can be resolved with the segregation of cortical architecture observed neurophysiologically, how a regular spherical percept of the spatial world of experience can be encoded in the convoluted slab of the cortical tissue, and how this convoluted space relates to the double mental image presented in chapter 1. This is done from both perspectives: from the inner perceptual world looking out at the objective physical world, and from the outer physical world looking in to the perceptual world.

THE ARCHITECT'S MODEL IN THE LOBBY

In order to discuss in general terms the spatial relation between different spaces, I employ the metaphor of an architect's model. An architect will often create a scale model of a building, as depicted in Fig. 7.1, to give an impression of the final appearance before committing to construction. After the building is complete, the model is sometimes displayed in a glass case in the lobby of the building of which it is a miniature copy. This offers a beautiful metaphor for perception, for the miniature replica of the building enclosed in a glass case, completely contained within the building of which it is a copy, is analogous to the perceptual copy of the world in a man's head, which is centered about the model of the man's body, embedded in a replica of local space, the entire model being completely contained within the man's physical brain. I use this metaphor to construct a more accurate mental image of the relation between the inner and outer worlds of epistemological reality.

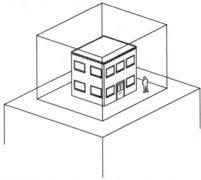

Fig. 7.1   An architect's model painted in full color, and enclosed in a glass case, provides a compelling metaphor for the world of perception modeled in the brain, especially if the model is located on a pedestal in the lobby of the building of which it is a miniature copy. A little man living in the model world could imagine the greater external world by scaling up the world in which he lives proportionally.

Let us start within the perceptual world, as if we were inside the glass case in the miniature world of the architect's model, for that represents the familiar world of phenomenal experience. We do not see ourselves as being in miniature, of course, because we cannot see the giant external world beyond the bounds of the glass case. However, if our world were indeed a miniature copy of euclidean space as is the case with the architect's model, we could imagine how the outer world would look if we could see it through the glass, for we need only scale up the world we see around us in linear fashion by the appropriate scaling factor. In terms of the real perceptual experience, we could imagine the dome of our nouminal skull hanging in space some distance above the perceived dome of the sky, and the bowl of the lower half of the skull extending deep below the perceived earth under our feet. A more accurate picture would have to include the fact that the image on the visual cortex is inverted and reversed relative to the external world. Therefore the foramen magnum, or hole in the bottom of our physical skull through which the brainstem connects to the spinal cord, should be imagined overhead above the zenith of the sky, rather than underfoot by the nadir.

Consider what would happen if the representational scale of the architect's model were not equal in all directions, but one dimension was flattened relative to the other two, as suggested in Fig. 7.2A. Because this warping is applied to the space itself rather than just to the objects in that space, it would distort the very units of measurement in the model space, so that the flattening would not be apparent to the little man in the miniature world. An external observer looking in from the euclidean space outside, on the other hand, would see a strange distortion as the little man moved about within the miniature world, especially when he rotated about his vertical axis. Viewed from the external world, his

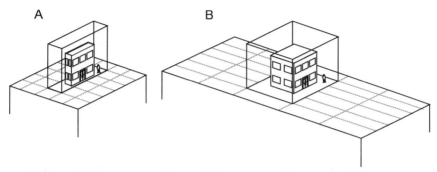

Fig. 7.2   (A) If the architect's model used a smaller scale in one dimension than in the other two, the model would appear flattened in that dimension, while remaining isomorphic with the world that it models. (B) The unequal scaling would not be apparent to the little man living in the model world, because his measure of distance would be compressed along with the compression of his space. If, however, the man could see out to the greater external world, he would observe an inverse scaling, or expansion in that same dimension relative to his internal model world.

body would be seen to morph alternately between being flattened front to back, like a gingerbread man, to a flattening left to right like a silhouette, and during the transition between these states the little man would morph continuously like a blob of clay that is rolled while pinched between thumb and index finger. None of this morphing would be apparent to the man in the miniature world. However, if the little man could see out through the glass to the greater world outside, he would see the inverse distortion applied to the external world, as suggested in Fig. 7.2B, where the square pedestal on which the model world is standing would appear distended in the same direction as the compression in Fig. 7.2A. The distortion of the outer world when viewed from the inside is the inverse of the distortion of the miniature world when viewed from the outside, in order to maintain a constant spatial relation between the two spaces when viewed from either perspective.

The inner and outer worlds in this hypothetical analogy would be isomorphic with one another, because every point in one space relates coherently to a unique point in the other space, although the isomorphism would be topological, preserving relations such as above-ness and between-ness as suggested by Köhler, rather than a strictly topographical isomorphism. A functional isomorphism is implied by the fact that the spatial transformation by which the little man rotates about his axis is not defined in euclidean space, but in the compressed space of the model world, which is why the little man appears to morph as he rotates when viewed from the external euclidean space. In other words, the morphing rotation in the model world is functionally isomorphic to a rigid rotation in euclidean space.

Consider now what would happen if the flattening of the model world were expressed as a nonlinear function, like a museum diorama or a theater set, in which the compression in the depth dimension increased in nonlinear fashion with proximity to the rear of the model space, and the rear face of the model, or back-plane painting, were to represent perceptual infinity, as suggested in Fig. 7.3A. Again, when viewed from the inside, this warping of space would not be immediately apparent, except for the fact that as in our perceptual world, objects that approach perceptual infinity would appear at progressively reduced resolution in depth—that is, it would be progressively more difficult to distinguish differences in depth between nearer and farther objects. At the singular surface at the rear of the space the perceptual resolution of depth would fall to zero, so that all objects beyond some limiting distance would appear as flat as the moon in the sky. If the little man in this distorted world could look out of his glass case, he would see a complementary nonlinear expansion of external space in the direction toward the back plane. For example in order for the little man to make progress toward the back plane in equal increments as measured in external coordinates, he would have to take ever larger steps toward the back plane as measured in internal units, and the last step to pass through the back plane itself would require a step of infinite length, at least as measured in the internal coordinates of his warped internal space. If we wish to picture the dome of our skull, therefore, out beyond the dome of the sky, the location of that bony dome must be imagined beyond the dome of the sky, although that is actually beyond infinity in internal terms, for even the farthest stars and galaxies in our perceived world are represented no farther than the surface of the dome of the sky.

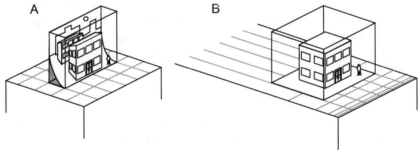

Fig. 7.3   (A) If the model world incorporated a nonlinear compressive scale in one dimension, like a diorama, this too would not be immediately apparent to the little man who lives in the model world, except for the fact that beyond a certain distance the spatial resolution in the depth dimension would fall to zero, due to limited resolution in the model space, as observed in our own perceptual world. (B) Viewed from inside this depth-compressed model, the external world would appear to exhibit a complementary expansion in that same dimension, expanding in scale with an exponential function whose slope goes to infinity at the distance of the back plane of the model, due to limited resolution in the model space.

The surface of the cortex is warped into great bulges and folds known as gyri and sulci. Figure 7.4A depicts the model world similarly bent into a great gyrus, or viewed from the other side, folded into a sulcus. How would the external world appear from within such a curved universe? Again the answer is found by applying the inverse curvature to the external world, as suggested in Fig. 7.4B, where the model world appears undistorted, but the external world appears relatively distorted by an inverse curvature, that is, in the direction of the convex curvature of the miniature world, the external world appears compressed laterally, because every degree of azimuth in internal coordinates covers many degrees in external coordinates. In the direction of the concave curvature, on the other hand, the external world appears stretched in the lateral dimension. However, the spatial relations between these two worlds remain the same whether viewed in internal or external coordinates. Given the many irregular gyrations of the cortex alternately concave and convex, the view of our skull from within this convoluted space would appear similarly convoluted by an inverse function, alternately approaching toward and receding from the sky in an inverse replica of the gyri and sulci of our brain. However irregular and ill-formed this mental image of our nouminal skull might be, one feature at least remains certain—that the entire convoluted surface of the skull as imagined from the inside must completely encompass our perceptual world as an irregular surrounding shell.

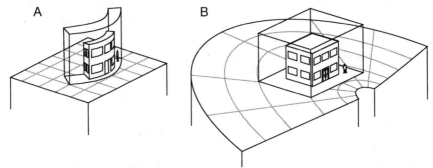

Fig. 7.4 (A) If the model world incorporated a curvature, like a gyrus in the cortex (or, viewed from the other side, like a cortical sulcus), this curvature too would not be apparent to the little man within the model world. (B) From the internal world looking out, an inverse curvature would be observed. This can be understood intuitively by imagining that the model and the pedestal in (A) are elastic, and considering what kind of deformation of the pedestal would be required to straighten out the curvature in the model space.

COUPLING BETWEEN CORTICAL AREAS

One of the most troublesome issues in neurophysiology is the fact that the visual cortex appears to be segregated into areas specialized for processing individual modalities such as color, motion, and binocular disparity. Other cortical maps exist to represent auditory and somatosensory information. How can this segregated architecture possibly be resolved with the unity of the conscious experience? This issue has come to be known as the *binding problem*. The following hypothetical model can help clarify these issues, at least with respect to a functional isomorphism. Imagine that the architect's model is constructed in duplicate, and the two models of the same building stand side by side in the lobby. Let us suppose further that the two models are not identical, but each is specialized for depicting certain properties of the building. One model is painted in full color to depict the external appearance of the building, whereas the other is constructed of clear plastic to depict internal structures, such as the internal subdivision of rooms and floors. By definition these two models represent the same space, and it is only in external coordinates that they are separated into different spaces. Therefore in the internal context within the model world, the painted surface of the colored model is by definition superimposed on the front surface of the transparent model; that is, the representation is unified by definition to express different aspects of the same building, and this relation would hold, even if one model world was warped or scaled differently from the other. It is in this manner that the physically separate cortical maps can be conceived to relate to the unity of conscious experience.

The view of the external world from within these two models is not identical, because they are spatially separated in external space, and therefore they see the external world from different perspectives. From the perspective of the unified internal world, therefore, the external world would have to appear as a double image, with two alternative perspectives of the lobby that appear superimposed on one another from within the model world. If the two models are built to different scales, and are warped to different curvatures, then each of the superimposed images of the external world would be correspondingly warped with the appropriate inverse function. Given the multiple cortical maps in the visual cortex, and the additional somatosensory and auditory maps identified neurophysiologically, our mental image of the dome of our skull is now even more convoluted and confused, appearing something like a fuzzy superposition of a number of complex convoluted surfaces, but again, all of these surfaces must completely enclose our perceptual world. It is in this rather confused sense that it is true to say that the dome of our physical skull is located beyond the dome of the sky, as a topological rather than topographical fact.

FUNCTIONAL ISOMORPHISM AND THE HOMUNCULUS PROBLEM

This more elaborate model of spatial experience raises anew some fundamental issues relating to consciousness and the "problem of the homunculus." In the literal analogy of the two models in the lobby, nobody would claim that these models have any intrinsic consciousness as such, and although they might be considered to represent the same external objects, they are not spatially superimposed but are physically separate structures. So how are we to account for the unity of conscious experience, given the physical separateness of the different cortical maps in the brain? The solution to this problem relates to the issue of functional isomorphism, as opposed to the structural or topological isomorphism that was just addressed.

Functional isomorphism is necessarily defined with respect to certain transformations or functional connections between the spaces in question. Spaces that are functionally as well as topologically isomorphic are causally linked in some manner, so that changes in one space have specific consequences in the other. Imagine, for example, that the twin models in the lobby are coupled in some fashion so that if you were to press on one model with your fingertip such that its wall flexes under the strain, the wall of the other model would flex in a similar way at the corresponding location. To extend this fanciful analogy, let us suppose that the modal model, being merely a facade, offers little resistance to your finger and flexes easily under the stress. If, however, the three-dimensional structure of the amodal model is more rigid, it would help resist the force of your finger even though you are pressing on the modal model, due to the dynamic coupling between them. Whatever the mechanism of this coupling might be, if two models are functionally coupled in this manner, they would behave functionally as a single structure, even though they are actually constructed as two.

This principle would work even in an artificial intelligence whose behavior could be designed to operate *as if* it experienced a unified percept of the world that was actually distributed across physically separated representations, as long as those mechanisms were functionally coupled. In fact, this is exactly the principle behind Vannevar Bush's differential analyzer, discussed in chapter 1, whose component parts are physically connected by the same functional relations as the mathematical variables that they represent by analogy. The reason why this concept has been so difficult to express in the digital computer is that the most fundamental component of that device, the logical gate, is an input–output device—that is, with a unidirectional causal connection in which the output has no influence on the input—and this same concept is also expressed in the neuron doctrine in the distinction between the dendrites and axon of the cell. This paradigm of computation has constrained our whole concept of computation as an input–output process, which necessarily separates the output from the input. Consider by contrast a pair of pendulums rigidly connected by a rod, so as to constrain them to swing together, by a bidirectional causal connection. Such a system behaves as a single system, even though it is distributed between separate sub-systems. Dewan (1976) proposed that the unity of conscious experience is analogous to emergence as observed in the entrainment of coupled oscillators. Dewan invoked the metaphor of the electrical power grid, whose alternating current is supplied by a network of interconnected power generators, each generator being controlled by a local governor to maintain a constant rate of rotation. However, the stability and accuracy of the system of generators are far greater than those of any single unit, because the various generators couple across the grid, automatically loading down generators that run fast and boosting generators that run slow. Therefore the network of coupled generators behaves like an emergent larger "virtual generator" with a virtual inertia equal to the sum of the inertias of all of its component generators. I propose exactly this kind of bidirectional causal connection in the brain between different representational maps, so that perceptual information calculated in one modality is immediately communicated to other modality maps, where that information is expressed in the form appropriate to the modalities of those other maps.

A mental image will help clarify this concept. Imagine a set of identical marionettes, each constructed with hinges and pivots at elbows and knees, to replicate the freedom of movement of the human body. Imagine further that these marionettes are all functionally coupled, so that raising the arm of one of them will automatically raise the same arm on all of the other marionettes in synchrony. Finally, imagine that the mechanism that couples the marionettes can even function when the marionettes are translated or rotated relative to each other, so that raising the arm of one of the marionettes will raise the arm of the others, even those that are currently upside-down or facing backward. If a spring is installed on one of these many marionettes so as to tend to hold the arm down toward the feet, then the reaction force due to that spring will be transmitted to all of the other marionettes in parallel, including the one whose arm is being pushed upward, where the effect of that spring force will be felt remotely. The effect of that resistance will therefore be replicated in all of the marionettes in the set, whose arms will all rise in synchrony only to the height allowed by the balance between the lifting force and the depressing spring. Now if every marionette in the set were equipped with a different set of springs pulling different limbs in different directions, the joint effect on the collective "virtual marionette" would be the same as if all of those springs were installed on a single marionette. It is in this sense that physically separate cortical maps can be conceived as functionally unified, because the different aspects of the percept are completed functionally *as if* the various diverse abstractive and filling-in operations in the different maps were actually occurring in a single space that encoded all the perceived properties in a single unified map.

A NONANCHORED REPRESENTATION OF SPATIAL STRUCTURE

Neurophysiological studies suggest that the image on the primary visual cortex is anchored to the retinal surface. However, phenomenological examination of the visual world suggests instead a representation anchored to external coordinates, for as we rotate our head or eyes relative to the world, our percept is of a stable world with our head or eye rotating within it. To express this concept in our spatial analogy, let us switch the analogy to a model ship installed on the bridge of a real ship of which it is a miniature copy. When the greater external ship turns from one heading to another, the model ship in the glass case turns with it, like the lubber line of a compass that remains fixed to the orientation of the ship as a whole. However, the model of the local environment surrounding the model ship in the glass case remains fixed in orientation relative to the external world, like a compass card in a turning ship whose north pointer points always to the north in external coordinates, even as the compass housing with its lubber line rotates around it with the greater ship. In the internal coordinates of the ship, therefore, the rotation of the ship is modeled by a counterrotation of the modeled environment around the fixed model ship, whereas in external global coordinates it is the model environment that remains fixed while the real and model ships rotate in synchrony within it. This is the kind of representation suggested by the experience of turning one's head in the world, which suggests that the pattern of activation in our brain that represents the structural world around us rotates relative to the tissue of the brain as we turn our head in the world.

There is an alternative way in which a model ship can be designed to behave: like a moving map display on a computer screen that depicts north always at the top, so the ship traveling east would be depicted pointing to the right, whereas when westbound it is depicted pointing to the left. The map itself, however, is fixed to the coordinates of the ship, as depicted on a computer monitor that is bolted to the deck. The invariance in the proposed coupling mechanism would allow both types of model to be present simultaneously in the same ship, and the two models would be coupled to each other through the invariance relation.

This kind of coupling across rotation is necessary to account for the way that the visual world recorded on the eye-anchored retina can be related to the somatosenaory world recorded on the body-anchored body surface so that I can point precisely to the point in visual space where I feel an itch on my body, and I can anticipate in somatosensory space where a fly will be felt as I see it land on my body. The relation between these two body-anchored spaces can only be meaningfully mediated through an intermediate world-anchored representation that can be updated from either of those body-anchored maps despite variations in body posture and direction of gaze.

VOLUMETRIC SPACE IN FLAT CORTEX

The one remaining obstacle to completing the relation between phenomenology and physiology is that the cortex appears to be a two-dimensional space whereas perception is essentially spherical. How can this aspect of perception be accommodated in the physical structure of the brain? An answer to this question can be found by the principle of functional isomorphism, by applying topological distortions to the perceptual spherical space to flatten it out into a sheet, while preserving the interconnectivity between regions of the representation, thereby maintaining a functional isomorphism with the spherical space.

Imagine the following topological operation performed on the sphere of perceptual space. First we insert a vector into the perceptual manifold from the rear, extending radially from the outer surface in to the center of the space, as suggested by the arrow in Fig. 7.5A. This hole is then widened into a cylindrical cavity, as suggested in Fig. 7.5B, but as the hole is widened, the perceptual tissue is pushed aside topologically, while preserving its functional connectivity, as suggested by the warped grid lines in Fig. 7.5B. The interior surface of this cylindrical cavity therefore now represents the radial vector at a single point at the back of the head, and the computations of collinear and coplanar completion follow the distorted lines of collinearity depicted in the figure, so as to proceed isomorphically as if performed in a geometrically continuous space. The cylindrical hole can be further expanded in this manner, eventually molding the entire perceptual sphere into a hollow bowl shape as suggested in Fig. 7.5C, like a "pinch pot" made out of a ball of clay by pressing a thumb into the center of the ball from one side. The entire rim of this bowl-shaped structure now represents the single point at the back of the head. The thickness of this concave disk of tissue represents the depth dimension of the visual world replicated in bas-relief, with the inner surface of the bowl representing the surface of the face, and the outer surface representing perceptual infinity. It is therefore perfectly conceivable that a geometrically flat surface of finite thickness, like the cortical surface, can be wired to be functionally isomorphic with a spherical perceptual space. Indeed, the discovery of binocular disparity-tuned cells arranged in a regular array of increasing disparity (Barlow, Blakemore, & Pettigrew, 1967) is consistent with this kind of representation.

I propose therefore that a section of cortical tissue from the primary visual cortex encodes the spatial structure of the visual world by spatial regions in the volume of the cortex, as suggested in Fig. 7.5D, in which the different colors in the figure represent volumetric regions of cortical tissue that are in different electrochemical states, corresponding to the subjective experience of opacity or transparency and perceived color currently represented in that visual space. The exact representation depicted in Fig. 7.5D is of course highly speculative, for it attempts to unite information from two disparate realms of knowledge, the phenomenological and the neurophysiological. However, unless we take the incredible position that phenomenology exists somehow independent of physiology, there must be some kind of neural substrate to the phenomenal experience, and that substrate must encode all of the information present in the subjective experience. In an epistemological sense, therefore, the most speculative component in Fig. 7.5D is the neurophysiological

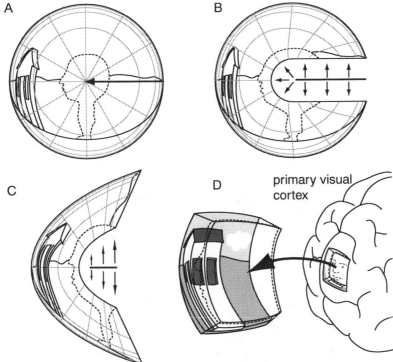

Fig. 7.5   The spherical world of perception can be mapped to the flat space of the cortical surface as follows. (A) First a vector is inserted from the posterior side of the perceptual space, as indicated by the arrow. (B) The perceptual sphere is then expanded outward topologically while preserving the connectivity of the spherical representation. (C) When opened up enough, the space becomes a domed surface, like a cortical gyrus, which now resembles the mapping of the primary visual cortex. (D) In other words, a section of the cortical surface maps objects in perceived space by volumetric regions of the cortical tissue reified in depth, with the far surface representing infinity, and the near surface representing the surface of the face, depicted in dotted lines, which is perceived amodally as the nearest object in perceived space.

portion, for all of our scientific knowledge of the external world is indirect, built on inferences and indirect measurements that are all ultimately grounded in subjective experience. Therefore the regions of different colors in Fig. 7.5D are epistemologically more certain to exist in the brain in some form than the neurons and electrical signals postulated by neurophysiology. Those colors and structures are experienced directly, whereas neurons and electrical signals are detected only indirectly by specialized instruments, which in turn are viewed through the veil of conscious experience. All that remains uncertain is the neurophysiological form taken by those subjective components of experience in the physical brain. Figure 7.5D expresses the hypothesis that some physical quantity in the brain corresponding to those perceived colors is spatially distributed in the cortex in a pattern corresponding to the patterns of that experience.

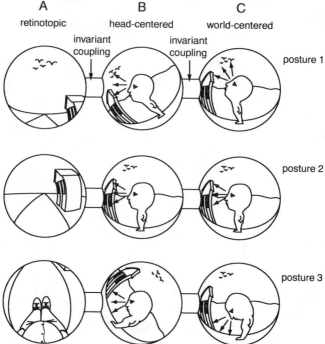

Fig. 7.6 A schematic depiction of a hypothetical scheme for various cortical mappings, to demonstrate the invariance relation that must hold between different maps. (A) The retinotopic map, as in the primary visual cortex, shown for three different views. (B) A head-centered map in which the image of the world rotates as the man moves his head, but the head remains fixed at the center of the space. (C) A world-centered mapping, presumably like a parietal representation, in which the image remains oriented to the coordinates of the external world. These different representations remain tightly coupled despite their differences in reference frame, so that changes calculated in one map are communicated immediately to the other two.

I propose that each of the various topographical maps of visual space encodes such a spherical space within the flat tissue of the cortical surface, and that the many physically separate maps are functionally coupled by bidirectional connections so as to define a single unified perceptual structure to explain the unity of conscious experience. The dynamic images of the perceived world in these maps are synchronized, like the pictures on an array of television sets in a shop window, all tuned to the same channel, except that the synchrony of the cortical maps is not because they are all presenting identical copies of the same scene, but because each contributes its own influence to a common perceptual model or representation that is distributed among those maps. Figure 7.6 depicts a schematic conceptualization of the relations between various cortical maps, expressed this time in functionally isomorphic rather than neurophysiological terms. Each of these spheres therefore represents the spherical information encoded in a circular slab of flat cortical tissue. In column C, rows 1–3 depict three viewing poses, looking up, forward, and down, respectively, as expressed in a world-centered coordinate system perhaps like the representation in the parietal cortex. Column A shows the retina-anchored cortical image for each of these views, resembling the mapping of the primary visual cortex. Each of the three views is projected to a different region of world-centered space, as suggested by the arrows depicted in column C. Any number of intermediate cortical maps might exist in order to assist the invariant transition between these different cortical representations. For example, column B represents a head-anchored representation intermediate between the retinotopic map of column A and the world-anchored map of column C, in which the world and body images rotate about a head that remains fixed at the center of the representation.

OBJECT-CENTERED AND BODY-CENTERED COORDINATE SYSTEMS

The rotation invariance between coupled cortical maps offers a different perspective on the operation of the temporal lobe in perception. The temporal lobe has been identified as the cortical area dedicated to object recognition. The coordinates in a temporal lobe visual map therefore might be expressed in object-centered coordinates, with axes labeled top, bottom, front, back, left, and right, relative to the object under consideration. When viewing an object like a house, perceptual effigies of the house in the primary visual or parietal cortices would be depicted in its spatial context as it appears in the scene, presented at the orientation from which it is viewed. Another copy of the house percept would appear in the temporal lobe map, this time rotated to a canonical orientation. Because these representations remain coupled, any mental computation performed on this object-centered image—for example, an amodal completion of its hidden rear face— would be immediately communicated in parallel to all of the other cortical maps, where that same amodal percept would be rendered at the orientation specific to that map. This object-centered map encodes only the object or feature in the scene that is currently the focus of attention. If the focus of attention is shifted, without moving the eyes, to a component feature like the door of the house, for example, the image of the house in the primary visual and parietal maps remains unchanged, whereas the image of the door in the temporal cortex map expands to fill the whole of the object-centered space, allowing perceptual computations to occur at high resolution in that space. The results of this focused completion are nevertheless reflected at lower resolution in the other cortical maps. This kind of model would account for the subjective experience of shifting your focus of attention without moving your eyes, which seems to bring the object of attention into clearer view, as if seen at higher resolution and somehow centered focally, without changing its perceived location or spatial relation to the rest of the scene. Walker and Young (1996) presented evidence from a patient who showed neglect for the left sides of individual objects, regardless of where they were located in the visual field, suggesting damage to this kind of object-centered map.

If this object-centered map could be decoupled from the primary visual and parietal maps under voluntary control, hypothetical or imaginary perceptual operations could be performed on the objects in that map. For example, in order to imagine the view of the back of a house that is present in front of you, that image can be formed where it rests, as if viewing through a transparent model of the house, as is typical of engineering and architectural depictions. Alternatively, the object-centered map can be decoupled from the other cortical representations in order to allow the image of the house within it to be rotated so as to expose its rear face to mental view—that is, the right side of the house now appears on the left side of the image of the back of the house. This creates a double mental image of the house from front and rear views simultaneously, although the rear view is entirely amodal, and its orientation remains under voluntary control. The fact that we are capable of forming such an image can be easily demonstrated by asking subjects to sketch the imagined rear face of an object currently viewed from the front. This imaginary copy of a perceived house can be manipulated and scrutinized mentally, like a model held in your hands. Any conclusions drawn from that mental manipulation can be readily projected to the modal percept of the scene in front of you by simply reestablishing the coupling between the object-centered map and the rest of the cortex. The manipulation of mental imagery is discussed at greater length in chapter 9.

Other cortical maps in the somatosensory and motor areas might be expressed in body-centered coordinates, similar to the object-centered representation except with an image of your own body permanently resident at the center, with coordinate axes labeled rostral, caudal, dorsal, ventral, left, and right. The body image in this body-centered map would remain fixed in orientation, like a man hanging from a parachute harness, whose limb movements cannot change his orientation in space. This body-centered map would nevertheless remain coupled to the parietal or world-centered representation, so that the body movements in the two spaces would remain identical. If a man performs a handstand, his body image rotates relative to a fixed world in the world-centered map, whereas in the body-centered map the world would rotate around the body image, giving the man the subjective impression of holding the world above his head. The subjective experience of a handstand seems to express both of these perspectives simultaneously. The mapping of the primary somatosensory and motor areas seems to suggest an even finer breakdown of the body map, into separate maps for particular body parts. For example, a hand-centered map might contain an effigy of the hand, permanently fixed in a canonical orientation, in order to map the fine movements of the fingers relative to the hand as a whole. An instruction to flex your finger would be initiated in this hand-centered map, whereas an instruction to raise your finger upward in global coordinates would be computed first in the world-centered map. Either way, the outcome of the spatial computation is communicated to all other maps in parallel, through the invariant couplings by which they are functionally connected.

I propose that the cortical area in the somatosensory map devoted to a single finger does not correspond directly to the surface of that finger, as is often supposed, but rather that region delimits the range of motion of an as-yet-undetected higher order representation of that finger as a spatial pattern of energy, whose nonanchored manifestation in that cortical area represents the current posture of that finger. In other words, as the finger is flexed back and forth through its full range, a pattern of energy flexes back and forth through the cortical area devoted to mapping that finger, and that space represented by that cortical area, and the motions of the represented finger within it, are expressed in a full three-dimensional space, although with the depth dimension flattened as in a bas-relief sculpture. Similarly, the patterns of energy in the primary visual cortex that represent the visual scene take the form of dynamic three-dimensional patterns of energy that drift back and forth across the cortical tissue in synchrony with the perceived scene. These patterns are virtually invisible to the brain-anchored electrodes used in neurophysiological recordings, which seem to indicate instead brain-anchored cells with large receptive fields. The entire edifice of modern neuroscience is built on brain-anchored assumptions, but the evidence for that paradigm is chiefly based on the brain-anchored electrode, which is optimized for detecting brain-anchored signals. However, a brain-anchored system cannot plausibly account for the many invariances apparent in perception.

The more general principles that are exemplified by this concept of cortical representation are that the sensory surface both of the retinal and the skin surface receptors are necessarily tissue anchored at the lower levels of representation, and therefore if the information from the different senses is to be meaningfully interrelated, it must be translated into a nonanchored code expressed in the only coordinates that are meaningful for interaction in the world. Only this kind of explanation can possibly account for the experience of conscious perception as observed phenomenologically. Those who would deny an explicit volumetric coding of the spatial percept in cortical tissue, the onus is on them to explain how *else* the information plainly manifest in subjective experience could possibly be coded in the brain. In the absence of an alternative explanation, the present model at least accounts for the subjective experience of perception, and therefore sets the constraints for any neurophysiological theory of perceptual representation. Only when we have taken the full measure of the informational transformation required for sensory perception can we possibly hope to unravel the neurophysiological mechanism that performs that incredible transformation. I propose that the reason why the primary cortical areas have been mapped topographically in neurophysiological recordings, although no such mapping has been found in higher association areas of the cortex, is not that those areas are not topographically mapped, but that the spatial code in those higher areas is no longer a brain-anchored code but one anchored to coordinates that can shift with respect to the neural substrate, which makes those patterns essentially undetectable by the brain-anchored electrode. In the next chapter I present the harmonic resonance theory as a plausible mechanism to implement the improbable transformations observed in perception.

Chapter 8

Harmonic Resonance Theory

A HARMONIC HYPOTHESIS

The properties of perception as observed phenomenally and described by Gestalt theory are truly baffling when it comes to proposing a computational mechanism to account for those properties. However, there is one physical phenomenon that exhibits exactly those baffling properties observed in perception: the phenomenon of harmonic resonance, or the representation of spatial structure expressed as patterns of standing waves in a resonating system. This tantalizing similarity cannot be coincidental, considering especially that no other physical mechanism or phenomenon has ever been identified that exhibits these same enigmatic properties. The unique properties of harmonic resonance were recognized already by Lashley (1942), who argued for a harmonic resonance representation specifically to address invariance in perception. However, Lashley did not propose any details as to the mechanism and how it relates to specific perceptual phenomena. The theory presented in this chapter is also somewhat vague, but one step closer to a fully specified model. I describe the properties and principles of harmonic resonance that relate to perceptual phenomena, and discuss how these relate to recent findings in embryological morphogenesis, where a similar standing-wave representation has been identified as the mechanism that determines the geometrical structure of the developing embryo. The harmonic resonance theory also relates to recent work on synchronous firing between remote cortical regions, and the *temporal correlation hypothesis* (Eckhorn et al., 1988; Nicolelis, Baccala, Lin, & Chapin, 1995; Murthy & Fetz 1992; Sompolinsky, Gollomb, & Kleinfeld, 1990), as well as to the holographic theory of neural representation (Pribram, 1971; Pribram, Nuwer, & Baron, 1974) and the concept of cortical cells as Fourier frequency detectors (De Valois, De Valois, & Yund, 1979, De Valois & De Valois, 1988).

GENERAL PROPERTIES OF HARMONIC RESONANCE

The most remarkable property of harmonic resonance is the sheer number of different unique patterns that can be obtained in even the simplest resonating system. A pioneering study of standing-wave patterns was presented by Chladni (1787), who demonstrated the resonant patterns produced by a vibrating steel plate. The technique introduced by Chladni was to sprinkle sand on top of the plate and then to set the plate into vibration by bowing with a violin bow. The vibration of the plate causes the sand to dance about randomly except at the nodes of vibration where the sand accumulates, thereby revealing

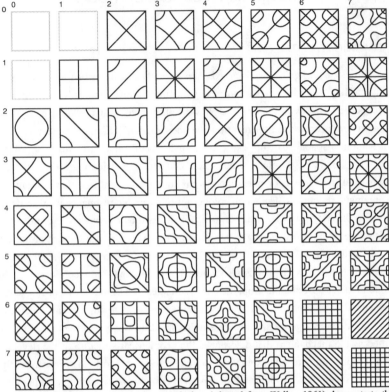

Fig. 8.1   Chladni figures for a square steel plate (adapted from Waller, 1961) demonstrate the fantastic variety of standing-wave patterns that can arise from a simple resonating system. A square steel plate is clamped at its midpoint and sprinkled with sand. It is then set into vibration either by bowing with a violin bow, or by pressing dry ice against it. The resultant standing-wave patterns are revealed by the sand, which collects at the nodes of the oscillation where the vibration is minimal.

the spatial pattern of nodes. This technique was refined by Waller (1961) using a piece of dry ice pressed against the plate, where the escaping gas due to the sublimation of the ice sets the plate into resonance, resulting in a high-pitched squeal as the plate vibrates. Figure 8.1 (adapted from Waller, 1961, p. 69) shows some of the patterns that can be obtained by vibrating a square steel plate clamped at its midpoint. The lines in the figure represent the patterns of nodes obtained by vibration at various harmonic modes of the plate, with each node forming the boundary between portions of the plate moving in opposite directions: that is, during the first half cycle, alternate segments deflect upward while neighboring segments deflect downward, and these motions reverse during the second halfcycle of the oscillation. The different patterns seen in Fig. 8.1 can be obtained by touching the plate at a selected point while bowing at the periphery of the plate, which forms a node of oscillation at the damped location, as well as at the clamped center point of the plate. The plate emits an acoustical tone when bowed in this manner, and each of the patterns shown in Fig. 8.1 corresponds to a unique temporal frequency, or musical pitch. The lowest tones are produced by the patterns with fewer large segments shown at the upper left of Fig. 8.1, and higher tones are produced by the higher harmonics, depicted toward the lower right in the figure. The higher harmonics represent higher energies of vibration and are achieved by damping closer to the central clamp point, as well as by more vigorous bowing. There are many more possible patterns in a square plate than those depicted in Fig. 8.1; these would be revealed by suspending the plate without clamping, allowing patterns which do not happen to exhibit a node at the center of the square. Of course there are many more patterns possible in plates of different shapes (Waller, 1961), and many more still in volumetric resonant systems such as a vibrating cube or sphere, which define three-dimensional subdivisions of the resonating volume, although these have not received much attention due to the difficulty in observing the standing-wave patterns within a solid volume or volumetric resonant cavity. Faraday (1831) extended Chladni's phenomenon by observing standing waves on the surface of liquids, which produces geometrical arrays of standing waves on the surface of the fluid in the form of concentric rings, parallel ridges, grid and checkerboard patterns, arrays of conelike points, and even brick patterns. This work has been extended more recently by Cristiansen, Alstrøm, & Levinsen (1992), Kumar and Bajaj (1995), Kudrolli and Gollub (1996), Kudrolli, Pier, and Gollub (1998), and others, who have demonstrated patterns of equilateral triangles, regular hexagons, superlattice, and quasi-crystal array patterns by driving the oscillation of the fluid layer with a controlled waveform. Figure 8.2 shows some of the patterns produced by Kudrolli et al. It seems that this work is only touching the surface of the full potential of this phenomenon for producing complex geometrical patterns by relatively simple driving oscillations.

The utility of standing wave patterns as a representation of spatial form is demonstrated by the fact that nature makes use of a resonance representation in another unrelated aspect of biological function, that of embryological morphogenesis, or the development of spatial structure in the embryo. After the initial cell divisions following fertilization, the embryo develops into an ellipsoid of essentially undifferentiated tissue. Then, at some critical point a periodic banded pattern is seen to emerge as revealed by appropriate staining techniques, shown in Fig. 8.3A. This pattern indicates an alternating pattern of concentration of morphogens, i.e. chemicals that permanently mark the underlying tissue for future development. This pattern is sustained despite the fact that the morphogens are free to diffuse through the embryo. The mechanism behind the emergence of this periodic pattern is a chemical harmonic resonance known as *reaction diffusion* (Turing, 1952;

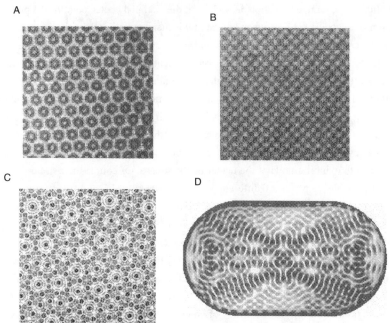

Fig. 8.2   Various patterns of standing waves on fluid surfaces generated by vibrating the containing vessels with various driving frequencies, producing (A) hexagonal, (B) rectangular lattice, and (C) quasi-crystal patterns, among many more. (D) This pattern is defined more by the shape of the walls of the container than by the driving waveform, showing how interference patterns in the resonating system tend to subdivide the resonating system into periodic and symmetric subpatterns in an essentially Gestalt manner.

Prigogine & Nicolis, 1967; Winfree, 1974; Welsh, Gomatam, & Burgess, 1983) in which a continuous chemical reaction involving a morphogen P catalyzes the production of more morphogen P as well as of a morphogen S, but the concentration of morphogen S in turn inhibits production of morphogen P (see Gilbert, 1988, pp. 655–661, for a summary). The result of this circular reaction is analogous to the periodic patterns of a resonating steel plate. The chemical harmonic resonance in the embryo can thereby define a spatial addressing scheme that identifies local cells in the embryonic tissue as belonging to one or another part of the global pattern in the embryo by way of the relative concentration of certain morphogens. For example, one resonance divides the embryo into two halves, with high and low morphogenic concentrations to distinguish the head from the tail. Another morphogen produces a low–high–low pattern of concentration, which subdivides the embryo into medial and distal divisions, producing by combination with the first morphogen a total of four divisions: distal-head, medial-head, medial-tail, and distal-tail. Higher harmonics of chemical standing waves further subdivide this pattern, providing a chemical addressing scheme whereby the local concentration of a few morphogens uniquely address each distinct segment in the embryo (Kauffman, Shymko, & Trabert,

1978) with a binary code that can specify 2^N unique zones in the embryonic tissue given N different morphogens. Note how the boundaries between adjacent zones seen in Fig. 8.3A are defined at higher spatial resolution than the discrete cell bodies of which the tissue is composed. Perhaps the most visible example of the kinds of patterns that can be defined by reaction diffusion systems are those seen in animal markings, such as the stripes of the zebra or the spots of the leopard which have also been attributed to reaction diffusion processes (Murray, 1981, 1988). Most of the markings on animal skins are for the purpose of camouflage, and therefore those patterns are generally somewhat irregular for adaptive reasons. However, there are cases where animal and plant markings are intended to attract attention, and in those cases the true potential of morphogenic processes is demonstrated as a representation of geometrical form. This is seen for example in poisonous animals, like the caterpillar shown in Fig. 8.3B, as well as in a variety of poisonous snakes that show periodic geometrical patterns of rings, diamonds, or stripes, as well as in animals that display for mating purposes, like the plumage of a peacock, and of various birds of paradise, and in the plant kingdom it is seen in the forms of flowers. The symmetry and periodicity observed in these examples can be seen as both evidence of the properties of morphogenesis, and at the same time, as properties of biological vision, whose particular sensitivity to periodicity and symmetry are exploited by those morphogenic markings in order to attract visual attention.

In the case of animal coat markings, the chemical patterns only define different patterns of coloration. But the same spatial addressing scheme is also responsible for defining the pattern of tissue types in the embryo, for the pattern of concentration of these morphogens during a critical period of development has been shown to be responsible for permanently marking the tissue for subsequent development into bone versus muscle tissue, and so on. This explains some of the geometrical regularities observed in the shape of the muscles, bones, and internal organs of the body. The periodicity in morphogenesis is ultimately responsible for the periodic segments observed in the bodies of worms and insects and in the vertebrae of vertebrates, and similar resonances have been implicated in many other symmetries and periodicities in plant and animal forms, including the bilateral symmetry of the human body, the pentalateral symmetry of the starfish, the angular and radial periodicity of the bones in the human hand and fingers, and the geometrical forms observed in plant and flower structures. Newman and Frisch (1979) proposed a chemical harmonic resonance explanation for the phenomenon that the bones in animal limbs exhibit a progression from single bones proximal to the body, as in the upper arm and leg, double bones more distally as in the lower arm and leg, and with increasing numbers of bones distally, as in the human hands and feet. Newman and Fisch explained that as the growing embryonic limb bud increases in physical size, the chemical harmonic resonances

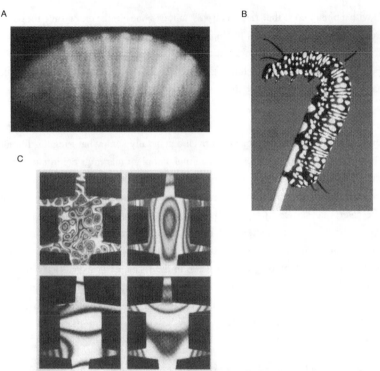

Fig. 8.3   (A) A periodic banded pattern revealed by chemical staining emerges in a developing embryo, due to a chemical harmonic resonance whose standing waves mark the embryonic tissue for future growth. (B) This chemical harmonic resonance has been identified as the mechanism behind the formation of patterns in animal skins, as well as for the periodicity of the vertebrae of vertebrates, the bilateral symmetry of the body plan, and the periodicity of the bones in the limbs and fingers. (C) Murray (1988) showed the connection between chemical and vibrational standing waves by replicating the patterns of leopard spots and zebra stripes in the standing-wave resonances in a vibrating steel sheet cut in the form of an animal skin.

in it jump from a first, to a second, to progressively higher harmonics for the same reason that it is easier to blow higher harmonics in a long horn than a short horn or whistle, which tends to resonate only at its fundamental frequency. The spatial-period doubling of the pattern in the growing limb bud leaves a branching pattern of future bone tissue in its wake. Murray (1988) made the connection between chemical and vibrational standing waves, showing how a variety of different animal coat patterns can be produced as standing waves in a steel plate cut in the shape of an animal skin, shown in Fig. 8.3C.

There has been much interest recently in the phenomenon known as chaos theory (Gleik, 1987), in which a spatial or temporal pattern is seen to emerge unexpectedly in otherwise disorganized systems. In fact, chaos is somewhat of a misnomer, because the phenomenon is better described as *unexpected order* rather than disorder. Furthermore, many of the phenomena that fall under the rubric of chaos theory, such as period doubling and limit cycles, are actually manifestations of harmonic resonance, which is an orderly self-organizing rather than chaotic principle.

There are several properties of the harmonic resonance model that are suggestive of human recognition. Unlike a rigid template, the pattern defined by a standing-wave representation is elastic and adaptive. This can be seen in the manner in which the spatial patterns of animal skins are defined. The parameters of the reaction diffusion that distinguish between the spots and stripes of the tiger, zebra, leopard, and giraffe are encoded as general rules for the generation of those patterns, rather than as a spatial template of any one such pattern. For example, if a spot or stripe were to be fixed at one point as the pattern was emerging, the rest of the pattern would redistribute itself to adapt to that fixed feature while maintaining the general character of the encoded pattern. This invariance in the representation allows one set of parameters to generate an infinite variety of exemplars of any particular pattern type, or to adapt most flexibly to any fixed constraints or boundary conditions. In fact, the morphogenic patterns in the developing embryo have been shown to be anchored in exactly this manner by specialized cells at the head or tail end of the embryo that release one or another morphogen, thereby fixing the phase of the chemical resonance at that end. This property of the harmonic resonance representation explains the adaptiveness of the body plan in morphogenesis to variations in the geometry of the embryonic tissue. This adaptiveness is seen in most dramatic form in mutations such as Siamese twins, where the body plan is observed to split like a mirror reflection, bifurcating every bone, muscle, tendon, and blood vessel as if it were part of the original plan. This kind of invariance to distortion is a prominent characteristic of human recognition also, as seen in the ease with which we recognize wildly distorted caricatures of familiar faces or distorted reflections in a curved mirror.

EMERGENCE IN HARMONIC RESONANCE

A soap bubble is the classical physical analogy used in Gestalt theory (Koffka, 1935, p. 107; Attneave, 1982) to exemplify the principle of emergence. However, the standing wave offers an even more dramatic example of the principle of emergence and of the kind of holistic processes identified by Gestalt theory. Like the soap bubble, a standing-wave pattern in a flute, for example, is the result of relatively simple local interactions at the molecular level. Yet the effects of these interactions are as global as the resonating system itself. Unlike the soap bubble, the resonance can define a whole set of unique patterns corresponding to the fundamental and its higher harmonics, as seen in the Chladni figures. The emergent patterns defined by those harmonics are not rigid, or templatelike, but more like an elastic template that automatically conforms to irregularities in the resonating cavity. For example, if a flute is curved, or flared at the end like a trumpet, or bulging in the middle like a barrel, the periodic pattern of the resonance will be correspondingly deformed, defining periodic segments of equal volume, although of unequal geometry. In other words, the resonance defines the topology, rather than the topography of the encoded forms. Resonances in connected systems, such as the engine and chassis of your car, have a natural tendency to synchronize or couple with each other (Dewan, 1976; Strogatz & Stewart, 1993) so as to produce a single emergent oscillation that exhibits higher harmonics, which are characteristic of each component resonator, embedded in a fundamental waveform that captures the resonance of the system as a whole. Finally, a special condition is observed in resonating systems that exhibit a circular symmetry—for example, a circular flute that closes on itself like a torus, or standing waves in a spherical cavity. Although the harmonics in a toroidal or spherical cavity also subdivide that cavity into periodic segments, that pattern of subdivision can occur at any orientation. In other words, the standing-wave pattern breaks free of the resonating substrate and can rotate freely within the cavity. It is this unique property of harmonic resonance that accounts for rotation invariance in human perception.

HARMONIC RESONANCE IN THE BRAIN

Oscillations and temporal resonances are familiar enough in neural systems and are observed at every scale, from long-period circadian rhythms, to the medium period rhythmic movements of limbs, all the way to the very rapid rhythmic spiking of the single cell, or the synchronized spiking of groups of cells. Harmonic resonance is also observed in single-celled organisms like the paramecium in the rhythmic beating of flagella in synchronized traveling waves. Similar waves are observed in multicellular invertebrates, such as the synchronized wavelike swimming movements of the hydra and the jellyfish, whose decentralized nervous systems consist of a distributed network of largely undifferentiated cells.

The fact that such unstructured neural architectures can give rise to such structured behavior suggests a level of computational organization below that of the switching and gating functions of the chemical synapse. Vertebrates too exhibit prominent rhythmic motions, most evident in simpler vertebrates such as caterpillars and worms; even larger vertebrates such as snakes, lizards, fish, and eels exhibit a graceful undulating motion suggestive of an underlying wavelike computational mechanism. Golubitsky, Stewart, Buono, and Collins (1999) provided mathematical models for central pattern generators in insect and animal locomotion expressed in terms of coupled oscillators. Strogatz and Stewart (1993) even characterized the movement of larger mammals in terms of oscillations, showing, for example, how the various gaits of a horse (trot, canter, gallop, etc.) correspond to the various modes of oscillation of four coupled oscillators. At the cellular level, the muscle of the heart provides perhaps the clearest example of synchronized oscillation, for the individual cells of the cardiac muscle are independent oscillators that pulse at their own rhythm when separated from the rest of the tissue in vitro. However when connected to other cells they synchronize with each other to define a single coupled oscillator.

The idea of oscillations in neural systems is not new. However, the proposal advanced here is that nature makes use of such natural resonances not only to define rhythmic patterns in space and time, but also to define static spatial patterns in the form of electrical standing waves, for the purpose that is commonly ascribed to spatial receptive fields. Although the specific neurophysiological evidence for this pattern formation device remains to be sought out and identified, I next show that as a mechanism for defining spatial pattern, the standing wave offers a great deal more flexibility and adaptiveness to local conditions than the alternative receptive field model, and that a single resonating system can replace a whole array of hard-wired receptive fields in a conventional neural network model. Finally, I show how the properties of resonant standing waves exhibit exactly those Gestalt properties of global emergence and invariance that are so difficult to account for using hard-wired neural receptive field concepts.

PHYSIOLOGICAL AND PSYCHOPHYSICAL EVIDENCE

The neurophysiological basis for a standing-wave theory of neural representation is supported by the observation that blocks of neural tissue that are connected by electrical synapses, or *gap junctions*, to form a *neural syncytium* have been shown to exhibit synchronous spiking activity (Kandell & Siegelbaum, 1985). Dermietzel and Spray (1993) identified gap junctions in cortical and subcortical tissue and showed that gap junctions are ubiquitous in the brain and nervous system. Peinado, Yuste, and Katz (1993) also implicated gap junctions in local cortical circuits. Bremer (1953) observed in the cat spinal cord electrical oscillations that maintain synchronization from one end of the cord to the other, even when the cord is severed and reconnected by contact alone. Bremer observed that the electrical synchrony along the spinal cord propagates faster than electrical impulses. Gerard and Libet (1940) published similar observations for the rabbit. In more recent literature, widely varied kinds of oscillations were associated with the visual, somatosensory, and motor cortices, suggesting that they may mediate functional integration of sensory or motor information processing in the brain (Eckhorn et al., 1988; Murthy & Fetz, 1992; Nicolelis et al., 1995; Sompolinsky et al., 1990). Several researchers proposed that such synchronous oscillations are related to the integration of the conscious experience (von der Malsburg, 1987; Edelman, 1987; Llinás, 1993; Crick &

Koch, 1990; Singer et al., 1993; Eckhorn et al., 1988; Zeki, 1993; Bressler, Coppola, & Nakamura, 1993). Hashemiyoon and Chapin (1993) reported retinally derived dark-spontaneous fast frequency oscillations, throughout the subcortical visual system of rats, and these are suppressed by tonic light stimulation. They remain remarkably phase coherent while fluctuating between multiple frequencies approximating 10, 20, and 40 Hz. Gray, Koenig, Engel, and Singer (1989) reported stimulus induced ~40-Hz oscillations in the visual cortex and suggested a functional role for these oscillations in visual processing.

Psychophysical evidence was also reported in support of some kind of oscillations in perceptual processing. Kristofferson (1990) showed how the linear plot of the Weber function for a temporal discrimination task becomes a step function after extensive practice, when the task becomes overlearned. The step function is composed of a series of flat plateaus within which the discrimination threshold remains constant, separated by sudden increases in discrimination threshold, so that the step function straddles back and forth across the nonlinear function predicted by Weber's law. A period doubling is observed between successive plateaus; that is, each plateau is double the length of the previous plateau, as discussed by Geissler (1997). In other words, the microstructure of Weber's law is not a smooth logarithmic function, but a discontinuous step function rising in octaves like those of a musical scale. Geissler (Geissler, 1987; Geissler, Schebera, & Kompass, 1999) interpreted this phenomenon as evidence for a phase locking between coupled oscillators of a range of different frequencies.

The neurophysiological and psychophysical study of synchronous neural activity, however, is handicapped by the absence of a plausible theory to lend structure to these observations, and to guide future experiments to test specific hypotheses. Although the theory presented here is not yet formulated with enough precision to explain all of these phenomena, there is mounting evidence for some kind of resonance processing in the brain, even if its functional significance remains obscure. In the following sections the properties of harmonic resonance are discussed in more general terms to clarify the functional potential they offer as a representation of spatial structure in biological vision, in order to motivate a more targeted neurophysiological search for such resonances in the brain.

PATTERN RECOGNITION BY TUNED RESONATORS

The standing wave and the patterned receptive field share the property that each defines a spatial pattern in the neural substrate. In the conventional neural network paradigm, the cell body acts as the focal point, whose state of electrical activity represents the presence or absence of a corresponding pattern of activation sampled in the cell's receptive field. The standing-wave pattern, on the other hand, appears at first sight to be a more distributed representation, in that the presence of such a pattern in the neural substrate establishes a patterned interaction between the resonating neurons: that is, the activation of any one cell depends on the total pattern of activation in all neighboring cells, but there is no single cell that is active in the presence of a particular pattern and inactive in the absence of that pattern, as is the case with the cell body in the neural network paradigm. This focal point is crucial, because it would seem to be the very essence of a recognition system to reduce a complex spatial match to a single match value. There is, however, a quantity that is associated with each pattern of resonance. In the case of the Chladni figures depicted in Fig. 8.1, each individual pattern is associated with a unique temporal frequency of oscillation, or audible tone. Therefore an audio recording of the vibrating steel plate could be used to uniquely identify which pattern was present on the plate during recording. Furthermore, an audio playback of that frequency in the presence of the plate would have the effect of regenerating that same pattern of resonance back on the original plate. The audio tone can therefore be considered as an abstracted representation, or reduced-dimensionality encoding, of the spatial pattern on the plate. Thus, matching the tone generated by a vibrating plate to a tone stored in memory corresponds to a recognition of that spatial pattern, just as the activation of a cell body in a receptive field model represents a recognition of the spatial pattern present in its input field. The item in the resonance model corresponding to the cell body in the receptive field model can be envisaged as some kind of tuned resonator, perhaps a cell with a natural tendency to spike at a characteristic frequency.

The principle behind this concept of recognition can be demonstrated using a Chladni plate coupled to an array of acoustical resonators tuned to the specific harmonic frequencies of that plate. Figure 8.4A shows three resonators coupled to a Chladni plate, tuned to three selected patterns of standing waves from Fig. 8.1. For convenience these are called the +, X, and / patterns. When the plate is set into vibration, the standing-wave pattern that appears on the plate activates the resonator tuned to that pattern as suggested for each pattern in Fig. 8.4A. The system automatically incorporates reification with recognition, because just as the vibration of the plate with a particular standing-wave pattern activates its corresponding resonator, so also does the vibration of the resonator at its characteristic frequency automatically regenerate its characteristic pattern back on the plate, as suggested in Fig. 8.4B.

INPUT PATTERN APPLIED BY DAMPING

Waller (1961) described how different patterns of standing waves are produced on a steel plate. In Waller's technique the resonance is energized by a piece of dry ice pressed against the plate, where the gas generated by sublimation of the ice produces a gap

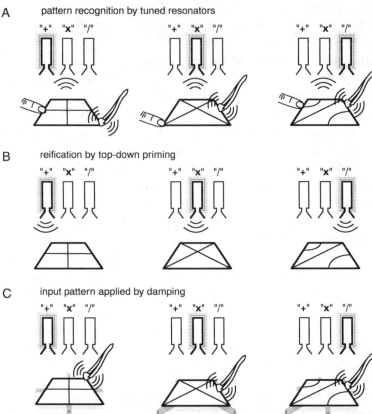

Fig. 8.4   (A) A bank of three resonators tuned to the frequencies of three specific standing-wave patterns is coupled to the plate to behave as feature detectors that become active whenever their pattern of standing waves is present on the plate. (B) The system automatically performs reification with recognition, for the activation of any of the resonators regenerates its characteristic standing-wave pattern back on the plate. (C) If the plate is resting on rubber ridges in the form of one of the standing-wave patterns, the ridges behave as an input pattern, forcing the resonance on the plate to conform to the pattern of the input.

between the ice and the plate that opens and closes periodically as the gas escapes. The significant property of this method of energizing the oscillations is that it does not force the oscillations at any particular frequency, but allows the natural resonance of the plate to determine the period of the vibration. A similar principle is seen in musical instruments. For example, the sound of a trumpet is energized by the pulsing of the trumpeter's lips. However, that pulsing is triggered by the sound waves reflected back from the far end of the trumpet, so the final resonance is determined not by the local dynamics of the lips as much as by the resonance of the trumpet/lip system as a whole, with every part of the resonant cavity contributing to the final oscillation. Waller described how higher harmonic patterns are achieved by pressing the dry ice harder against the plate, just as a trumpeter can jump to a higher octave by pursing his lips and blowing harder, which in turn doubles the spatial frequency of the standing-wave pattern in the body of the trumpet.The full range of Chladni figures is obtained by damping the plate at various points, either with the touch of a finger or by resting the plate on rubber studs or ridges. The damped points restrict the standing wave patterns to those that exhibit stationary nodes coincident with the damped points. This is the same principle used in a flute, where an open hole damps the vibration of air at that point in the tube, allowing only standing-wave patterns to emerge that have a node at the location of the open hole. The pattern of damping can therefore be seen as corresponding to the input pattern in the receptive field model, because the pattern of damping calls up a corresponding pattern of standing waves that matches the pattern of the input, as suggested in Fig. 8.4C, where the plate is shown resting on rubber ridges that match the nodes of the three standing-wave patterns corresponding to the three resonators. A nonspecific energization of the plate while resting on these ridges therefore calls up the standing-wave pattern that matches the pattern of damping, and that standing wave in turn activates the resonator tuned to its characteristic frequency, which represents the recognition of the pattern of damping present on the plate.

There is an interesting concept of representation expressed in the harmonic resonance theory. An impulse function, or sharp rap, applied to a Chladni plate energizes that plate at all vibration frequencies simultaneously, thereby reifying standing wave patterns of all spatial frequencies on the plate. The damping effect of the rubber studs or ridges, representing an applied input, quenches every oscillation that does not have a node at the damped location, leaving active every possible resonance which is consistent with that pattern of damping. This ability to reify every possible interpretation of a stimulus consistent with a particular input, has implications for a cognitive representation which is discussed in chapter 9.

EMERGENCE, REIFICATION, MULTISTABILITY, AND INVARIANCE

There are several significant differences between the receptive field or template model of recognition and that of the harmonic resonance model. The harmonic resonance model automatically exhibits the Gestalt properties of emergence, reification, multistability, and invariance, not as specialized circuits or mechanisms contrived to produce those properties, but as natural properties of the resonance itself. Emergence in the harmonic resonance model is seen in the fact that there is no need for a set of specialized spatial receptive fields devised to match all of the patterns to which the system is tuned, because the spatial patterning mechanism in harmonic resonance occurs in emergent fashion in the natural vibrational modes of a homogeneous steel plate. This defines a basis set of geometrical patterns in an ascending order of complexity, corresponding to the eigenfunctions of the plate. The tuned resonators that respond to these vibrational modes are very simple devices, which could either be tuned individually to the harmonics of the plate, or be devised to adjust their own tuning adaptively to match the temporal frequencies commonly produced by the plate to which they are coupled. Emergence therefore offers a simple mechanism whose dynamic behavior is very much more complex than its architecture would suggest. The simple plate and resonator system is functionally equivalent to a much more complex neural network model with special patterned receptive fields tuned to detect every pattern to which the system responds. It is the emergent nature of this central mechanism of pattern detection that accounts for the other Gestalt properties of the system: reification, multistability, and invariance.

Reification occurs automatically with no additional mechanism required, for the vibration of the resonator at its characteristic frequency automatically regenerates its characteristic pattern back on the plate. Therefore if a noisy or irregular or incomplete pattern of damping is presented on the plate, the resonance resulting from that input pattern will set up the nearest matching standing-wave pattern, which in turn will activate the corresponding resonator. The vibration of that resonator in turn will reify or complete its pattern back on the plate, automatically filling in any missing features, as suggested in Fig. 8.5A. This property of the harmonic resonance model corresponds to the perceptual tendency to perceive complete objects even when portions of them are occluded. It also offers an explanation for the phenomenon of amodal completion of the hidden rear faces of objects on the basis of their visible front faces. In order to define a neural network model with the equivalent functional behavior, it would be necessary to posit not only bottom-up feature detectors with templatelike receptive fields, but each of these detectors would have to have a corresponding top-down projective field to print a copy of its characteristic pattern back down on the input field.

Multistability is also an intrinsic property of the harmonic resonance model. Not only does this make the model consistent with the properties of perception, but the multistability itself provides interesting functional properties to the recognition system. Figure 8.5B depicts a damping input pattern which might be interpreted as either half of an X pattern, or the central diagonal of the / pattern. In the presence of this input therefore the system becomes multistable between these two standing-wave interpretations, each pattern appearing alternately on the plate in a random sequence. The activation of the two resonators will also alternate in synchrony with the alternation of patterns on the plate— that is, the recognition of the identity of the patterns alternates with the patterns themselves. There is no need to postulate lateral inhibition between the two feature nodes, because the resonance on the plate itself naturally resists any kind of combined pattern and

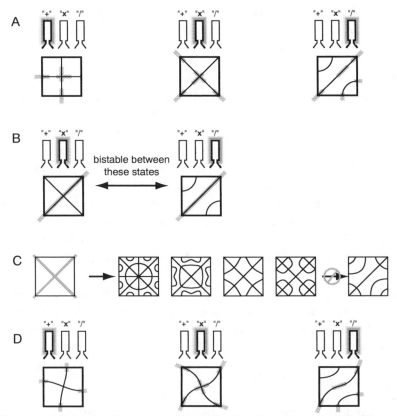

Fig. 8.5   (A) In the case of noisy or incomplete input patterns, the system automatically fills in or completes the missing portions of the pattern, while registering the identity of the recognized pattern in the resonator response. (B) In the case of ambiguous patterns, the system becomes multistable between alternative interpretations. (C) Even for simple inputs the system can be multistable when stimulated to higher energies, interpreting the input with any standing wave that contains the input as a subset. This excludes the last pattern on the right. (D) The system is invariant to elastic deformations of the input pattern, as long as the global gestalt is preserved.

will fluctuate in a random bistable manner between these two interpretations of the ambiguous input. Any additional evidence present in the input will bias this competition. For example, if one of the undamped corners of the plate is lightly damped with the touch of a fingertip, this will immediately favor the X-feature interpretation, which is damped along that diagonal, and that tiny bias factor results in the complete X-feature pattern being reified on the plate. This is consistent with the observed properties of bistable stimuli such as the Necker cube, in which every portion of the percept appears to invert with the inversion of the spatial interpretation of the stimulus, suggesting a complete inversion of a high-resolution, low-level rendition of the perceptual experience, rather than the flipping of a pair of higher level abstract feature recognition nodes. The Necker cube can also be stabilized in one or the other state by providing tiny gaps in the lines where they cross, suggesting one edge occluding another, and this tiny variation in one small portion of the figure will stabilize the entire perceptual structure.

Multistability has further implications for the properties of harmonic resonance as a recognition system. In fact, the response of the system to a given input is not confined to a single standing-wave pattern, but as Waller explained, higher harmonics of that pattern can also be evoked by pressing the dry ice harder against the plate, driving the system to higher energies, just as a trumpeter jumps to higher octaves by pursing his lips and blowing harder. For example if the plate is damped in the pattern of an X as suggested in Fig. 8.5C, the lowest energy standing wave in response to this input would be the one with the X-shaped pattern of nodes as already described. However, if the plate is excited to higher energy states by pressing the ice harder against the plate, then patterns of higher harmonic standing waves can emerge in response to the same stimulus, including the four patterns depicted to the right in Fig. 8.5C (among others), because all of these patterns share in common the X-shaped nodal pattern across the diagonals of the square. The standing wave pattern depicted on the far right in Fig. 8.5C, on the other hand, could not appear in the presence of the X-shaped input, because that pattern requires the freedom to oscillate along one of the diagonals that are damped by the input pattern. The input pattern thus does not call up the one and only encoded pattern to which it matches best as in the case of the template model, but rather the system tends to call up any of the many encoded patterns of which the input is a subset.

In the presence of the input, therefore, the system is multistable, with the lowest energy state representing the simplest encoded pattern that matches to the input, but with additional energy the system can be made to match more complex patterns to the input, as long as those patterns contain the input pattern as a subset. This kind of system can therefore be made to "search through" its catalog of encoded patterns for any given input, by energizing the oscillations to greater or lesser magnitude, corresponding to pressing the ice harder or softer against the plate. As each pattern is matched against the input, that pattern is reified on the plate in full spatial form, and as that pattern appears on the plate, its corresponding resonator becomes energized, thereby labeling the spatial pattern with the identity encoded by the resonator. The lowest energy patterns are represented by the lower harmonics, which define the simplest or least elaborate patterns. The simplest patterns are the most stable, and therefore are the most likely to be perceived, corresponding to the Gestalt notion of prägnanz, or "Gestalt goodness," which relates to the intrinsic constraints discussed in chapter 4. This principle might also be described as a perceptual expression of Occam's Razor, whereby the simplest possible explanation that fits the available evidence is most likely to be the correct one.

Invariance is also a natural property of a harmonic resonance representation, which is a direct consequence of the emergent nature of the encoding. The spatial pattern is encoded not as a rigid template, but as a complex dynamic interaction between elements in a continuous resonating system. Recognition is therefore invariant to elastic deformations of the pattern on the plate, as long as they maintain their essential global structure. For example, the standing-wave patterns shown in Fig. 8.5D subdivide the plate into the same number of regions with equal area as those in Fig. 8.5A, and therefore these resonances will activate the same feature detectors despite the distortion in the pattern. The issue of invariance in recognition is often confused in theoretical discussions with a *blindness* to variation; that is, a system is considered invariant to a certain stimulus variation if its response is identical across that variation. However invariance in perception does not have that character, as seen in Fig. 3.5, where the various rotations, translations, scales, perspectives, and elastic distortions of the object are clearly perceived as variations of the basic shape, even as the basic shape is recognized independent of those variations. This suggests a two-level response, with invariance at the higher level that is nevertheless coupled to a lower level reified representation in which those variations are plainly evident. This is exactly what occurs in the harmonic resonance model, because the pattern completion occurs in the reified representation with respect to the deformations of the pattern as seen in Fig. 8.5D, whereas the higher level recognition represented by the resonator response remains invariant to those distortions. This unique property of harmonic resonance, so clearly manifest in the subjective experience of vision, is virtually impossible to account for with a neural network model due to the rigid templatelike property of the neural receptive field.

ROTATION INVARIANCE IN RECOGNITION AND COMPLETION

Invariance of an even more impressive form is observed in standing waves generated in a circular symmetric resonator. Figure 8.6A (adapted from Waller, 1961, pp. 9 and 27) depicts some of the standing-wave Chladni figures that can be produced on a circular steel plate clamped at its midpoint, sorted by the number of diameters and concentric circles present in the pattern. (The patterns [0,0] and [0,1] expressed in terms of [diameters, circles] are not actually possible to produce on a steel plate for technical reasons, and are depicted here for theoretical completeness of the representation.) These patterns are shown with one node line oriented vertically. However, as a consequence of the symmetry of the plate, these same patterns can actually occur at any orientation, while maintaining the same frequency of vibration. Figure 8.6B (adapted from Waller, 1961, p. 9) plots the vibration frequency of some of these patterns as a function of the number of diameters in the pattern (corresponding to the columns in Fig. 8.6A), and the number of concentric circles (corresponding to the rows in Fig. 8.6A). The frequencies are expressed as multiples of a fundamental frequency. For example the X or + shaped pattern [2,0] with two diameters and no circles has a vibration frequency of 1, whereas the asterisk pattern [3,0] has a vibrational frequency between 2 and 3. Waller noted that no two frequencies are exactly equal, and that therefore the frequency uniquely encodes the range of possible patterns. The diagram can be extended indefinitely to greater numbers of diameters and circles, although the higher harmonics require ever increasing energy of vibration.

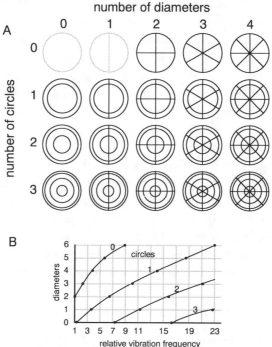

Fig. 8.6 (A) Chladni figures for a circular plate, sorted by number of [diameters, circles] in each pattern. These patterns can appear at any orientation on the plate. Each distinct pattern has a unique vibration frequency, plotted in (B). The vibration frequency therefore offers a rotation invariant representation of the pattern present on the plate.

The rotation invariance relation between the spatial pattern of standing waves and the corresponding vibration frequency is significant. It means that in the presence of an "input pattern," that is, a pattern of damping, the plate will resonate at the frequency corresponding to that pattern, and that frequency will remain unchanged as the input pattern is rotated to any angle. A bank of resonators tuned specifically to the fundamental frequencies of vibration of the plate thus encode a rotation invariant representation of those patterns in exactly the manner suggested for invariant recognition discussed in chapter 6. The unique property of harmonic resonance is in the coupling between the frequency and its pattern. If a resonator is activated top-down, in the absence of any input stimulus, the activation of that resonator in the vicinity of the plate will tend to regenerate its corresponding pattern on the plate. If the resonator is activated at a lower amplitude in the absence of any input stimulus, this will result in an indeterminate pattern on the plate, because the pattern is attempting to reify itself at all orientations simultaneously, as suggested in Fig. 8.7A. However if the top-down activation of the resonator is applied at sufficiently high amplitude, the pattern will emerge on the plate at a random orientation, and because the orientation of the emergent pattern is unconstrained by the top-down signal, the reified pattern will be free to spin on the plate like a compass needle as suggested in Fig. 8..7B. This is reminiscent of the properties of mental imagery, which can take on a characteristic form while remaining unconstrained in location and orientation, although with sufficient concentration the mental image can be fixed to a particular location and orientation. With sufficient top-down priming the mental image can even become a hallucination, indistinguishable from a sensory stimulus.

In the presence of a weak or partial input applied simultaneously to a moderate top-down prime, the input will anchor the orientation of the pattern projected top down, resulting in a bottom-up/top-down resonance, in which the input pattern is interpreted and filled in in the context of the current top-down prime. For example a top-down priming of the circular plate with an X-feature oscillation could potentially regenerate that X pattern at any orientation. A touch of a finger on the rim of the plate during this priming would fix that X pattern at an orientation where one node line coincides with the damped point, as suggested in Fig. 8.7C. The standing-wave model also mirrors several properties of recognition in the bottom-up mode. In the absence of a top-down priming signal, a noisy or ambiguous input pattern will stimulate the appearance of the nearest matching pattern encoded in the harmonic representation, and that best matching pattern will be reified on the plate, with any missing details filled in, as suggested in Fig. 8.7D. It is this property of bottom-up top-down matching across an invariance relation that represents the greatest promise of the harmonic resonance theory as a representation of perceptual processes, for it provides a mechanism for the invariance observed in perception as discussed in chapters 6 and 7. A functionally equivalent neural network model would have to be improbably complex, because it would require a set of spatial detector templates for every one of the patterns shown in Fig. 8.6A, and another equal set of corresponding top-down templates to account for reification, and every one of these bottom-up and top-down templates would have to be replicated at every orientation, and additional lateral inhibition or competition must be invoked to account for the multistability between ambiguous interpretations. With

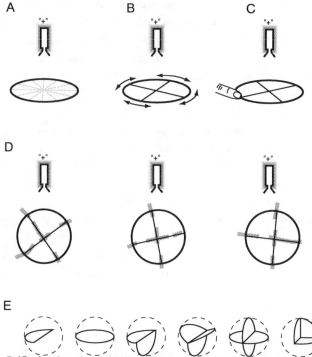

Fig. 8.7   Reification through rotation invariance. (A) With a weak top-down priming of a "+"
feature, the reification is indeterminate, as the pattern attempts to reify itself at all orientations
simultaneously. (B) With a stronger prime the pattern is reified at some arbitrary orientation, but
remains free to spin like a compass needle. (C) A touch on the plate with a finger breaks the
symmetry and locks the reified pattern to an orientation that matches the damped input. (D) A noisy
pattern is reified and completed at the orientation that best matches the primed pattern. (E) One
possible series of three-dimensional standing-wave patterns that extend the representation of the
occlusion, coplanarity, and orthogonality fields described in chapter 4 with higher order patterns of
symmetry at planar intersections.

additional mechanisms required to account for invariance to perspective and elastic
deformation, the neural network model becomes hopelessly implausible as an explanation
for the observed properties of visual experience.

Rotation invariance has long been a serious obstacle to models of perceptual processing
Great effort has been expended in psychophysical experiments to attempt to demonstrate
that perception is in fact not rotation invariant, and thus to dispose of this troublesome
issue. Although it is true that recognition is not completely invariant to rotation, and
counterexamples have been found, those examples generally involve complex stimuli that
are hard to absorb perceptually in a single glance. For simple stimuli like the geometrical
structure depicted in Fig. 3.5 invariance is clearly manifest even at a casual glance.

Although the harmonic resonance theory offers a mechanism that can exhibit rotation invariance, this does not imply that human perception is incapable of distinguishing different orientations, for clearly we can distinguish "p" from "b," and "6" from "9," although this task is difficult for dyslexics and for young children, suggesting that invariance is perhaps more basic than rotation variant perception. However, the harmonic resonance model can also account for rotation-variant perception, that information is recorded in the phase component of the resonance, as in a Fourier representation. In other words, the harmonic resonance theory allows for invariance in recognition, but does not require it in all cases.

The invariance relation described earlier holds between two levels of the representation. But the same principle can apply between every pair of levels in a hierarchical representation, with each level of the hierarchy conferring an additional dimension of invariance to the highest level representation, and yet reification can proceed nevertheless from the highest to the lowest levels, with the inverse of invariance—that is, specification occuring progressively from higher to lower levels down the hierarchy. This principle explains how recognition can be invariant to certain transformations, whereas at the same time the recognized feature is completed perceptually in the context of its exact configuration as represented throughout the visual hierarchy.

AN ALTERNATIVE PARADIGM OF COMPUTATION

The description of the harmonic resonance theory just given, presented by comparison with embryological morphogenesis and in terms of the properties of vibrating steel plates, is open to the criticism that the theory is presented merely by analogy, and that no rigorous or mathematical specification is provided for the actual computational transformations performed by the resonance. The Western scientific tradition has always emphasized reduction of physical systems to simpler mathematical terms, and virtually all problems in physics are traditionally addressed in that form. However, this procedure can give the physicist a biased view of physical reality. In fact, the vast majority of physical systems and phenomena are far too complicated to be reduced to such analytical terms except by way of simplifying assumptions, although a typical physical education carefully avoids those troublesome realms to focus on those phenomena for which analytical solutions have been devised. There are certain classes of physical systems that simply do not succumb to mathematical analysis because the phenomena in question are already the simplest model of themselves; there is no way to reduce the phenomena to simpler mathematical terms without setting prohibitively restrictive constraints on the parameters of the system. In all but the simplest cases, harmonic resonance has exactly this property, and it is those very properties that represent the most interesting aspects of harmonic resonance as a representation in the brain. For example, Chladni and Waller both referenced work by various authors who provided mathematical solutions to the equilibrium states of various standing-wave patterns found on steel plates. Basic physics texts offer formulas to calculate the fundamental frequency of flutes and organ pipes based on their length and diameter etc. But these analyses are an abstraction or meta-level description of the real mechanism of harmonic resonance, which is actually a fine-grained process involving molecular interactions throughout the resonating system in a holistic global manner. The mathematical solutions for steel plates have only been developed to account for the simplest of these patterns, like those for circular or square plates, and the equations for organ pipes apply only to geometrically simple straight pipes with circular cross section and uniform diameter along their length. This kind of analysis is invalid in the case of irregular or arbitrarily-shaped steel plates, or plates of nonuniform thickness, or organ pipes that are curved, or flared, or barrel shaped, or with any other irregularity in their form. Yet it is this very flexibility that represents the most interesting aspect of the resonance. If the discussion were limited to the simple cases for which analytical solutions have been found, the theory would degenerate to a template theory and would thereby lose its most appealing properties.

Physical systems that defy mathematical characterization are often addressed numerically, using computer simulations. This is the approach used for example to predict the behavior of the atmosphere, which is approximated by quantization of the system in space and time to tiny local elements which are simple enough to be treated as discrete points. However, this approach too has its limitations, for the quantization in space and time inevitably introduce inhomogeneities into the system. For example, a computer model that simulates the interactions between vibrating molecules of air in an organ pipe must begin with a subdivision of that pipe into discrete cells or "voxels" (volume pixels), but the rectilinear nature of that grid of voxels introduces artifacts due to the fact that vertically and horizontally adjacent voxels in the grid are closer than diagonal or other voxels. Because resonance is such a fine-grained phenomenon that operates in an essentially continuous analog medium, it is impossible to accurately model the phenomenon in a digital simulation with any confidence that the simulation is correct in any but the simplest possible cases, to say nothing of the enormous computational load of an iterative algorithm operating on volumetric data. The case of harmonic resonance is even more problematic for numerical simulations than a model of the atmosphere, because atmospheric parameters such as temperature, pressure, and humidity tend to diffuse isotropically into adjacent regions in a relatively simple manner, so that these parameters can be computed fairly accurately by considering only nearest neighboring regions. In the case of a standing-wave pattern in a resonating system on the other hand, the local value of the pattern (i.e., whether a particular point is a node or anti-node of the standing wave) depends on the configuration of the entire resonating system as a whole, and cannot be even approximated from the values of adjacent regions of the system, because resonance does not simply diffuse between adjacent points in the system but is influenced by the entire configuration of the system as a whole. The very fact that harmonic resonance exhibits this Gestalt-like nature and the fact that these kinds of systems are so difficult to characterize both mathematically and computationally provide all the more reason to investigate these phenomena as a possible property of biological computation, to account for exactly those aspects of perception that have defied characterization in more abstracted terms.

If this work must be done "by analogy" using vibrating steel plates, that does not in any way invalidate the results, for the vibrating steel plate is itself a computational mechanism, albeit one whose operational principles are radically different from any known computational device: therefore, the "output" of the steel plate is no less valid in principle than the output of a digital computer simulation. The fact that resonance exhibits similar properties, whether expressed as a physical, electrical, chemical, or acoustic resonance, indicates that resonance is a general principle that transcends any particular physical instantiation, and thereby represents a higher order organizational principle of physical matter and energy. Considered as a computational paradigm, harmonic resonance has unique emergent properties that cannot be meaningfully reduced to an equivalent Turing-machine description. The message of Gestalt theory is that it is exactly this kind of unconventional enigmatic computational principle that should be sought out in the brain to account for the enigmatic properties observed in perception. The fact that harmonic resonance of a different sort is observed in embryological morphogenesis is solid and concrete evidence that harmonic resonance both can and does serve the purpose of a representation of spatial structure in biological systems. In doing so, it exhibits unique properties that happen to correspond to those same enigmatic Gestalt properties observed in perception. The hypothesis that the same principle is also active in neurocomputation is therefore a solid and worthwhile proposal that deserves further investigation, even if (or especially if) that investigation takes us into uncharted computational and theoretical territory.

THREE-DIMENSIONAL SPATIAL STRUCTURE

The standing-wave patterns due to harmonic resonances occur just as readily in three dimensions as they do in two, and a spherical resonating system would exhibit a full three-dimensional rotation invariance. The primitives of such a system would be defined in terms of spherical instead of circular harmonics, with patterns of periodicity expressed in circumferential as well as radial dimensions. In the simplest form, such standing-wave patterns offer a plausible mechanism for coding a descriptor of geometrical form based on the pattern of symmetry of the objects vertices, as suggested in Fig. 6.7. Furthermore, the standing-wave model would also suggest a mechanism to express the occlusion, coplanarity, and orthogonality fields described in chapter 4 and in the appendix, as local standing waves that emerge spontaneously where the perceived surfaces meet, and to extend those patterns with a regular series of corner types defined in terms of patterns of symmetry around a line of intersection, as suggested in Fig. 8.7E.

DYNAMIC PATTERN FORMATION

One of the most compelling features of a harmonic resonance representation is that the same mechanism that defines static patterns of standing waves is also capable of generating complex dynamic patterns of the sort that are most likely responsible for the sinusoidal oscillations in fish and snakes and the periodic cyclic pattern of motion of the centipede's feet. Such complex patterns can be generated by interference between spatial waves driven at slightly different frequencies, resulting in a cyclic rotation of the standing-wave pattern at a rate that is proportional to the frequency difference between the component waveforms. In other words, the orientation and rate of rotation of a spatial standing wave pattern can be controlled by the phase shift between component driving oscillations, in the manner of the rotating Lissajou figures on an oscilloscope, generated by plotting two sinusoids against each other in x and y axes on the scope. As with the Lissajou figures, complex dynamic figures can be generated by addition of more component waveforms, which can result in patterns such as two circular periodic star-shaped patterns rotating slowly in opposite directions, which can combine to form a single star shape that pulses periodically in amplitude, or a rotating star shape with individual fingers appearing and disappearing in some cyclic sequence, and so forth in endless combination from a small set of pattern primitives.

RESONANT TISSUE

What kind of properties would the neural tissue of the brain have to have in order to exhibit the properties just described? I propose that the elemental local behavior of neural tissue is of a resonator designed to amplify any temporal frequency detected at any local point in the tissue. In other words, if a local point in the brain is subjected to an electrical oscillation at a particular frequency, the tissue would respond by "dancing to that rhythm," generating an amplified oscillation at that same frequency and waveform, as suggested by Geissler (1987; Geissler, Schebera, & Kompass, 1999). In fact Llinás (1988; Llinás, Grace, & Yarom, 1991) showed that neural cells behave like tuned oscillators, so this property would be achieved by a population of neurons tuned to a range of frequencies. If a continuous block of tissue were constructed with this local behavior expressed at every point, an oscillation stimulated at one point in the tissue would tend to radiate outward like the expanding rings when a stone is thrown into a pond, except that these waves could be self-sustaining, rather than damped like the waves in a pond, and they could generate a range of spatial and temporal frequencies, rather than a single frequency as seen in the rings in a pond. The propagating wave would reflect from the boundaries of the block of tissue, and the reflected waves would interfere in the volume of the tissue, producing a complex pattern of volumetric standing waves by interference, like the standing-wave patterns seen in Fig. 8.2D. If the entire block were stimulated with a white-noise signal through a range of frequencies, the block would tend to resonate as a whole at its own natural resonant frequency, which is related to the time it takes for a single wave to sweep from one end of the block to the other. This in turn would subdivide the block into volumetric regions that are integer fractions of the volume of the whole.

I propose that the brain is a resonator of this sort, whose natural frequency of oscillation as a whole is observed in the global oscillations detected in the electro-encephalogram. This fundamental oscillation sweeping across the whole brain establishes a reference frame or coordinate system in the form of a spatial standing wave. The higher harmonics on this standing wave represent the spatial percepts of objects perceived in the world, with the phase of those harmonics relative to the fundamental determining the location of the percept in the perceived world. This concept of the function of brain rhythms as a rasterlike scanning device is analogous to the raster scan of a television monitor, which serves to transform a periodic temporal signal into a spatial one, proposed by Walter (1950) and Brazier (1950); the same concept is expressed in more recent work by Shevelev (1988).

TIME-REVERSED RECONSTRUCTION

When I was a professional flight instructor, I had plenty of opportunity to look down on the world while the student was flying the plane. I noticed a curious phenomenon on the lakes below, whenever I saw a motor boat following the curved path of a circular arc. Because the speed of a motor boat is fast relative to the speed of the surface waves on the water, the wake is like a wavefront that travels essentially perpendicular to the path of the boat. Whenever the boat follows a curved path, the waves on the inside of the curve converge towards a focal point at the center of curvature, with the first waves arriving at that focal point usually long after the boat has gone by. The amplitude of the waves increases as they converge to that point, reaching a peak at that focal point, marking the center of circular curvature with a high-amplitude bobbing of a single point in the water. A similar phenomenon can be imagined to occur in three dimensions in the visual representation to explain the amodal abstraction of central symmetry, as described in chapter 6. If a portion of a spherical or cylindrical shell were immersed in a fluid and energized with a white-noise vibration, that surface would generate three-dimensional wavefronts in the fluid normal to the vibrating surface, and these wavefronts would converge in three dimensions to the focus of curvature of the spherical or cylindrical shell, producing a point or line of high-amplitude activity at the center of symmetry of the form. In a resonant neural tissue this point of high amplitude oscillation might stimulate the cells at that point to oscillate in synchrony, thereby reifying the complete sphere around that central point as suggested in Fig. 6.6A, and similar resonances would account for the completion of other regular geometrical forms. A similar phenomenon is observed in Fig. 8.2D where the standing waves at the center of the resonating system appear somewhat like a central axis of symmetry of the resonating cavity. This phenomenon has a distinctly Gestalt nature, for the same symmetry response could be evoked by a number of disconnected fragments of a spherical surface, as long as they were properly arrayed about the same center. The symmetry response therefore does not depend on the exact geometry of each fragment as much as on the global configuration of the various fragments. This relates perceptual processing to a concept known as time-reversed acoustics (Fink, 1996, 1997), in which an array of microphones picks up the a three-dimensional pattern of sound waves emitted by a source. The source is then reconstructed by a set of loudspeakers placed in the same pattern as the original microphones. The synchronized playback of the recorded sound from this array of speakers reconstructs the original sound source in time-reversed manner. There is an analogous phenomenon in light, known as the phase conjugate mirror (Yariv, 1991; Pepper, 1982, 1986), in which a light wave entering the device is reflected back out as an exact replica of the incoming wave travelling backwards in time. I propose that a similar principle is active in perception in order to reconstruct the central symmetry of perceived objects from the patterns generated by their surfaces in the perceptual manifold, as suggested in chapter 6 and illustrated in Fig. 6.6.

If the resonating tissue of the brain were in the form of a homogeneous sphere, the resonance of this sphere would produce a single dominant frequency as determined by the time it takes a wave to cross the sphere, like the ringing of a bell. I propose, however, that the tissue of the brain is not homogeneous, but rather that its physical properties vary with distance from the center of the sphere such that a wave propagating through this inhomogeneous medium would traverse equal "perceived distance" (in the perceptual representation) in equal time. In other words, a wave travelling outward from the center of the perceptual sphere would propagate more and more slowly as it approached the surface of the sphere, as would a percept of a moving object receding from the percipient at a constant speed in external space. A pattern of straight, parallel wavefronts therefore would travel through this inhomogeneous medium in the pattern of the grid lines of Fig. 4.9B, moving faster through the center, and ever slower towards the periphery. In a standing wave representation the nonlinear variation in the speed of wave propagation defines the nonlinear geometry of the represented space, because a standing-wave pattern resonating in such an inhomogeneous sphere would subdivide the sphere with a spatial periodicity that varies with distance from the center of the sphere, with larger scale cycles near the center, and smaller scale cycles near the periphery, like the patterns of standing waves on the basilar membrane in the presence of structured sound. This property would allow a finite-sized resonator to simulate the properties of an infinite resonator using a variable representational scale. This principle is depicted conceptually in Escher's print "Circle Limit IV," shown in Fig. 8.8A.

Fig. 8.8   This print by M. C. Escher ("Circle Limit IV" © 2002 Cordon Art B. V. - Baarn - Holland. All rights reserved) demonstrates how a finite representational space can represent an infinite pattern by use of a nonlinear scale. This kind of pattern could be coded in the form of standing waves in a spherical resonator whose physical properties vary in nonlinear fashion as a function of radial distance from the center, so that the speed of wave propagation diminishes with distance from the center at a rate that matches the reduction of spatial scale from the center. If the speed of wave propagation approaches zero at the periphery, that periphery will represent an infinite distance from the center.

THE UNITY OF CONSCIOUS EXPERIENCE

The harmonic resonance theory finally provides a plausible computational principle to account for the unity of the conscious experience, for it is in the very nature of resonances in different resonators to unite when the resonators are coupled, to produce a single coherent coupled oscillation of the system as a whole, as discussed by Dewan (1976). It is also in the nature of harmonic resonance to form multiple identical or similar copies of a particular waveform, sometimes replicated in mirror-reversed symmetry, as seen for example in the top right Chladni figure in Fig. 8.1 [0, 7]. This pattern is symmetrical about a diagonal, and therefore the patterns of resonance on opposite sides of the diagonal can be considered as two separate copies of the same resonant half-pattern that are coupled to each other in a single resonance. This in turn suggests how different cortical maps might be dynamically coupled into a single coherent entity by a global resonance that generates similar or complementary patterns in the different cortical areas. Neurophysiological mapping of the somatosensory cortex, which was originally thought to define a simple somatotopic map, has on closer examination revealed multiple copies of the body map often in mirror-reversed patterns (Kolb & Whishaw, 1980, p. 176) suggestive of a standing-wave representation.

Identical copies of a cortical map are not very useful. However, if the dynamic properties of the resonating substrate were slightly different in different cortical regions, specialized dynamic properties of each different cortical area would enhance or emphasize specific aspects of the resonance in those areas, while maintaining a dynamic coupling to other areas with slightly different dynamic properties. However, the special features enhanced in one brain area would not remain isolated to that area, but rather the effects of any resonance in any brain area would immediately modulate the resonance in all other areas simultaneously, as seen in the phenomenon of audio filtering, as when various acoustical cavities are coupled to each other. This principle is also observed in analog RF (radio frequency) circuits, where the addition of different components at different points in the circuit does not process the signal in an input-output manner "downstream" of the added component as in digital circuitry, but rather it modulates the signal in the circuit as a whole, enhancing certain aspects of the waveform in all of the components of the circuit simultaneously, although the exact waveform observed within each component exhibits subtle variations. Harmonic resonance offers a computational mechanism to account for the bidirectional causal coupling between cortical areas across an invariant relation as suggested by the properties of conscious experience, as discussed in chapter 7.

The harmonic resonance theory therefore offers a computational principle that reflects the most troublesome and enigmatic properties of perception as identified by Gestalt theory, and it exhibits these properties as a natural property of the resonance itself. I propose that the decades of neurophysiological study since the invention of the single-cell recording electrode have been largely a chase down a blind alley. The noisy static discharge of the single cell cannot possibly reflect the true significant code of the nervous system. I can see that code from the inside, and it appears as a crystal-clear and stable picture of the world. I can hear that code from the inside, and it sounds like a highly structured and organized auditory experience. I propose that what we are picking up with our microelectrodes is not the significant signal in neural processing, but rather the noisy system that energizes the more patterned oscillations, like the rasping scratch of a bow on a violin string, or the rude "raspberry" of the trumpeter's lips, as opposed to the harmonious resonance that they engender in the body of the instrument as a whole. I propose that until we begin to pick up music with our microelectrodes, we must be tuned to the wrong channel in the brain.

Chapter 9

Image Theory of Language and Cognition

THE IMAGERY DEBATE

Language and the cognitive function that it requires are the crowning glory of human mental achievement, and this function most clearly distinguishes us from our animal ancestors. Although perception involves concrete structural representations closely coupled to the sensory stimulus, language and cognition inhabit a higher more abstracted realm of representation, much more independent of the concrete sensory and perceptual worlds. Surely human language and cognition did not appear out of nowhere; they must have evolved incrementally from the lower functions of sensation and perception. In this chapter I argue that the fundamental code behind language and cognition is the mental image, and that mental imagery is in turn a more abstracted and elaborate form of amodal perception. Consistent with classical Gestalt theory, therefore, I propose that language and cognition are not as different from perception as they might initially seem, but rather that difference is more a matter of degree of complexity, rather than any fundamental difference in principle of operation.

The last hundred years or so have seen a running debate between those who accept the phenomenal evidence of mental imagery at face value and those who would deny the very existence of mental imagery as some kind of illusion that has no correspondence to actual processes in the physical brain. To a large extent this debate hinges on the choice between direct and indirect realism. By denying that the vivid spatial structure of the phenomenal world is an explicit product, or output of perceptual processing, the naive realist perspective suggests a very much simplified or abstracted view of the perceptual function. For this reason, the naive realist has difficulty recognizing the capacity of the brain to generate the dynamic three-dimensional volumetric structures observed in mental imagery. The insight of indirect realism, on the other hand, clearly demonstrates the capacity of the brain to generate the vivid spatial structures of phenomenal experience, and this in turn makes it much more plausible that the brain can also generate the more vague and tenuous but fully spatial structures observed in mental imagery and cognition.

After a century of vigorous denial, the pendulum is now beginning to swing back in favor of acknowledging the explicit spatial reality of the mental image. This more recent trend has been due largely to a series of ingenious psychophysical experiments. For example, Shepard and Metzler (1971) showed that the time required to rotate a mental image has a linear relation to the angle through which it is rotated. Stephen Kosslyn and his coworkers

179

established that the time it takes to scan between two points on the mental image of a memorized map is in direct proportion to the distance between the points, just as with a real map (Kosslyn, Ball, & Reisner, 1978). In addition, it takes subjects approximately the same amount of time to scan a real map as it takes them to scan their visual image of a map memorized from a verbal description (Denis & Cocude, 1989). Kosslyn (1975) showed that mental images take a finite time to zoom up or down to a different size, as when comparing the mental image of an elephant immediately following an image of a rabbit. Visual pathologies offer further striking evidence for the spatial nature of mental images. Patients with unilateral neglect, who ignore objects in one half of visual space, also ignore objects in the same half of their mental image space (Bisiach & Luzzatti 1978). Llinás and Paré (1991) observe that neglect patients report a similar lack of perception in their dreams, and that the people inhabiting the dreams of prosopagnosic subjects are faceless. Levine, Warach, and Farah (1985) found that patients who had lost the ability to perceive either shape or location, had corresponding difficulties in mental imagery tasks. These findings suggest that mental imagery serves a concrete function that employs the same, or similar machinery as that used in perception.

But the issue remains a contentious one, not only because of the continued dominance of naive realism in contemporary philosophy, psychology, and neuroscience, but also because of some fundamental problems that remain to be addressed. The most serious challenge to the concept of mental imagery as the basis of cognition was raised by Locke, with respect to the representation of abstract concepts. Cognition is necessarily concerned not only with concrete concepts that are easily expressed in image form, but also with generalities that relate to many possible images. How then can thinking be based on individual images? Locke presented the example of the concept of a triangle, which must necessarily include all of the various different types of triangles including acute, obtuse, equilateral, and isosceles, in all their possible configurations, not to mention the infinite possible rotations, translations, and scales of every one of those triangle types. What kind of mental image could possibly encode a general concept of this sort?

Arnheim (1969b) proposed that this kind of abstraction can be expressed as a *dynamic concept*—rather than picking a single triangle as the prototypical exemplar, the dynamic concept represents the full sweep of the total range of the concept. For example, the concept of an angle appears in the mental image somewhat like two rulers connected by a hinging pivot that allows them to sweep to any angle, or even to somehow exist in an indeterminate state that represents all angles simultaneously, or can be restricted to some subset of that range, as in the concept of an acute or obtuse angle. The dynamic concept of a triangle is composed of three such dynamic angles, flexibly connected so as to be able to morph effortlessly through the full range of possible triangular forms, while adhering to the essential laws of the triangle's characteristic structure. The idea of a dynamic concept is exemplified in the principle of the differential analyzer discussed in chapter 1. Once the mechanism of the differential analyzer is set up to express some mathematical relation between certain variables, the mechanism represents the whole problem in the abstract, through all possible combinations of the values of those variables, independent of the particular values of those variables at any one moment. For example, if shafts a, b, and c represent the internal angles of a triangle, they can be interconnected through an analog adder mechanism to shaft d, which in turn is clamped to a value of 180 degrees, to express the relationship between the angles of a triangle: $a + b + c = 180°$. In the absence of any contextual influence, the dynamic concept tends to relax back to its canonical form, where it manifests itself in prototypical form. In the differential analyzer this corresponds to installing a gentle spring force on each of the shafts a, b, and c that tends to push each of them toward a median value of 60 degrees. With these springs in place, the lowest energy state of the system as a whole would be that of an equilateral triangle, although this is only a preference and the mechanism can still deviate from that canonical form in response to additional forces or influences.

The evidence for this dynamic form of spatial concept can be found phenomenologically, by inspecting the appearance of mental images under various conditions as described here. As soon as we recognize that thought is a real manifestation of actual physical processes in the brain, this opens the possibility of examining those processes introspectively. The main obstacle to phenomenological observation of mental imagery in the past has been the fleeting evanescence of thoughts and mental images, which tend to morph rapidly into different forms, or disappear altogether under scrutiny. But that very evanescence and ethereality can be seen as a characteristic property of mental images themselves. Rather than being an obstacle to observation, the fleeting and tenuous nature of mental images provides direct evidence for a fleeting and tenuous physical process in the brain. The harmonic resonance theory presented in chapter 8 offers a representational paradigm that exhibits some of that fleeting and tenuous character, as well as an ability to represent a kind of fuzzy superposition of states characteristic of the mental image. In this chapter I present a phenomenological analysis of the mental image explored in a series of thought experiments designed to tease out the key properties of mental imagery, and how they relate to a cognitive and linguistic representation of the world.

THE STRUCTURE OF LANGUAGE

Language is a highly structured affair. The meaning of a sentence is determined by the structural relationships between the words in the sentence, which determine which words are to be interpreted as the subject, object, or verb of the sentence. There are critical connecting words such as "if" and "but" or "otherwise," which act as branch points, connecting whole sections of text in a meaningful way. The structures of language have been formalized in the rules of grammar, which prescribe the proper sequences of grammatical units around the connecting words. The nature of grammatical form is exemplified in its most pure form in formal languages such as computer languages, whose grammatical structure is defined in even more precise and rigid terms than are the rules of natural language. These rules can be expanded in lawful manner to generate arbitrarily complex structures using a finite set of rules. The precision and definiteness of such a formal language allow it to express a greater depth of grammatical complexity than is possible in a natural language. For example, "if" statements in a computer language can be nested inside each other to arbitrary depth. Such grammatical complexity is natural to computer interpretation, but goes beyond the complexity allowed in casual speech, where such complex structures would have to be broken into smaller, more digestible pieces.

The structure of formal languages is inspired by the grammatical structure of natural language, and thereby reveals by imitation an essential aspect of natural language grammar. However, formal language is very much less tolerant of error or ambiguity. In such a formal language the accidental omission or insertion of a single word or punctuation mark can render the entire block of text meaningless. The fault tolerance of natural language suggests that it operates on fundamentally different principles than do formal language systems, whose behavior is undefined in the presence of grammatical error. For example, a human has no problem understanding a statement such as "me want food" or "no go now." One possibility is that interpretation of such agrammatical statements simply involves more rules to handle such exceptional cases. The violation of strict proper grammar evident in such examples would, by this theory, automatically kick in a different system of agrammatical or slang rules to interpret them. If a sentence is inconsistent with one set of rules, then other sets of rules might be tried on it. However, this would require an infinite set of rule systems to process not only all possible classes of grammatical errors, but also combinations of erroneous rule systems. In fact, natural language has never been successfully formalized sufficient for practical interpretation of common speech, and indeed, there is reason to believe that this might be impossible in principle. Furthermore, the rules of slang systems must be learned from an experience of these errors, but people can parse even grammatical errors that they have never heard before. For example, this here sentence bad word-follows and word-choosings have that nobody none did hear before-time likely, but people know-think what it say noless, even if it no pretty music-sound speech makes to hear.

There are several lines of evidence that suggest that the complex grammatical structures of language corresponding to the rules of formal language systems are not the principal vehicle for communication of meaning, but rather that meaning is carried mainly by a lower level, more general and fault-tolerant system of thought, of which the formal rules of grammar are but an imperfect reflection. This evidence can be found in six general areas:

- Evolution of language in humans.
- Development of language in the child.
- Prosody.
- Metaphor.
- Grammatical flex.
- Meaning.

Evolution of Language in Humans

Human language appears to be qualitatively different from the next nearest form of communication in the animal kingdom. This might seem to suggest that the emergence of language represented a quantum leap or abrupt discontinuity in the nature of thought that sharply distinguishes human from animal thought. It would be more parsimonious, on the other hand, if it could be shown that language evolved incrementally from something more primitive that is shared in common with our animal ancestors, although formal language systems give no clue as to what its animal precursor might have been.

Development of Language in the Child

The adage "ontogeny recapitulates phylogeny" loosely applied to the evolution of language suggests that the earliest forms of ancestral language might be similar to the language seen in young children who are just beginning to learn it. Unlike early evolutionary language, children's speech is available for us to study. Characteristic of such early speech are agrammatical statements such as "me want food" or "no go now". Prominently absent from such primitive speech are the vital connecting words that serve such a pivotal role in formal language systems. This raises the question of how meaning is reliably extracted in the absence of the connecting words, or correct grammatical form that are so indispensable for formal language systems.

Prosody

The prosody, or melodic intonation of speech is present from the earliest development of a child's language, being present perhaps as early as the infant's first cry for maternal service. Children can comprehend the meaning of the words communicated by prosody long before they master the intricacies of grammar. Even our pets comprehend the prosodic content of speech, as when we say "Bad dog!" or "There's a good boy!" Although prosody receives little attention in linguistic circles, the primal nature of prosody suggests that it plays a central role in the communication of meaning, even in the written word, where the prosody is not even recorded except with the occasional punctuation. The prosody nevertheless is reconstructed in the reader's mind, to the point that if the reader misinterprets the intended prosody, he will almost certainly also miss the intended meaning. Again, there is no evidence of prosody in formal language systems.

Metaphor

Metaphor is fundamental to human thought and language. There is no end to the combinations of thoughts and concepts that can be combined to generate new thoughts and concepts. Many metaphors have become integrated into the language, such as the head of a department, the head of a line, the head of a page, and the head of a hammer or of a nail. However, the reason why such metaphorical constructs find their way into common usage in the first place is because of our natural ability to see meaning even in new and unfamiliar metaphorical combinations. For example, almost any physical object can be seen to possess parts of the body. Although by common usage a chair has legs and sometimes arms, it would also be generally understood what is meant if one spoke of the head or the feet of a chair. The head of a lamp might be the light bulb, whereby the lamp shade would be the hat of the lamp. A lamp may have a foot and shoulders too, and if the lamp narrows in the middle then it also has a waist, whereas if it widens in the middle it has a belly. A nail drives its toe into the heart of a plank; a stapler bites into paper, leaving its teeth in the ear of the page. The ability to construct and comprehend such metaphorical constructs is often considered to be an aspect of higher level thought, as are the production and interpretation of poetry and riddles. Does the appreciation of metaphorical riddles reflect a higher level intellectual function, or a primitive function fundamental to language? If the former were the case, one would expect metaphor to be the last to emerge as a child learns language. However children delight in metaphorical fantasies, such as the man in the moon, the dish that ran away with the spoon, Humpty Dumpty who sat on a wall, and so on. Metaphor is seen frequently in children's books and cartoons, where physical objects are constantly taking on human form. The headlights of cars turn into eyes, and the radiator grille into a toothy grin. Trees sprout faces and arms, as do bottles, plates, forks, houses, and just about any other objects in the cartoon world. Not only do children naturally comprehend metaphor, but in fact, metaphor appears to be a central part of children's thought. The central role of metaphor in children's thought and literature suggests that metaphor is fundamental to human thought and language, although there is little evidence of it in formal language systems, where the meanings of words are strictly defined and do not transfer meaningfully to other words without a formal definition.

Grammatical Flex

There is another troubling issue for the concept of natural language as a formal language system. Although the dictionary categorizes words as either nouns or verbs, pronouns or prepositions, and so on, in natural language these distinctions seem to have much less significance. The word "go" is listed in the dictionary as a verb, but anyone would understand the statement that "Gasoline puts the *go* in cars." The word "fist" is listed as a noun, but anyone would understand the statement "Fist the clay until it is soft." In fact, virtually any word can be used as virtually any part of speech, although the results are often somewhat awkward or unfamiliar, but comprehensible nevertheless. Many of these examples of grammatical cross dressing have made it into the dictionary. These metaphors must have appeared initially in common usage before they were recorded in the dictionary, because the dictionary is a catalog of common usage rather than the original authority on word usage. Thus we have colorful phrases such as "table the motion," "seat the crowd," "foot the bill," "face the front," "nail it shut," "wall it in," "I was floored," "pencil me in," "hand me a book," "knee him in the crotch," "belly up to the bar," "box my shopping," "bottle your beer,"and so on.

Meaning

Finally we come to a most central issue of language, the question of meaning. How is the meaning of a sentence encoded in the brain? The interactive activation model (IAM) of language (McClelland & Rummelhart, 1981; Rummelhart & McClelland, 1982) suggests that meaning is represented by a network of "nodes" that represent concepts. Hearing a word causes its corresponding concept node to "light up" like a light bulb, or become "activated." The concept nodes in turn are interconnected syntactically through the network, such that any active concept node automatically lights up related concept nodes and suppresses the activation of contradictory or mutually exclusive concept nodes. For example, the word <u>astronomer</u> when heard in a sentence supposedly lights up the "astronomer" node in the listener's mind, and this node in turn lights up syntactically related nodes such as "telescope," "planet," and "star." The "star" node that represents the concept of a celestial body in turn suppresses the activation of an alternative interpretation of the word <u>star</u> as a celebrity. In this view of language, understanding of speech corresponds to the lighting up of particular concept nodes, like the warning lights flashing on the instrument panel of a jet airplane, to indicate such conditions as "landing gear down" or "oil pressure low." However, it cannot be said that the airplane understands these concepts in any sense, just because a particular light blinks on on the instrument panel, and similarly, the lighting up of a set of abstract concept nodes is not a satisfactory explanation for the comprehension of concepts in language.

MENTAL IMAGERY AS A BASIS FOR LANGUAGE

The time has come to re-examine the old notion that the fundamental basis of human thought and language is an elaborate system of mental imagery. That the comprehension of the meaning of a sentence corresponds to the formation of a mental image in the listener's mind of the meaning of the spoken sentence. For example when a person hears the word table, I propose that a comprehension of that concept corresponds to the appearance of a mental image of a table in their mental image space. The sentence "The book is on the table" generates a mental image of a book on a table. This, I propose, is a far more satisfactory model of language comprehension, because an experience of a mental image is somewhat like a faint or ghostly perception of the imaged scene, and therefore understanding, by this theory, is essentially similar to experience.

The hypothesis that human cognition is a form of mental imagery immediately raises several questions about the nature of mental imagery that must be addressed for the theory to be at all viable. Specifically:

- What is the nature of mental imagery?
- Which of the infinite possible images of a concept should be selected to represent that concept?
- How can abstract concepts be represented by a mental image?
- How are mental images manipulated or combined?

These questions are addressed next.

The Nature of Mental Imagery

I propose that mental imagery evolved from perception, and inherited from perception its essential properties—that is, that the nature of the representation of perception and that of mental imagery are essentially similar: They use the same representational scheme. Perception of an object can be described as the generation of an internal mental copy of the external physical object. Mental imagery can therefore be described as the generation of an internal mental entity that is similar in essential properties to a percept of a real object, except that the imaged object, unlike the perceived object, need not be immediately present in external space. It is essential, however, for mental images to be clearly distinguishable from percepts—otherwise, the mental image would become a hallucination. Indeed, the existence of hallucinations and dreams demonstrates the capacity of the mind to generate elaborate mental images. Under normal perceptual conditions the mental image is distinguished from the percept by being very much less salient, or less vividly experienced, having the quality of a ghostly or transparent percept. In this sense the mental image is similar to amodal perception, like the perception of the hidden parts of a partially occluded object. I propose that mental imagery evolved as an extension of amodal perception, and that therefore amodal perception is actually a primitive, or lower-level form of mental imagery. Figure 9.1A illustrates a simple form of amodal perception, where the invisible portion of the occluded object can be easily completed by collinearity from the visible portions. This kind of amodal perception is very similar to modal illusory contours, as seen in the Kanizsa figure.

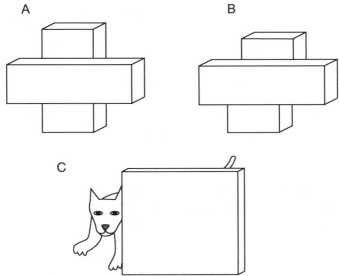

Fig. 9.1   (A) Amodal completion of an object through occlusion. (B) A more ambiguous case of amodal completion in which the completion path is uncertain. (C) A still more uncertain amodal completion, and yet a spatial percept nonetheless. Notice how the amodal image of the cat changes if you consider the feature on the right not as the cat's tail, but as some other extraneous object, which makes the amodal percept of the cat pull away from it, like an elastic blob after removal of an anchor point.

Which Image to Represent a Concept?

There are generally many possible mental images that correspond to any single concept. This is even true for very simple concrete concepts such as the concept of "table", for if a mental image is conceived of as a pictorial depiction, any particular table can be depicted from an infinite number of perspectives; furthermore, the table itself can be depicted in any number of different colors, shapes, or furniture styles. If a mental image is to represent such a concept, a choice must be made from this infinite set of possible images. How is this selection to occur?

The answer to this question is suggested by examining the amodal percept. In Fig. 9.1A the hidden portion of the occluded figure is pretty much specified by the visible portions of that figure, such that it would be easy to sketch in those missing parts of the picture with a pencil, and most anyone would probably sketch them in the same way. Figure 9.1B illustrates a more ambiguous case, where the exact shapes of the occluded edges are not so clearly specified, although the two visible ends of the occluded figure can still be perceived to be connected behind the occluder; alternatively, this figure can be seen as two separate blocks abutting, or partially occluded by a larger block. The nature of such vaguely specified visual edges is illustrative of the nature of mental imagery, as this case can be seen as essentially similar to the still less specified amodal completion shown in Fig. 9.1C. In the latter case the details of the occluded cat are so unspecified as to be practically invisible, or so faint and ghostly as to seem essentially nonexistent, or purely "cognitive." I propose, however, that the amodal percept is not entirely unspecified, but only seems so because of the large degree of variability that it possesses. Consider again, for comparison, the case of Fig. 9.1B. There are a number of likely completions of this figure, three of which are depicted in Fig. 9.2, A through C, and there are also an infinite number of less likely, or less predictable, completions. The central concept of the present hypothesis is that the visual system addresses such ambiguity by constructing an essentially infinite set of possible completions, and completing all of them simultaneously. The resultant amodal percept is experienced somewhat like a simultaneous superposition of ghostly renditions of all of these completions, with the more likely completions being represented with greater salience, whereas the less likely completions are experienced in a more ghostly or indistinct manner.

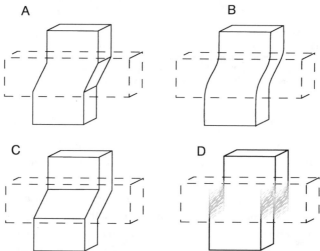

Fig. 9.2   (A through C) Several possible completion percepts for the amodal completion shown in Fig. 9.1B. (D) A spatial probability field that represents a probabilistic superposition of all possible completion paths of the amodal percept of Fig. 9.1B, with a higher density (darker shade) along lines where many of the possible completion paths coincide.

I propose that the amodal completion of Fig. 9.1B generates a percept somewhat like Fig. 9.2D, where the multiple alternative percepts appear overlaid on top of each other somewhat like the view of a spinning propeller, with the individual views of the propeller blades at each individual orientation superimposed perceptually to produce a ghostly image of a semitransparent disk through the plane of rotation. The density of the perceived disk of a rotating propeller is not uniform, because a stone thrown through the disk near the hub is more likely to strike a blade than a stone thrown through the disk near its outer rim. The image of the disk is correspondingly more dense near the hub, where it blends smoothly with the solid percept of the spinning propeller shaft that is seen as completely solid, becoming progressively more transparent with distance from the center. In the same way, the amodal percept is most concrete or vivid at the point where the visible edges disappear behind the occluding block in Fig. 9.1B, indicated by the darker shading in Fig. 9.2 D, because virtually all of the possible completions pass through these points, and the percept becomes progressively less distinct with distance from these points, where the different possible completion paths diverge.

The disk of a spinning propeller blade is quite different in nature from a circular disk of glass, even if the transparency of the glass is made to vary with distance from the center to look like a spinning propeller, because the propeller is not actually at all orientations simultaneously but exists at any one moment at only one of the possible orientations. In a similar manner, the multiple alternative completions depicted in Fig. 9.2D are actually mutually exclusive in regions where their paths diverge, so that although all of the completions are simultaneously possible, only one can reflect the true configuration of the hidden structure. Like the spinning propeller, therefore, I propose that these multiple alternative completions can be considered to be both simultaneously present, or superimposed, like the propeller disk, and at the same time to be mutually exclusive, like the instantaneous position of the propeller at any one time. In other words, I propose that the visual system cycles through the multiple alternatives so rapidly that they essentially blur into one. This cycling, I propose, is not necessarily regular or periodic, as in the case of the propeller, but can be more like the random path of an electron occupying the probability field of its atomic orbital. More generally, I propose that perception behaves like a dynamic system that wanders randomly throughout its energy landscape, spending proportionally more time in regions of greater stability, corresponding to greater perceptual likelihood, producing a spatial probability field, or superposition of states, much like an electron orbital, resulting in a ghostly spatial percept.

The evidence for this hypothesis comes from a careful study of the nature of modal illusory contours, where the path of the uncertain percept can be observed directly. A modal illusory contour, as in Fig. 9.3A, is distinguished from an amodal contour as in Fig. 9.1B in that it is experienced more vividly; that is, the visual system not only generates a hypothesized contour, but also postulates that this contour is exposed to the viewer, and thus is expected to be visible and is therefore rendered so perceptually. The amodal contour, on the other hand, although constructed by the same process and having the same spatial properties, is expected by the visual system to be occluded, and therefore to be invisible to the viewer. This, I propose, does not affect the form of the amodal contour, but it does affect its appearance, being "seen" in a more abstract or "cognitive" manner. The modal illusory contour therefore is more easily observed in order to study its properties, but reveals a nature that is common to both types of contour.

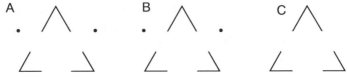

Fig. 9.3   (A) A modal illusory triangle whose corners are defined by three dots. (B and C) The sides of the illusory triangle fade progressively in salience with removal of the anchoring dots, although they remain visible in a ghostly uncertain manner.

Consider the three triangles depicted in Fig. 9.3. Fig. 9.3A produces a vivid modal percept of an occluding foreground triangle that is based on rather scanty evidence. A progressive elimination of visual cues progressively diminishes the salience of the percept. In Fig. 9.3B the elimination of one corner-anchoring dot causes the corresponding vertex to become rather fuzzy and indistinct. With an effort, the triangle can still be seen as a closed figure, but the lower vertex remains at best fuzzy, and the boundaries of the triangle extending towards it fade with distance from the inducers above. Alternatively, this figure can be seen to be truncated abruptly at the lower set of "V" features, or perhaps the illusion is totally destroyed by the elimination of one dot. Likewise, the elimination of all three vertex-anchoring dots as in Fig. 9.3C can either be seen as a triangle with faded corners or a triangle with rounded corners, or again, the illusory figure can fail to appear altogether. The salience of these illusory percepts varies with the observer, with some people being able to see almost a complete triangle in Fig. 9.3C, whereas others have difficulty even with Fig. 9.3A. Whatever the individual variabilities, certain principles hold for all observers: The salience of the observed illusory edges is a function of the amount of evidence supporting that contour; when the evidence for a contour is scanty, the contour appears faded and indistinct, and its exact path becomes uncertain, although portions of the contour near the inducers can appear locally more distinct, fading progressively with distance from the inducer. In ambiguous cases the percept appears unstable, shifting restlessly between different configurations. Significantly, the actual percept experienced can be modified somewhat by cognitive factors, that is, by an effort to see it one way or another.

This same principle can also be seen in the amodal percept of the occluded cat, shown in Fig. 9.1D. The occluded parts of the cat near the edges of the occluder are perceived most clearly, with the rest of the cat being very vague or unspecified. However, the fact that it is perceived as a spatial image rather than a pure abstraction can be demonstrated by the fact that people are capable of sketching in the missing portions of the cat, indicating that they can see some kind of spatial picture to guide their sketch. The variability or instability of that picture is demonstrated by the fact that even the same person can sketch a variety of different possible cats, each of which forms a spatial picture consistent with the visible portions. Note how the appearance of the tip of the tail at the upper right corner of Fig. 9.1C has a strong influence on the configuration of the unseen portions of the cat, stretching it out to the right to be consistent with that tail. Note also how this influence can be eliminated by the cognitive consideration that this feature is not the cat's tail, but is some other extraneous feature. With this fact in mind, the image of the rest of the cat pulls back to the left like an elastic blob rebounding after release of one anchor point. The way this amodal image of the cat can be manipulated by cognitive thought is illustrative of the nature of mental imagery. The amodal nature of the image is also characteristic of mental images, which, unlike hallucinations, are positively not expected by the visual system to be visible, and are therefore experienced in a very abstract or nonsensory manner. It is this nonsensory and indistinct nature of the mental image that has made it possible for vision theorists to deny the very existence of mental imagery.

The Representation of Abstract Concepts

The idea of abstraction is intimately related to the superposition of multiple images, because abstraction represents a one-to-many relation between the general concept and its multiple manifestations. For example, the concept of "furniture" includes the concepts of "chair," "table," "bed," "stool" and so on, each of which corresponds to multiple perspectives of those items in a multitude of colors, shapes, and furniture styles. The human ability to manipulate such abstract concepts corresponds, according to the present theory, to a manipulation of the vague and ghostly mental images representing the superposition, or simultaneous consideration of all possible variations of the concept. For a concept as abstract as this, the lowest levels or most concrete manifestations of it may be so tenuous as to be essentially imperceptible, like the rim of a spinning propeller disk that is so tenuous as to be completely invisible. For this reason, the higher levels of conceptual abstraction are experienced subjectively as if they were totally abstract, like the concept nodes in the interactive activation model (IAM). However, I propose that reification is an essential property of a semantic representation, without which the abstract nodes of the network would be completely devoid of meaning. This becomes evident if one persistently questions the meaning of abstract concepts, as in the following hypothetical exchange:

"What is furniture?"

"Furniture is things you can sit on, or put things on, like tables and chairs."

"What is a table?"

"A table is a thing with four legs and a flat surface".

"What is a leg?"

"The legs of a table are vertical pieces of wood that support the table top"

"What is wood?"

"Wood is the substance that comes from trees. A tree is cut into pieces to make the legs of a chair."

"What is a tree?"

"A tree is like that thing over there—with branches and leaves."

And so on. Although ordinary conversations rarely descend to such low levels, anyone who cannot decompose a concept in this manner demonstrates that they do not really understand that concept. At the lowest level of this descent, concepts rest on images that correspond to direct observations or experiences, which are, I propose, the ultimate basis of the concepts built on them.

Reification of a similar sort is also essential to recognize a general concept in a specific situation. Consider for example the concept of "democracy," which is often considered so abstract as to be entirely divorced from concrete images. In the first place, the concept would decompose as in the previous example into something like:

"What is democracy?"

"It is a form of government where people in power are chosen by election."

"What is an election?"

"Well, they have a thing called a ballot box, and the people line up and cast their ballots."

"What is a ballot?"

"It is a piece of paper with the name of the candidate they wish to support."

This hypothetical exchange illustrates how even this most abstract notion decomposes ultimately into concrete images, although of course I present only one possible sequence of questions and answers, which could have proceeded in an infinite number of alternative ways, leading to an infinite set of alternative images underlying this abstract concept. Nevertheless, the lowest level always decomposes to mental images that are irreducible beyond that point.

"What is a piece of paper?"

"A piece of paper is like this thing here that you are holding in your hand. See this? This is paper, and so is this, and this. They are all paper."

Indeed, this is exactly how we learn language from childhood, learning first the most concrete concepts by direct experience, and then building abstractions from those concrete images. In the absence of this lowest level imaging stage, a purely cognitive or verbal system would be like referring to dictionary definitions for each concept. For example, the last question in the preceding exchange could have been answered by quoting the dictionary definition of paper, which in turn would lead to more dictionary definitions of the words used in that definition, and so on. Ultimately, such a purely verbal representation of the world is necessarily circular, and thus ultimately meaningless.

Although the cognitive processing of the concept of democracy rarely descends to such low levels as in the given example, anyone who understands the concept can match it against specific images or experiences. For example, a photograph of people being herded into polling stations by soldiers armed with machine guns would immediately be recognized as a violation of the concept of democracy, even though the dictionary definition never explicitly precludes this exact combination of concepts. How, then, is so abstract a concept matched against such a specific image of a scene? I propose that this can only be accomplished by matching the components of the concept against features in the photograph, something like: "This is the polling station, and these are the people lining up to vote, but what are these soldiers with guns doing here?" Ultimately, the conceptual mismatch occurs at the level of the image. In this example the image of the soldiers cannot be matched to an essential component of democracy, and in fact, the coercion suggested by the presence of armed troops explicitly violates the conceptual requirement that an election be free and fair. This demonstrates that the observer must have translated an abstract concept into a low level image by reification, using the specific photograph to guide this reification toward that particular instance of the concept, and matched the components of the resultant image with specific features in the photograph. The unmatched images of armed troops are also abstracted to a concept of coercion, which is also matched against the abstraction of democracy. A different photograph of democracy might have generated a completely different set of images. So even if the word <u>democracy</u> is normally processed exclusively at a higher level of abstraction, as when processing the statement "Democracy is a form of government," true comprehension of the concept requires an ability to reify the concept in an infinite variety of different forms, which at their lowest levels are constructed of mental images, which in turn correspond to a ghostly or amodal type of sensory experience.

There are some concepts that are so abstract as to seem entirely devoid of imagery. What, for example, could be the mental image corresponding to the concept of a "thing"? A "thing" could represent just about any object, and therefore can have any size, shape, or color. By extension from the foregoing discussion, this concept might be expressed as a ghostly superposition of all such possible things. This concept is so insubstantial as to appear at first to be totally insensible or impossible to experience. However, the concept of a "thing" can be imagined as a center of symmetry, or a nucleus of perceptual condensation, known in Gestalt theory as a <u>gestalt</u>. I propose that the image of a "thing" can have location, without any other sensible properties. However at that location, the image is energized perceptually—that is, it has a powerful tendency to become an image of something more definite, while remaining in balance between all of the possible images that can form at that location.

The human ability to manipulate abstract concepts suggests that the imaging system is capable of manipulating or processing such potential images. The fact that such abstractions are spatial rather than immaterial entities is evidenced by the fact that a "thing" can have a location, and a size, when these are specified. For example it is possible to imagine a "small thing" in your hand, or a "big thing" behind you, although the mental image of these concepts remains transparent and invisible. The spatial nature of the abstract image is seen as soon as the "thing" is more precisely specified. For example, if the "thing" is further qualified to be a piece of furniture, or more specifically, a chair, then a more substantial and spatial image appears at the location formerly specified as the location of the "thing." Observe the progressive development of the mental image resulting from the following sequence of instructions: "Picture a thing—a big thing, in front of you right now, a big blue thing, it is a piece of furniture, a chair, an old-fashioned overstuffed armchair." The mental image appears to evolve progressively with each additional qualifying adjective, and those adjectives can be supplied in any order, resulting in any number of possible intermediate partially specified mental images.

As for the location of mental images, they can seem to appear in a separate disconnected space, as when you are instructed to "imagine a chair." If that image is sufficiently reified so as to appear in detail as viewed from a particular perspective, it appears to occupy a location that can perhaps be related to the space of the world around you, although remaining separated from that world, like a reflection in a pane of glass, that appears spatially superimposed on the world seen through the glass, but at the same time remaining completely separated from that world—that is, its spatial superposition on that world appears to be coincidental and inconsequential, having no interaction with that world. As with the reflection in the glass, attention tends to focus either on the world or on the image in its separate space. A mental image can also appear embedded in the world around you, as when you are instructed to "imagine a chair on the floor in front of you." In this case, if the image is sufficiently reified, it is possible to indicate with the palm of your hand the exact spatial location and spatial extent of the chair, as well as the orientations of individual surfaces of the imagined chair. Indeed, it is possible to act in every way as if the imagined chair were real, picking it up and moving it around, or holding it upside down over your head so that its imagined feet are perceived to just touch the real ceiling above you.

The possibility of imagining an abstract "thing" can be similarly demonstrated by the ability to pretend to hold "something" in your hand, to pick it up or put it down, using generic grasping motions, and to otherwise manipulate it as if it were a real object, all the while seeing it mentally as merely a nondescript "thing." If the human mind is capable of physically manipulating such abstractions in real space, an ability that can be clearly demonstrated even by children, then it is unlikely that this powerful imaging capacity would not be employed in the comprehension and manipulation of concepts in thought and language.

Manipulation of Mental Images

To elaborate the hypothesis of imagery as a basis of thought, I propose that mental images can be manipulated and combined, and that such manipulations form the fundamental basis of language and cognition. In the first place, as suggested earlier, I propose that we have control over the level of reification applied to any concept. When asked to imagine a table, it is possible (and perhaps more natural) to imagine it in abstract form, not committing to any particular perspective, scale, or furniture style. We clearly also have an ability to reify further, with artists and sculptors routinely reifying all the way to concrete images, as do plumbers, carpenters, and other tradesmen who build things with their hands that originate from concepts in their minds. When intentionally reifying to a concrete image, there does appear to be a tendency to image concepts in canonical form. For example, when picturing a table, we are unlikely to imagine a round table with a single central leg, but rather we tend to imagine a rectangular table with four legs, and a median aspect ratio, with a length perhaps 1.5 times its width. This is not rigidly specified, however, since one can actually imagine any kind of table, and one can even modify the image on the fly, for example when asked to "imagine a table—a long table." The image in our mind's eye appears to stretch dynamically, much like a cartoon table is apt to do. In fact, I propose that the mental image medium is very much like the cartoon world, where even supposedly rigid objects, like tables, chairs, buildings, and so on are elastic, and can bend or stretch, bulge outward as if under pressure, and wobble like a jelly when they collide with other objects. The canonical form of a mental image therefore appears to represent its lowest energy state, requiring extra mental energy or verbal specification to deviate from that form. A concept such as "long" or "fat" acts as a modifier of such forms, capable of acting on virtually any concept, even on abstractions, as in a "long thing." However, I don't believe these modifiers are fundamentally different from generic concepts, because object concepts can also be employed as modifiers of other object concepts. For example, a "table mountain" is a mountain with tablelike properties, and a "coat tree" is a treelike structure for hanging coats. Indeed, it is this general ability to combine essentially any two concepts that underlies the most fundamental aspect of language, that appears to be more primitive than grammar itself, which is why children first learning language make use of such conceptual combinations to describe unfamiliar objects.

Another essential property that is evident in cartoons is a tendency toward anthropomorphization, that is, to see the human form in inanimate objects. For example, cars seem to have faces, and their wheels seem like feet. This tendency may originate from the fact that the perceptual mechanism used for the representation of objects evolved from the perceptual representation of the body itself, and inherits from that more basic mechanism the same essential coordinate system. In any case, the anthropomorphic tendency offers a familiar coordinate system for the purpose of orientation. For example, a brick standing on end can be related to the human body, having a head and a foot, a front and a back, and a left and right side, although some of these relations will be bistable—for example, the front and back, which are reversible by symmetry, and the left and right sides, which are coupled to the front and back orientations. A cubical block, being more completely symmetrical, takes its body orientations exclusively from its orientation to the world, with the upper and lower faces being the head and foot respectively, whereas any inherent asymmetry in an object tends to anchor the body orientation. For example, a ceramic tile has a face and a back, being normally installed face up, exposing the finished face to view.

Fig. 9.4   (A and B) Two possible reifications of the concept "box man." (C) One possible form of the compound concept "bevel box man." (D) One possible form of the concept "wavy box man."

The mapping is not always self-consistent, as the face of the page includes both its head and its foot, appearing somewhat like the depiction in children's books of the dish that ran away with the spoon, whose legs and arms sprout directly from the face of the dish. The head can also appear either at the top of an object, like a human head, or at the front, like an animal head, which is why a locomotive is seen as the head of a train in cartoons, and why the face of a car usually appears near the radiator grille rather than at the top of the passenger compartment. This is also why the head of a table is found at one end, rather than at the top. These anthropomorphic designations are used extensively by engineers to describe mechanical parts, such as the cylinder head, the jaws of pliers, the teeth of a saw, the elbow of a pipe, the cross-arms of a telephone pole, the shoulder of a road, and so on. Notice how in these examples the configuration of the human or animal form is warped or distorted to match the object in question, like a cartoon caricature of an animated rendition of that object, after which that caricature can be used to express spatial relations between parts of the object in body coordinates.

The compound images produced by combinations of concepts are not always specified unambiguously, but often suggest multiple distinct interpretations. For example, the combination "box man" might be interpreted as a man who is concerned with boxes, like an assistant at the supermarket, or a box with manlike features, as shown in Fig. 9.4A, or a man composed of boxlike elements, as shown in Fig. 9.4B, or any number of other possibilities, which would have to be disambiguated by context. Indeed, this model is fundamentally context sensitive, and compound concepts can be further modified by other concepts; for example, the "bevel box man" shown in Fig. 9.4C combines the concepts of "box man" with the concept of "beveled", which has the effect of beveling the corners in the box-man image, while the "wavy box man" in Fig. 9.4D combines the concepts of "box man" with "wavy." Note that each of these concept modifiers seeks out the corners or edges in the image to which the concept applies, beveling or wobbling each edge wherever it is found in the image in a context-sensitive manner. In this way the same concept can have very different effects when applied to different objects—that is, the concept is expressed in the context of the image to which it is applied.

IMAGERY AND GRAMMAR

The combination of simple concepts into compound concepts forms the fundamental basis of the proposed model, whereas the power of human language is in its ability to construct complexity composed of higher order combinations of these more basic concepts or compound concepts. This is achieved by grammatical connecting words that relate compound concepts to each other to form higher orders of structure in the image. The fundamental basis of this grammar, too, is the mental image, in this case in the form of images of relations, as shown next with some examples.

In the sentence "The box is on the table," the word *on* relates the concepts of "box" and "table" by way of a specific spatial relation. Phenomenological examination suggests that the word "on" itself evokes a spatial mental image of one "thing" on top of another "thing." To further specify the relation, we can say that on means "this," or "this thing"—that is, the subject of the relation—on top of "that," or "that thing," the object. The mental image of the word "on" therefore is somewhat like Fig. 9.5A, where the concentric star-shaped symbol represents the abstract notion of some solid center of symmetry, or nucleus of perceptual energy—that is, a "thing," whose only specified properties are identity, unity, and perhaps spatial location. While the location of a single "thing" is not necessarily specified in absolute space, a "this" on top of "that" is specified at least in relative terms: on either side of the "on" relation, represented by the sagging divider depicted in dashed lines in Fig. 9.5A. This divider is depicted as curved to denote the fact that the weight of "this" is supported by "that," which, in the elastic cartoon world suggests that "that" must sag

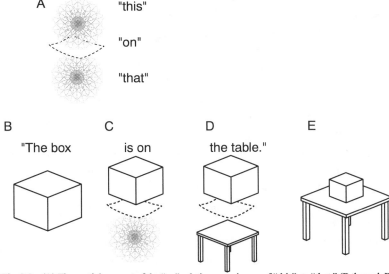

Fig. 9.5   (A) The spatial concept of the "on" relation as an image of "this" on "that." (B through D) Progressive construction of the mental image of the statement "The box is on the table." (E) Final, fully reified form of the resultant mental image.

somewhat under the weight of "this", whatever those two abstractions might represent. The location of both "things" and the "on" relation between them is unspecified in world coordinates, and therefore this mental image appears in a disconnected separate mental image space. The whole sentence "The box is on the table" would be interpreted in sequence as follows. First, the words The box generates a mental image of a generic box in canonical form, at the center of the image space, as shown in Fig. 9.5B. The words is on generate momentarily an image as in Fig. 9.5A, that is, of the "on" relation, or "this" on top of "that." Because the box image already resides in the image space, it becomes immediately associated with "this thing," producing the compound image shown in Fig. 9.5C, of a "box" on top of "that," the "that" remaining unspecified, like an open question, waiting to be specified. Finally, the words the table generate momentarily an image of a canonical table, which becomes immediately associated with "that," producing an image of a box on top of a table, as shown in Fig. 9.5D. This compound image then relaxes dynamically as the image components conform to each other, and because the generic box is generally smaller than a generic table, the box shrinks somewhat as the table expands, the bottom surface of the box conforms to the top surface of the table, the orientation of the box aligns with the orientation of the table, and finally, the table sags somewhat under the weight of the box, but not too much, because tables are typically rigid, producing a final compound image as shown in Fig. 9.5E. I propose that this compound mental image, as it forms in the mind's eye, remains variable, or largely unspecified; that is, the images of the box and the table can be viewed from any angle, and therefore their size, location, and orientation in space remain unspecified. However, the image of the box remains coupled with the image of the table, so that as the table materializes at one location, size, or orientation, the box will necessarily appear on top of it with a tendency to appear at an appropriate scale and orientation.

The spatial specificity of the notion "on" can be demonstrated with the following thought experiment. What is the locus, or spatial extent of the "on" relation? Although in general the concept appears abstract and nonspatial, as depicted in Fig. 9.5A, as soon as a specific table is specified as the object of the relation, the "on" relation becomes a spatial field whose perimeter conforms to the edge of the table, whatever shape or size that might take. The height of the "on" relation remains similarly vague and unspecified, like a mist clinging to the table top and fading with distance from that surface. It too takes on a sharper form, however, as soon as a particular box is specified as the subject of the relation, because the "on" relation becomes abruptly untrue as soon as the box levitates off the surface of the table, and in fact it might even lose some of its truth if the box is no longer supported by the table—for example, if its weight is supported by a rope even while the box remains in contact with the table. Similarly, the horizontal extent of the "on" relation is bounded at the point where the center of gravity of the box moves beyond the edge of the table, for a box that overhangs too much will either tumble off the table, or require additional support from some other object, which would therefore have to share the "on" relation with the table. The "on" relation therefore exhibits strictly delimited spatial dimensions which depend, however, on the exact dimensions of the related objects. It is only when these objects are themselves spatially unspecified that the "on" relation itself becomes abstract and nonspatial. Whatever the physiological mechanism that encodes this relation, these spatial properties are clearly essential to the meaning of the relation, and therefore the "on" relation can be considered as a spatial entity as opposed to a pure abstraction.

It may very well be that in normal conversation the reification of a sentence like "The box is on the table" may not necessarily proceed to completion, and that the mental image might never evolve beyond the stage of a symbolic box hovering over a symbolic table, both appearing as icons of equal size, as shown in Fig. 9.5D, that appears somewhat like the symbols used in company logos, heraldic symbols, religious icons, or pictures on playing cards. Or perhaps the box and table images never reify to a specific scale or orientation, producing a vague image, as in Fig. 9.5A. However, the fact that the image is capable of evolving to a mature state is evidenced by the ability of artists, sculptors, and carpenters to reify compound concepts in a more realistic form. Note that the grammatical structure in this model is by no means as sensitive to a rigid word sequence as in formal language systems, because the same mental image can be generated by the more basic childlike sentence of "Box on table." Indeed, the influence of prosody is also seen here, because it is exactly those three words that receive prosodic emphasis in the sentence "The box is on the table." The prosody can further emphasize aspects of the image. For example, if "box" is given extra emphasis, as in "The *box* is on the table," this would direct extra perceptual energy on the image of the box; that is, the box in the image would be highlighted, as if rendered at higher contrast, brightness, or perceptual salience, suggesting visually, in the mental image, that it is the box, as opposed to some other object, that is to be found on the table. The prosody therefore highlights objects or relations that are essential to the image of the sentence.

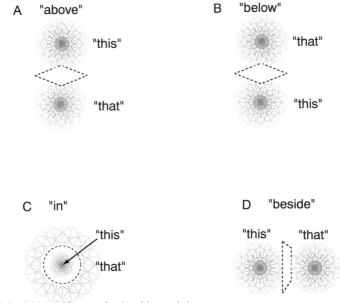

Fig. 9.6   (A) Mental images of various binary relations.

Other spatial relations can be represented in similar manner. For example, "above" is represented by a "this" above "that". In this case the weight of "this" does not impinge on "that," but rather, it hovers over it, as suggested in Fig. 9.6A, and "under" or "below" is represented by "this" below "that", as shown in Fig. 9.6B. The relation "in" is represented by "this" inside of or surrounded by "that," as shown in Fig. 9.6C, and "beside" is represented by "this" adjacent to "that," as shown in Fig. 9.6D.

The concept of numbers can be similarly abstracted. For example the concept "three" is represented as three "things," as suggested in Fig. 9.7A. The three things might in canonical form appear in a triangular configuration; alternatively, they might appear in a horizontal line. These arrangements, however, are independent of the concept of "three," and therefore the three things can actually appear in any configuration, with the canonical configuration representing merely the lowest energy condition, or the configuration that would appear in the absence of additional contextual influences.

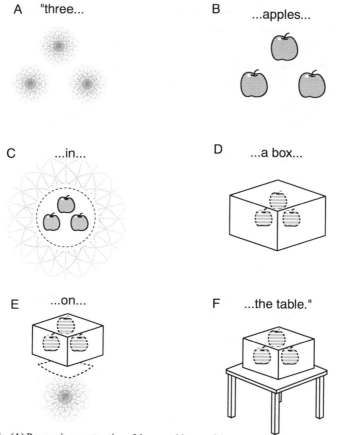

Fig. 9.7   (A) Progressive construction of the mental image of the statement "Three apples in a box on the table."

The relations just discussed are binary relations, relating "this" to "that," but these relations can be used in combination to construct more complex scenes. Consider for example the sentence "Three apples in a box on the table." The word <u>three</u> generates an image of three "things," as shown in Fig. 9.7A, which, combined with the concept "apples" produces an image of three apples, as shown in Fig. 9.7B. The concept "in" shrinks these three apples and encloses them in a surrounding "that," as shown in Fig. 9.7C, and then the word "box" generates a canonical box that expands to encompass the three apples, as shown in Fig. 9.7D. The three apples are perceived amodally in the mental image; they are not expected to be visible from outside of the box, although they are still perceived to be present within the box. The word <u>on</u> shrinks this compound image and places it over "that," as shown in Fig. 9.7E, and finally the words <u>the table</u> replace "that" with a canonical table image as shown in Fig. 9.7F. In this manner, arbitrarily complex scenes can be constructed by combinations of these binary relations presented in a sequence. Note that, as in natural language, the final image produced is not dependent on the word order, as the same image would be produced from the sentence "On the table there is a box containing three apples."

LANGUAGE GENERATION

The interpretation of language involves a transformation of a linear sequence of words into a spatial image of the described scene. The inverse function of language generation involves the decomposition of a spatial structure into a linear sequence of words. Because a scene can be described in a number of alternative ways, there must be a number of alternative ways to disassemble a scene into a linear sequence. How is this transformation to be achieved? How is a complex three-dimensional scene to be disassembled into a linear sequence of words describing that scene?

The inspiration for the following description comes from the practice of counting objects— for example, if you are instructed to count the dots depicted in Fig. 9.8A. The counting operation can proceed in any order, although it is important to mentally mark each dot as it is counted in order to count each dot once only. In other words, this task also requires the transformation of a spatial pattern into a linear sequence, and, as in describing a scene, that sequence can occur in a number of different ways. The grouping or structure of the configuration of dots, however, is used as a guide to counting. For example, this pattern can be seen as two groups of dots, with the upper group being composed of two subgroups, one of four dots and the other of three, whereas the lower group can also be separated into two subgroups, one of three and another of two dots.

A Gestalt-inspired algorithm for performing this counting might be to count the most salient group first, and to proceed by decomposing that group recursively into subgroups until all the dots have been counted. For example, if the dots are imagined to be like weights resting on a horizontal elastic sheet, attentional focus will concentrate on the lowest point, or the point of highest concentration of weights, like the point where water would accumulate if it were poured on to the elastic sheet. Each dot or group of dots in turn is checked off, or marked in some manner as it is counted, to ensure that no dot is counted twice. This marking might occur by making the dot appear less salient

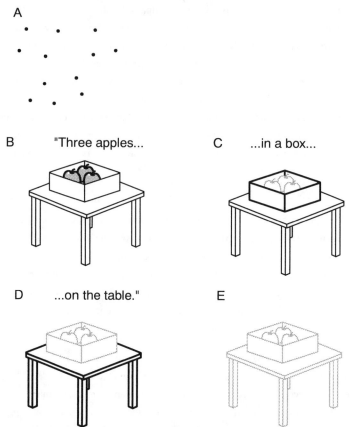

Fig. 9.8 (A) Dots that are counted in some spatial sequence, as an analogy for the sequence of breaking down a spatial scene into a verbal sequence. (B through E) Progressive changes in attentional salience of a perceived scene as it is decomposed into the verbal sentence "Three apples in a box on the table."

attentionally, thereby attracting attention automatically to the remaining uncounted dots or groups of dots. In the elastic sheet analogy, this would correspond to removing weights from the sheet as they are counted, causing the "attentional water" to pool at the next lowest point on the sheet. When groups of dots are of essentially equal salience, such as the upper and lower groups of dots in this example, the sequence is arbitrary; that is; it occurs randomly, or perhaps it follows a rough raster scan, but in any case, whichever group is selected for counting, it effectively disappears in an attentional sense, to allow the counting to proceed to the rest of the dots.

In the verbal description of a scene, a similar algorithm can be defined. For example Fig. 9.8B depicts a scene similar to the one discussed earlier, of three apples in a box on a table. The verbal decomposition of the scene can begin at some arbitrary location, possibly the most salient or interesting object in the scene—for example, the three apples in the box, which would stimulate the production of the first words of the sentence, "Three apples... ." As these words are spoken, the image of the three apples abruptly fades attentionally, as suggested in Fig. 9.8C. This in turn directs attention to the object most directly related to the apples, the box, and the relation between the last mentioned apples and that box, i.e.the "in" relation, resulting in the words "...in a box... ," whereupon the images of the apples and the box both fade from attention, as suggested in Fig. 9.8D. This in turn focuses attention on the next related object to the apples/box combination, that is, the table, together with the "on" relation by which they are bound, evoking the words "...on a table..." whereupon the image of the table also fades attentionally, as suggested in Fig. 9.8E. All the significant features of the scene have now been verbally described, and the entire scene fades from attentional focus. Note that this same scene could have been described equally well beginning with the table, in which case the words "On the table..." would have caused attention to shift to the box, followed by the words "...is a box..." and finally "...containing three apples."

ATTENTION

The idea of reification as an integral part of cognitive function offers a new perspective on the nature of attention. Early theories of attention suggested that attention operates somewhat like a spotlight, which can be directed at different parts of a scene, and psychophysical studies showed that perceptual performance is improved in regions where attention is focused. Like a spotlight with a zoom lens, the effectiveness of attention also appears to be attenuated when the attention is distributed over a larger area, as if a limited attentional resource can be either concentrated on a small area, or distributed over a larger region. However, attention is not merely a generic energizing force, because studies have shown that attention can be made featurally specific, enhancing certain specific features at the expense of others, suggesting a featural as well as a spatial aspect of attention. Searching specifically for a red triangle enhances the perception of red objects, and of triangular objects, either of which will consequently pop out more readily from a field cluttered with distractor items. The present model allows for exactly this type of spatial and featural tuning of attention, in that attention, in this example, is essentially similar to an attempt to imagine something red and triangular, with the additional requirement that the red triangular "thing" be actually present in the field of view, so that it is perceived modally rather than imagined amodally. The shape and color of the object are specified, whereas its location, orientation, and size are not. As soon as the object is located in the field of view, these parameters too become perceptually specified. The act of searching for such an object is therefore analogous to the example of searching for democracy in a photograph of a scene, and operates by the same principles, only at a lower level of abstraction, with less variability in the number of possible scenes that can match the searched-for description. According to the present theory, therefore, attention is not a separate and distinct perceptual function, but I propose that attention, perception, and cognition are different manifestations of the same basic computational mechanism, involving a system of mental imagery whose images can be specified to greater or lesser extent, in either spatial or featural terms, as suggested by Gestalt theory.

CONDITIONAL STATEMENTS

The relations discussed so far, "on," "in," "near," and so on, are essentially spatial relations, and therefore naturally expressed in mental imagery. What about more elaborate grammatical relations such as the conditional relation of "If <this> then <that>"? How are such abstractions to be related to concrete images? Again, the solution can be found using the same general principle: that an abstraction has meaning only by way of its reification into concrete images, which can therefore be matched against specific scenes. Consider the following conditional statement: "If the flag is up, then there is a letter in the mailbox." Although it is not explicitly stated, the converse is also implied by this statement—that if the flag is down, then there is no letter in the mailbox. The image components of these statements are simple enough; the image of the flag can appear either up or down, and the image of the mailbox does or does not contain an amodal image of a letter inside it. What the conditional statement does is establish a connection between the position of the flag and the possible presence of a letter. A conditional statement necessarily refers to two alternative possibilities. These do not, however, refer to two copies of the scene, because there is only one mailbox and one flag, and possibly one letter; it is the same mailbox that may or may not contain the letter or sport the flag. Applying again the idea of superposition of states, we can say that the image of the mailbox is bistable. That is, the amodal image of the letter in it is fleeting, alternately appearing and disappearing within the mailbox. The image of the flag is also bistable, alternately flipping between "up" and "down" positions. The message of the conditional is that the position of the flag is synchronized or causally linked with the presence of the letter, such that when the flag is up the letter is present, and when it is down, the letter is absent. This bistable synchronized mental image therefore corresponds to the meaning of the conditional statement. The two alternative states of the image can be examined or manipulated in turn; for example, the words "If the flag is up" stabilize the image in this alternative state, allowing the following words "there is a letter in the mailbox" to be associated exclusively with that state, that is, to complete the mental image corresponding to that state. If the conditional statement were followed by another statement beginning with the word "otherwise," the rest of that statement would apply exclusively to the alternative condition. At the end of both statements the bistable mental image would be complete, and could be cognitively flipped or flopped into either state at will as each alternative is considered in turn, or allowed to flip randomly between the two states to reflect the uncertainty inherent in the statement.

In the absence of the converse "otherwise" statement, the converse conditional will be assumed by contrast with the explicitly stated portion: that is, the converse of the first half of the conditional, "the flag is down," is linked to the converse of the second half, "there is no letter in the mailbox." This natural appearance of the converse notion following activation of a concept can be considered the cognitive correlate of spatial or temporal contrast effects observed in perception, which is consistent with the general theme of the present theory that perception and cognition are essentially similar processes that operate by the same essential principles. The appearance of a bright red light results in a green afterimage by the successive contrast effect, and, a grey square on a red background appears tinged with green, by the simultaneous contrast effect. In the same manner, a contemplation of the cognitive notion of war brings to mind the concept of peace, love brings to mind hate, heat reminds us of cold, and so forth. Therefore as soon as the conceptual combination of "flag is up → letter is in the box" is released, the converse conceptual combination appears, i.e. "flag is down → no letter in the box".

GENERAL PRINCIPLES OF COGNITIVE REPRESENTATION

Once again, the significant aspect of the present proposal is not so much the details of the preceding descriptions, but rather the general principles that they illustrate by example. In most general terms, the present hypothesis suggests that cognition is essentially similar to perception in that it is capable of generating three-dimensional spatial structures or probability fields that represent objects and surfaces in the world, with the distinction that the structures built by cognitive processes refer not to objects necessarily present in the immediate environment, but to possible or potential objects and events, which can be manipulated independently of the local perceived environment but can also be related to the environment as and when required. The properties of the cognitive world can be examined phenomenologically, and measured psychophysically, as can those of the perceptual world. Abstract concepts are represented as they appear phenomenologically as a fuzzy, unstable superposition of many possible spatial interpretations of the concept, and the various dimensions of such fuzzy constructs can be independently sharpened or constrained at will, thereby reducing the range of possibilities of the probability field, even down to a single, sharply focused mental image. However, the image remains flexible and malleable, being able to be rotated, translated, and scaled at will while maintaining its spatial structure, or morphed into different forms by cognitive manipulation of the concept. As such, the concept is a slippery customer, resisting rigid confinement to a fixed spatial configuration, which is why cognition has most often been mistaken for a nonspatial representation. However, the fact that cognitive structures *can* be reified into specific three-dimensional spatial structures whose spatial boundaries can be outlined by morphomimesis demonstrates that they are fundamentally spatial in nature, much like an amodal percept.

The functional utility of a structural representation in cognition can be clarified in contrast with the purely abstract representation of the differential analyzer discussed in chapter 1. One of the applications that motivated the development of the differential analyzer was the problem of calculating the trajectory of an artillery shell, taking into account variations of air density with altitude, Coriolis force due to the rotation of the earth, and so on. This is essentially a spatial problem that can be represented in a spatial model of the gun set in a miniature model of the local environment, with a parabolic trajectory arching up from the gun and back down to the ground at the strike point some miles distant. The differential analyzer did not make use of a spatial model, employing instead an abstract, nonspatial representation in which variables such as the azimuth and elevation of the gun would be set on the appropriate shafts as input variables, whereas the coordinates of the strike point, expressed as range and azimuth, would be read off as output variables by human operators. Let us imagine a spatial version of this analogical mechanism, in the form of an explicit spatial model in which variables such as azimuth and elevation angles are expressed literally in the model gun, whose model barrel would be adjusted directly by pushing it up, down, or sideways. The spatial structure of the model can be used to perform some of those spatial computations by analogy. For example, a synthetic gravity in the model world would pull massive objects downward, even cognitive structures like the parabolic trajectory of the artillery shell projecting from the gun. The curve of its arching flight path can be computed in the cognitive mental image somewhat like the sagging of an elastic rod under its own weight. Moving the model gun barrel would automatically update the spatial profile of the parabolic trajectory depicted in the spatial model, thereby automatically updating the calculated strike point in the model. Because any variable in the model can be designated as input or output, the problem can also be solved in inverse form by taking hold of the strike point itself, that is, the far end of the curving trajectory in the model, and moving that strike point directly onto the desired target point. As the strike point is moved around in this manner, this spatial version of the differential analyzer would automatically and continuously compute the inverse problem, depicting the model gun always at the azimuth and elevation corresponding to the current location of the strike point.

There is a problem with this concept of inverse computation that was glossed over in our initial discussion of the differential analyzer in chapter 1. Not all functions are mathematically invertible, and in fact the artillery problem is a case in point, because there are generally two different elevation angles for every given range of shot, one for a high-lobbing trajectory and one for a flatter horizontal trajectory. How should the analogical computational paradigm respond to such nonunique solutions? The concept of superposition of states, developed earlier, offers the conceptual framework required to address this issue: The inverse of the artillery problem produces two solutions, and therefore both solutions should be computed in parallel by the device. The response of the model to a setting of the strike point should therefore be a double image, with the barrel depicted simultaneously at both elevations corresponding to the given strike point. Because the solution space is shared by these two elevations, each solution should be rendered at half magnitude. That is, each of the two barrels at the two different elevations appears semitransparent in the model, as do the two parabolic trajectories projecting from those two barrels. But this does not mean that the barrel should be actually split in two, sending the shell along both trajectories simultaneously, because only one elevation can actually be set at any one time. These two solutions are mutually exclusive, and therefore the system should be bistable between these two states.

In fact, the arching trajectory is itself a superposition of all the positions momentarily occupied by the shell in flight, and that trajectory can be seen in the mental image either as a linear trail, or as a sequence in a short movie of the shell progressing along the trajectory. That "movie clip" can be played at will, either in one rapid real-time flash, or examined more carefully in slow-motion; or it can be frozen in time at any point along its trajectory, or rewound and played again as desired. Whatever the mechanism in the human brain that performs this remarkable representational function, this is the level of control that I observe phenomenologically over my own mental image of the artillery problem. And it is by this imagery that I feel that I "understand" the problem. The human mental imagery system is not very good at producing accurate quantitative answers, which is why we resort to mathematics or computers when precision is required. But mental imagery is well suited to producing qualitative answers, based on an intuitive understanding of the problem. For example I can "see" the effect on the trajectory of the shell of modeling gravity not as a constant downward force, but as one that diminishes with distance from the earth, which would raise the peak of the trajectory by a small amount, and thereby increase the range slightly. I can "see" the effect of Coriolis force, which deflects northbound shells eastward, and southbound shells westward (at least in the northern hemisphere) although by how much, I don't know without doing the math. But it would be hard to do the math without first understanding the problem to know what the numbers actually mean.

An interesting corollary of this concept of cognitive representation is that the system of driving forces that sets the analogical mechanism into motion, or that deviates the model in a certain direction, are what corresponds to incentive, or drive—that is, the "emotional" function of the mechanism. Like the delicacy in the shop window that deviates our path as we succumb to the influence of its attractive force, a force applied to any part of the analogical cognitive model represents a desire for it to move so as to relieve that force. Pain and dispair correspond to unrequited forces that arise when the system is blocked from relieving the forces applied to it, whereas pleasure and satisfaction correspond to the act of advancing toward, or relieving an applied desire force. Of course there is no guarantee that a man-made analogical device actually experiences anything like pleasure or pain. All we can say is that this motive force in an analogical model performs a function similar to that produced by pleasure and pain in human behavior, that is, attraction and avoidance responses respectively.

It is this kind of manipulation of spatial concepts which are meaningfully coupled to each other in an integrated spatial model of external reality which represents the essential principles of cognitive function. The grammatical processing of words and symbols in language and logic is merely the tip of the iceberg of this mechanism of spatial reasoning, because words by themselves are meaningless when disconnected from the spatial concepts that they represent. When meaningfully coupled to the analogical representation, words and symbols act as handles for manipulation of distinct aspects or components of the spatial model, which can be pulled or pushed as desired to explore the implications of various cognitive hypotheses.

Chapter 10
Motor Control and Field Theory

THE GENERALITY OF THE MOTOR CODE

The most remarkable aspect of motor control as observed in human and animal behavior is not so much the synchronization of many muscles and joints in a complex motor act, for complex synchronization is easily achieved in man-made machines by way of cams and cogs. The unique property of biological motor control is the adaptability and generality of the motor code. The mechanical synchronization by way of cams and cogs is rigid and stereotyped, the motor control equivalent of templates in visual recognition. Much more difficult to replicate is the generality exhibited in biological motion, when the regular sequence of the motor pattern is modulated in analog fashion to avoid obstacles, or to conform a complex pattern of steps to an irregular terrain. The generality of the motor code is seen most clearly in the way that a person adapts their gait to accommodate a prosthetic leg, or crutches, or the way a waiter carrying a loaded tray opens a door with his knee, or when a man tied up by an intruder wriggles across the floor like a worm, lifts the telephone receiver with his mouth, and dials the police with his nose. This adaptability in motor representation is seen from the earliest months of development. For the patterns of motion observed in infants when they first learn to crawl varies considerably across individual infants. Some babies locomote by rolling like a log; others shuffle and scrape along the floor using a bewildering variety of strategies, much like a person tied up by a burglar. After eventually learning to walk in the conventional fashion, even young children can easily adapt to bizarre variations such as walking sideways or backward, or walking in a straight line while rotating slowly like a top.

Gestalt theory proposed a holistic fieldlike approach to address the generality observed in motor control. The secret of the Gestalt approach is to model the organism and its local environment in a reified spatial replica of the external world, as suggested earlier in the context of visual perception. The problem of motor control can then be addressed by spatial analogy in this representation. I will show how this reified approach offers a solution to some of the most challenging problems of motor control, by defining the elements of motor action not in terms of individual joints or muscles, but rather in terms of global spatial patterns of synchronized motor activity, expressed as fieldlike forces defined in the model of local space both inside and outside the body. I begin by describing a simple control system modeled on the hydraulic arm of a backhoe, and demonstrate how this control system can be reformulated to operate in an isomorphic manner as suggested by Gestalt theory. I then present the field theory of motor control as discussed by the

Gestaltists (Koffka, 1935; Lewin, 1936/1969) and by Gibson and Crooks (1938), whereby perceptual processes assign a valence to objects in the environment that acts as an attractive or repulsive force, and motor processes respond to this motor valence field much like the way that charged particles respond to electric fields. Whatever the neurophysiological mechanism is that underlies motor control, this approach at least offers an accurate description of human and animal motor behavior, and that description is also consistent with the subjective experience of motor behavior. The fieldlike nature of the motor signal is most clearly evident in the movement of elastic organs like the tongue, a snail's body, or an elephant's trunk, and in multilimbed organs like the human hand or the body of an octopus. The harmonic resonance theory offers a plausible fieldlike computational mechanism in the brain to account for the global field-like properties of motor behavior. The wavelike character of the motor code is most evident in the sinusoidal motions of snakes and eels, and in the cyclic motions of a caterpillar's legs, although it is present in more subtle form in the periodic oscillations of the walking or running cycles, and appears in exaggerated form in human dance.

THE BACKHOE ANALOGY

Consider a simple control system similar to the hydraulic controls of a backhoe, where the individual joints of the backhoe are moved by hydraulic pistons, each controlled by its own hydraulic lever, as suggested in Fig. 10.1A. For simplicity let us assume a simple linear relation between the deflection of the lever and the rate of rotation of the joint. In other words, if the lever is deflected to a particular angle L, the angle of the joint A will begin to change at a steady rate that is proportional to the deflection of the lever. If the lever is then returned to the neutral position, such that $L = 0$, then the joint will stop where it is, and remain at that angle until the lever is moved again. A deflection of the lever in the opposite direction, to a negative value of L, causes the joint to rotate in the opposite direction. Expressed mathematically,

$$\frac{dA}{dt} = L$$

This simple control system is next progressively elaborated in the direction of an isomorphic model, in order to demonstrate the capabilities of an isomorphic representation for solving problems of motor control.

We can add a simple feedback loop to the backhoe control system, so that instead of having the lever control the rate of rotation of the joint, the lever will instead indicate the desired joint angle, and an automatic mechanism rotates the joint to that angle. This is how the flap lever works on an airliner, where the pilot sets the lever to the required angle, and the hydraulic control system automatically runs the flap motor until the flaps reach that angle. This type of control system is more isomorphic than the simpler backhoe system, because the operator has more of a sense that the lever represents the joint arm itself, although the motion of the arm always lags a bit behind the angle set by the lever.

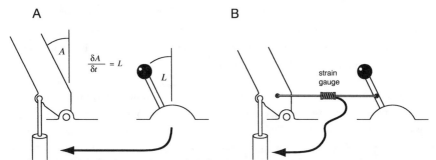

Fig. 10.1   (A) A simple control system is depicted as seen in a backhoe, where a fixed deflection of the hydraulic control lever L causes a constant rate of rotation of the arm A. In a more isomorphic control system the lever is moved to the desired angle, and the arm moves automatically to duplicate the angle of the lever. (B) An even more isomorphic system has the arm and its control lever mechanically coupled by a connecting rod, so that the angle of the lever always duplicates the angle of the arm. When pressure is applied to the control lever, a strain gauge on the connecting rod commands the arm to move, and the movement of the arm causes the lever to duplicate that motion.

An even more isomorphic system can be devised in which the motion of the lever is coupled to the motion of the arm, so that the operator does not move the lever itself but instead, applies force to the lever in the direction he wishes the arm to move, and that force is registered by a strain gauge, as depicted in Fig. 10.1B. The strain signal in turn is interpreted as a command for the hydraulics to move the arm in that direction. The lever is mechanically linked to the arm by a connecting rod, depicted in Fig. 10.1B, so that as the arm moves, the lever duplicates its motion, indicating to the operator by feel the angle of the arm at any point in time. This is the kind of control system seen in the primary flight controls of larger aircraft, to give the pilot a feel of the exact deflection of each control. One advantage of this control system if it were installed in the backhoe is that if the arm is blocked by an obstacle, the operator gets tactile feedback on the location of that obstacle by the resistance of the control lever to motion in that direction. With this kind of control system even a blind operator could use the arm to explore the terrain and to map out the pattern of obstacles in a three-dimensional space by feel.

Besides making the control system more intuitive to operate, this concept of isomorphism in control systems offers an elegant solution to the multijointed limb problem for robotic control. For the multiple joints of the arm can be replicated in effigy in the control lever itself, as suggested in Fig. 10.2B, whose joints and segments are designed to duplicate the geometry of the backhoe itself, shown in Fig. 10.2A. In this hypothetical control system the operator applies a force to the knob at the end of the multijointed control stick, and that force in turn registers on individual strain gauges installed at each of the joints on the control stick. Those multiple strain signals in turn are interpreted as commands to the hydraulic actuators at each of the corresponding joints on the backhoe, which respond by deflecting their respective joints in proportion to the strain. As the multiple joints begin to move, the jointed control stick replicates the configuration of the backhoe at any moment, thereby giving the operator the sense that he is moving a model of the backhoe with his hand simply by pushing on it in the desired direction.

The problem of targeting a multijointed limb is underconstrained when there is a larger number of joints, because there are often several different configurations of joint angles that lead to the same position of the end-effector. In biological motion the limb is usually observed to take on a smooth curvature when reaching for a target, in which the deflection is distributed equally among the multiple joints. This constraint can also be expressed in the isomorphic backhoe by installing nonlinear spring forces at each of the joints of the control lever, or the internal effigy of the limb, that tend to return each joint to its neutral position of zero deflection. The nonlinearity in the spring force ensures that a large deflection by one joint results in greater spring tension than two smaller deflections in adjacent joints. Therefore, the nonlinear springs will tend to distribute the joint deflections equally among all of the joints of the limb while reaching for the target point. The beauty of this control system is that it automatically solves the complex trigonometrical problem of the multi-jointed arm by analogy, that is, by building a spatial replica of the forces involved, and allowing that physical model to distribute the forces between the multiple joints automatically. This allows the control signal to be expressed in terms of the desired motion of the end effector, rather than in terms of individual joints and actuators. The requirement to distribute the limb deflection equally amongst its various joints is also expressed in terms of actual physical forces that push the system toward the desired objective. The principle automatically generalizes to any configuration of joints with any number of degrees of freedom. The operator no longer needs to calculate which joints to move in what proportion, he simply directs the model arm in the direction he wishes it to move, and the model takes care of the rest.

However, the real strength of the isomorphic approach is that it allows the operator to be replaced more easily by an automatic control system expressed isomorphically, given that the control lever is installed within an isomorphic spatial replica of the physical environment in which it is to operate, as suggested in Fig. 10.2C. A command to move the arm toward a particular target can then be expressed simply as a force of attraction between the target and the tip of the arm, and this very simple command signal in turn automatically results in the perfect combination of joint motions in order to direct the arm in a straight line towards the target. Gestalt theory suggests that our phenomenal world incorporates exactly this kind of spatial replica of the external world, and that motor intentionality—for example, a decision to reach for an object—is expressed in this phenomenal space in spatial form as an attractive force between the end of the arm and the target object. This is perfectly consistent with the subjective experience of motor control, in which our conscious awareness is of simple motions in phenomenal space, rather than of the complex patterns of motions of individual joints.

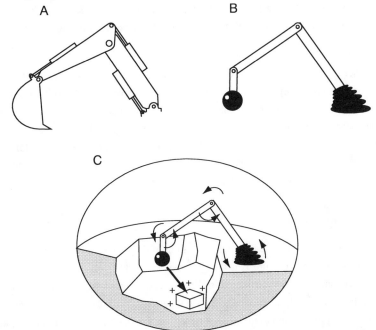

Fig. 10.2 The isomorphic backhoe solves the multijointed limb problem by duplicating the configuration of the arm (A) in the configuration of the control lever (B), which remains mechanically coupled to the configuration of the arm. Strain gauges installed at every joint in the lever command the corresponding joints of the backhoe. This allows the backhoe to be controlled simply by pushing on the end effector. (C) If the isomorphic backhoe control lever is installed in a spatial replica of the local environment, a command to move toward an object—for example, the box depicted with positive valence—can be expressed as a force of attraction between the object and the end effector, which in turn is automatically converted to the appropriate pattern of torques at each joint of the compound arm.

A FIELD THEORY OF MOTOR CONTROL

The idea of a field theory in biological motor control and navigation has been proposed by several authors, including Koffka (1935), Lewin (1936/1969), and Gibson and Crooks

(1938). Although this concept occasionally resurfaces in the contemporary literature on robotics (Khatib, 1986; Schoner, Dose, & Engels, 1995) and is still favored in the Gibsonian or ecological psychology circles (Brett, Warren, Temizer, & Kaelbling, 2001), the idea has generally fallen from favor in recent decades because it is difficult to relate to modern concepts of neurophysiology. However, the insight of indirect realism, in conjunction with Gestalt theory and harmonic resonance theory, offers a computational framework in which motor fields can be expressed not only as patterns of activation in an internal muscle space, or as discrete signals to individual muscles, but as spatial fields in an internal model of the external environment. The backhoe analogy just described explains how a simple force vector between an end-effector and a target object can be translated into a complex combination of synchronized muscle commands to move a limb towards a target.

I next present a more elaborate model of motor control that is consistent with the field theory models proposed by Koffka and Gibson, in which motor intentionality is expressed as a structured field in phenomenal space, and individual muscles receive different motor command vectors depending on where the perceptual copy of the muscle is currently located in phenomenal space. In other words, each muscle samples the local motor field in phenomenal space, so a single field can direct muscles in one place to move up, while directing muscles in another place downward, depending on where they are located within the motor field.

A Field Theory of Posture

Body posture is perhaps the clearest demonstration of the spatial nature of at least this one aspect of thought, for a posture is a thought, experienced in consciousness as a unitary gestalt, which can either be considered in the abstract, as when thinking for instance of a crouch, or be immediately expressed as a spatial pattern of muscles and joints. The ability to conceive of a posture, and to maintain it rigidly, or to cycle through rhythmic sequences of postures in locomotion or in dance, demonstrates the ability of the brain to express mental activity in the form of static or dynamic spatial patterns, which are communicated in parallel to the muscles of the body. This behavior is difficult to explain in the template-like paradigm of spatial receptive fields, but is more naturally explained in terms of standing wave patterns. Standing waves define static and dynamic spatial patterns, and different standing wave patterns naturally interact with one another to produce endless combinations of compound patterns, whose individual components can nevertheless be manipulated independently.

Gestalt theory has always emphasized the fact that there are certain general themes or guiding principles in the brain that manifest themselves in different guises in various

general postural code expressed in field-theory terms

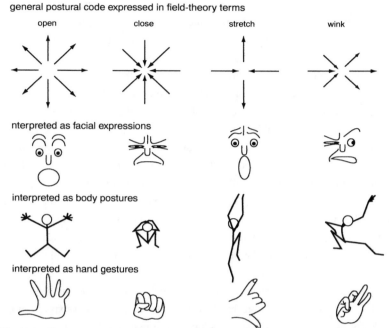

Fig. 10.3   The language of posture appears to be universal, whether expressed in face, body, or hand postures, as shown here. The general postural primitives, expressed as field patterns, are depicted in the top row, and examples of their expression are illustrated in the lower rows.

functions of the brain. In the case of posture, Arnheim (1988, p. 158) drew a connection between the postures of the body and those of the face and the hand, suggesting a general purpose posture language for control of these diverse geometrical structures. A field theory offers the appropriate level of generality in the motor code. In terms of field theory, a posture can be described as a patterned deformation of an elastic body from a canonical or neutral central posture. Figure 10.3 demonstrates some postural primitives and how they might be applied to the posture of the body, face, and hand. The atom of motor control therefore is not a command for the contraction of a single muscle, but the spatial field of limb position or motion vectors that apply to many muscles simultaneously in a structured spatial code, as suggested by Gestalt theory. The fieldlike nature of these motor primitives can be seen most clearly when expressed in a multipart organ like the human hand, or the tentacles of an octopus, that open or close in unison like the petals of a flower, or generate more complex configurations as when a hand prepares to grasp tools of various shapes. This fieldlike description of postural primitives can be related to the representation of geometrical form proposed in chapter 6, expressed in terms of patterns of symmetry of the vertices about a center. The zeroth harmonic would therefore represent a huddled posture with all appendages retracted (or its inverse, with all appendages extended); the first harmonic represents extension in one direction only; the second harmonic represents extension in two opposite directions; the third harmonic represents a "Y"-shaped configuration, either with arms extended outward overhead, or with legs splayed outward; and so on. Note that the postures depicted in Fig. 10.3 are not the only possible interpretation of those commands. For example, the stretch is depicted with one leg flexed and the other extended, but it could also be interpreted as both legs extended, or with only one arm extended, and so on. Similarly, the hand gesture depicted for stretch is only one of several possibilities. This represents the real power of the field-theory approach, because a field pattern does not rigidly dictate the exact body configuration, but rather it generates a fieldlike attractor which can accommodate a number of alternative interpretations of that pattern. This allows the motor patterns to adapt to local conditions, or to the previous posture of the body in a flexible manner. The connection between the geometrical representation of objects in the world and body and hand postures can be seen in the way that carpenters, plumbers, and engineers communicate geometrical concepts to each other with geometrical hand gestures, where the hands can represent planks or beams or pipes or bolts that join in various configurations. It is also seen in the way that children naturally express the geometrical configuration of alphabetic characters in hand and body pantomimes. The conversion from hand, to body, to external object expression occurs immediately and effortlessly, suggesting a low-level primitive process.

Edith Kaplan (1990) observed that axial body movements, centered on the spine, are learned earlier by children, and preserved later in progressive deterioration of mental function with age and disease, whereas distal movements of the limb, and even more so with the fingers, are learned later by children, and lost earlier in disease. For example, when asked to imitate a windshield wiper, a young child waves their whole body from side to side, whereas older children tend to wave two arms in pantomime, and a still older child or adult will tend to use only a pair of index fingers instead, and the reverse pattern is observed in progressive loss of motor ability. This suggests that axial or whole-body motions are the most primitive and robust, whereas distal movements are more advanced and fragile. This is consistent with a hierarchical representation in which axial whole-body motions are expressed as a fundamental standing-wave pattern, on which are superimposed the higher harmonics that direct the configuration of the limbs, and still higher harmonics direct the patterns of motion of the fingers and toes.

A Field Theory of Balance

The motor patterns involved in maintaining balance are also best described as fieldlike patterns of synchronized motor activity. For example, when standing up on tippy-toes, we can feel the balls of our feet rolling this way and that, shifting the center of upward thrust

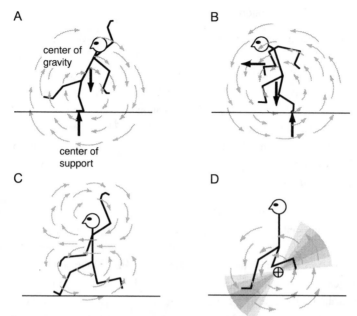

Fig. 10.4   (A) The imbalance due to misalignment between center of gravity and center of support can be expressed as a field, indicated by the gray arrows, which can be used as a motor field to restore the balance, moving parts of the body in the direction indicated by the arrows of the motor field. (B) Maintaining a constant imbalance or tilt results in locomotion in the direction of tilt. (C) A more generalized motion field is expressed by a directed motion of the core of the body, with a balancing countermotion of the limbs in the periphery. (D) A phasic component to the motor field defines a rotating vortex that directs the two feet to rotate in counterphase.

from the floor laterally in order to keep it under the shifting center of gravity, in much the same way that a broomstick handle is balanced vertically on a fingertip. This dynamic can also be expressed most generally as a corrective field constructed on the basis of two forces, the upward-directed center of support, and the downward-directed center of gravity. Whenever these two forces fall out of alignment, as suggested in Fig. 10.4A, this results in an overall toppling moment represented by the field lines in the figure, in this case showing the man about to fall over backward. Because action and reaction are equal and opposite, the balance can be restored by interpreting these same field lines as a motor command field, in this case by pushing forward against the ground with the feet, or, pushing backward against overhead hand holds, if available. The balance can also be restored by taking small steps backward, as suggested by the rotary pattern of the motor field as a whole. The complex ballet of balance can therefore be reduced to the emergence of this field pattern in response to any perceived imbalance between the support vector and the body's center of gravity vector, and the same motor field applies regardless of the number of limbs or their articulation.

A Field Theory of Locomotion

Given this very general mechanism of balance control, a locomotion signal can be added in the form of a simple unbalancing mechanism that expresses a desire to move in a certain direction by leaning the body in that direction, just as a helicopter, or the lunar module hovering on its rocket exhaust, translates laterally by tilting its lift vector in the desired direction of motion. If a certain angle of inclination is maintained with respect to the vertical, then the automatic balancing function just described will result in a constant force of locomotion in that same direction, as suggested in Fig. 10.4B. This pattern of locomotion, however, only applies to walking with vertical posture. A more general pattern must be used for crawling, swimming, and flying.

The most general principle of locomotion, which applies to locomotion on land, sea, and air, is Newton's principle of action and reaction, whereby progress in a particular direction can be made by pushing back on the world in the opposite direction. The more resistance that is felt in a backward push on the world, the more forward thrust is achieved by that push. This general concept can be expressed by the field pattern shown in Fig. 10.4C, that represents a directed vector of the core of the body in a particular direction in space, balanced by a complementary field of motion in the opposite direction in the periphery, defining a balanced circulatory field somewhat like a convection cell. When applied to a body, this motor field is superimposed in three-dimensions on the model of the body in perceived space, where the field forces command different limbs to move in different directions depending on their location in the field. Any limbs that are outstretched in the periphery are commanded to move backward forcefully, whereas limbs that are proximal to the body, and the body itself, fall into the forward-directed portion of the field. This field therefore expresses the concept of forward locomotion in its most general form. In this form, motor control can account for the infants early attempts at locomotion. This also suggests a common general propulsive principle expressed in the various forms of human swimming strategies such as the dog-paddle, breast stroke, and the crawl. This general locomotory field would be further specified or elaborated to conform to the specific geometry of the body. In the case of walking animals, the feet must be recovered from behind the body and advanced forward for the next step. In the most general terms, this constraint can be expressed as a center of cyclic rotation located between the body center and the ground, as depicted in Fig. 10.4D. In combination with the general locomotor field, this generates a rotary vortex about the center of rotation of the feet. This cycle determines the general path of the feet during walking, although it does not define the exact articulation of the knees and hips to achieve that rotary objective; those details must be worked out as in the isomorphic backhoe concept, using a spatial analog of the jointed limb to follow the end-effector as it moves in response to motor fields.

A further level of specification would define the phase of the cyclic rotation, suggested by the gray shading in Fig. 10.4D. This would depend on the number of feet in each cycle. For a bilateral symmetric biped this means a two-phase cycle for the two feet, as suggested in the rear view of the motor field depicted in Fig. 10.5A, where the two feet remain in counterphase during the rotation. This counterphase motion of the lower body introduces an eccentric oscillation in the gait, which can be balanced by a complementary oscillation of the upper body, resulting in a swinging of the arms, as suggested in Fig. 10.5A. This balancing of motions in the perceptual representation in turn minimizes the deviation of the center of gravity of the physical body from the smooth, generalized locomotor pattern. When calculated as in the isomorphic backhoe, this balanced pair of complementary oscillations in the upper and lower body would likely induce a sinusoidal oscillation of the spine, as suggested also in Fig. 10.5A. Cutting, Proffitt, and Kozlowski (1978) described the perceived motion of the body during locomotion as the flexing of a flat spring, with limbs in symmetrical motion around it.

OBJECT-ORIENTED MOTOR CONTROL

A similar field-theory analysis can be applied to more specific motor goals that relate to objects in the environment. For example, the desire to push a box is experienced as a motor field or force vector attached to the perceived object; that same motor field is observed to map differently to the body depending on how the body is applied to the box, as suggested in Fig. 10.5B. This kind of invariance in the motor code is seen in the way that ants cooperatively dragging a large crumb back to the nest tug on it in all different orientations—some ants pulling from ahead, others pushing from behind, some standing on top of the crumb and pushing back against overhead obstacles, and some ants hanging upside-down from the bottom of the crumb, pushing backward on the ground, all this without losing their global sense of the direction toward the nest. The generality of the motor code is also seen when a player manipulates a soccer ball, striking it with the foot, knee, chest, or head, depending on which part of the body is most conveniently aligned with the ball, as suggested in Fig. 10.5C.

More complex motor intentions are expressed as more complex motor fields. For example, a desire to pull a cork from a bottle with a corkscrew is expressed first in perceptual coordinates as a balanced pair of force vectors pulling the cork and the bottle in opposite directions, as suggested in Fig. 10.5D. This spatial thought is anchored to the orientation of the perceived bottle; that is, the desired force vectors are perceived subjectively to rotate and translate with the bottle as it moves about in space. When transformed into a motor field, that same pair of opposed vectors or dipole applies itself to motor space in the most general way, such that the action can be accomplished in principle at any orientation

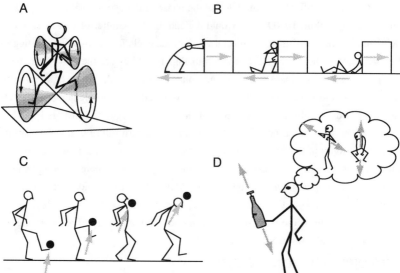

Fig. 10.5 (A) The synchronization between different parts of the body during walking can be modeled as a biphasic rotary cycle of the feet, meshed with a counterrotating sub-cycle of the shoulders and arms that remains coupled to the primary cycle like meshed cogs. (B) The intention to move a box is experienced as a force vector attached to the box, opposed by a traction vector against the ground. (C) The generality of the motor code can be seen in the flexibility with which a soccer player handles the ball, using any body part to apply the desired force. (D) The intention to uncork a wine bottle is perceived as a motor dipole of opposed vectors as an amodal spatial percept that remains locked to the bottle as it rotates and translates through space. The dipole inspires dipolelike thoughts of opposed pairs of muscles, and the motor plan reduces to aligning the dipole perceived on the bottle with a motor dipole of the body.

and using any set of opposed muscles in the body in any posture, provided only that a proper grip and opposed force can be applied. This general motor intentionality can be expressed in field terms as follows.

First, the dipole force pattern perceived on the bottle is considered in the context of the body, where the dipole concept seeks out any possible expression on the body. For example a simple force dipole can be created by pulling the fists in opposite directions across the chest, or a more powerful dipole can be achieved across the body as a whole, pulling the hands and feet against each other using the muscles of the back. Once the motor strategy has been selected, moving the bottle into the proper configuration is achieved by allowing the bottle dipole and the body dipole to match to each other, like two magnets floating freely in a three-dimensional space, which would simultaneously drift together and rotate into alignment by mutual attraction. In other words, the final configuration with the motor and bottle dipoles both aligned and superimposed represents the minimal energy configuration whenever these concepts are considered together. The bottle seems to drift effortlessly into place for the pull, propelled by the arms in response to the motor fields. The required contribution of each muscle to this global action is computed as in the isomorphic backhoe analogy, by configuring a spatial replica of the body or motor homunculus around a perceptual model of the bottle, and applying the force dipole to this model at the points where the body grips the bottle and cork. The details of this description of motor performance can be determined phenomenologically, by observing the direction that the bottle "wants to go" when held in the hand as soon as the concept "pull the cork" becomes active. The appropriate field lines could in principle be measured psychophysically by observing the motion of the bottle from various starting points when the command to pull the cork is given, just as electric field lines can be mapped by observing the tracks of charged particles released at various points in the field.

FIELD THEORY OF GESTURE

Field theory offers a novel perspective on the phenomenon of gesture, or the communication of spatial information by way of hand or body movements. Gesture is a very primal form of communication, for it emerges early in development, is universal across cultures, and can often serve as the only form of communication between people who do not share a common language. It is difficult to suppress the urge to gesticulate, especially when making an emphatic or emotional point, and people even gesticulate unconsciously when talking on the telephone, where the listener cannot possibly benefit from the added information. Gesture is also employed extensively in noisy environments, as when a workman directs a driver backing up a truck, or a crane operator maneuvers a heavy load at a construction site. The hand signals used in these circumstances are very literal and direct, as if the signaller were actually reaching out and grabbing the truck or the load, and pushing it with a hand in the direction of intended motion, although the gesticulating hand is usually well out of reach of the object being directed, suggesting instead a larger, fieldlike motion extrapolated outward from the moving hand. The hand is often paddled in a circular motion, as if swirling a fluid substance whose flow is intended to drift the load in the intended direction. These gestural patterns can be understood in field-theoretical terms by assuming that the perceptual matrix in which the gesticulator is perceived is indeed suffused with fieldlike patterns of energy, whose flow lines are indeed controlled by moving objects in the environment. The view of a rotating windmill, for example, is perceived not only as the rigid rotation of a structure; that rotation carries with it a fieldlike rotational vortex in the perceptual representation. Gesticulation makes use of this invisible substance, paddling it like a hand swirling the water in a bathtub, generating flow fields that extend well beyond the gesticulating hand. The patterns of gesture can therefore be seen as a direct manifestation of the field-like forces of motor control present in the mind of the gesticulator and in the mind of the person interpreting the gesticulation.

COMBINATIONS OF MOTOR PRIMITIVES

The greatest promise of a standing-wave representation is seen in the way that different wave patterns can be combined to modulate one another to generate more complex compound patterns. I do not propose to specify the neurophysiological details as to how this is achieved, but merely to suggest the promise of this concept with a hypothetical model of compound motor fields, to demonstrate the most general principles of such a system as a reified hypothetical exemplar.

Many forms of biological locomotion are expressed as periodic cycles of motor action. These can be generally categorized into wavelike motions as in the body undulations of fish and snakes, and rotary motions as in the general cycle of the limbs during walking or running. The cyclic and wavelike motions are seen in combined form in the movements of a centipede, whose globally wavelike motions of limbs are expressed as the synchronized cycling of individual feet. A fish or a snake steers its body by applying a global curvature to the body as a whole. This global curving is superimposed on the propulsive undulations, although these components of the combined motor patterns are addressable individually as separate commands to advance and to steer. In similar fashion, the subjective experience of human walking feels like a smooth continuous flowing motion, where the motor intention to walk faster or slower, or to steer left or right, is experienced independent of the cycling propulsive motion of the feet, giving a subjective impression somewhat like a smooth ride on a motorcycle, rather than the jerky stepping motion of a robotic legged vehicle.

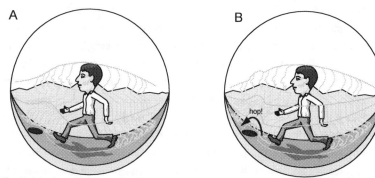

Fig. 10.6 A planned trajectory is perceived amodally as a snakelike trail, like an amodal projection of the body profile forward into perceived space, with the proper perspective applied, filled in with a periodic pattern of planned footsteps. The negative valence occasioned by a perceived obstacle in the path causes (A) the planned trajectory to deviate smoothly around that perceived obstacle, or (B) the periodicity of the stepping pattern to be modulated so as to step over the obstacle.

Figure 10.6A depicts the subjective experience of walking down a road, where the planned trajectory appears as an amodal snakelike percept overlaid invisibly on the terrain in three dimensions somewhat like a linear projection of the body profile out into perceived space. This amodal percept is not experienced as a spatial structure as such, like the hidden rear faces of solid objects. In fact, one would be inclined to say that there is nothing perceived in our path as we walk, whether perceptual or structural—just an empty void. However, there is a spatial zone within which the sudden appearance of obstacles would cause us to hesitate, or duck, or to deviate our path to avoid a collision, and that zone has fairly precise spatial limits, as suggested in the figure. For example we can tell in advance whether an overhead obstacle will require us to duck or divert our path as we pass it, or whether a narrowing in the path will require us to pull in our arms, or to turn sideways to squeeze through. This fieldlike zone can therefore be considered as a quantitative description of observed behavior *as if* breaking this field triggered the behavioral response. In fact, this description can also be seen as a computational algorithm, or, a fieldlike decision strategy that specifies how that observed behavior might be computed in a robotic system, given that that system is capable of computing a volumetric projection of the body profile forward into a volumetric model of perceived space. In the example shown in Fig. 10.6A, the trajectory deviates smoothly to avoid an open manhole in the road. It is the negative valence represented by the obstacle that causes the deviation in the planned path. The spatial extent of this snakelike percept could be measured psychophysically by observing how long subjects can continue to walk around obstacles after their vision has been unexpectedly occluded, or how far away the sudden appearance of an obstacle would cause a deviation in the subject's path. The planned trajectory also encodes the pattern of footsteps, as suggested in Fig. 10.6A and B, although this step planning does not seem to occur out as far as the planned path.

The range of step planning could also be determined psychophysically by measuring how far away an obstacle that suddenly appears in the path affects the periodicity of the steps. Figure 10.6B depicts a different strategy to avoid the open manhole in the walker's path, which in this case causes the walker to plan to take a couple of shorter steps, followed by a longer step to hop over the manhole. In a more complex natural environment, every part of the terrain is marked by irregular patches of positive and negative valence, which direct not only the sinuous path of the planned trajectory percept, but also the periodicity of the stepping pattern. Like a pinion cog rolling across a toothed rack, the phase of the stepping rotation locks itself to the pattern of valences in the terrain, except in this case the pinion wheel must warp or deform in order to anticipate the irregular spacing of the teeth on the rack, with step points chosen to match positive valence regions, and intervals between steps aligning themselves with regions of negative valence, while maintaining maximal periodicity and smoothness in the path profile. Whenever such variations are made in the walking pattern, every component of the complex synchrony of movements of the feet, hips, shoulders, and arms is automatically modulated in analog fashion to match the modified pattern of periodicity. Whatever the neurophysiological underpinnings of this behavior, these are the observed properties of motor synchronization. A coupled oscillator (Dewan, 1976; Strogatz & Stewart, 1993; Cutting et al., 1978) or harmonic resonance model offers a computational mechanism with these properties because harmonic resonance has a natural tendency to couple between connected systems and thereby to maintain synchronization between its component oscillating parts.

SYNCHRONIZED DANCE AND MILITARY DRILL

One of the most interesting aspects of motor performance observed in human behavior across cultures is a common tendency for geometrical arrays of people to move in synchronized patterns, as seen in a chorus line, in ballet, in tribal and folk dances, and in more crisp and rigid form in military drill. The principle of indirect realism in conjunction with harmonic resonance theory offers an explanation for this peculiar behavior. The images of other people's bodies appear as a data structure in phenomenal space, just as does the image of one's own body, and therefore it is as natural to see the common pattern in a line of dancers at a distance as it is to share that common pattern by being one of the dancers in the line. This kind of synchronization is also observed in the schooling of fish and the flocking of birds, where each individual locks their bodily motions to the global pattern defined by the flock or school. In a very real sense the individuals in a flock or school are coupled by bidirectional causal reactions into a larger collective entity, in much the same way that different cortical areas are coupled in the brain.

The perceptual relation between one's own body and that of another person also offers an account for the otherwise mysterious phenomenon that very young infants are able to mimic facial expressions. Phenomenological examination suggests that we can perceive our own facial expression as an amodal spatial percept, somewhat like viewing a mask from the inside, and that the motor representation of facial expression is encoded as a spatial field that generates an elastic deformation of a canonical face. The nature of the vertex representation of spatial structure presented in chapter 6 is indifferent to whether the object is viewed from the inside or from the outside. For example, a cube possesses an eightfold symmetry of vertices, whether you are viewing a cube in your hand or standing inside a cubical room.

The field-theoretical concepts introduced in this chapter to account for the fieldlike control of motor behavior therefore suggests that similar fieldlike principles are also employed in perception to make sense of the body motions of other persons and animals. When we see a person walking, we immediately apprehend the global pattern of their motion, as if seeing smooth sinusoidal oscillations that seem to carry the body with their motion, as seen in exaggerated form in the motion of cartoon characters. This is the kind of explanation that is required to account for the perception of biological motion in the experiments of Johansson (1973), in which subjects view moving bodies in a dark room with tiny point lights attached at key points. The motion of the lights alone is sufficient to generate a percept of the body as a whole, as if the point lights were being carried by swirling vortices whose global patterns reveal the essential motions of the body.

FIELD THEORY OF NAVIGATION

Koffka (1935, pp. 42–46) proposed a model of local navigation in terms of valence fields that attract or repel the body percept in a perceptual model of the world. Brett et al. (2001) found supporting psychophysical evidence for a field theory of navigation in the pattern of paths taken by subjects in a virtual world on their way to a target object. Hartgenbusch (1927) presented a clear example of this concept in a soccer game, where the opponent's goal serves as the positive valence, attracting the players of one team wherever they stand on the field. The player who has control of the ball responds to this global attractive force, but responds also to the many local negative valence fields represented by players from the opposing team who threaten to block his path. At any moment in time, the field of valences on the soccer pitch could be mapped like a set of flow lines. All the player has to do is to follow the path of least resistance along the strongest flow lines toward the goal. This suggests that the thought patterns used for navigational calculations are not expressed as logical decision sequences, as suggested in the algorithmic paradigm of digital computation, but that navigational thoughts can take the form of spatial fields in the brain built to match the perceived terrain.

The reason why such thought processes have been traditionally described as logical decision sequences is that the higher level selection of alternative paths, or the navigational decision-making process, is indeed experienced in the form of discrete decisions, especially when expressed at the verbal level of conscious decision making. The choice between two paths is indeed a logical decision process, somewhat analogous to the bistability of the Necker cube, for a decision to pursue one particular path eliminates alternative paths from consideration. However, the elements of that decision—the perceived paths themselves, and the perceived promise and risk of each path—are expressed at the lowest level as fieldlike entities in the brain. The field of forces is in a state of constant flux, and is not necessarily identical in different players' perceptions. The field in a particular player's head changes abruptly whenever he notices a new threat, or a new opening to the goal.

Gibson and Crooks (1938) proposed a similar field theory model of driving. They proposed that obstacles generate a negative valence field, and a moving obstacle—that is,

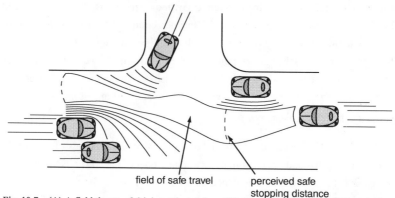

field of safe travel   perceived safe
                                    stopping distance

Fig. 10.7   (A) A field theory of driving, adapted from Gibson and Crooks (1938). Every obstacle presents a field of threat, and moving obstacles present a larger field of threat in the direction of motion. A driver steers his vehicle through a field of safe travel, which is perceived as a snakelike field of influence that winds its way between perceived obstacles.

another vehicle—projects a field of negative valence out in the direction of motion. The spatial range of that valence field is modulated by that vehicle's perceived speed and momentum; the higher the speed, the more stopping distance the vehicle requires, and therefore the longer its field of threat is perceived to extend out in front of it. This concept is depicted schematically in Fig. 10.7. The strength of the field is also modulated by the presence of perceived obstacles in the vehicle's path. If the straight path of a rapidly moving vehicle is blocked by an obstacle, the field of threat is perceived to spill out to either side of the obstacle wherever an opening is perceived, and the intensity of this diverted field in any direction is inversely proportional to the number of alternative openings available, thereby representing the perceived probability of that vehicle's taking any particular path.

As in the case of walking, the perceptual computation required to construct a field of intended progress of a vehicle in motion can be described as a linear projection of an amodal extension of that vehicle in the direction of motion. This perceptual computation is similar in principle of computation to the kind of projection proposed earlier to model the perceived propagation of light through space by forward ray-tracing, except that this projection can also express smooth deviations from a straight path as required to avoid obstacles. When viewed from within the vehicle, this projected path is subject to foreshortening by perspective; therefore, this amodal percept can be used to estimate the clearance between obstacles in the vehicle's path in terms of the vehicle's lateral and vertical dimensions.

LONG-RANGE NAVIGATION

The navigational function just described involves navigation to points that fall within the perceptual sphere. A different kind of computation is required for longer range navigation to points so distant that the path cannot be represented in the immediate sphere of local space. This kind of navigation requires some kind of abstraction of the geometry of the intended path. Introspective examination suggests the following properties of that abstracted representation. Consider the image that comes to mind when given the directions "take the first right, then right again, and then the first left." Note that in this typical format for informal directions, no distance is necessary for the individual legs, except if a leg is much longer or shorter than other legs. There is a great deal of invariance in the typical directions to variations in the exact geometry of the path, being more of a topological rather than topographical descriptor. This makes perfect sense given that no specific action is required along each of the individual legs except to continue until the next landmark. The turns need not even be exact right angles, being described only in sufficient detail to eliminate alternative wrong choices. These properties are not unique to navigation in our man-made environment of roads and intersections, but apply also in natural environments as when following rivers, coastlines, well-worn tracks, or any other discernible linear contour dividing dissimilar patches of terrain.

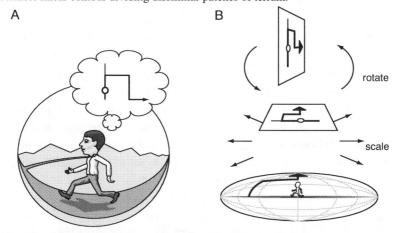

Fig. 10.8   (A) For navigation beyond the range of immediately perceived space, a mental map appears in a disconnected mental space, in a manner somewhat like the experience of consulting an actual map. Usually the mental map appears with the forward direction uppermost. (B) This mental map can be rotated and scaled mentally, and it can even be scaled up to full size and superimposed on the perceived world, with the proper perspective distortions automatically applied.

I propose that the mental image of this example appears somewhat as shown in the "thought cloud" of Fig. 10.8A. I find that I can manipulate this mental map, rotating it clockwise or counter-clockwise in my mind, and scaling it up or down, independent of my current direction of progress, although I find the map easiest to use when oriented with the frontal direction at the top, or perhaps with north or some other cardinal direction at the top, as when reading a real map. In other words, the representation appears to be invariant to translation, rotation, and scale, although in order to image it I must view it mentally at a particular orientation and scale. Furthermore, it is also possible to see the map projected in the proper orientation on the world around me, for otherwise the map would be useless for navigation in the real world. In other words, I can rotate the map mentally into the horizontal plane, and scale it up to full size, as suggested in Fig. 10.8B, and superimpose it amodally on the world model in the perceptual sphere, with the proper perspective distortion automatically applied. In this configuration most of the map, except for the part representing the immediate vicinity, is squashed by perspective onto the horizon line. This concept is illustrated schematically in Fig. 10.8, where the mental map, depicted in the "thought cloud" as a separate spatial representation, can be coupled to the perceptual sphere, where the mapped path is projected at the proper scale and location in the percept of the external world.

Confirmation of this phenomenological observation comes from the fact that people given verbal directions can relate them spatially either to a sketch on a piece of paper, or to the external world of immediate experience, and they can relate those two representations feature for feature with one another, thereby demonstrating a coupling between different spatial representations through an invariance relation. An isomorphic coupling between the two mental spaces ensures that manipulations performed on one copy of the path have an immediate effect on the other copy. For example, the thought "which turn is that up ahead?" might be expressed as a kind of question mark superimposed on the percept of the turn in the road up ahead, and the attentional lighting up of that perceived feature at that point in space would in turn highlight the corresponding feature in the mental map. The lighting up in the global map represents the answer to the self-posed question, coupling the feature in local space to a feature in the global map, allowing the view of that feature in the world to update the man's perceived position in the global map.

Once again, the models described here to illustrate the concepts presented are necessarily somewhat speculative, and the details remain to be confirmed with quantitative psychophysical tests. However, these speculations are perfectly consistent with the subjective experience of motor control. The more general message of the present modeling approach is therefore that the subjective experience of motor control, like that of perception and cognition, is a valuable source of evidence into the nature of the computational processes underlying those experiences. The models presented here merely demonstrate one way that these subjective observations can be quantified in computational models of motor control, both as a quantitative description of behavior and as a model of perceptual computation.

Chapter 11

A Psycho-Aesthetic Hypothesis

THE BIOLOGICAL COMPONENT OF CULTURE

If human nature is factored into biological and cultural components, the biological component of behavior is likely to manifest itself in properties observed across all cultures through space and time, whereas the cultural component of behavior is likely to vary from one society to the next. Arnheim (1988, pp. 1–2) extended this argument into the world of aesthetics. Although there is a great degree of variation in the arts of different cultures, there is also much that is common among them. In particular, factors such as balance, harmony, symmetry, and periodicity, as well as an elegant simplicity of the component forms, are universal laws of aesthetics. This suggests that these aspects of aesthetic judgment are likely to be properties inherent in the human mind. One of the most prominent features of human aesthetics is a pronounced preference for symmetry and periodicity. This preference is seen in all of our decorative arts, especially the patterns of ornament with which we adorn our clothing, carpets, wallpaper, floors, vases, lamps, and such—in fact virtually every artifact that we use, and most especially those items of symbolic and ceremonial use in which we place the most value. It can hardly be an accident that these most general properties of aesthetic preference are also characteristic properties of harmonic resonance: symmetry and periodicity both in simple and compound hierarchical form, as well as simplicity and elegance of the basic repeating elements.

The patterns of ornament observed across cultures appear to be reified manifestations, or ideal exemplars of the Gestalt laws of perceptual grouping, which have been shown to be significant factors in perception. The principles of similarity, proximity, good continuation, closure, symmetry, periodicity, and so on are characteristic of virtually all human art and decorative design. These patterns of regularity and spatiotemporal order are not confined to the visual arts, but extend into every dimension of aesthetic and functional activity, including music, rhythm, poetry, dance, and architecture, and even into the abstract world of mathematics. Several authors have proposed that the properties that we find to be pleasing in all aspects of aesthetic activity are pleasing exactly because those properties are easily represented in the internal code of our perceptual mechanism (Arnheim, 1969a; Herzberger & Epstein, 1988); that the beauty in music, art, and dance reflects a similarity between the beautiful work and the natural structure of the mind; and that beauty is perceived in objects that are complex enough to fully engage our perceptual system without overloading it with excess complexity, and when that complexity is expressed in a form that is naturally and efficiently encoded by our perceptual mechanism (Sander, 1931). This relationship between the laws of aesthetics and the structure of mind might be called a *psycho-aesthetic* hypothesis. The psycho-aesthetic hypothesis offers a promising avenue toward an eventual *consilience*, or unification of the disparate worlds of science and the humanities, an objective that Edward O. Wilson (1998) identified as the greatest enterprise of human intellectual discovery.

If the psycho-aesthetic hypothesis is correct, then the principle can also be inverted, to deduce the properties of the perceptual representation by the common properties observed in human art across cultures. I begin therefore with a discussion of the similarities across aesthetic media, which are therefore likely to reflect properties of the human mind. I then show how these common properties suggest a periodic basis set underlying the mental representation, as suggested by the harmonic resonance theory. I show how the properties observed in art, such as balance and harmony in visual and auditory composition, as well as in poetry and dance, can be used to derive properties of this representation. I suggest further that those special aspects of religion and spirituality that are common across cultures also reflect properties of the mind, and that many aspects of human spirituality can be seen as an unconscious recognition of the truth of indirect realism. I conclude the chapter with a discussion of how the properties of harmonic resonance as a mechanism for mental representation might be explored in greater depth in future research.

Although there has been some measure of speculation throughout this book, in this final chapter that speculation soars to new heights. There has always been a segment of the scientific community that looks askance at speculation as an activity unworthy of true science. A prominent subtheme of this book has been a defense of speculation and vivid mental imagery not only as a secret indulgence of scientists performed in private, but even as a public, publishable activity, for speculation is the very essence of mental imagery and thought experimentation. In fact, there is no clear dividing line between hypotheses and speculation, for both are the legitimate tools of science to penetrate deeper into the fog of mystery. The more rigorous quantitative analysis and logical proofs practiced in "normal science" (to use Kuhn's terminology) can be seen as merely the mopping-up operation after speculation has done its work (Kuhn, 1970). Those scientists who delight in speculation and "thought experimentation" are sometimes undervalued or even shunned in science, in the mistaken belief that speculations are not valid scientifically until they have been confirmed beyond a shadow of doubt. In fact, nothing could be farther from the truth, for in reality science is the art of speculation, and, *cogito ergo sum* notwithstanding, all of science is nothing more than an elaborate system of speculations, whose truth is validated not by definitive proof, as much as by consensus in the scientific community. No theory has ever been proven beyond a shadow of doubt, for theories are built upon axioms, which are themselves no more than speculations. This is not to suggest a kind of scientific relativism whereby all theories are equally valid, for science assumes the existence of an objective external world with properties that are objectively real, and therefore some theories must be necessarily closer to that objective reality than others. However, science is forever denied any absolute certainty about its foundational assumptions and should therefore remain eternally receptive to alternative paradigmatic hypotheses.

Speculation and mental imagery are particularly important when the case being argued has a Gestalt character—that is, when no single definitive *experimenta crucis* can yet be devised to decide the issue because the evidence lies scattered across a broad range of diverse phenomena that all point to the same unifying central hypothesis. Evidence in the abstract world of ideas can often take a form similar to the evidence for the dog in the dog picture of Fig. 1.4, which requires some kind of emergent process of mental judgment as opposed to the hard logic of absolute certainty often held up as the scientific ideal. In fact, Kuhn pointed out that many of the great debates in science seem to have had this Gestalt nature, where the same facts that appear convincing to some leave others unconvinced, because the very interpretation of the evidence is colored by one's basic assumptions, which are exactly what is in question. In Kuhn's words (Kuhn, 1970, pp. 156–157): *Paradigm debates are not really about relative problem-solving ability... . Instead, the issue is which paradigm should in the future guide research on problems many of which neither competitor can yet claim to resolve completely. A decision between alternate ways of practicing science is called for, and in the circumstances that decision must be based less on past achievement than on future promise. ... Something must make at least a few scientists feel that the new proposal is on the right track, and sometimes it is only personal and inarticulate aesthetic considerations that can do that.* This chapter is an appeal to the aesthetic judgment of the reader to see the evidence for a harmonic resonance in biological computation scattered far and wide through a great variety of diverse human activities and behaviors.

COMMON PROPERTIES ACROSS THE ARTS

Let us begin with periodicity in its simplest form, and how it manifests itself in visual, auditory, and motor modalities. Consider, for example, the regular beat of a metronome, marking off equal intervals of time. We only need to hear three or four beats to perceive the sound as a finite sample from an infinite pattern of regularity stretching to infinity in past and future directions, although that pattern is perceived amodally, based on the limited given sample, which is itself experienced as a modal percept. Notice the transformation that occurs in the perception of the temporal structure in the following example. Consider the stimulus of a metronome, or regular drum beat, that begins with a number of beats equally spaced in time:

tum tum tum...

In the instant that the next beat should occur, that beat is anticipated perceptually, based on the rhythm established by the earlier beats. If the next beat should fail to occur where expected, or if it should occur in a different form, that violation of expectation is experienced in the form of a new perceived pattern. For example, the sequence

*tum tum tum **boom**...*

immediately suggests the infinite compound pattern

*...tum tum tum **boom** tum tum tum **boom** tum tum tum **boom**...*

Now observe the development of this pattern given a longer stimulus of the form

*tum tum tum **boom** tum tum tum (rest)...*

where the (rest) is an unexpected silence instead of a beat. This stimulus immediately suggests the repeating pattern

*...tum tum tum **boom** tum tum tum (rest) tum tum tum **boom** tum tum tum (rest)...*

and all subsequent auditory stimuli are experienced with respect to this expected pattern. In other words, if the stimulus continues in accordance with this pattern, no further information is gained from it as more beats are heard. This perceptual completion of a periodic stimulus is likely to be a low-level or primitive function of perception, because a similar phenomenon has been observed in simple animals such as rays and turtles, under the name of *omitted stimulus potential* (Bullock & Hofmann, 1991; Bullock, Karamürsel, & Hofmann, 1993). A periodic series of stimuli, such as clicks or flashes of light, are presented to the animals, whose scalps are wired for electro-encephalogram (EEG) recording. Each stimulus spike produces a corresponding spike in the EEG recording. When an unexpected pause occurs in the series, a prominent potential spike is observed in the EEG recording, occurring exactly at the time when the omitted stimulus would have been expected.

Meyer (1967) drew a connection between patterns of music and information theory, and suggested that such latent expectations represent the necessary conditions for the communication of musical information, while the disturbances, or breaks in the musical pattern, are the carriers of the information in the musical message. This is directly analogous to the spatial completion of patterns discussed in chapter 6, where a finite sample is presumed to be representative of the pattern as a whole, and is completed accordingly in amodal form.

The direct analogy between the perceptual completion of spatial and temporal patterns suggests a common mechanism or principle for the representation of spatial and temporal pattern in the brain. It suggests a representation of pattern that uses a periodic basis set, like a Fourier representation, for the unseen portion of the pattern filled in amodally is periodic in nature. The compound patterns seen in visual ornament, as exemplified in Fig. 6.8, are reflected in similar compound structures in music, as observed in a Bach fugue, with its nested patterns of symmetry and periodicity. In fact, the Gestalt principles of symmetry, proximity, good continuation, closure, and so on have all been identified as properties of musical as well as of visual form (Coren et al., 1994). The property of invariance is also manifest in the perception of melody, for the identity of a melody remains unchanged when transposed to different keys, or when heard at different tempos, or when played on different instruments. In fact, the invariance of melody as described by von Ehrenfels (1890) was one of the key factors in the launching of the Gestalt movement. The invariance to changes in tempo can even survive a tempo of zero rate, as if the pattern of the melody were somehow frozen in time. Consider for example the first seven notes of the tune "Ma-ry had a lit-tle lamb-." It is possible to stop the tune in mid-stride at this or any other point, like a suspended animation, and to continue again in stepwise manner one note at a time, with arbitrary pauses in between, as is done routinely in musical analysis, or when learning a tune on a musical instrument. The melody is therefore experienced in a sense somehow outside of time, as an eternal static pattern, although that pattern can be replayed at will at any tempo or key. The tendency toward closure in musical form suggests a circular representation, like the representation of geometrical form proposed in chapter 6 based on a pattern of symmetry about a center, along with a dynamic component as suggested in chapter 8 in the section on dynamic pattern formation.

The fundamental periodicity observed in perception is also seen in the more abstracted world of mathematics, whose unit is the number, a periodic entity that subdivides the number line into equal intervals, just like the bars of a spatial grid, or the regular ticks of the metronome, extending to infinity in opposite directions. The unitary interval of the number line that sets the scale for the entire pattern is a dimensionless interval that adapts itself to whatever units are required for the task at hand, in exactly the same manner that spatial and temporal perception adapts itself to the periodicity of whatever finite pattern is given as a stimulus, for the periodicity of perception is defined relative to the stimulus itself, rather than to any objective unit of space or time, such as a meter, or a second.

The relationship between music and motor control can be examined by playing music and observing how it provokes a spontaneous reaction in people, who exhibit an almost insuppressible urge to tap a toe or finger to the rhythm, and when all social inhibitions are released to gyrate their whole bodies to the beat, in a most elegant demonstration of the true capacities of the motor system. Tiny tiddley tunes are suggestive of smaller tapping movements of the extremities, whereas heavy thumping tunes suggest more powerful pounding of the feet, and extravagant flowing melodies suggest a disembodied free flight of the spirit, as expressed in the waltz and in ballet. It is interesting that music, when interpreted as a motor signal in dance, does not dictate precise movements of the limbs, but rather music appears to encode a more abstracted motor signal defining the general character of the movement in an essentially Gestalt way. Like mathematics, therefore, music represents a higher order of invariance independent of any particular sensory stimulus or modality.

A PERIODIC BASIS SET

The concept of a basis set is an interesting one. The idea is that a pattern is encoded in terms of its similarity to some selected basis function. The basis function can be virtually any waveform. For example, the Fourier transform represents pattern in terms of a sinusoidal function, whereas the Hadamard transform uses a square-wave basis function. The basis function need not even be periodic, as seen for example in the wavelet transform that uses a basis function that does not extend to infinity, but represents pattern in terms of a finite functional form in space or time. Although virtually any pattern can be expressed to arbitrary precision using virtually any basis function, different types of pattern are expressed more efficiently in different basis sets, in the sense that in one basis function the entire pattern might be captured in just a few low-order terms, whereas using a different basis function that same pattern would require an infinite set of higher order terms. For example, a smooth, rolling pattern is more efficiently expressed in the smooth sinusoids of a Fourier representation, whereas a pattern with abrupt step-like transitions between flat plateaus is usually expressed more efficiently in the square wave of a Hadamard code. Similarly, a pattern containing a lot of periodicity is usually encoded more efficiently with a periodic basis set, whereas a nonperiodic pattern is more efficiently encoded using a nonperiodic basis set.

Although in theory a basis set can use an infinite set of high order terms for the encoding, in a real physical coding system the signal is necessarily band limited. In that case, the use of an inappropriate basis function results in artifacts in the coded signal. For example, a single square-wave pulse encoded in the Fourier representation using a finite set of terms (or equivalently, applying a low-pass filter) results in periodic sinusoidal wavelike artifacts appearing in the decoded signal. Figure 11.1A shows a two-dimensional input image, which is then transformed to a Fourier representation; a low-pass filter is applied, and then an inverse Fourier transform is applied, producing the image shown in Fig. 11.1B. This image therefore expresses the portion of the pattern that is captured in the low order terms of a band-limited Fourier representation. Figure 11.1C depicts a high-pass filtered version of the image, showing the part of the information from Fig. 11.1A that was lost in Fig. 11.1B. If the low-pass and high-pass images are added, pixel for pixel, this produces an exact a reconstruction of the original image. Figures 11.1D through Fig. 11.1F show band-pass filtered versions of the same image using three different spatial frequency bands from low to high, to indicate the kind of information that is encoded in each band of spatial frequency. A prominent "ringing" artifact is observed in these filtered images that suggests intuitively how the nonperiodic patterns of the image are expressed in terms of the periodic basis function, and a similar but more subtle ringing is also observed in the low-pass and high-pass filtered images.

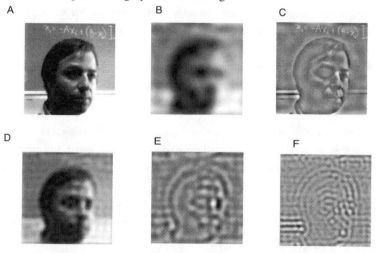

Fig. 11.1   (A) Original image. (B) Fourier low-pass filtered version of the original, in which the higher harmonic frequencies are eliminated. (C) Fourier high-pass filtered version in which lower frequencies are eliminated. (D through F) Band-pass filtered versions of the original, at three different spatial frequency bands, showing how the irregular pattern of the input image is expressed in terms of patterns of periodicity in the imge. Note that the ringing artifacts observed in these images reflect the global Gestalt-like features of the image, such as the circular head centered in the square frame.

A similar kind of ringing is observed in patterns that appear spontaneously in the visual field under intoxication by psychedelic substances, such as LSD or mescaline. Heinrich Klüver (1966) categorized various constant pattern types observed under mescaline intoxication, which subjects described using terms such as lattice, fretwork, filigree, honeycomb, and chessboard patterns, as well as cobwebs, tunnel, and funnel patterns. The form constants were further characterized by varied and saturated colors, intense brightness and symmetrical configurations. Klüver made the crucial observation that these form constants appear in a wide variety of hallucinatory conditions, which, counting also conditions identified by later researchers (Siegel, 1977), include falling asleep, waking up, insulin hypoglycemia, the delirium of fever, epilepsy, psychotic episodes, advanced syphilis, sensory deprivation, photostimulation, electrical stimulation, crystal gazing, migraine headaches, dizziness, and of course a variety of drug intoxications. Siegel (1977) extended this work to investigate more complex hallucinated scenes, in which subjects reported seeing religious symbols and images, animals, and humans, many in the nature of cartoons and caricatures. These images were often projected against a background of geometric forms, which frequently combined, duplicated, and superimposed on each other. Siegel also mentioned that during the peak hallucinatory periods subjects frequently described themselves as having become part of the imagery, with a feeling of dissociation from their bodies. Siegel commented that some of these patterns are strikingly similar to the primordial or archetypal forms such as the mandala, the mystic symbol of the universe employed in Hinduism and Buddhism as an aid to meditation. Moreover, as many anthropologists have noted, the hallucinogen-inspired art of many primitive peoples often contains similar geometrical patterns of form, color, and movement (Lewis-Williams & Dowson, 1988).

I propose that these spontaneous patterns of regularity reflect the natural resonance of the visual system in response to the ambient noise, which is apparently amplified (or insufficiently suppressed) under the influence of psychedelic drugs or other conditions of high stress, in the manner of the Fourier band-pass images shown in Fig. 11.1. These features also bear a certain resemblance to paintings by artist Louis Wain. Wain made a career of depicting generally realistic pictures of cats. But after he was afflicted with a progressive psychosis, his pictures progressively deteriorated into periodic and symmetric patterns, as shown in Fig. 11.2. As in the case of psychedelic drugs, I propose that these periodic patterns are evidence of a periodic basis set that is used to encode spatial form in the visual system. A similar property is observed in the patterns of ornament, as seen in decorative patterns on carpets, or the elaborations of architecture that adorn a building or archway, for these decorative patterns are most often devised to subdivide or multiplicate some basic interval. Figure 11.3 shows some patterns of ornament from a range of different historical styles selected somewhat arbitrarily from Speltz (1910), except that I have endeavored to select nonrepresentational or abstract patterns of ornament, to illustrate that the regularities in these patterns are not just copied from the regularities of nature. However, inevitably some representational features appear in these designs,

Fig. 11.2   Artist Louis Wain, who made a career of painting realistic pictures of cats, was afflicted with a progressive psychosis, which revealed itself in his art by a progressive increase in the symmetry and periodicity of his depictions of cats. (A) First only the textured regions succumb to periodicity. (B) Next, local features such as tufts of fur begin to exhibit more periodicity and similarity to neighboring tufts. (C and D) Finally the entire figure takes on the appearance of an ornamental pattern, characterized by a global symmetry adorned with hierarchical patterns of local symmetry.

especially in floral motifs, and human and animal forms are common themes in ornamental design. This too is consistent with the general theme of the present hypothesis: that there is no clear dividing line between the abstract geometrical forms of perception, and the more deliberate representational forms in cognition. This blending of the two is readily apparent in the patterns of ornament. Note that the various subpatterns in visual ornament are often seen replicated in mirror-symmetric arrangements, or at a variety of translations, rotations, and scales, or the same visual pattern is seen replicated in different variations at different places, like the variations on a theme in musical form, which is suggestive of a harmonic resonance representation. The fact that geometrical similarity is apprehended preattentively across variations of rotation, translation, and scale, as seen in visual ornament, is clear evidence for invariance in perception manifest through art.

A periodic basis set has the advantage that when a pattern is found to match a particular basis function, that match automatically generates predictions and postdictions out into the past and future, or extrapolates outward spatially in both directions, as observed in

Fig. 11.3   A number of patterns of ornamental design selected somewhat arbitrarily from Speltz (1910) from a wide variety of diverse cultural sources. These patterns demonstrate the universal human tendency to fill blank regions with periodic and symmetrical patterns.

perception. A nonperiodic basis set, on the other hand, while perhaps accurately expressing isolated events to which a match is found, tells nothing about the implications of one event for other events into the past or the future. This, I propose, is the reason why the brain makes use of a periodic basis set. The latticework patterns seen in Fig. 11.2 and 11.3 are a modal depiction of a structure that remains amodal in normal vision and represents the spatial "predictions" made by the visual system based on the visible sample of the scene by the representative sample principle. A similar phenomenon in the cognitive realm is captured in the adage "History repeats itself." In fact, nothing could be farther from the truth, for history has never repeated itself; every historical event is unique to the smallest possible detail. However, whatever the vague global similarities are that might be found between past and present events, those similarities are of particular interest for the human observer, for they allow us to "predict" the future from the present (in a very uncertain manner) based on the patterns from the past.

The periodicity in the patterns of ornament can be seen either as a subdivision of an existing space, as in the case of the doorways shown in Fig. 11.3, or as a repetition or multiplication of a basic element, depending on whether the pattern is considered outward from the element, or inward from the larger design. These patterns in perception correspond to the concepts of multiplication and division in mathematics. I propose that these ornamental variations are an expression of the kinds of patterns that would be stimulated in the mind of the observer of a plain unadorned doorway or panel of the same dimensions. The difference is that in normal perception, the percept remains in an unstable balance between all of the infinite variety of ornamental patterns, with each one being perceived in a subliminal and fleeting form, whereas only one pattern is frozen and reified in the ornamental design. Siegel (1977) wrote that the geometric patterns observed under psychedelic intoxication are reported to morph into different patterns at a rate of up to 10 times per second. I propose that the purpose of these multiplicative and divisive periodicities is to offer a reference frame or grid, like that of a ruler or of graph paper, but expressed explicitly in relative terms, relative to the unit size of the given object in perception. It is this kind of invisible or amodal latticework generated by perceptual processes that helps us to estimate the midpoint of an interval, as when hanging a picture on a wall between other objects with a pleasing balance, or to extrapolate from a given unit, as when expressing distance in car lengths, or hand spans.

The concept is well illustrated in the perception of musical pitch. When two musical notes are compared either simultaneously, as in a chord, or successively, as a two-note "melody," each pitch is perceived relative to the other. If one tone is held constant, as a reference tone f_0, and the other tone f_1 is varied up and down as a test tone, a periodic pattern is found in a plot of the *consonance* or measure of pleasing harmony between the two tones. Helmholtz (1863//1954) proposed that the principle behind this pattern of consonance is an interaction between the higher harmonics of the two tones, thereby drawing a connection between aesthetic judgement and the principle of harmonic resonance. Figure 11.4 shows the consonance plot as calculated by a modern refinement of Helmholtz's theory (Sethares, 1998). Figure 11.4A plots the consonance between two notes as one is held at a reference frequency, marked f_0 in the figure, while the other ranges from that frequency to the next higher octave or $2 \times f_0$, and Fig. 11.4B plots the consonance from f_0 down to the next octave below, or frequency $.5 \times f_0$.. The consonance

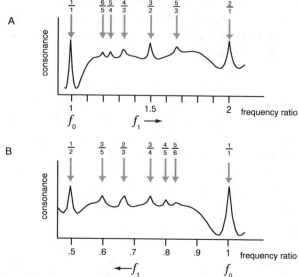

Fig. 11.4   Plots of consonance between two notes as a reference tone f_0 is held fixed at one frequency (normalized here to frequency $f_0 = 1$) while a test tone f_1 is varied (A) from that frequency to the octave above (frequency $f_1 = 2$), and (B) from that same frequency (frequency 1) down to the octave below (frequency $f_1 = 0.5$). The peaks in these plots mark the points of consonance, which define a structured pattern at integer ratios between the frequencies of the reference and test tones.

function is characterized by a pattern of peaks that occur where the test tone hits frequencies that are either integer multiples or fractions of the reference tone, that is, at frequencies $f_0 \times 1, 2, 3, \ldots$ and $f_0 \times \frac{1}{2}, \frac{1}{3}, \frac{1}{4}, \ldots$ and so on. The consonance function depends on the timbre, or composition of higher harmonics of the two tones. This phenomenon is a direct analogy of the spatial periodicity in Fig. 11.3, for the percept of a single note generates a subliminal ringing at all of its lower and higher harmonics, creating a subjective auditory experience of a rich complex tone composed of the fundamental and its higher harmonics, even when the stimulus is a pure tone without higher harmonics. In fact this ringing effect, known as "Kemp's echo," has been recorded as a physical vibration of the basilar membrane in the cochlea when presented with a pure tone stimulus (Khanna, Ulfendahl, & Flock, 1989a, 1989b). These subliminal percepts correspond to the visual ringing seen in patterns of ornament, which are also expressed as higher and lower harmonics of spatial frequency in the visual domain. The harmony between musical tones therefore also relates to the concepts of multiplication and division in mathematics. For example, a scale that goes up by octaves from C_0 to C_1 to C_2 and so on is like the two-times multiplication table, whereas a descending octave scale is like the successive division by two. Irrational numbers like π, according to this analogy, correspond to a dissonant interval between two notes, where the reference tone represents the unit value, or 1, which is why Pythagoras was so distressed to discover that the circular circumference is related to its radius by such an inharmonious relation. As in Fig. 11.3, these interactions are not really of a binary nature as in the comparison of two tones, but more of a synergistic harmony between all of the features in a visual scene, or all of the notes in a symphony interacting across frequency and time.

The relative measure between a reference quantity and the comparison quantity might also account for the phenomenon of Weber's law in psychology, whereby the psychophysical measure of many perceived quantities (brightness, loudness, weight, etc.) often follows a logarithmic function. For example, if an object were to suddenly double in size, this growth would be perceived as a more salient change than if it were subsequently to grow by an equal increment to three times the original size. In order to produce perceptually equal increments in size, that object would have to double its size every time; that is, the progression 1, 2, 4, 8, 16, when expressed in some perceptual quantity is usually experienced as somehow regular or uniform, whereas the progression 1, 2, 3, 4, 5, is perceived in some sense as a decelerating growth, because the second step doubles in size, whereas the last step represents a growth of only $^4/_5$ or $1^1/_4$ times the size of the previous stage. This is why the measure of perceptual sensitivity is usually expressed in terms of relative change, or Weber fraction, for that quantity has been found to remain approximately constant across a large range of perceptual magnitudes. For example the "just noticeable difference" (JND) in perceived weight varies with the weight of the object: a small difference in weight is detectable in light objects, whereas only larger differences are detectable in heavy objects. Perhaps the purest example of such a relative scale is in the perception of musical pitch itself. For example, the octave jumps on a piano keyboard, which are perceived to define equal intervals in pitch, actually represent a frequency doubling with each octave. I propose that the explanation for Weber's law in perception can be traced to a harmonic resonance representation in which the magnitude of sensory stimulation—for example, the frequency of a musical note—is encoded perceptually in terms of its harmonics, as in the musical scale. This is consistent with the harmonic resonance model presented in chapter 8, where the spatial patterns of standing waves in a resonating system are encoded in terms of a bank of oscillators tuned to the frequencies of the various harmonics of the system, where each oscillator of a series is tuned to the next integer multiple of the frequency of the fundamental. Waller's plots of frequency versus pattern, shown in Fig. 8.6B, are thereby analogous to the logarithmic plot of Weber's law.

The subdivision of the musical scale into harmonic intervals provides further evidence for the relationship between harmonic resonance and perceptual aesthetics. Figure 11.5 plots the relationship between frequency F and perceived pitch P, which follows a logarithmic relation of $P = \log_2(F)$, plotted here as the inverse function $F = 2^P$. The frequency in this plot is expressed in units of Hz/261.626, which is the frequency of middle C, so that the frequency of middle C is equal to 1 in these units. A rise of pitch in octaves from C_0 to C_1 to C_2 and so on is perceived as a rise in equal intervals, even though this corresponds to a successive doubling in frequency from 1 to 2 to 4 to 8 and so on. However, the intervals between the octaves in the pitch dimension exhibit a further perceptual subdivision, for the next most consonant interval besides the octave is the interval of the "fifth". The reason for this can be seen in the diagram, for if we rise in equal intervals in frequency, that is, from 1 to 2 to 3, the frequency 3 corresponds to a pitch of 1.585 (rounded to three decimal places), which is 0.585 times the octave interval, just over half way from one C to the next in the pitch dimension, corresponding to the note G. The next most consonant interval in the musical scale is the interval of the third, and the reason for this too can be seen from the diagram, for the frequency 5 corresponds to a pitch of 2.322, which is 0.322 times the distance from one C to the next in the pitch dimension, corresponding to the note E. The major triad, which is the most harmonious combination of three notes in the key of C, is composed of the notes C, E, and G, or 1, 1.322, and 1.585 times the pitch of middle C. The study of musical temperament, or the subdivision of the octave into smaller intervals of a musical scale, is enormously more complex than this brief introduction might suggest, revealing a great depth of structure in the auditory code. However, that code is clearly organized on lawful principles that relate to higher order properties of harmonic resonance. Therefore, the study of music offers a unique window into the organizational structure of mind.

Much of the complexity of musical temperaments stems from the effort to organize the irrational intervals of the musical scale into a regular or periodic pattern on the perceptual pitch scale. For example the Pythagorean tuning is based on the observation that the irrational interval of the fifth, that is, 0.584962..., is almost equal to the rational fraction $7/12$, which actually works out to 0.583333... . Therefore, 12 steps up from middle C, each of the interval of the fifth relative to the previous note, takes us *almost* exactly back to 7 octaves above middle C—actually to 7.01955... times middle C, which is too high by only 0.01955. In the process, these 12 steps encounter every note of the musical scale: C + fifth = G, + fifth = D, and so on to A, E, B, F♯, C♯, A♭, E♭, B♭, F, and then back to C, *almost*. This is the basis of the "circle of fifths" concept of tuning that defines the most basic musical scale. Poor Pythagoras must have been driven to distraction by the residual irrationality of this almost perfect relation. The Western "equal temperament" scale is an attempt to correct this annoying discrepancy by shifting the final note down by 0.01955 to

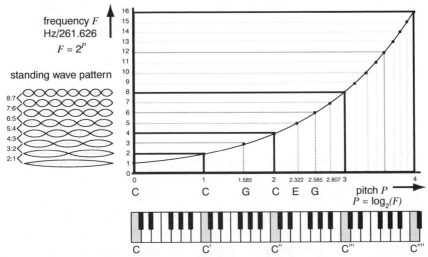

Fig. 11.5   Plot of perceived pitch P, in units of octaves above middle C, as a function of frequency F, expressed in terms of Hz/261.626, which is the frequency of middle C. The pitch is perceived to rise in equal intervals with each octave from C to C' to C'', etc., whereas the frequency doubles with each octave. The linear rise of frequency in integer units from 1 to 2 to 3 creates finer subdivisions of the pitch scale at frequencies 1, 1.585, 2, 2.322, 2.585, etc., and these subdivisions correspond to the subdivision of the octave interval in musical scales. Different tempered scales are proposed to subdivide the octave into rational intervals, in an attempt to impose a periodicity on the pitch dimension. This urge for order in the pitch dimension reflects a hierarchical tendency in search of periodicity of periodicity.

an exact octave, and redistributing the tiny errors between the intervening intervals equally among the various notes of the scale. Ultimately the effort is merely a compromise, and to this day musical theorists bemoan the residual problems due to the stubborn resistance of nature to conform to the rational mind of man. But why should the perceptual scale of pitch even be expected to divide into equal intervals besides the octaves by which that scale is defined? The equal intervals are a feature only of the frequency dimension rather than the pitch dimension, and it is the irrational nature of the logarithmic function that is ultimately responsible for the ugly intervals of the musical scale in the pitch dimension. This persistant search for regularity in the pitch dimension suggests a hierarchical organization in musical pitch perception that seeks to find periodicity of periodicity.

The subdivision of the octave interval need not have stopped at 8 divisions (counting whole notes, as in a major scale), but could just as well have proceeded to much smaller intervals. I propose that this choice of granularity in the representation relates to Miller's magic number of 7 ± 2 (Miller, 1956) as the limit of the number of items that can be stored in short-term memory, and the perceptual limit of six or seven dots on dice that can be counted at a glance, also seen as the limit of the number of wavelengths in Fig. 11.5 that can be counted, and the limit of the platonic solids series as suggested in Fig. 6.7A before the shapes lose their individual character, as well as the number of distinct colors perceived in the spectrum. I propose that these all reflect the basic limits of granularity of the representational code of the human mind.

Although there are similarities between the Fourier band-pass filtered images in Fig. 11.1 and the visual resonances depicted in Fig. 11.2 and 11.3, there are also prominent differences, for the perceived patterns exhibit a sharp square-wave component—regions of uniform color or brightness separated by sharp dividing boundaries, which is suggestive of a square-wave Hadamard code as opposed to the smooth sinusoids of the Fourier code. The properties of art seem to suggest *both* representations, as decorative motifs often use the harsh rectilinear of lines, zigzags, squares, and battlement patterns together with the smooth curves of paisley, floral, and heart motifs in endless combination. We see also both aspects in dance, with smooth flowing motions in ballet, and rigid robotic motions in military drill. In fact, a harmonic resonance representation suggests an answer to this question, for a square-wave function is expressed in Fourier terms as an infinite series of higher harmonics whose frequencies define periodic patterns in frequency space as integer multiples of a fundamental. The frequency spectrum of a square-wave signal is like the spectrum of a musical chord, a harmonious combination of simultaneous notes whose stepwise rise defines an arithmetic sequence in frequency. For a representation that is tuned to periodicity, this *periodicity of periodicities* can be detected as a higher order periodicity, given the proper hierarchical representation. This is the concept behind *Cepstral filtering*, in which a Fourier filtering is performed on a Fourier transform of the original signal, in order to detect the periodicity of the Fourier code. A hierarchical representation based on sinusoidal basis functions would therefore account for square-wave patterns by a waveform composed of a fundamental with a series of higher harmonics, like the notes in a harmonious chord. The smooth curving forms of paisley and ballet represent a more languid compliant feminine nature, because they are captured in the lower harmonic components of a Fourier code, whereas the rigid square-wave features of the checkerboard grid, the Nazi goose step, and the solid blocky structures seen in bank and prison architecture suggests stability, determination, and force, as reflected in the higher energy required to maintain these rigid forms and motions in a standing-wave representation.

THE MISSING FUNDAMENTAL PHENOMENON

A Fourier or harmonic resonance representation of temporal perception suggests an explanation for another otherwise mysterious auditory phenomenon known as the restoration of the missing fundamental. Complex tones such as those produced by the human voice or by musical instruments are composed of different Fourier components, characterized by a fundamental frequency and its higher harmonics. The fundamental corresponds to the frequency that a human listener would describe as the pitch of the perceived note, whereas the higher harmonics are not perceived as separate tones, but are perceived as the characteristic quality, or *timbre,* of the sound, which is the quality that differentiates the sound of a violin from an oboe from a trombone. The higher harmonics are found at integer multiples of the fundamental frequency, and therefore addition of the higher harmonics to the sinusoidal waveform of the fundamental results in a more complex or irregular waveform structure, although that irregular pattern remains periodic, repeating exactly in each cycle of the fundamental.

The reason why the higher harmonics always occur at integer multiples of the fundamental can be traced to the harmonic resonance of the vocal cord, or of the musical instrument that generates the sound. A complex resonating system of this sort oscillates in the same way as a system of massive balls connected by springs. When a ball-and-springs model is energized by a white-noise vibration, it responds by oscillating in a complex harmonic dance, with individual pieces of the structure vibrating in synchrony, although smaller subcomponents will oscillate at integer multiples of the frequency of the structure as a whole. The pattern of this complex oscillation can be understood intuitively by comparison with human dancers gyrating to music, who might shift their weight from foot to foot every second beat of the music, while oscillating their hips vertically with every beat, and swinging their arms in counterphase to the gyration of their hips, and so on, for the human body naturally mimics this kind of compound oscillation, as described by Cutting et al. (1978). The human ear is specifically tuned to detect such compound oscillations in the sound signal, being specifically tuned to detect periodicity. In fact, a real oscillation of a physical system is never perfectly regular, so a real waveform is never perfectly periodic. But the human ear automatically segments a harmonic signal into a percept of a purely periodic signal, in which the various harmonic components are perceived as an integrated whole, together with a percept of noise, like a hissing sound, that appears perceptually distinct from the harmonic signal. Furthermore, if an artificial waveform is constructed of higher harmonics of a fundamental that is missing, then the human ear fills in the missing fundamental as if it were there. For example, a wave composed of frequencies $2f + 3f + 4f$ is perceived as being of frequency f, together with a characteristic timbre defined by the pattern of those higher harmonics.

But this filling in is not merely a perceptual phenomenon. One of the most explicit examples of reification in sensory processing is seen in the basilar membrane, the transducer in the cochlea of the ear that converts the physical vibration of sound into an electrical signal in the auditory nerve. It has been shown that the basilar membrane is not just a passive device like the diaphragm of a microphone, but is an active device like a loudspeaker, capable of generating sound on its own; this sound has been recorded by tiny microphones inserted into the cochlea. The restoration of the missing fundamental therefore appears to be a dynamic property of the basilar membrane, for the restored fundamental frequency has been picked up as an actual sound generated by the basilar membrane. The basilar membrane therefore appears to be a dynamic resonating system whose self-amplified vibration adapts itself to match the incoming sound signal. I propose that this property is not just a bizarre peculiarity of this unique organ, but that it exemplifies the principle of operation of all perceptual processing: that is, that perception operates by generating a reified signal that is tuned to replicate and elaborate on the pattern of regularity picked up by the sensory organ from the environment, and that pattern is expressed in terms of a harmonic resonance representation. I propose that there is a fundamental similarity between the properties of neural tissue and that of the basilar membrane, in that they are both designed to generate resonances expressed as spatiotemporal patterns that are tuned to match the sensory input. Indeed, a visual correlate of the missing fundamental phenomenon has been identified in visual perception (Campbell, Howell, & Robson, 1971; Campbell, Howell, & Johnstone, 1978) in which high-pass filtered images, such as the one shown in Fig. 11.1C, tend to "fill in" perceptually, restoring a percept of large regions of bright and dark between the sharp brightness transitions, which were eliminated by the high-pass filtering. This is the basis of the Craik–O'Brien–Cornsweet illusion (Cornsweet, 1970).

SYMMETRY VERSUS PERIODICITY, RELATIVE VERSUS ABSOLUTE

There is an interesting relationship between the relative and the absolute that can be seen in the contrast between symmetry and periodicity. A periodic pattern suggests an absolute scale that extends to infinity in all directions, like the regular spacing of the number line. A symmetrical pattern, on the other hand, is centered on an origin, which defines the axis of symmetry. This is seen on the number line at the origin, where the countdown of the negative numbers switches to a countup of the positive numbers, like a reversal in a musical scale that reaches a climax before stepping back down again, or like the pattern on a Persian carpet that steps outward in opposite directions from a center. These two paradigms of representation are used in endless combination in art to represent the patterns of the world.

In fact, in a periodic basis set, every solitary pattern in space or time is actually represented as periodic by considering the opposite limits of the pattern to be contiguous with each other. This is seen for example in the Fourier representation of a single image, like Fig. 11.1A, which is encoded mathematically in the Fourier code as if it were a single cycle in an infinitely repeating pattern of identical replicas of that image like a tile pattern extending to infinity in all directions. In the same way, the unitary interval on the number line is the solitary pattern that is repeated to eternity in both directions. When unitary patterns are encoded in a periodic basis set, their opposite sides become adjacent and contiguous in the representation, fusing the isolated unique pattern into a continuous closed space. In the case of a two-dimensional image, this is as if the two-dimensional pattern were painted on the surface of a sphere or torus, thus losing the significance of the transition at the edges of the pattern. This adjacency of opposite boundaries is revealed in a Fourier low-pass filtering of the image, which tends to blur sharp step edges into smoother rolling transitions. This blurring occurs also across the opposite boundaries of the image, because opposite edges that are dissimilar in brightness represent a sharp step function in brightness across the boundary. This sharp transition is blurred like any other edge by the low-pass filtering, resulting in a bleeding of brightness across the boundaries of the image. For example, the top edge of Fig. 11.1B shows a faint light–dark–light echo of the brightness pattern of the bottom edge of that same image, because the patterns from the top and bottom edges tend to bleed into each other with the loss of the higher harmonics, as do the left and right edges of the image.

This bleeding through the limits of the pattern might explain a most curious property of color perception, that the extreme ends of the spectrum of visible light, whose wavelengths are the most dissimilar, appear perceptually as a circular continuum, with red blending to violet through a range of "nonspectral hues," colors that do not correspond to any single wavelength in the physical spectrum. This suggests that color is encoded in the brain in some kind of cyclic phase representation that wraps around on itself in the manner of a Fourier representation. This explanation is also consistent with the aesthetic phenomenon of color balance or harmony. It has been known for some time that colors appear harmonious, or produce a pleasing match, when they define periodic subdivisions of the color circle. A two-tone pattern appears balanced when composed of complementary colors such as red and green, or blue and yellow, which are separated by about 180° on the color circle, whereas a three-tone pattern appears balanced when its colors are separated by 120° on the color circle, like the combination of red, green, and blue. Brightness and saturation, on the other hand, do not exhibit such a closure across the limits. However, closure is observed in spatial perception, where the opposite boundaries of a visible object tend to merge across the hidden rear face, just as the percept of the surrounding world seems to merge behind the head. Closure is also seen as a property of melody, poetry, and decorative design, which implicates a periodic representation.

BALANCE IN VISUAL ART

Since the earliest recorded cultures, the patterns of art have been observed to express certain laws of composition, involving symmetry and balance. Arnheim (1969a) described the laws of visual balance as observed in art, making frequent mention of the connection between visual and musical harmony. From the perspective of the psycho-aesthetic hypothesis, these rules can also be interpreted as indications of the laws governing the visual system. For example, Fig. 11.6A appears harmonious, and the position of the central dot is rapidly assimilated and easily remembered, whereas the patterns of Fig. 11.6B through 11.6D reflect progressively reduced visual harmony, as described by Arnheim (1969a). Arnheim proposed that the reference square, when probed in this manner with a test dot, reveals a fieldlike pattern of visual harmony as suggested in Fig. 11.6E (adapted from Arnheim, 1969a) where the shaded lines represent lines along which the test dot rests more comfortably, in pleasing balance with the square. The single square also suggests a regular array of identical squares in a grid. The patterned field of visual harmony suggested by a single square is reminiscent of the periodic and symmetrical patterns in Figs. 11.2 and 11.3, and therefore this too suggests a periodic basis set in vision.

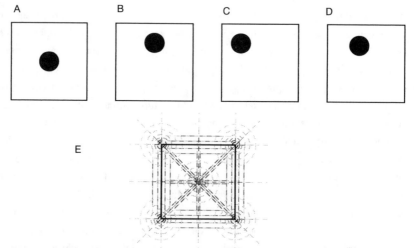

Fig. 11.6   The fields of visual balance due to a square can be explored by moving a circular test dot around within that square, as suggested by Arnheim (1969a). In the progression from (A) through (D), the dot appears increasingly unbalanced relative to the square. The pattern depicted in (E) (adapted from Arnheim) suggests the fieldlike influence generated by the square, where regions of denser dashed lines represent regions of greater visual balance. This field appears to define a central skeleton composed of axes of symmetry.

The same kind of explanation holds for the golden ratio, in which a rectangle is judged to be most pleasing when its ratio of height and width conforms to the ratio of 34:21, as measured psychophysically by Fechner(1871). The reason behind this exact ratio seems to be that it represents a curious fractal-like resonance, for if the golden rectangle is trimmed off to a square whose side is equal to the smaller dimension of the rectangle, the remaining section is itself another golden rectangle, which suggests a recursive trimming to ever smaller scale in a fractal manner. The perceptual significance of fractal self-similarity, seen in patterns such as the Fibonacci series, can be explained as a higher order periodicity, or periodicity of periodicities, because each cycle or level of the fractal pattern is a scale replica of the patterns of adjacent levels, with a constant scale factor going from level to level. This is analogous to the fractal pattern of the musical scale, whose periodicity in the pitch dimension reflects a fractal pattern in the frequency dimension. Fechner (1871) found other preferred ratios between height and width, as manifest in the frames of pictures in museums. For upright pictures the favorite ratio was 5:4, and for horizontal ones about 4:3. I propose that this relates to a resonance or harmony between the vertical and horizontal dimensions of the rectangle. In other words, if a rectangle were stretched continuously from an elongated vertical to an elongated horizontal aspect ratio, the visual harmony of the shape would wax and wane in a periodic pattern, with greater harmony for integer ratios between height and width, in a manner exactly analogous to the pattern of consonance of the musical interval.

There has been much discussion of the concept of tension in visual composition. For example, Arnheim (1969a) described the inharmonious percept of the dot in Fig. 11.6D as a tension, or restoring force, that pulls the dot inward toward the center, or alternatively, an eccentric force that holds the dot outward against the attraction of the more comfortable central position. Similarly, a rectangle squeezed well beyond the golden ratio appears as if under tension, as if it were being pulled out by an eccentric force, or alternatively, as if it were trying to pull itself back together to a more stable square form. This raises the question of whether the force of tension in composition is an eccentric or a restoring force. The answer is, *both*, and the two opposing forces are in balance with each other. If form is represented as a periodic pattern of vertices about a center, as suggested in chapter 6, the canonical form of the quadrilateral is its most symmetrical form, the square shape. Any quadrilateral that deviates from that canonical form must be held in its eccentric configuration by a force that modulates the basic form of the square, like a higher harmonic that modulates the pattern of the fundamental, expressing the rectangle as a square with a certain coefficient of eccentricity. A low-pass filtering, or dropping of the high energy terms, corresponds to the rectangle relaxing back to the more comfortable symmetry of the square. The square in turn can be seen as a circle with a higher harmonic of fourfold symmetry, so a low-pass filtering of the square would return it to the simpler circular form. This kind of code can be seen either as a symmetry code, expressing visual form in terms of its symmetries, or when considering the action of a higher harmonic on its fundamental, it can be seen as a deviation-from-symmetry code, expressing square form by its various deviations from the perfect symmetry of a circle, and the rectangle by its deviation from the symmetry of the square. Early Gestalt experiments studied the relative stability of various shapes by the phenomenon of *flicker fusion* (Hartmann, 1923; Koffka, 1935). When viewed through an *episcotister*, a spinning wheel with a small gap, the figure appears to flicker for slow rates of rotation, but the flicker is replaced by a steady percept at higher rotational speeds. The *critical fusion velocity* at which the flicker disappears depends on the complexity of the figure observed, with a circle surviving slower rotation rates than a square, and the square surviving slower rotation than a rectangle. The Gestalt explanation of this phenomenon is that the cyclic reappearance of the figure viewed through the episcotister means that the visual system must repeatedly reconstruct the perceptual structure from scratch, as suggested by indirect realism. Because more complex forms take slightly longer to construct, they exhibit a slower critical fusion velocity. The relative complexity of various figures as represented in perception can be measured using this technique to deduce the primitives of the visual representation. The stubby rounded forms seen so often in children's and infant's toys, like the airplanes with stubby wings and tail, or bulbous little cars with oversized drivers, can be seen as a relaxation of the more realistic shape by a dropping of higher harmonics in a three-dimensional spatial code, resulting in both a loss of sharp corners and a return to a simpler pattern organized around a single center of symmetry.

A HIERARCHICAL PROGRESSION IN ART

There is an interesting pattern observed in the progressive development of children's art, mirrored in the development of art through the history of our culture. The earliest depictions of children's art tend to represent objects in canonical form, with faces depicted in frontal view, as a symmetrical pattern, or in stark profile view, and bodies appear in symmetrical posture with arms and legs outstretched, or later as simple vertical lines. Art from early history also exhibits a tendency toward the canonical form, as seen in ancient Egyptian statues and pagan idols, as well as early Christian art. The level of realism in art can be seen as a measure of the advancement of a culture, as in an individual, with features such as the three-quarter view and apparently accidental rather than rigidly posed postures emerging with increasing sophistication, as if capturing a momentary percept at some arbitrary time, rather than a kind of high-level summation or representative posture averaged over a longer time, as embodied in the canonical view. I propose that this pattern of development in art reflects the hierarchical order of representation in the brain, where the early attempts at art of the individual and of the culture depict the highest level, most abstracted and regularized representation in the mind, although of course reified to concrete form in the actual art work. This kind of exaggeration of Gestalt grouping principles is seen especially in symbolic forms, like religious icons, company logos, symbols on playing cards, and graphical symbols for planets, elements, gender, and such. Artistic sophistication progresses top-down from the symbolic timeless general concept toward the low-level immediate experience of the arbitrary moment of consciousness.

Science and art address the opposite faces of the perceptual coin; science seeks to describe the objective world, whereas art attempts to communicate the subjective conscious experience. Science takes a left-brained or reductionist approach of reducing reality to a minimum number of laws and equations in an attempt to capture the constant or invariant in the world, whereas art has taken the right-brained reified approach of filling in the conscious experience in all its rich spatial detail. For example, a mathematician might describe a log as a cylinder, abstracted to a line of central symmetry with a radius and a length. The artist, on the other hand, depicts that same log in reified form, completing every detail of its irregular texture and form. In fact, the artist's rendition is itself more regular than the object being depicted, for the artist comprehends and expresses irregular forms by way of simpler geometric primitives. The process of decomposing an irregular object into its component primitives is clearly described in "how to draw" books, where the proper technique is to begin with a few sketch lines that capture the central skeleton as suggested by the global gestalt, and fill in the details from that sparse skeleton using sketched ovals, rectangles, and simple geometrical primitives to flesh out the skeleton to volumetric form, and finally to dress up the sketch with a veneer of irregular textures to complete the illusion of a real object. The skeleton is the artist's version of abstraction, a depiction of the central symmetries from which the reification proceeds in lawful manner, and the sketched geometrical primitives on that skeleton represent the amodal percept of organized structure underlying the otherwise chaotic confusion of texture that comprises the immediate conscious experience. Naive art and children's art are expressed closer to the invariant, with uniform regions clearly delimited by bold contours, using simple geometrical forms that are easily assimilated perceptually, whereas realist art approaches closer to the immediate conscious interface with the world, where the "rubber" of the perceptual interpolation mechanism meets the "road" of irregular surfaces and volumes of the world, which that mechanism attempts to match.

What is missing in mathematics and in science in general is the perceptual interface with the world. Like logic, law, and language, mathematics relies on human observers to enter the numbers into the equations describing the properties of the world. What is missing is a mathematics that can extract the pertinent numbers from a local view of the world and automatically express what it sees in abstracted form in as much complexity as required to model the observed forms and motions. Mathematics should also emulate art in the practice of reifying or extrapolating outward from the abstraction in order to compute the spatial implications of the abstract code, in a form that can be compared directly with the sensory stimulus. The points where nature breaks out of the predicted patterns we impose on it are the points of greatest interest, for these points offer an opportunity to update the model to account for the anomaly. Perception, humor, and science all highlight the importance of novelty, for we naturally take pleasure in the unexpected, and that pleasure is lost once the novelty is gone.

Our scientific understanding of the world will be more complete and symmetrical once we have formalized the rules of art sufficient to automate the process of extraction of geometrical primitives from the world itself, while maintaining the ability to reify the abstracted forms, in order to express the full spatial implications of the detected invariances. This bidirectional coupling between the world and our mathematical representation of it is the missing component in our attempt to formalize our understanding of the world. The principles behind this missing functionality are to be found at the intersection where art and science meet, using an abstracted representation expressed in terms of centers of symmetry and regularities, as in mathematics, but with the elastic deformable character of the sketch lines in art, together with the reification component of art that fills in or completes the pattern as far as possible in conformance to to the patterns of regularity detected in it.

SPIRITUALITY AND THE PARANORMAL

There are certain common cross-cultural themes observed in supernatural and spiritual beliefs that, in the context of the psycho-aesthetic hypothesis, might also be seen as evidence for the structure of the mind. One of the most general principles of spirituality is the belief in an alternate reality of the spirit world, which is almost universally recognized as immaterial, usually invisible, insubstantial, and not subject to the laws of the physical world. Although superimposed on the physical world, the spirit world is in a separate plane of existence, which can occasionally make contact with the physical world, often by way of a human medium. Spirits are also often described as dominating certain environments, like forest nymphs or gods of the sea or the heavens, or they can be seen as ruling abstract concepts like love or war. I propose that the dualism inherent in the notion of separate material and spiritual worlds is an unconscious recognition of indirect realism, or the ultimate unreality of the world of perception. The existence of illusory percepts, and of dreams and hallucinations, clearly shows that there is not a direct relation between reality and experience, and this in turn casts doubt on the objective reality of all experience. The ghostly images sometimes observed in the world around us are, I propose, none other than mental images projected by the mind, and their properties as described by those who see them are exactly the properties of mental images. Our failure to recognize them as products of our mind has been largely because they do not appear within our heads where we consider our minds to be located, but appear out in the world around us. Once we recognize the world around us as an internal representation, and once we recognize the ability of the brain to construct vivid spatial entities in that representation, these phenomena become much less mysterious, for they are revealed to be merely spatial thoughts in the brain, superimposed on perceptual structures also in the brain.

The properties of the spirit world are consistent with the properties of thought and mental imagery, as proposed in chapter 9. For thought is abstracted and nebulous, and yet it can materialize as semitransparent spatial constructs much like a ghost. These ghostly thoughts are often weightless and insubstantial, and can pass through walls, levitate, teleport, and morph from one form to another. There is also a curious tendency for ghosts, as described in many cultures, to come into existence in response to dramatically emotional or tragic circumstances, such as disastrous battles, or gruesome murders, the very factors that promote the formation of vivid memories. Ghosts also tend to display curious stereotyped behavior, like the ghost of Hamlet's father, who would pace back and forth, usually paying no attention to people around him, like a fragment of a memory replayed repeatedly. Ghosts often reappear at periodic intervals that are meaningful to human observers, like a repeating echo of the past event. This is reminiscent of our propensity to celebrate great events either annually, or at intervals of decades or centuries, as is natural for a mind that organizes its perceptions in terms of patterns of periodicity.

PSYCHEDELIC AND MYSTICAL EXPERIENCE

Into the most ancient times of prehistory, our ancestors discovered that geometrical patterns and ghostly apparitions could be conjured up by ecstatic drug intoxication, reinforced by rhythmic chanting or dancing, or in the sensory-deprived caverns of the underworld (Lewis-Williams & Dowson, 1988)—exactly the environmental circumstances known to induce hallucinations, or at least vivid mental imagery. In more reserved religions, more subtle and peaceful visions are conjured up by prayer, often characterized by a symmetrical canonical posture, with the hands closing on themselves rather than on the world, or with eyes closed and head bowed, or turned against a blank wall or the floor, to disconnect from the external world in order to focus on the internal world from whence the spirits originate. In the modern scientific context these experiences are nothing more than subjective illusions. But for people who perceived them as something objectively real, these experiences were viewed as a valuable glimpse into a mysterious and magical alternate world of spiritual existence. The concept of the soul being distinct from the body, and being capable of independent existence, is supported by the daily experience of sleep and dreaming, followed by a return to the material world upon awakening the next day. As the daily cycle of day and night is echoed by the larger annual cycle of the seasons, so also it is reasonable for a periodic mind to suppose that the daily cycle of wakefulness and sleep would be mirrored by a larger cycle of death and rebirth. It would be surprising if early man did not arrive at these conclusions, given the evidence of everyday experience.

The potential of the psychedelic experience as a means of exploring the nature of mind has been recognized in modern times also, as seen in the very meaning of the word *psychedelic,* which translates to "mind-revealing." For some the experience is religious, as if revealing an alternate world of separate reality. However in the context of indirect realism, the experience can also be scientific, for the illusory percepts and hallucinations conjured up by the drug experience are very real manifestations of the informational interactions of the mind. If the subjective experience of consciousness is accepted as a valid object of scientific scrutiny, the psychedelic experience offers a different perspective on that same entity, less encumbered by the familiarity that tends to hide some of its most prominent features. In the words of Huxley (1963, p. 25), "Visual impressions are greatly intensified and the eye recovers some of the perceptual innocence of childhood, when the sensum was not immediately and automatically subordinated to the concept." A phenomenologist who eschews the use of mind-altering substances is like a linguist who declines to study foreign languages, and whose observations are thereby limited to those based on his familiar native tongue.

Not surprisingly, the notion of indirect realism is one of the common themes reported in the psychedelic experience. Here is how it was described by Alan Watts (1958, p. 135):

> *I became vividly aware of the fact that what I call shapes, colors, and textures in the outside world are also states of my nervous system, that is, of me. ... I did not appear to be inspecting [those perceived forms] from outside or from a distance, [but] the awareness of grain or structure in the senses seemed to be awareness of awareness, of myself from the inside. ... The distance or separation between myself ... and the external world seemed to disappear. I was no longer a detached observer, a little man inside my own head, having sensations, I was the sensations, so much so that there was nothing left of me, the observing ego, except the series of sensations which happened—not to me, but just happened—moment by moment, one after another.*

Timothy Leary (1983 p. 32) offered the following description after consumption of magic mushrooms in Mexico:

I gave way to delight, as mystics have for centuries when they peeked through the curtains and discovered that this world—so manifestly real—was actually a tiny stage set constructed by the mind.

and later, on p. 119:

Since [my first LSD trip] I have been acutely aware that everything I perceive, everything within and around me, is a creation of my own consciousness. And that everyone lives in a neural cocoon of private reality. From that day I have never lost the sense that I am an actor, surrounded by characters, props, and sets for the comic drama being written in my brain.

Solomon Snyder (1986, p. 181) wrote:

Even more extraordinary is the ineffable change that takes place in the user's sense of self. Boundaries between self and nonself evaporate, giving rise to a serene sense of being at one with the universe. I recall muttering to myself again and again, 'All is one, all is one'.

Aldous Huxley (1963) expressed the same concept:

We live together, we act on, and react to one another; but always and in all circumstances we are by ourselves ... From family to nation, every human group is a society of island universes. (p. 12)

I spent several minutes—or was it centuries?—not merely gazing at [the legs of a chair], but actually being them—or rather being myself in them; or, to be still more accurate (for "I" was not involved in the case, nor in a certain sense were "they") being my Not-self in the Not-self which was the chair. (p. 22)

These insights are reminiscent of the Buddhist view of the world, with which the psychedelic experience is often compared.

Another common theme in the literature of drug experiences is the report of repeated periodic patterns, described as elaborate latticework, or grids, funnels, spirals, and arabesques, suggestive of a harmonic resonance representation. Alan Watts (1958, p. 135) wrote:

I noticed, for example, that all repeated forms—leaves on a stem, books on shelves, mullions in windows— gave me the sensation of seeing double or even multiple, as if the second, third, and fourth leaves on the stem were reflections of the first, seen, as it were, in several thicknesses of window glass. ... As I then concentrated upon this sensation of doubling or repeating images, it seemed suddenly as if the whole field of sight were a transparent liquid rippled in concentric circles as in dropping a stone into a pool.

This insight is reminiscent of Plato's concept of ideals, or pure concepts, which exist only in unitary form, but exhibit many imperfect copies or reflections of that unitary concept. This relates to the invariant representation proposed in chapter 6, in which any number of cubes or spheres anywhere in the visual field all stimulate a single cube or sphere node, that represents the common form of all exemplars of that form currently present in the visual field. The various cubes in the visual field are therefore coupled to each other through the one invariant universal cube, which makes them shimmer and waver in synchrony when viewed under LSD. Huxley (1963, p. 26) expressed a similar observation: "*In the final stages of egolessness there is an 'obscure knowledge' that All is in all—that All is actually each.*"

Mystical and spiritual teachings down through the ages have spoken about the fundamental interconnectedness of all things, and that the microcosm somehow contains the macrocosm. A beautiful and legendary image of this is the "jeweled net of Indra" in the Avatamsaka Sutra, in which the universe is represented as an infinite network of pearls, each of which reflects all the others. This relation between the single concept and its many manifestations relates also to the phenomenon of *polyopia* (Klüver, 1966, p. 30), in which a hallucinated form often appears singly, and then divides into multiple copies of the same pattern, often in synchronized patterns of motion.

> *A little man is standing there changing continually in appearance, sometimes he has a beard, sometimes not, the covering of his head is also changing ... [the man divides, and] now the little men increase again in number until there is a whole line of them ... one of them twirls his moustache, and at once all of them twirl their moustaches.* (Klüver, 1966, p. 30)

This same principle is illustrated most impressively in the inebriated dream of Dumbo in the Walt Disney cartoon movie, where an imaginary pink elephant splits and splits again into a multitude of identical copies, all dancing and marching in synchrony, or in symmetrical geometrical patterns.

LEFT-BRAINED VERSUS RIGHT-BRAINED THOUGHT

There has been some debate recently challenging the neat segregation of "left-brained" and "right-brained" functions into their corresponding cerebral hemispheres. But whatever the neurophysiological reality behind hemispheric specialization, the terms *left-brained* and *right-brained* do convey a conceptual distinction between two distinct modes of thought, or computational strategies in perception and cognition, which is meaningful regardless of the hemispheres in which they are actually computed. My use of these terms therefore relates to the atomistic versus holistic character of the two modes of thought, rather than to their location in the brain. It is curious that the rigid templatelike view of the mind, as suggested by the spatial receptive field paradigm, and the computer-like logic gates, is much more readily proposed and accepted in the scientific community than the holistic, field-like view of mind introduced by Gestalt theory. One reason is that the aspect of conscious experience that most clearly manifests these Gestalt properties is the integrated holistic percept of the world, which is often confused with the world itself, as suggested by the naive realist view. West (1997) suggested that the overt concerns of modern culture appear to be almost entirely dominated by the modes of thought most compatible with the left hemisphere, that our view of the world, our education system, our system of rewards, our aspirations, and our value systems are all effectively focused on reinforcing the operation of the left hemisphere, often referred to as the "dominant hemisphere," whereas the more basic contributions of the right hemisphere are largely ignored or seen as primitive. West (1997, p. 14) observed that one of the most important recent developments that arose from research on the functions of the two hemispheres is the idea that the right hemisphere is actually thinking at all—that is, the clear demonstration that consciousness and thought are indeed possible without words.

The biggest obstacle to recognizing the contribution of the right hemisphere is that the principal product of that organ is the solid and stable picture of the world we see around us, which is commonly mistaken for the world itself. The analytic reductionist left-brained thinking that has been advanced to such a high degree of sophistication in the human mind does indeed seem to have the character of sequential logic as in the digital computer. What is less well recognized, however, is that the elements or building blocks of the logical mental function are themselves composed of right-brained holistic images. For example, a logical statement such as "cows eat grass" is dependent on the concepts of cows and of grass, which themselves are not pure abstractions reducible to a Boolean true/false binary element, but are complex spatial concepts that require the highest right-brained function for recognition or identification in the world. This fact is often overlooked due to the ease with which we routinely recognize and identify objects like cows, so we take their identification for granted. The problem has been that the lower levels of mental processing, such as the identification of a cow, occur preattentively and automatically, leaving little trace in consciousness, except of course for the vivid spatial experience of the cow in immediate consciousness. And that entity is mistaken for the cow itself, rather than a mental construct. The logical structures composed of these elements, on the other hand, are vividly experienced as conscious mental manipulations. This has given us a biased view of the world of thought, which is generally described as of a logical nature, for the holistic Gestalt aspects of thought tend to be considered as properties of the world and of the objects within it, rather than a property of mind.

Another reason for the general resistance to Gestalt ideas is a general bias in academic and educational institutions toward the rigorous analytical left-brained thinking that reflects the reductionist view of science, which has dominated academia at least since the days of

Descartes. One striking example of this bias is seen in the intense research effort currently under way to investigate the human genetic code expressed in human DNA, while a very small effort is directed at investigating the mechanism of chemical harmonic resonance by which that abstracted or reduced code is expanded into the reified spatial structures of the body. In fact, very few scientists are even aware of this aspect of the expression of the DNA code, despite the fact that the mechanism behind it has been established for quite some time. Yet the DNA code by itself is meaningless without the mechanism to decode it, like a telephone number without the telephone network to make the connection. It is the unique combinatorial properties of chemical harmonic resonance that allow the DNA code to be decoded into the complex geometrical structures of the body.

Right-brained spatial thinking has been consistently undervalued as a component of scientific thinking (Arnheim, 1969b, West, 1997), despite the fact that many of the great discoveries of theoretical science were originally arrived at by the process of mental imagery, including those of Einstein, Maxwell, Faraday, Hadamard, Poincaré, Tesla, Mandlebrot, and Gleik, who were all intensely visual thinkers (West, 1997). The mathematical details of their theories were painstakingly worked out after the initial insight, as a means of objective verification and precise quantification of the concept. The abstracted or reductionist view usually follows where the mental image leads the way, and therefore the process of mental imagery should be given much greater acknowledgment as a valid and fruitful scientific procedure. In the words of Poincaré, "It is by logic that we prove, but by intuition that we discover" (Arnheim, 1969a, p. 274).

I remember well in my own scientific education that the equations we were given to learn, relating current and voltage and resistance in electric circuit, seemed so hollow and meaningless until a visionary teacher[1] gave meaning to those equations by explaining the water analogy to electricity: that current is like the flow of water, and voltage is like pressure. Only after I had grasped this vivid imagery did the bare equations take on real meaning. Years later, when I learned about capacitors and inductors, I was again perplexed by the differential equations that described their function. It was only weeks after the class had moved on rapidly to other topics that I finally figured out for myself the proper water analogies, that the capacitor is like an elastic membrane stretched across the cross section of a water pipe, and the inductor is like an inertial turbine wheel spun up by the flow of current. Only then did the equations describing their behavior begin to make sense to me at an intuitive level. Similarly, the processes of differentiation and integration in calculus were taught to me as a meaningless manipulation of symbols. I only grasped

---

1. Mr. Sarfas of the Oratory School—deepest thanks for filling my young head with images. Thanks also to Ron Horgan, for many great spatial intuitions at an impressionable age.

the concept behind them years later when I discovered that the derivative is like the lever of the simple backhoe model presented in chapter 10, whose static deflection results in a steady motion of its hydraulic piston. A double derivative can therefore be modeled by connecting the piston of one system to the lever of the next, and integration is like trying to calculate the position and motion of the control lever by observing the movement of the piston that it controls. What was amazing to me was that most of my teachers seemed to find such spatial analogies irrelevant to the presentation of the material, although these concepts must have originally appeared in the minds of Newton and Leibnitz in spatial form, and only later been translated into mathematical symbolism. Although equations are clearly a useful shorthand to encapsulate the spatial knowledge in unambiguous terms, and to communicate them from one mind to another, I have always felt that true understanding comes directly from the mental image rather than from the equation. Knowledge that is learned exclusively in the form of equations does not generalize outside of the narrow domain in which the equations are defined. The mental image, on the other hand, reaches out and makes contact across different realms of knowledge in remotely related disciplines.

There is yet another reason why academia has been inclined to favor the abstracted over the reified representation of the world. Although mental imagery and spatial analogies are helpful in learning abstract material, it is very difficult to objectively test a student's power of mental imagery ability, or creativity and originality, which are related to it. These factors can be recognized only through informal personal interaction, but not by formal tests or examinations. There is no way to determine whether a student answers a problem in calculus by a meaningless manipulation of symbols, or by the flash of intuition occasioned by the right mental image. Students who are weak in mental imaging ability can compensate with extra effort in learning the symbol manipulations. Word problems in mathematics are designed specifically to test the ability to map a real situation to an abstracted mathematical formulation. However weakness in this ability can be covered up by more practice with similar problems, learning many particular solutions instead of grasping a single general principle. It is impossible to distinguish these two strategies in the answers given to a mathematical exam, for the really creative imaginative solution to a problem, once found, is easily parroted by less creative souls.

Sadly, much of a typical scientific education involves a parroting of the knowledge of great scientists of the past, rather than developing the skill to find original solutions to physical problems by way of mental imagery. In the most competitive schools, a large work load is often used to select between students of different abilities. But the best students are not always those who assimilate knowledge most rapidly, or with the patience for endless practice and repetition. Students who "waste their time" trying to elaborate their mental image understanding of the material might fall behind in the class work of memorizing the details of the equations, and often ultimately lose interest in science as too dry and boring an enterprise. Consequently, some of the most brilliant minds at the head of our academic institutions are not necessarily people with a broad general grasp of the essential principles of their field, but often they are people with powerfully focused minds, capable of great depth of penetration into specific problems, rather than breadth of generality over a broad range of problems, whereas some of the most creative and ingenious spatial thinkers, like Rudolph Arnheim, seek refuge in the world of art, where their way of thinking receives the recognition it deserves. This has had the unfortunate consequence of misrepresenting the true nature of science to the world, for science is often perceived by the public and by lesser scientists as a pedantic pursuit of minute details, rather than a broad-fronted general pursuit of the greater mysteries facing mankind.

FUTURE WORK

If harmonic resonance is indeed a significant principle of computation and representation in the brain, how are we to pursue the investigation of this fascinating phenomenon? There are three possible approaches that come to mind for the direction of future research: perceptual modeling, neurophysiology, and the study of physical resonances. Perceptual modeling is the study of the informational transformation apparent in perception, as presented in chapters 4 through 6. Although this approach is not entirely new, most recent attempts at modeling perceptual processing have followed a hybrid approach, expressing the elements of perceptual computation and representation in neural network terms in the interests of perceived "neural plausibility." The pure perceptual modeling approach breaks free entirely from contemporary concepts of neurocomputation, allowing the use of seemingly "implausible" concepts such as an emergent reified structural representation of the external world that is free to translate and rotate relative to the tissue of the brain. The structural representation of the perceptual model can serve therefore as a framework to unify many of the perceptual phenomena identified psychophysically that have not found convenient expression in neural network terms.

The psycho-aesthetic hypothesis extends the science of psychophysics also into the aesthetic domain, where the laws of artistic composition and the principles of ornamental design can be seen as evidence for the laws of visual structure as encoded in the brain. Similarly, the laws of musical form and the structure of musical scales offer clues to the code for auditory perception, and for the perceptual organization of temporal sequences of events, whereas the patterns of dance and military drill offer clues to the code of the motor representation.

Harmonic resonance in the brain can also be investigated neurophysiologically, as synchronous neural activity between spiking neurons, and analog or graded potential oscillations measured by way of microelectrodes, while more global resonances of the brain as a whole are measurable by Electroencephalogram (EEG) recordings. Although this research is already under way, as discussed in chapter 8, this investigation would be considerably more focused if it were guided by a theoretical understanding of the principles of a resonance representation, that is, what information might be expected to be encoded or processed by a resonance representation. For example, the harmonic resonance theory presented in chapter 8 suggests that a promising avenue of research might be to investigate the effects of stimulus variation on the phase, magnitude, and waveform of the oscillations measured in sensory neurons, and in cortical sensory areas. Similarly, the motor code might be investigated by observing the effect of different postures and motor behaviors on the phase and magnitude of electrical oscillations in motor neurons and in cortical motor areas. A very simple test of the harmonic resonance theory would be to see whether an electrical signal from a signal generator applied to the motor nerve of a dismembered frog's leg might be able to move the leg in a more controlled manner than the simple jerk produced by a pulse of DC current.

The study of harmonic resonance as a principle of representation in the brain can also be conducted by investigating the properties of inanimate resonances in physical systems, continuing the seminal work of Chladni (1787), Faraday (1831), and Waller (1961), and the more recent work of Cristiansen et al. (1992), Kumar and Bajaj (1995), Kudrolli and Gollub (1996), and Kudrolli et al. (1998) on resonances in fluids. However, the focus of all of those investigations has been on the dynamic properties of physical matter. This research could be fruitfully redirected as an investigation of a principle of representation in the brain. First, the investigation could be extended to standing waves in a three-dimensional medium, like a resonating sphere, or spherical acoustical cavity. The principal difficulty here would be devising a means to measure and record the resulting patterns. In fact, there are so many different ways to stimulate standing waves in physical systems, including acoustical, vibrational, electrical, electromagnetic, electrochemical, chemical, optical laser, maser, and so on, that the hardest choice would be to select the best physical medium for investigating the phenomenon. There are also many promising new electro-optical devices that have been developed in recent decades, such as phase-conjugate mirrors (Pepper, 1982; 1986, Yariv, 1991) and acousto-optic modulators (Yariv, 1991), which are sure to play a significant role in the investigation, although only an expert in this fast moving field would be competent to identify the most promising mechanism for research into the properties of resonance as a representation of pattern in the brain.

There are two other directions of resonance research that might prove to be fruitful. One is to investigate the effect of damping in a variety of configurations on the resultant standing wave pattern. This is analogous to opening the holes in a flute to modulate or constrain the resonances within it, and therefore this investigation is directly related to the scientific study of the operational principles behind various musical instruments. Whether performed in two dimensions on a circular plate, or in three dimensions in a spherical resonator, it would be interesting to attempt to "recognize" a pattern of damping in a rotation-invariant manner by way of a resonator tuned to the frequency of the pattern of damping, and to design the system to reify the missing portions of the pattern as observed in perception as discussed in chapter 8.

The potential of a harmonic resonance representation for motor control could also be investigated in a resonance model by using sensors attached at various points to a resonating Chladni plate to define the postural configuration of a robotic body based on the pattern of standing waves currently present on the plate. For example, a circular plate with eight sensors evenly spaced around its perimeter could be used to control the eight legs of a robotic spider, using the phase and magnitude of the standing wave at each sensor location to control the direction and magnitude of flexion of the corresponding leg. The advantage of using a standing wave for this purpose is that each standing wave defines a complete postural configuration for all the limbs in a single variable of coded information. Furthermore, different standing waves that are energized simultaneously tend to couple with each other to produce a combined standing wave, whose individual components can nevertheless be manipulated independently. With the right kind of driving waveform, the limbs could be made to oscillate in synchronous waves, like the legs of a centipede during walking, or to replicate the periodic and symmetrical stepping patterns of a walking insect, or the sinusoidal oscillations of a slithering snake or a swimming fish. But the real promise of harmonic resonance as a code for motor control is that it offers a simple means to modulate the local stepping pattern of the individual limbs with a larger global control signal, also represented by a standing wave. For example, the command to walk more quickly or slowly, or to steer left or right, or to step over an obstacle in the path, requires a modulation of the pattern of motion of each individual leg in analog fashion in conformance with the spatial structure of the controlling standing wave. The controlling standing waves can also be used in combination—for example, as a command to walk more quickly, steer left, and step over an obstacle all at the same time. This combinatorial property of harmonic resonance allows it to escape the combinatorial explosion that would encumber a neural network or template-based solution to this problem.

Another interesting variation of resonance research would be to vary the physical properties of a circular or spherical resonating system as a function of distance from the center, in order to give it the properties of the perceptual sphere developed in chapter 4: that a standing wave in the system would be larger at the center and progressively smaller with proximity to the edges, as suggested in Escher's print in Fig. 8.8. This would provide a finite representational space capable of encoding an essentially infinite pattern.

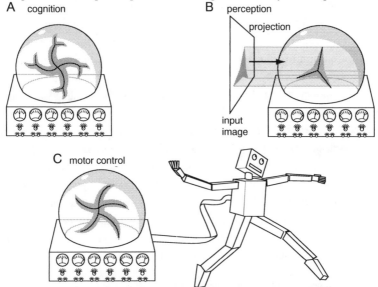

Fig. 11.7   An artist's conception, or functional specification of an imagined artificial mind. (A) The cognitive function is subserved by a spherical resonator or "crystal ball," capable of generating three-dimensional spatial standing-wave patterns in conformity with the settings on a control panel. (B) The perceptual function is added by making the standing wave pattern responsive also to images projected into the sphere. (C) Motor function is then added by coupling the crystal ball to an android body in such a way that the servos in the android body always drive the limbs to match the configuration of the "body image" standing wave permanently located at the center of the resonator. At the same time, the "body image" standing wave is also designed to always mirror the configuration of the android body, with a bi-directional causal connection between the body and its perceptual image.

A FINAL MENTAL IMAGE

A prominent subtheme of this book, as discussed in chapter 1, has been to emphasize the value of vivid mental imagery as a vehicle for communicating abstract ideas in more concrete terms. I present therefore a final mental image of how I imagine the future investigation of artificial intelligence might proceed if it is conducted along the lines suggested in this book. The long-term objective of this research is to produce an artificial mind that works on the same essential principles as our own. Although it is impossible to say exactly what form that artificial mind might ultimately take, what follows is a description of the functionality, or "user interface specification," to demonstrate by example what I believe to be the essential functional principles required of a simple artificial mind, as it might be implemented in a harmonic resonance mechanism.

I envisage a dynamic volumetric mechanism, somewhat like a crystal ball or spherical resonator, capable of generating three-dimensional images within its volume as suggested schematically in Fig. 11.7A, expressed as a spatial variation of some measurable physical property, such as the phase or amplitude of vibration of a standing-wave pattern present in the system. The images in the sphere are controlled by a panel with knobs that modulate the driving waveform to represent a variety of spatial concepts. For example one knob might control the number of vertices of the waveform that appears at the center of the sphere, so that turning that knob progressively would cause the standing wave pattern to morph through a sequence of Platonic solids as suggested in Fig. 6.7A. Another knob might control the peripheral symmetries on this central symmetry as suggested in the hierarchical code depicted in Fig. 6.7D and 6.7E, while still other knobs would control the degree of "bloat" (as discussed in chapter 6) and other characteristics of the generated form. With the proper settings of the control panel, therefore, the system could generate a wide variety of volumetric spatial patterns expressed as explicit reified standing waves in the spherical resonator. Other knobs, pads, or joysticks would be provided to control certain spatial parameters of the reified form, such as the size and orientation of each form as it appears, and the location of the object within the spatial representation.

Each of the parametric controls on the control panel should have two additional control knobs labeled "tolerance" and "focus." The tolerance knob determines the level of specificity for that component of the reified form, or how strictly it must adhere to the exact value specified by the parametric control. For example, a third harmonic resonance with low tolerance value would produce only a third harmonic pattern, whereas with increased tolerance values it would cycle randomly through a range of spatial forms either side of the third harmonic, such as from second through forth harmonic, or from first through fifth harmonic, depending on the tolerance setting. Each parameter should also have an associated "focus" knob that would fix the level of specification of that component of this synthetic concept whenever the tolerance control allows multiple interpretations. A soft focus would allow the system to remain in intermediate states, with multiple possible configurations superimposed on each other as spatial probability fields, whereas a sharp focus would reify different possible variations of the synthetic concept in sequence, like artist's sketches of the same basic concept expressed in a number of alternative ways. In fact, the the soft focus mode may be no different from a very rapid cycling between different spatial patterns in sharp focus mode, except that this cycling occurs so rapidly that the patterns essentially blur into each other as a fuzzy superposition of states, like the transparent disk swept out by a spinning propellor. For example, if the location is rigidly specified but the orientation is left indeterminate, the standing-wave pattern would tumble randomly through every orientation at a fixed location in sharp focus mode, whereas in soft focus mode it would exist essentially at all orientations simultaneously in a fuzzy uncertain manner. If, on the other hand, the location is left unspecified, or restricted to a subset of the representational space, the pattern will either shift around randomly within that region, or in soft focus mode it would spread out uniformly throughout the allowable range in a ghostly, semitransparent manner. Tuning such a system to produce the right kind of dynamics could be guided by the patterns seen in visual ornament; that is, in free-wheeling hallucination mode the system should spontaneously generate an endless stream of ornamental patterns like those in Fig. 11.3, and as observed in psychedelic hallucinations as described by Klüver (1966) and Siegel (1976), whereas in soft focus mode it would exist in a state of balance between all of those possible patterns.

The mechanism responsible for energizing the patterns of standing waves in the spherical resonator takes the form of an array of tuned resonators coupled to that sphere, with each one tuned to a different fundamental vibration frequency of the spherical resonator. Activating these individual resonators in various combinations at different magnitudes would generate different compound forms, in the manner of a Fourier descriptor that defines spatial structure in the form of its component Fourier coefficients. I propose that the functionality embodied in this hypothetical mechanism corresponds to the cognitive function of the brain. This includes not only the ability to encode information in an abstracted or symbolic form, which is normally considered to be the essential function of cognition, but also an ability to reify that abstracted information in an analogical spatial representation as proposed in chapter 9.

The perceptual function would be added to this cognitive mechanism by making the synthetic concepts, or reified geometrical patterns in the system, responsive also to "sensory" images projected into the spherical resonator, to define the extrinsic constraints on the emergent synthetic percept, as suggested schematically in Fig. 11.7B. When attending to an input, the knobs on the control panel should be set to high tolerance and soft focus mode, in order to balance the system equally between different perceptual interpretations, allowing the final stable state to be determined principally by the configuration of the input. As a particular standing wave emerges in the system in response to a particular stimulus, that standing wave would automatically activate the corresponding pattern of Fourier coefficients of the array of individual resonators as shown on the control panel, representing a "cognitive" recognition of the pattern detected perceptually. So, for example, if an ambiguous input stimulus produced a multistable resonance response that alternated spontaneously between two or more standing-wave patterns, the unstable alternation between these patterns would be accompanied by a corresponding alternation between the Fourier coefficients in the array of tuned resonators, as described also in chapter 8. The Fourier coefficients would register on a set of dials on the control panel to indicate the control-knob settings that would be required to generate that same spatial pattern endogenously. The control panel therefore represents the "left-brained" analytical description of the percept broken down into its component elements, as they would be encoded in language or stored in memory, whereas the reified spatial image in the resonating sphere represents the "right-brained" integrated reconstruction of that scene, corresponding to the immediate conscious experience or the mental image.

The motor function could then be added to this system by connecting the spherical resonator to a mechanical robot body, as suggested in Fig. 11.7C, whose limbs would be designed to automatically track or mirror the configuration of limbs in a "body percept" or standing-wave pattern permanently established at a special location at the center of the spherical the resonator. For example, the human body configuration might be encoded by a fifth harmonic of spherical resonance, or a five-limbed standing wave at the center of the resonator (or more precisely, a hierarchical $2^{(3,4)}$ pattern, as suggested in Fig. 6.7E). Subharmonics on this standing wave would act as command signals, modulating the local configuration of the limbs in accordance with the pattern of the command standing wave, as suggested in the field-theory code suggested in Fig. 10.3, and the android body would be designed to automatically reflect or mimic the postural configuration encoded in the standing wave pattern in the spherical resonator. At the same time, the configuration of the standing waves in the spherical resonator should also be responsive to the configuration of the android body, so that a physical deflection of the android body due to external forces would automatically result in a corresponding deflection of its body image in the standing-wave replica in the spherical resonator. In other words, a bidirectional causal relation must be established between the robotic body and its perceptual image, so that forces applied to either one are automatically communicated to the other. The best way to achieve this bidirectional coupling would be to employ a harmonic resonance code in the android body itself to control its limbs, so that the coupling between the resonance in the spherical resonator and that in the android body would synchronize the pattern of standing waves in those two systems, much like the coupling between cortical areas proposed in chapter 7.

The three functions of cognition, perception, and behavior depicted individually in Fig. 11..7A through 11.7C, would have to be integrated to form a single coupled system.

Exactly how this coupling might occur in a harmonic resonance representation is perhaps too early to say at this point. But the functional principles required of the system are perfectly clear if the evidence of subjective experience is to be believed. The phenomenological evidence suggests that the three functions should be coupled to each other by the same principle in which each of them is coupled internally: by way of bidirectional causal links that bind all the parts of the system into an integrated whole, as suggested also by Gestalt theory. The various components of the system would then be coupled to each other like the variables in the differential analyzer presented in chapter 1, with the exception that the variables in the perceptual representation need not be limited to abstract algebraeic variables expressed as individual real-number values, but they could also take the form of analogical representations, as extended spatial fieldlike entities that interact with one another by way of spatial fieldlike forces. The standing waves must therefore be devised so that they can exert spatial forces on each other—for example, to model the attraction between the body image and an attractive stimulus in the environment—and that attractive force should be designed to modulate the shape of the body percept standing wave, resulting in a motor response that propels the body toward the geographic origin of that attractive stimulus.

In order to model physical laws, the standing waves would also have to be endowed with physical properties like those that the system is intended to model. For example, a standing-wave pattern can be made to model solid matter by making it resist penetration by other standing waves that also represent solid matter; that is, patterns representing solid matter should repel each other powerfully whenever they attempt to occupy the same volume of perceived space. The resistance of the body percept to penetrating the perceived ground keeps the two entities spatially separate even when they come into contact. Similarly, the force of gravity can be simulated in the perceptual model by a force that draws all standing-wave patterns that represent solid matter downward toward the perceived ground underfoot, as an analogical replica of the real force of gravity in the external world. The solid structure of the body percept is therefore held against the solid ground by this synthetic gravity, producing a perceptual experience not only of structure, but also of structured forces in a state of balance. A standing wave capable of mimicking the spatial impenetrability of solid matter could also represent an articulated mechanism, like the human body, whose head and torso are balanced on its legs and feet, braced against the downward pull of synthetic gravity by an opposing force of structural support. This kind of representation would then be capable of motor computations by spatial logic, as suggested with the isomorphic backhoe concept described in chapter 10.

The functionality outlined in this hypothetical mental image goes far beyond the functionality described in chapter 8 as the known properties of a harmonic resonance representation. Whether or not the principle of harmonic resonance is capable of all of the complex spatial and analogical functions already described therefore remains very much an open question at this point. However, whether it is performed by harmonic resonance or by some other principle of computation in the brain, the functionality of the hypothetical mechanism described here does correspond to certain essential principles of mental function. Cognition is not exclusively an abstract or symbolic function, because any abstract cognitive concept can be reified at will into an explicit mental image, or matched feature for feature against an explicit visual image of that concept, as discussed in chapter 9. This ability to reify an abstract concept is intimately related to an understanding of that concept. Similarly, perception is not just a matter of recognition of features in the stimulus, as it is often described in the contemporary neural literature, but involves the construction of an explicit reified rendition of the perceived object in a volumetric representation of perceived space, as discussed in chapters 4 through 6. The Gestalt principles of emergence, reification, multistability, invariance, and non-anchored representation, which are so clearly manifest in the observed properties of the world of conscious experience, just happen to be natural properties of a harmonic resonance representation, but are very difficult to account for in any other terms. Therefore, if it is not by harmonic resonance that these properties of perception and cognition are subserved, then some other alternative paradigm of neurocomputation would have to be invoked to account for the observed properties of phenomenal experience.

The development and refinement of an artificial mind that operates on a harmonic resonance principle are likely to comprise a long and involved process, for like Stradivarius's pursuit of the perfect violin, the search to understand the full potential of harmonic resonance as a representation of spatiotemporal structure is likely to be a search with no well-defined end. But what else could we expect in the investigation of the mechanism that underlies human conscious experience? It would be truly incredible if the mechanism behind the "enchanted loom" were not itself an enchanted principle. And the enchantment of the principle of harmonic resonance was recognized long ago, when man first blew life into the inanimate matter of a hollow horn or shell. That early man surely recognized the sonorous tone that emerged as a haunting echo of some essential quality of the human spirit.

APPENDIX

THE COPLANARITY FIELD

The mathematical form of the coplanarity interaction field can be described as follows. Consider the field strength F due to an element in the opaque state at some point in the volume of the spatial matrix, with a certain surface orientation, depicted in Fig. A.1A as a vector, representing the normal to the surface encoded by that element. The strength of the field F should peak within the plane at right angles to this normal vector (depicted as a circle in Fig. A.1A) as defined in polar coordinates by the function $F_\alpha = \sin(\alpha)$, where α is the angle between the surface normal and some point in the field and ranges from zero, parallel to the normal vector, to π, in the opposite direction. The sine function peaks at $\alpha = \pi/2$, as shown in Fig. A.1B, producing an equatorial belt around the normal vector as suggested schematically in cross section in Fig. A.1C, where the gray shading represents the strength of the field. The strength of the field should actually decay with distance from the element, for example with an exponential decay function, as defined by the equation

$$F_{\alpha r} = e^{-r^2}\sin(\alpha)$$ as shown in Fig. A.1D, where r is the radial distance from the element.

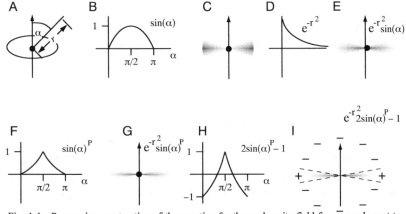

Fig. A.1   Progressive construction of the equation for the coplanarity field from one element to another, as described in the text.

This produces a fading equatorial band, as suggested schematically in cross section in Fig. A.1E. The equatorial belt of the function described so far would be rather fat, resulting in a lax or fuzzy coplanarity constraint, but the constraint can be stiffened by raising the sine to some positive power P, producing the equation $F_{\alpha r} = e^{-r^2}\sin(\alpha)^P$ which will produce a sharper peak in the function as shown in Fig. A.1F, producing a sharper in-plane field depicted schematically in cross section in Fig. A.1G. In order to control runaway positive feedback and suppress the uncontrolled proliferation of surfaces, the field function should be normalized, in order to project inhibition in directions outside the equatorial plane. This can be achieved with the equation $F_{\alpha r} = e^{-r^2}[2\sin(\alpha)^P - 1]$ which has the effect of shifting the equatorial function half way into the negative region as shown in Fig. A.1H, producing the field suggested in cross section in Fig. A.1I.

The field described so far is unoriented—that is, it has a magnitude, but no direction at any sample point (r,α). What is actually required is a field with a direction, a field that would have maximal influence on adjacent elements that are oriented parallel to it, that is, elements that are coplanar with it in both position and orientation. We can describe this orientation of the field with the parameter θ, which represents the orientation at which the field F is sampled, expressed as an angle relative to the normal vector; in other words, the strength of the influence F exerted on an adjacent element located at a point (r,α) varies with the deviation θ of that element from the direction parallel to the normal vector, as shown in Fig. A.2, such that the maximal influence is felt when the two elements are parallel (when $\theta = 0$), as in Fig. A.2A, and falls off smoothly as the other element's orientation deviates from that orientation as in Fig. A.2B and Fig. A.2C. This can be expressed with a cosine function, such that the influence F of an element on another element in a direction α and separation r from the first element and with a relative orientation θ would be defined by

$$F_{\alpha r \theta} = e^{-r^2}[2\sin(\alpha)^P - 1]\left|\cos(\theta)^Q\right|$$
(EQ 1)

This cosine function allows the coplanar influence to propagate to near-coplanar orientations, thereby allowing surface completion to occur around smoothly curving surfaces. The tolerance to such curvature can also be varied parametrically by raising the cosine function to a positive power Q, as shown in Equation 1. So the in-plane stiffness of the coplanarity constraint is adjusted by parameter P, while the angular stiffness is adjusted by parameter Q. The absolute value on the cosine function in Equation 1 allows interaction between elements when θ is between $\pi/2$ and π.

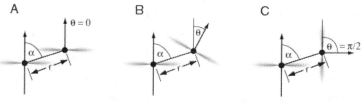

Fig. A.2   Orientation of the field of influence between one element and another. For an element located at polar coordinates (r, α), the influence varies as a cosine function of θ, the angle between the normal vectors of the two interacting elements.

THE OCCLUSION FIELD

The orthogonality and occlusion fields have one less dimension of symmetry than the coplanarity field, and therefore they are defined with reference to two vectors through each element at right angles to each other, as shown in Fig. A.3A. For the orthogonality field, these vectors represent the surface normals to the two orthogonal planes of the corner, whereas for the occlusion field one vector is a surface normal, and the other vector points within that plane in a direction orthogonal to the occlusion edge. The occlusion field G around the local element is defined in polar coordinates from these two vector directions, using the angles α and β, respectively, as shown in Fig. A.3A. The plane of the first surface is defined as for the coplanarity field, with the equation $G_{\alpha\beta r} = e^{-r^2} \sin(\alpha)^P$. For the occlusion field this planar function should be split in two, as shown in Fig. A.3B, to produce a positive and a negative half, so that this field will promote surface completion in one direction only, and will actually suppress surface completion in the negative half of the field. This can be achieved by multiplying the equation just shown by the *sign* [plus or minus, designated by the function sgn( )] of a cosine on the orthogonal vector, that is, $G_{\alpha\beta r} = e^{-r^2} \sin(\alpha)^P \mathrm{sgn}[\cos(\beta)]$. Because of the negative half field in this function, there is no need to normalize the equation. However, the oriented component of the field can be added as before, resulting in the equation

$$G_{\alpha\beta r\theta} = e^{-r^2} \{ \sin(\alpha)^P \mathrm{sgn}[\cos(\beta)] \} |\cos(\theta)^Q| \qquad \text{(EQ 2)}$$

Again, the maximal influence will be experienced when the two elements are parallel in orientation, when $\theta = 0$. As before, the orientation cosine function is raised to the positive power Q, to allow parametric adjustment of the stiffness of the coplanarity constraint.

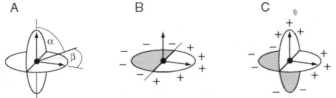

Fig. A.3   (A) Polar coordinate reference vectors through each element. (B) Occlusion field. (C) Orthogonality field.

THE ORTHOGONALITY FIELD

The orthogonality field H can be developed in a similar manner, beginning with the planar function divided into positive and negative half-fields, that is, with the equation $H_{\alpha\beta r} = e^{-r^2} \sin(\alpha) \mathrm{sgn}[\cos(\beta)]$ but then adding another similar plane from the orthogonal surface normal, producing the equation

$H_{\alpha\beta r} = e^{-r^2}\{\sin(\alpha)^P \text{sgn}[\cos(\beta)] + \sin(\beta)^P \text{sgn}[\cos(\alpha)]\}$. This produces two orthogonal planes, each with a negative half-field, as shown schematically in Fig. A.3C. Finally, this equation must be modified to add the oriented component to the field, represented by the vector θ, such that the maximal influence on an adjacent element will be experienced when that element is either within one positive half plane and at one orientation, or is within the other positive half plane and at the orthogonal orientation. The final equation for the orthogonality field therefore is defined by

$$H_{\alpha\beta r\theta} = e^{-r^2}\{\sin(\alpha)^P \text{sgn}[\cos(\beta)]|\cos(\theta)^Q| + \sin(\beta)^P \text{sgn}[\cos(\alpha)]|\cos(\theta)^Q|\} \quad \text{(EQ 3)}$$

EDGE CONSISTENCY AND INCONSISTENCY CONSTRAINTS

There is another aspect of the fieldlike interaction between elements that remains to be defined. Both the orthogonal and the occlusion states are promoted by appropriately aligned neighboring elements in the coplanar state. Orthogonal and occlusion elements should also feel the influence of neighboring elements in the orthogonal and occlusion states, because a single edge should have a tendency to become either an orthogonal corner percept, or an occlusion edge percept along its entire length. Therefore, orthogonal or occlusion elements should promote like states and inhibit unlike states in adjacent elements along the same corner or edge. The interaction between like state elements along the edge is called the *edge-consistency constraint*, and the corresponding field of influence is designated *E*, whereas the complementary interaction between unlike-state elements along the edge is called the *edge-inconsistency constraint*, whose corresponding edge-inconsistency field is designated *I*. These interactions are depicted schematically in Fig. A.4.

The spatial direction along the edge can be defined by the product of the two sine functions $\sin(\alpha) \sin(\beta)$ defining the orthogonal planes, denoting the zone of intersection of those two orthogonal planes, as suggested in Fig. A.4E. Again, this field can be sharpened by raising these sine functions to a positive power *P*, and localized by applying the exponential decay function. The edge consistency constraint *E* therefore has the form $E_{\alpha\beta r} = e^{-r^2}[\sin(\alpha)^P \sin(\beta)^P]$. As for the orientation of the edge-consistency field, this will depend now on two angles, θ and ϕ, representing the orientations of the two orthogonal vectors of the adjacent orthogonal or occlusion elements relative to the two normal vectors, respectively. Both the edge-consistency and the edge-inconsistency fields, whether excitatory between like-state elements or inhibitory between unlike-state elements, should peak when both pairs of reference vectors are parallel to the normal

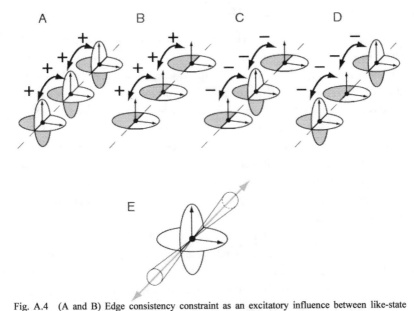

Fig. A.4 (A and B) Edge consistency constraint as an excitatory influence between like-state elements along a corner or edge percept. (C and D) Edge inconsistency constraint as an inhibitory influence between unlike-state elements along a corner or edge percept. (E) The direction along the edge expressed as the intersection of the orthogonal planes defined by sine functions on the two orthogonal vectors.

vectors of the central element—that is, when θ and φ are both equal to zero. The full equation for the edge-consistency field E would therefore be

$$E_{\alpha\beta r\theta\phi} = e^{-r^2}[\sin(\alpha)^P\sin(\beta)^P]\cos(\theta)^Q\cos(\phi)^Q \qquad \text{(EQ 4)}$$

where this equation is applied only to like-state edge or corner elements, whereas the edge-inconsistency field I would be given by

$$I_{\alpha\beta r\theta\phi} = e^{-r^2}[\sin(\alpha)^P\sin(\beta)^P]\cos(\theta)^Q\cos(\phi)^Q \qquad \text{(EQ 5)}$$

applied only to unlike-state elements. The total influence R on an occlusion element therefore is calculated as the sum of the influence of neighboring coplanar, orthogonal, and occlusion state elements as defined by

$$R_{\alpha\beta r\theta\phi} = G_{\alpha\beta r\theta\phi} + E_{\alpha\beta r\theta\phi} - I_{\alpha\beta r\theta\phi} \qquad \text{(EQ 6)}$$

and the total influence S on an orthogonal state element is defined by

$$S_{\alpha\beta r\theta\phi} = H_{\alpha\beta r\theta\phi} + E_{\alpha\beta r\theta\phi} - I_{\alpha\beta r\theta\phi} \qquad \text{(EQ 7)}$$

INFLUENCE OF THE VISUAL INPUT

A two-dimensional visual edge has an influence on the three-dimensional interpretation of a scene, because an edge is suggestive of either a corner or an occlusion at some orientation in three dimensions whose two-dimensional projection coincides with that visual edge. This influence, however, is quite different from the local fieldlike influences described earlier, because the influence of a visual edge should penetrate the volumetric matrix with a planar field of influence to all depths and should activate all local elements within the plane of influence that are consistent with that edge. Subsequent local interactions between those activated elements serve to select which subset of them should finally represent the three-dimensional percept corresponding to the two-dimensional image. For example, a vertical edge as shown in Fig. A.5A would project a vertical plane of influence, as suggested by the light shading in Fig. A.5A, into the depth dimension of the volumetric matrix, where it stimulates the orthogonal and occlusion states which are consistent with that visual edge. It would stimulate corner and occlusion states at all angles about a vertical axis, as shown in Fig. A.5A, where the circular disks represent different orientations of the positive half fields of either corner or occlusion fields, and this influence would be felt at all depths throughout the plane of influence of the edge, as suggested in Fig. A.5B. But a vertical edge would also be consistent with corners or occlusions about axes tilted relative to the image plane but within the plane of influence— for example, about the axes depicted in Fig. A.5C—and again this influence would propagate throughout the plane of influence of that edge, as suggested in Fig. A.5D.

When all elements consistent with this vertical edge have been stimulated in the plane of influence of the edge, local fieldlike interactions between adjacent stimulated elements will tend to reinforce any chance alignments between elements that are aligned in collinear configurations, resulting in the emergence of long strings of active elements within the plane of influence, as suggested in Fig. A.5E. Mutual inhibition across the depth dimension will suppress competing strings of active units at different depths, resulting in the emergence of a single corner or occlusion edge, as suggested in Fig. A.5E. The corner or occlusion percepts along this emergent depth edge would interact further along the edge, randomly selecting either the corner or occlusion state throughout the entire edge, as well as a consistent orientation of that corner or occlusion, as suggested in Fig. A.5F. At equilibrium, therefore, some arbitrary edge or corner percept will emerge within the plane of influence, as suggested in Fig. A.5G, which depicts only one such possible percept, whereas edge consistency interactions will promote like-state elements along that edge, producing a single emergent percept consistent with the visual edge. In the absence of additional influences—for example, in the isolated local case depicted in Fig. A.5—the actual edge that emerges will be unstable; that is, it could appear anywhere within the

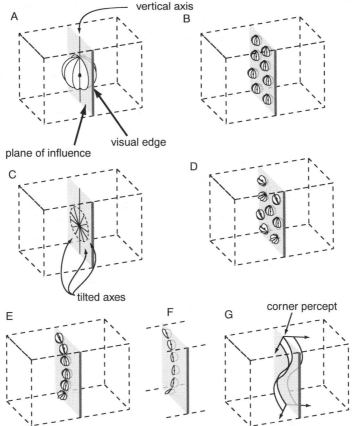

Fig. A.5   (A) The influence of a vertical edge is to (A) stimulate local elements in the corner or occlusion percept states at all orientations about a vertical axis, (B) and this stimulation occurs throughout the plane of influence projected by that edge. (C) The edge also stimulates corner or occlusion percepts about axes tilted from the vertical within the plane of influence, (D) and this stimulation also occurs throughout the plane of influence of the edge. (E) Mutual inhibition within the plane selects one dominant corner percept at some depth within that plane, whereas (F) mutual facilitation between these corner elements selects a consistent orientation among them, resulting in (G) a single self-consistent percept of a corner at some depth within the plane.

plane of influence of the visual edge through a range of tilt angles, and could appear as either an occlusion or a corner edge. However, when it does appear, it propagates its own fieldlike influence into the volumetric matrix. In this example, the corner percept would propagate a planar percept of two orthogonal surfaces that will expand into the volume of the matrix, as suggested by the arrows in Fig. A.5G. The final percept therefore will be influenced by the global pattern of activity, and the final percept will construct a self-consistent perceptual whole, whose individual parts reinforce each other by mutual activation by way of the local interaction fields.

A dynamic depletion and recovery mechanism can be incorporated in the elements of this representation so that active elements deplete their stored energy reserves, whereas inactive elements slowly recover their energy reserves, and thereby become more easily reactivated. With this dynamic in place, any particular percept will become unstable when it has been active for too long, which in turn would favor alternative perceptual interpretations that are otherwise equally likely in terms of the input stimulus. In other words, the system will tend to cycle randomly through the whole range of spatial configurations allowed by the input. For example, the corner percept depicted in Fig. A.5G would tend to snake back and forth unstably within the plane of influence, rotate back and forth along its axis through a small angle, and flip alternately between the corner and occlusion states, unless the percept is stabilized by other features at more remote locations in the matrix. If the outward-projected surfaces fall into a stable configuration with surrounding perceived structures to form coherent wholes, the percept will stabilize in that form or will flip unstably among a discrete number of equally stable states.

References

Arnheim, R. (1969a). Art and visual perception: A psychology of the creative eye. Berkeley: University of California Press.

Arnheim, R. (1969b). Visual thinking. Berkeley: University of California Press.

Arnheim, R. (1988). The power of the center. Berkeley: University of California Press.

Attneave, F. (1954). Some informational aspects of visual perception. Psychology Reviews, 61:183–193.

Attneave, F. (1955a). Symmetry, information, and memory for patterns. American Journal of Psychology, 68:209–222.

Attneave, F. (1955b). Perception of place in a circular field. American Journal of Psychology, 68:69–82.

Attneave, F. (1971). Multistability in perception. Scientific American, 225:142–151.

Attneave, F. (1982). Prägnanz and soap bubble systems: A theoretical exploration. In J. Beck (Ed.), Organization and representation in perception (pp. 11-29). Hillsdale, NJ: Lawrence Erlbaum Associates.

Attneave, F., & Farrar, P. (1977). The visual world behind the head. American Journal of Psychology, 90(4):549–563.

Ballard, D. H., & Brown, C. M. (1982). Computer vision. Englewood Cliffs, NJ:Prentice Hall.

Barlow, H., Blakemore, C., & Pettigrew, J. (1967). The neural mechanism of binocular depth discrimination. Journal of Physiology, 193:327–342.

Biederman, I. (1987). Recognition-by-components: A theory of human image understanding. Psychological Review, 94:115–147.

Bisiach, E., & Luzatti, C. (1978). Unilateral neglect of representational space. Cortex, 14:129–133.

Bisiach, E., Luzatti, C., & Perani, D. (1979). Unilateral neglect, representational schema and consciousness. Brain 102, 609–618.

Blank, A. A. (1958). Analysis of experiments in binocular space perception. Journal of the Optical Society of America, 48:911–925.

Blum, H. (1973). Biological shape and visual science (Part I). Journal of Theoretical Biology, 38:205–287.

Blumenfeld, W. (1913). Untersuchungen über die scheinbare Grösse im Sehraume. Zeitschrift für Psychologie, 65:241–404.

Boring, E. (1933). The Physical Dimensions of Consciousness. New York: Century.

Braitenberg, V. (1984). Vehicles: Experiments in synthetic psychology. Cambridge, MA: MIT Press.

Brazier, M. A. B. (1950). Neural nets and the integration of behaviour. In D. Richter (Ed.), Perspectives in Neuropsychiatry (pp. 35–45). London: H. K. Lewis.

Bremer, F. (1953). Some problems in neurophysiology. London: Athlone Press.

Bressler, S., Coppola, R., & Nakamura, R. (1993). Episodic multi-regional cortical coherence at multiple frequencies during visual task performance. Nature, 366:153–156.

Brett, R. F., Warren, W. H., Temizer, S., & Kaelbling, L. P. (2001). A dynamical model of visually-guided steering, obstacle avoidance, and route selection. In Press: International Journal of Computer Vision.

Brooks, R. A. (1991). Intelligence without representation. Artificial Intelligence, 47(1/3):139.

Bullock, T.H., & Hofmann, M. H. (1991). Apparent expectation in interstimulus-interval-specific event related potentials to omitted stimuli in the electrosensory pathway of elasmobranchs. Society for Neuroscience Abstracts, 17:303.

Bullock, T. H., Karamürsel, S., & Hofmann, M. H. (1993). Interval-specific event related potentials to omitted stimuli in the electrosensory pathway in elasmobranchs: An elementary form of expectation. Journal of Comparative Physiology A, 172:501–510.

Campbell, F. W., Howell, E. R., & Robson, J. G. (1971). The appearance of gratings with and without the fundamental fourier component. Journal of Physiology, London, 217:17–19.

Campbell, F. W., Howell, E. R., & Johnstone, J. R. (1978). A comparison of threshold and suprathreshold appearance of gratings with components in the low and high spatial frequency range. Journal of Physiology, London, 284:193–201.

Charnwood J. R. B. (1951). Essay on Binocular Vision. London, Halton Press.

Chladni, E. E. F. (1787). Entdeckungen über die Theorie des Klanges. Leipzig: Breitkopf und Härtel.

Coren, S., Ward, L. M., & Enns, J. T. (1994). Sensation and perception. Fort Worth, TX: Harcourt Brace.

Cornsweet, J. N. (1970). Visual perception. New York: Academic Press.

Crick, H., & Koch, C. (1990). Towards a neurobiological theory of consciousness. Seminars in the Neurosciences, 2:263–275.

Cristiansen, B., Alstrøm, & Levinsen, M. T. (1992). Ordered capillary-wave states: Quasicrystals, hexagons, and radial waves. Physical Review Letters, 68(14):2157–2160.

Cutting, J. E., Proffitt, D. R., & Kozlowski, L. T. (1978). A biomechanical invariant for gait perception. Journal of Experimental Psychology: Human Perception & Performance, 4:357–372.

Denis, M., & Cocude, M. (1989). Scanning visual images generated from verbal descriptions. European Journal of Cognitive Psychology, 1:293–307.

Dermietzel, R., & Spray, D. C. (1993). Gap junctions in the brain: Where, what type, how many, and why? Trends In Neurosciences, 16(5):186–191.

De Valois, K. K., De Valois, R. L., & Yund, W. W. (1979). Responses of striate cortex cells to grating and checkerboard patterns. Journal of Physiology 291:483–505.

De Valois, R. L., & De Valois, K. K. (1988). Spatial vision (Oxford Psychology Series No.

14). New York: Oxford University Press.

Dewan, E. M. (1976). Consciousness as an emergent causal agent in the context of control systems theory. In: G. Globus (Ed.), Consciousness and the brain: A scientific and philosophical inquiry. (pp. 181–198). New York: Plenum Press.

Eckhorn, R., Bauer, R., Jordan, W., Brosch, M., Kruse, W., Munk, M., & Reitboeck, J. (1988). Coherent oscillations: A mechanism of feature linking in the visual cortex? Biolgical Cybernetics, 60:121–130.

Edelman, G. (1987). Neural darwinism: The theory of neuronal group selection. New York: Basic Books.

Faraday, M. (1831). On a peculiar class of acoustical figures and on the form of fluids vibrating on elastic surfaces. Philosophical Transactions of the Royal Society of London, 225:563–576.

Farah, M. J. (1990). Visual agnosia. Cambridge MA: MIT Press.

Fechner, G. T. (1871). Zur experimentalen Aesthetik. Leipzig: Hirzel.

Fifer, S. (1961). Analog computation: Theory, techniques, and applications (4 volumes). New York: McGraw-Hill.

Fink, M. (1996). Time reversal in acoustics. Contemporary Physics, 37(2):95–109.

Fink, M. (1997). Time-reversed acoustics. Physics Today, 20:34–40.

Foley, J. M. (1978). Primary distance perception. In R. Held, H. W. Leibowitz, & H. J. L. Tauber (Eds.), Handbook of sensory physiology, Vol VII Perception. Berlin: Springer Verlag. (pp. 181–213).

Galli, A. (1932). Über mittels verschiedener Sinnesreize erweckte Wahrnehmung von Scheinbewegung. Archiv für die gesamte Psychologie, 85:137–180.

Geissler, H.-G. (1987). The temporal architecture of central information processing: Evidence for a tentative time-quantum model . Psychological Research, 49:99–106.

Geissler H.-G. (1997). Is there a way from behavior to non-linear brain dynamics? On quantal periods in cognition and the place of alpha in brain resonances . International Journal of Psychophysiology, 26, 381–393.

Geissler, H.-G., Schebera, F.-U., & Kompass, R. (1999). Ultra-precise quantal timing: Evidence from simultaneity thresholds in long-range apparent movement. Perception & Psychophysics, 61(4):707–726.

Gerard, R. W. & Libet B. (1940). The control of normal and 'convulsive' brain potentials . American Journal of Psychiatry, 96:1125–1153.

Gibson, J. J. & Crooks, L. E. (1938). A theoretical field-analysis of automobile driving. American Journal of Psychology 51(3):453–471.

Gilbert, S. F. (1988). Developmental biology. Sunderland MA: Sinauer Associates.

Gleik, J. (1987). Chaos: Making a new science. New York: Penguin Books.

Golubitsky, M., Stewart I., Buono, P.-L., & Collins, J. J. (1999). Symmetry in locomotor central pattern generators and animal gaits. Nature, 401:693–695.

Graham, C. H. (1965). Visual space perception. In C. H. Graham (Ed.), Vision and visual perception (pp. 504–547) New York: John Wiley.

Gray, C. M., Koenig, P., Engel, K. A., & Singer, W. (1989). Oscillatory responses in cat visual cortex exhibit intercolumnar synchronisation which reflects global stimulus properties. Nature, 338:334–337.

Grimes, J. (1996). On the failure to detect changes in scenes across saccades. In K. Atkins (Ed.) Perception (Vancouver Studies in Cognitive Science, Vol. 5, pp. 89-110). New York: Oxford University Press.

Handel, S. & Garner, W. R. (1966). The structure of visual pattern associates and pattern goodness. Perception & Psychophysics, 1:33–38.

Harrison, S. (1989). A new visualization on the mind-brain problem: Naive realism transcended. In J. Smythies & J. Beloff (Eds.), The case for dualism (pp. 113-165). Charlottesville: University of Virginia.

Harnad, S. (1990). The symbol grounding problem. Physica D. 42:335–346.

Hartgenbusch, H. G. (1927). Gestalt psychology in sport. Psyche, 27:41–52.

Hartmann, L. (1923). Neue Verschmelzungsprobleme. Psychologische Forschung, 3:319–396.

Hashemiyoon, R., & Chapin, J. (1993). Retinally derived fast oscillations coding for global stimulus properties synchronise multiple visual system structures . Society for Neurosciences Abstracts, 19:528.

Heelan, P. A. (1983). Space perception and the philosophy of science. Berkeley: University of California Press.

Heider, F. & Simmel, M. (1944). An experimental study of apparent behaviour. American Journal of Psychology, 57:243–259.

Helmholtz, H. (1925). Physiological optics. Optical Society of America, 3:318.

Helmholtz, H. L. F. (1954). On the sensations of tone as a physiological basis for the theory of music. New York: Dover (Original work published 1863)

Hertzberger, B. & Epstein, D. (1988). Beauty and the brain: Biological aspects of aesthetics. Basel: Birkhauser Verlag.

Hillebrand, F. (1902). Theorie der scheinbaren Grösse bei binocularem Sehen. Denkschrift academische Wissenschaft Wien (Math. Nat. Kl.), 72:255–307.

Hochberg, J., & Brooks, V. (1960). The psychophysics of form: Reversible perspective drawings of spatial objects . American Journal of Psychology 73:337–354.

Hoffman, D. D. (1998). Visual intelligence: How we create what we see. New York: W. W. Norton.

Hollingsworth-Lisanby, S., & Lockhead, G. R. (1991). Subjective randomness, aesthetics, and structure. In G. R. Lockhead & J. R. Pomerantz (Eds.), The Perception of Structure (pp. 97–114). Washington, DC: American Psychological Association.

Huxley, A. (1963). The doors of perception. New York: Harper & Row.

Indow, T. (1991). A critical review of Luneberg's model with regard to global structure of visual space. Psychological Review, 98:430–453.

Johansson, G. (1973). Visual perception of biological motion and a model for its analysis. Perception & Psychophysics, 14(2):201–211.

Julesz, B. (1971). Foundations of cyclopean perception. Chicago: University of Chicago Press.

Kandell, E. R., & Siegelbaum, S. (1985). Principles underlying electrical and chemical synaptic transmission. In E. R. Kandell, & J. H. Schwartz (Eds.), *Principles of Neural Science* (pp. 89-107) New York: Elsevier.

Kanizsa, G. (1979). *Organization in vision.* New York: Praeger.

Kant, I. (1781). Critique of pure reason. V. Politis (Transl.) London: J. M. Dent (1993).

Kaplan, E. (1990). *Human Neuropsychology*. Boston: Boston University Medical School class BUMC ME 776.

Kauffman, S. A., Shymko, R. M., & Trabert K. (1978). Control of sequential compartment formation in Drosophila . *Science,* 199:259–270.

Kaufman, (1974). Sight and Mind. New York: Oxford University Press.

Khanna, S., Ulfendahl, M., & Flock, Å. (1989a). Modes of cellular vibration in the organs of corti. *Acta Otolaryngologica Stockholm, Supplement*, 467:183–188.

Khanna, S., Ulfendahl, M., & Flock, Å. (1989b). Waveforms and spectra of cellular vibrations in the organ of corti. *Acta Otolaryngologica Stockholm, Suppliment*, 467:189–193.

Khatib, O. (1986). Real-time obstacle avoidance for manipulators and mobile robots. *International Journal of Robotics Research*, 5:90–98.

Klüver, H. (1966). *Mescal and the mechanisms of hallucination*. Chicago: University of Chicago Press.

Koffka, K.(1935). *Principles of gestalt psychology*. New York: Harcourt Brace.

Köhler, W. (1924). *Die physischen Gestalten in Ruhe und im stationären Zustand: Eine naturphilosophische Untersuchung*. Erlangen: Verlag der Philosophichen Akademie.

Köhler, W., & Held, R. (1947). The cortical correlate of pattern vision. *Science,* 110:414–419.

Kolb, B. & Whishaw, I. Q. (1980). *Fundamentals of human neurophsycology,* (2nd ed.). New York: W. H. Freeman.

Kosslyn, S. M. (1975). Information representation in visual images. *C,ognitive Psychology* 7, 341–370.

Kosslyn S., M., Ball T., & Reisner B. (1978). Visual images preserve metric spatial information: Evidence of studies from image scanning. *Journal of Experimental Psychology: Human Perception and Performance,* 4:47–60.

Kovács, I, & Julesz, B. (1995). Psychophysical sensitivity maps indicate skeletal representation of visual shape . *Perception Supplement*, 24:34.

Kovács, I., Fehér Á., & Julesz, B. (1997). Medial point description of shape: A representation for action coding and its psychophysical correlates. (Tech. Rep. No. 33). New Brunswick NJ: Rutgers Center for Cognitive Science.

Kristofferson, A. B. (1990). Timing mechanisms and the threshold for duration. In H.-G. Geissler (Ed.), *Psychophysical Explorations of Mental Structures*, in collaboration with M. H. Müller & W. Prinz.(pp. 269–277). Toronto: Hogrefe & Huber.

Kudrolli, A., & Gollub, J. P. (1996). Patterns of spatiotemporal chaos in parametrically forced surface waves: A systematic survey at large aspect ratio. *Physica D*, 97:133–154.

Kudrolli, A., Pier, B., & Gollub, J. P. (1998). Superlattice patterns in surface waves. *Physica D*, 123:99–111.

Kuhn, T. (1970). The structure of scientific revolutions. Chicago: Chicago University Press.

Kumar, K., & Bajaj, K. M. S. (1995). Competing patterns in the Faraday experiment. *Physical Review E*, 52(5):R4606–R4609.

Lashley, K. S. (1942). The problem of cerebral organization in vision. *Biolological Simposia*, 7:301–322.

Leary, T. (1983). *Flashbacks–An autobiography*. Los Angeles: J. P. Tarcher.

Leeuwenberg, E. L. J. (1971). A perceptual coding language for visual and auditory patterns. *American Journal of Psychology*, 84(3):307–350.

Lehar, S. (1994). *Directed diffusion and orientational harmonics: Neural network models of long-range boundary completion through short-range interactions*. PhD thesis, Boston University. Also available at http://cns-alumni.bu.edu/~slehar/webstuff/thesis/thesis.html.

Lewin, K. (1969). *Principles of topological psychology*, F. Heider & G. M. Heider (Trans.). New York: McGraw-Hill. (Original work published 1936)

Lewis-Williams, J. D. & Dowson, T. A. (1988). The signs of all times: Entopic phenomena in upper paleolithic art. *Current Anthropology*, 29(2):201–245.

Llinás, R. R. (1988). The intrinsic electrophysiological properties of mammalian neurons: Insights into central nervous system function. *Science*, 242:1654–1664.

Llinás, R. R. (1993). Coherent 40-Hz oscillation characterizes dream state in humans. *Proceedings of the National Acadamy of Sciences*, 90:2078–2081.

Llinás, R. R., Grace, A. A., & Yarom, Y. (1991). In vitro neurons in mammalian cortical layer 4 exhibit intrinsic oscillatory activity in the 10–50-Hz frequency range. *Proceedings of the National Acadamy of Sciences*, USA, 88:897–901.

Llinás, R. R., & Paré, D. (1991). Of dreaming and wakefulness. *Neuroscience*, 44(3):521–535.

Luneburg, R. K. (1950). The metric of binocular visual space. *Journal of the Optical Society of America*, 40:627–642.

Marr, D. (1982). *Vision*. New York: W. H. Freeman.

Marr D., & Poggio, T. (1976). Cooperative computation of stereo disparity. *Science*, 194:283–287.

McClelland, J. R., & Rummelhart, D. E. (1981). An interactive activation model of context effects in letter perception: Part 1. An account of basic findings. *Psychological Review*, 88:375–407.

Meyer, L. B. (1967). *Music, the arts, and ideas*. Chicago: University of Chicago Press.

Michotte, A., (1963). *The perception of causality*. T. Miles & E. Miles (Trans.). London: Methuen. (Original work published 1946)

Michotte, A., Thinés, G., & Crabbé, G. (1991). Amodal completion of perceptual structures. In G. Thinés, A. Costall, & G. Butterworth (Eds.), Michotte's experimental phenomenology of perception (pp. 140–167). Hillsdale, NJ: Lawrence Erlbaum Associates. (Original work published in 1967).

Miller, G. A. (1956). The magical number seven, plus or minus two. *Psychological Review*, 63:81–97.

Müller, G. E. (1896). Zur Psychophysik der Gesichtsempfindungen. Zeitschrift für Psychologie, 10.

Murray, J. D. (1981). A pre-pattern formation mechanism for animal coat markings. *Journal of Theoretical Biology*, 88:161–199.

Murray, J. D. (1988). How the leopard gets its spots. *Scientific American,* 258(3):80–87.

Murthy, V., & Fetz, E. (1992). Coherent 25- to 35-Hz oscillations in the sensorimotor cortex of awake behaving monkeys. *Proceedings of the National Academy of Sciences*, USA, 89:5670–5674.

Newman, S. A., & Frisch, H. L. (1979). Dynamics of skeletal pattern formation in developing chick limb. *Science*, 205:662–668.

Nicolelis, M., Baccala, L., Lin, R., & Chapin, J. (1995). Sensorimotor encoding by synchronous neural ensemble activity at multiple levels of the somatosensory system. *Science*, 268:1353–1358.

O'Regan, K. J., (1992). Solving the "real" mysteries of visual perception: The world as an outside memory. *Canadian Journal of Psychology*, 46:461–488.

Palmer, S. E. (1985). The role of symmetry in shape perception. *Acta Psychologica,* 59:67–90.

Peinado, A., Yuste, R., & Katz, L. C. (1993). Gap junctional communication and the development of local circuits in the neocortex. *Cerebral Cortex* 3:488–498.

Pepper, D. M. (1982). Nonlinear optical phase conjugation. *Optical Engineering,* 21(2):156–183.

Pepper, D. M. (1986). Applications of optical phase conjugation. *Scientific American,* 254:(1):74–83.

Pinker, S. (1984). Visual cognition: An introduction. *Cognition*, 18:1–63.

Pribram, K. H. (1971). *Languages of the brain*. New York: Prentice-Hall.

Pribram, K. H., Nuwer, M., & Baron, R. (1974). The holographic hypothesis of memory structure in brain function and perception. In R. C. Atkinson, D. H. Krantz, R. C. Luce, & P. Suppes (Eds.), *Contemporary developments in mathematical psychology* (pp. 416–467). San Francisco: W. H. Freeman.

Prigogine, I., & Nicolis, G. (1967). On symmetry-breaking instabilities in dissipative systems. *Journal of Chemical Physics*, 46:3542–3550.

Psotka, J. (1978). Perceptual processes that may create stick figures and balance. *Journal of Experimental Psychology: Human Perception & Performance*, 4:101–111.

Reed, E. S. (1988). *James J. Gibson and the psychology of perception*. New Haven CT: Yale University Press.

Rensink, R. A., O'Regan, J. K., & Clark, J. J. (1997). To see or not to see: The need for attention to perceive changes in scenes. *Psychological Science*, 8:368–373.

Rosenberg, G. H. (1999). On the intrinsic nature of the physical. In: S. R. Hameroff, A. W. Kaszniak, & A. C. Scott (Eds.), *Toward a science of consciousness III, The third Tucson discussions and debates* (pp. 33–47). Cambridge, MA: MIT Press.

Rubin, E. (1958). *Visuell wahrgenommene Figuren*. Copenhagen: Gyldendalske. [Exerpts translated and reprinted in D. C. Beardslee & M. Wertheimer (Eds.), *Readings in Perception* (pp. 194–203). Princeton, NJ: Van Nostrand. (Original work published 1921)

Rummelhart, D. E. & McClelland, J. R. (1982). An interactive activation model of context effects in letter perception: Part 2. The contextual effect and some tests and extensions of the model. *Psychological Review*, 89:60–94.

Russell, B. (1927). Physical and perceptual space. In *Philosophy* (pp. 137–143). New York: W. W. Norton.

Sacks, O. (1985). *The man who mistook his wife for a hat*. New York: Harper & Row.

Sander, F. (1931). Gestalt Psychologie und Kunsttheorie: Ein Beitrag zur Psychologie der Architectur. *Neue Psychologische Studien*, 8:311–333.

Schoner, G., Dose, M., & Engels, C. (1995). Dynamics of behavior: Theory and applications for autonomous robot architectures. *Robotics and Autonomous Systems*, 16:213–245.

Searle, J. R. (1992). *The rediscovery of mind*. Cambridge, MA: MIT Press.

Sethares, W. A. (1998). *Tuning timbre spectrum scale*. Berlin: Springer Verlag. See also http://eceserv0.ece.wisc.edu/~sethares/consemi.html.

Shepard, R. N. & Metzler, J. (1971). Mental rotation of three-dimensional objects. *Science*, 171(972):701–703.

Sherrington, C. S. (1941). *Man on his nature. The Gifford lectures*. Edinburgh: MacMillan. (Original work published 1937)

Shevelev, I. A. (1988). Visual recognition and the scanning process based on the EEG alpha wave. *Perception*, 175: 413.

Siegel, R. K. (1977). Hallucinations. *Scientific American*, 237(4):132–140.

Simons, D. J., & Levin, D. T. (1997). Change blindness. *Trends in cognitive sciences*, 7:261–267.

Singer, W., Artola, A., Engel, A. K., Koenig, P., Kreiter, A. K., Lowel, S., & Schillen, T. B. (1993). Neuronal representations and temporal codes. In: T. A. Poggio & D. A. Glaser (Eds.), *Exploring brain functions: Models in neuroscience* (pp. 179–194), Chichester, England: Wiley.

Smythies, J. R. (1994). *The walls of Plato's cave: The science and philosophy of brain, consciousness, and perception.* Altershot: Avebury.

Snyder, S. H. (1986). *Drugs and the brain.* New York: Scientific American Library.

Speltz, A. (1910). *The styles of ornament from prehistoric times to the middle of the XIXth century.* London: B. T. Batsford.

Sompolinsky, H., Golomb, D., & Kleinfeld, D. (1990). Global processing of visual stimuli in a neural network of coupled oscillators. *Proceedings of the National Acadamy of Sciences,* USA, 87:7200–7204.

Strogatz, S., & Stewart, I. (1993). Coupled oscillators and biological synchronization . *Scientific American,* 269(6):102–109.

Tampieri, G. (1956). Sul Completamento Amodale di Rappresentazioni Prospettiche di Solidi Geometrici. In L. Ancona (Ed.), *Atli dell' XI Congresso Degli Psicologi Italiani* (pp. 1–3). Milano: Vita e Pensiero.

Titchener, E. B. (1898). The postulates of a structural psychology. *Philosophical Review,* 7:449–465.

Tse, P. U. (1998). Illusory volumes from conformation. *Perception,* 27(8):977–994.

Tse, P. U. (1999). Volume Completion. *Cognitive Psychology,* 39: 37–68.

Turing, A. M. (1952). The chemical basis of morphogenesis. *Philosophical Transactions of the Royal Society, London, B,* 237:37–72.

von der Malsburg, C. (1987). Synaptic plasticity as a basis of brain organization. In P.-P. Changeux & M. Konishi (Eds.), *The neural and molecular bases of learning.* (Dahlem Workshop Report 38, pp. 411–431). Chichester England: Wiley.

von Ehrenfels, C. (1890). Über Gestaltqualitäten. *Vierteljaheresschrift für wissenschaftliche Philosophie,* 14:249–292.

Walker, R., & Young, A. W. (1996). Object-based neglect: An investigation of the contributions of eye movements and perceptual completion. *Cortex,* 32:279–295.

Waller, M. D. (1961). *Chladni Figures: A study in symmetry.* London: G. Bell & Sons.

Walter, W. G. (1950). Features in the electro-physiology of mental mechanism. In D. Richter (Ed.), *Perspectives in neuropsychiatry* (pp. 67–78). London: H. K. Lewis.

Watts, A. (1958). *This is it—and other essays on Zen and spiritual experience.* New York: Vintage Books.

Welsh, B. J., Gomatam, J., & Burgess, A. E. (1983). Three-dimensional chemical waves in the Belousov–Zhabotinski reaction. *Nature,* 304:611–614.

Wertheimer, M. (1923). Untersuchungen zur Lehre von Gestalt. *Psychologische Forschung,* 4:301–350. [Reprinted in part in W. D. Ellis (Ed., 1950), *A sourcebook of Gestalt psychology* (pp. 71–88). New York: Humanities Press.]

West, T. G. (1997). *In the mind's eye.* New York: Prometheus Books.

Wilson, E. O. (1998). *Consilience: The unity of knowledge.* New York: Alfred A. Knopf.

Winfree, A. T. (1974). Rotating chemical reactions. *Scientific American,* 230(6):82–95.

Wundt, W. (1873–1874). *Grundzüge der physiologischen Psychologie* (2 Vols.). Leipzig:

Wilhelm Engelmann.

Yariv, A. (1991). Phase conjugate optics—Theory and practice. In *Optical electronics* (4th ed., chap. 16). New York: Holt, Rinehart, & Winston.

Zeki, S. (1993). *A vision of the brain*. London: Blackwell.

Author Index

V
von der Malsburg C. 157

W
Wain L. 240
Walker R 145
Waller M. D. 150, 151, 159, 164, 165, 170,
245, 265
Walter W. G. 173
Watts A. 258, 259
Welsh B. J. 152
Wertheimer M. 45, 84
West T. G. 261, 262
Whishaw I. 176
Winfree A. T. 152
Wundt W. 34

Y
Yariv A. 174, 265
Young A. W. 145

Z
Zeki S. 158

Subject Index

295